# Off the Top of His Head

## "The Visor" Remembers Twelve Years Of Gator Football

Tony Papas
with commentary by Jeff Trippe

**Silent E Publishing Company**

Silent E Publishing Company
4446 Hendricks Ave, #141
Jacksonville, FL 32207

ISBN-10: 0-9755104-3-6
ISBN-13: 978-0-9755104-3-8

First Edition
**1 2 3 4 5 6 7 8 9**

# Foreword

Who – or what – is the Visor? This is a question asked by many and answered by few, but it can be defined on several levels.

On the most basic level, the Visor is the alter ego of my college roommate at the University of Florida, Tony Papas. Tony & I have been friends since the 7th grade, and I've never met a more dedicated fan of Gator football. Tony attends almost all home games, has supported the Gators at every SEC opponent's home field, and has attended all of Florida's national championship contests (football and basketball). He and I have a streak of Florida-Georgia games that dates, unbroken, back to 1979. This may not be a long streak compared to that of some in the Gator Nation, but give him time, he's still young.

On another level, the Visor is the headgear made famous by "The ol' Ball Coach." Coach Spurrier's legend is well-known in the Gator Nation and adds particular significance.

Most importantly, "The Visor" is a weekly column (during football season) that covers the happenings of all things Florida Football. Initially distributed via email to a select and privileged few, the column found a home at Gatorfootball.com in 1996 and has been a staple of the website to this day. This book is a compilation of "The Visor's" columns spanning the time between and including Florida's first three national championships. It's sort of a historical reference, if you will, serving to document the glorious and not-so-glorious years between 1996 and 2009.

So sit back in your favorite Gator chair this off-season and reminisce with The Visor, and don't forget to keep up online at www.gatorfootball.com.

Thanks to the original "Visor" followers: Brett "Gatorman" Mehring, Darren Edwards (who accompanied Tony on many a road trip), Roger Henderson, Tom Davidson, and Bill Houser. Special thanks also go out to Tony's wife Sina, who puts up with the trials and tribulations of a fanatic of this magnitude. Most importantly, thanks to fellow UF alum Jeff Trippe, who provided commentary, editing, moral support, and the occasional kick in the pants needed to get a project like this to press.

Go Gators!

George Foote
Silent E Publishing Company

# Table of Contents


| | |
|---|---|
| 1996 "Next Year" at Last | page 7 |
| 1997 Returning to Earth | page 11 |
| 1998 Hard Knocks up in Knoxville | page 21 |
| 1999 The Pothole at the End of the Road | page 35 |
| 2000 Brawl on Bourbon Street | page 55 |
| 2001 Big Events, Big Changes | page 77 |
| 2002 Zooking When They Should Have Zagged | page 103 |
| 2003 Sweating it Out | page 133 |
| 2004 Eight is Enough, But Seven Sends You Packing | page 155 |
| 2005 Urban Renewal | page 177 |
| 2006 No Room For Error | page 197 |
| 2007 Reloading the Young Guns | page 221 |
| 2008 True to His Word | page 243 |
| The Visor's All-Time Gator Greats | page 271 |

# 1996
## "Next Year" at Last

The '96 season went into the books as probably the most remarkable in the history of Florida football. The win in the National Championship game over Florida $tate was the culmination of the hard work of an extraordinary group of players, and it came after what had seemed a never-ending trail of tears and agony over many, many seasons. But more than that, it was also the result of a special relationship between one coach – Steve Spurrier – and one player – Danny Wuerffel.

I know, I know: Fred Taylor was on that team. Terry Jackson played an important part. The offensive line came together and rose above adversity. But the magic happened between the Head Ball Coach, who won the Heisman Trophy in 1966 as quarterback for the Gators, and Wuerffel, who won it exactly thirty years later. The image that lives in my mind is that of Spurrier with his hand on Danny's shoulder, on the sideline, the old sage and the young warrior. Still, that's only what everyone else got to see on TV. As the Visor, riding atop that endearing but lopsided cranium, I got to see the way it developed over time, the way it grew, through all the long hours on the practice field and all the brain-wearying scribblings on the chalkboard, all the conversations on planes and buses and in the locker room – and it was a beautiful thing.

On a long list of very fine college quarterbacks at UF, Wuerffel was our redeemer after ninety years of struggle. Still, this fellow Tebow has given a good account of himself, and it seems appropriate to note that these chronicles begin with Danny and the '96 season and end with Tebow, who was a big part of the next two Gators championships (although Chris Leak was clearly the leader in 2006).

I don't think many of the experts picked UF to win it all in 1996, but so much for them. Down here in Gainesville, we know that it's more about heart and determination than it is about the numbers or even the talent. Perhaps fifty years from now, if sport has reached that point at which the human character is no longer a key factor, some old man with an orange and blue tie on (or maybe a visor?) will gesture toward the spectacle on the field and say,

"Football? Well, these guys are all right, but let me tell you about a team I once saw… The Gators were 12 and 1 going into the National Championship game, having lost to F$U in their last regular season game…"

**Visor Flings, Week 19:**

## UF 52, F$U 20

It took ninety years, but it happened.

The Battle on the Bayou turned into a Beatdown, as the Gators crushed F$U 52-20 to win their first National Championship. What a great way for it to happen, as the best team in the country got its chance to show everyone who they really are, and to prove it by whipping their rival.

It was a complete and total team victory, as Florida dominated the entire second half. It was obvious that the better team won, and it's a shame that Florida was not this healthy on the offensive line for the game in Tallahassee, or else this match-up would not have even occurred.

Even after the Criminoles hit that big pass on their first possession, the tone was set when the defense stuffed Pooh Bear Williams on fourth and one, and then the offense went right down the field to score, as Ike Hilliard started what would be a huge night for himself with the touchdown reception. It was apparent that the O-line, even with center Jeff Mitchell remaining out, was going to do a much better job of pass protection than they did in Tallahassee. It also helped that the Head Ball Coach deciding to put Wuerffel in the shotgun for most of the night, allowing him enough time to shred the Semihole secondary.

F$U was able to stay close at halftime, though, mainly because of blown coverage in the secondary on a long pass to E.G. Green. They only put together one legitimate scoring drive the entire half. Each time F$U scored, though, the Gators responded with some huge pass plays, with Hilliard's stick move and reverse direction TD reception the highlight.

In the second half, Fred Taylor and Terry Jackson got the running game going, while the defense clamped down on Sad Busby and choked the life out of F$U. It was especially enjoyable, once again, to see the true colors of Mickey Andrews and his defense come out, as they picked up multiple late-hit penalties (the ones that weren't called in the last game) and the blowout commenced. What a bunch of losers.

Wuerffel's laser to Hilliard extended the lead to 31-20, then Danny himself pulled it down and scored on a third and long play when the field opened up. After that, it was all downhill. Jackson's long touchdown run on fourth and one sealed it, and the Gators got one more late to make the final 52-20.

This was a testament to an unbelievable senior class, who left with a 45-6-1 record. It's a great feeling to see guys like Lawrence Wright, Anthone Lott, Wuerffel, Mitchell, Donnie Young, and company go out on top.

It will be very interesting to see how the team does in 1997. There will be a tremendous loss of leadership and talent, even with so many young guys ready for their moment, and the team will have to work hard to avoid the letdown which often follows an outstanding season. Also, the Gators will have the largest target on their chests now, and will be hard-pressed to come close to their performance this season.

But for now, it's time to celebrate the Florida Gators being on top of the college football mountain for the first time ever. Congratulations to the entire team and coaching staff for a memorable and defining season. It took 90 years of heartbreaks and occasional bad luck, not to mention a crippling probation, but Florida is finally at the point where we might someday be considered one of the 'traditional' powers.

It really is great to be a Florida Gator today. Best wishes for the New Year.

Very Truly Yours,
The Visor

# 1997
# Returning to Earth

Small consolation though it may have been to Gators fans at the time, the 1997 season proved the growing volatility of the college football atmosphere. Even a team which had, through sheer willpower and tenacity (along with the grace of a second shot at their great rival), climbed to the top of the pile could fall to the status of also-ran in a single year's time. It would seem now that the days of the great dynasties – the Georgia Techs and Notre Dames of other ages – were done.

Most observers agree that the '96 championship firmly imbedded Florida in the American sports consciousness as a major power and perennial national threat, a team who, with the right break here and there, might go all the way in any given season, even with one loss…maybe even with two. Nonetheless, two critical losses in 1997 to LSU and Georgia undid the Gators' chances despite an uplifting victory early over a powerful Tennessee team with Peyton Manning at the helm.

Still, the game everyone seemed to remember most vividly from that season was UF's war against FSU, which many old-timers claimed unequivocally was the most intense and hard-fought contest they had ever witnessed in the Swamp. The Gators became proverbial spoilers, outlasting their nemeses after two lead-changes in the final two minutes before dragging the Criminoles down, 32-29. It was another compelling turn in the annual quest for the Governor's Cup.

There were also some stunning individual performances in '97. Both Fred Taylor and Fred Weary made the most of their senior seasons, and junior receiver Jaquez Green, at only 5-9 and 172 pounds, proved his mettle as one of the country's top receivers. Professional football stardom awaited all three – and is there any greater pleasure for the fan of a particular college football team to be able to say to his friends, when watching an NFL game, "Oh, yeah. That guy played for the Gators, you know."

Still, ten years-plus of perspective shows us that the road is long and arduous, and the mystery has only deepened. Big-budget programs no longer produce repeat championships, nor necessarily does the ascendance of the One, the touted athlete who is heralded as a savior. In all, it is still a team sport, and for something as difficult to attain as the BCS crown, many variables and unknowns must align themselves properly. Even then, injuries, crucial penalties, lapses in concentration, weather conditions…all things subject to the whims of the football gods, must be reckoned with and overcome. As we now see, the 1997 season was the beginning of a realignment and a journey which, like that of Odysseus, would take another ten years.

**Visor Flings: Week 1**
**UF 21, Southern Miss 6**

The title defense began this past Saturday with an uneven effort against the Eagles of USM. It's definitely a new look for the offense, as the entire unit struggled against the first of eleven opponents who have Florida circled on their schedule.

Doug Johnson was off-target quite often most of the night until late in the third quarter. He is definitely trying to force balls into coverage instead of checking down to short routes, and that has to improve. The running game was only okay, as Terry Jackson and company need more work as a unit. The loss of Jeff Mitchell and Donnie Young is already apparent. The receiving corps needs all the reps it can get. Jaquez Green is the only guy returning with quality experience. Jamie Richardson has a lot of hype, but has a lot of improving to do. And Nafis Karim is disappearing right now, strangely enough. All of the receivers will have to improve their timing with Johnson. There were some better plays in the second half as the nerves calmed, but we have a long way to go. Lots of room for improvement by the entire unit.

Bob Stoops looks to have another solid defense, even after losing some quality secondary help. The linebacker corps of Kearse, Rutledge, and Peterson could be the best in the SEC. They will have to play well all season, as the D-line looks to be okay at best. Stoops will have to do more with schemes this year than last to help out this group. Interesting move to put Eli Williams at cornerback, but necessary, as depth was seriously lacking there. He will see a lot of balls thrown his way until he proves he can handle the position. No problems with Fred Weary, who won't see a lot of action his way for now. Didn't get to see much from the new safeties, as USM's offense was vanilla and conservative most of the night until the Gators finally went ahead 21-6.

Central Michigan comes in for a beating to go along with a large paycheck next Saturday. Hopefully it will help the young players, because Tennessee has payback on their minds two weeks from now.

**Visor Flings, Week 2:**
**UF 82, Central Michigan 6**

It was nothing more than a glorified scrimmage, as the Gators destroyed CMU. A complete mismatch from the start, as the entire roster saw action, but how much did it help Florida prepare for Tennessee?

It's really difficult to say how well Florida played, but at least the starters got out early without injury. What stands out most on the stat sheet is 10-plus yards per rushing and passing attempt

The penalties are still too common, but there just couldn't be a very intense level of concentration from a bunch of guys so young in a game so easy.

Well, it's Tennessee week, and it's time to try and shut Peyton Manning out in this series and shut up (once again) the no-reason-to-boast Vol fans.

Phat Phil probably has his best offense ever this fall, and the Gator defense has to play its best for the entire sixty minutes. Coach Stoops will have to find a creative way to get pressure on Manning from both the line and linebackers, and rely on the secondary to hold up. The Head Ball Coach has to get Johnson and the offense to be efficient when they have scoring opportunities or this could result in a loss. A complete team effort will be required to pull this one off.

**Visor Flings, Week 3:**
**UF 33, Tennessee 20**

What a great win over Phat Phil and Tennessee on Saturday. The entire Gator team elevated its play and intensity for this one, and the fans made the Swamp, once again, the toughest place to play. The Vols had talked a lot about how they were finally the better team and were ready to beat Florida anywhere. Even Peyton Manning was quoted on how he liked the trash talk from the fans in the stadium, and how he looked forward to shutting them up. Well, not in this lifetime.

The defense set the tone right from the start, forcing the Vols to punt. Then Doug Johnson led the offense right down the field for a TD, with Jamie Richardson making a great catch. Coach Stoops had an effective scheme all day to keep Tennessee off balance, and the D-line, led by Ed Chester, was bringing heat all afternoon. Once they got a few hits on Manning, he reverted to his happy feet ways again, leading to Tony George's long interception return for a 14-0 lead that the Vols never could recover from. The secondary made sure that Tennessee had to earn its way the entire length of the field and played great coverage. This is a great linebacker corps: they can do it all, and really played both the run and pass equally well.

The offense still is not smooth in the passing game, due to a combination of Johnson's inaccuracy at times, and some inconsistent route-running. The running game should be relied upon more, because Fred Taylor and Terry Jackson are a great tandem. But will the Head Ball Coach ever do that? Taylor really hit some big runs early, and that seemed to slow down the Vols front seven. Then, he and T-Jack controlled the clock in the second half with key third-down runs to keep Tennessee's offense off the field. Doug has to get coached up some more – he still forces the ball into coverage too often, and is reluctant to check-down to short throws that are available. Jaquez Green needs some help from the other wide receivers as well, or he will see double-teams more often.

Now it's on to Kentucky, where Hall Mumme has Tim Couch doing what he should – throwing the ball all day long. They are very much improved from last season, and their fans have reason for hope, and Commonwealth Stadium will be sold out, looking for a big upset. This will be a good test for both the newer players and the staff to see if the team is sharp and focused from the outset for the Gators' first road game.

**Visor Flings, Week 4:**
**UF 55, Kentucky 28**

What a wild game in the Commonwealth Saturday against the Wildcats. The ball was in the air all day long, but Florida was simply too talented and too deep for Kentucky to keep up with.

The offense did a great job of taking the crowd out of the game from the start, as they scored four straight TDs to run out to a 28-0 lead. The defense forced a couple of turnovers early as well, and that seemed to shake the confidence of Tim Couch for the entire half as the Gators controlled the action. The Wildcats rarely ran the ball, using short dump-offs as the equivalent of a running game, but Florida's speed on defense was too much for them to overcome.

Johnson looked improved this week, albeit against a weak pass defense. He did not try to force throws and was more accurate than he's been yet. The running game was the difference in these offenses, as Florida could always rely on tough yards from Jackson and Taylor to eat up the clock and keep drives alive. Unfortunately, T-Jack limped off the field with what looks like a serious knee injury, and now the burden falls squarely on Taylor's shoulders. Actually, I hope Spurrier leans on him, because he can handle it, and could really blossom the rest of the season. Eugene McCaslin is a capable backup to spell Fred when needed. The O-line has been solid so far, and the run-blocking actually looks better than I expected so far this season.

Once again, Stoops earned his money with an effective game plan. Yes, UK scored 28 points, but they never scored quickly, nor were they ever really close or even in the game. Hal Mumme's offense is tough to deal with, but the Gators played a ton of guys all afternoon to try and stay fresh and keep the pressure on Couch, and it seemed to work. Not many teams have the manpower to do that.

A solid road win for Florida. Now it's back to the Swamp to welcome Arkansas.

**Visor Flings, Week 5:**
**UF 56, Arkansas 7**

It was an easier-than expected win over Arkansas at the Swamp. There's no way I expected a 56-7 blowout. Florida came out hot on offense, and simply buried the Hogs early. They simply do not have much firepower on offense, and after they fell behind so fast they were done. Well done.

Doug Johnson played fairly well again, and Quez Green is by far his favorite receiver. It worked this week, but he has to spread the ball around more against stronger teams. The running game once again provided some good balance, as Fred Taylor seems to have settled into his role as the main guy. Arkansas did have some success blitzing, though, even if the final score didn't reflect it. The O-line is still vulnerable somewhat up the middle, as Wyley Ritch has a ways to go at center.

The defense really had a field day, knowing that the Hogs were uncomfortable trying to play catch-up by passing the ball so often, and could dictate whatever rushing or blitzing package they chose. The D-Line did its job of shutting down the running game early, and once again the back seven looked very good – one of the best groups in the SEC. They racked up five more turnovers, which is important, as the offense still needs some help. We are spoiled by the successes of the past and by the big score this week, but there are some fundamentals that the QBs and O-line need to improve on.

Now it's on the road to Baton Rouge and Death Valley, against a Tiger team that was embarrassed by Florida 56-13 last year. The night-game crowd will be crazed. You can't underestimate that combination in the SEC.

**Visor Flings, Week 6:**
**LSU 28, UF 21**

It was payback time on the Bayou.

It took a combination of a determined LSU team and five turnovers, but the top-ranked Gators fell victim to a tough road atmosphere and inexperience at QB. Doug Johnson was simply horrible, throwing four interceptions, the first of which led to an early lead that got the crowd into it, and it was apparent that it affected his play the rest of the evening. Don't let the stats fool you, because long drives that end with bad passes don't mean much in the SEC. I suppose the news that came out after the game that Johnson violated curfew in Gainesville the night before the team left for the game shows that he has some maturing to do off the field as well.

Spurrier said he learned last season that the shotgun could help his pass offense, but he failed to use Fred Taylor enough throughout the game to counter a blitzing defense that didn't really care about Florida's running game. The yards were there for the taking, especially in the second half when the Gators started to rally, but the Head Ball Coach insisted on putting DJ on the spot, and he failed to deliver. The O-line was burned several times by the blitz, and struggled against it all night. Florida has gotten away with it against weaker teams, but against a strong defense, they were exposed. By the way, LSU nose tackle Booger MacFarland is a beast, and will be a stud in the NFL. He was un-blockable the entire game.

The defense was surprisingly beaten several times by the option runs of QB Herb Tyler, which is puzzling because that is a basic part of their game plan. Credit has to also go to the Tiger O-line, which whipped the Gator defense in the running game all evening, the perfect way to keep Florida's offense on the sideline and make Spurrier impatient.

What a nightmare scenario. The turnovers were just the fuel to accomplish this upset, and Johnson was only too happy to oblige. He has a ton of film work to do, but I wonder if he has the maturity to put the time in just yet. And it's time to lean on Fred Taylor, but will Coach go with that plan?

Now the SEC season hangs in the balance, as a second consecutive tough road trip comes up against Auburn, where Florida has historically struggled mightily. The Tigers/War Eagles/Plainsmen/whatever smell blood in the water, and the Gators have to re-focus and perhaps simplify things, in what will be a difficult environment.

**Visor Flings, Week 7:**
**UF 24, Auburn 10**

It was an "old school" win at Auburn, as the Gators did it with defense and the running game. Partly it was by necessity, as Doug Johnson was suspended for this game for his curfew violation before the LSU game. Jesse Palmer got the start, and looked nervous, throwing an early interception. What I didn't expect was to see Noah Brindise come in to manage the game, hand the ball off to Fred Taylor, and do just enough to get the win.

The O-line played its best game of the year, because this was on the road against a quality opponent who knew the Gator passing attack was not its usual self. They controlled the clock and moved the chains in the second and fourth quarters, and allowed Brindise enough time to complete safe throws. Great call by Spurrier to ice the game, running a reverse with Quezzie Green on third-and-goal inside the five. The Tigers were not expecting that call, and Green mad e a great run and leap to score.

On defense, Florida once again shut up Damyune Craig, who talked a lot of trash about how the Gators weren't the same as in 1996. He's right...but he's still a loser. The Gators shut down Auburn's running game completely, and forced three more turnovers. The front seven stepped up to the challenge and picked up the offense most of the afternoon.

Well, that was a huge gut-check win, and may prove beneficial down the road, as the team now knows it can run the ball even against a defense prepared for it, and the backup QBs saw a lot of snaps in a tough environment. Now it's on to Jacksonville, to try and continue Spurrier's dominance against the Dawgs. This looks like the toughest game for Florida in this series since 1992. Who knows who will play at QB? And, the defense has its third straight tough game, and is pretty beat up right now

**Visor Flings, Week 8:**
**Georgia 37, UF 17**

Well, that loss was as ugly as the score indicates. Even a third-quarter rally to tie the game wasn't enough to counter a carousel of QBs and a M*A*S*H unit of defensive linemen and linebackers. Georgia's senior leadership from Mike Bobo, Terrence Edwards, and Hines Ward on offense was too much to overcome. I'm still a little in disbelief as to Spurrier's decision to start yanking out any QB who struggled even for one series starting in the second quarter. I could see Johnson getting pulled after two interceptions, but I didn't expect to see Palmer only get a few plays before giving way to Brindise. Actually, Noah led the Gators to two consecutive TDs in the third quarter to tie the game, but after that the defense simply collapsed under the weight of so many injuries, and there was no way Brindise could continue to lead scoring drives, given his limited experience.

The Gator defense held on as long as it could, but when Peterson, Rutledge, and Kearse all left the game with injures, along with some dings on the D-line, Edwards was simply too good of a running back to hold at bay. Ward is a clutch player, and bailed out the Puppies many times with big third down receptions. Of course, the short field the Gator offense gave Georgia certainly made the upset easier. I was disappointed that Coach Stoops didn't pull out all the stops and start blitzing, even after losing so many starters, just to shake things up.

Wow – this one is hard to take. It has been quite the run by the Head Ball Coach in beating down the Puppies. And it's frustrating to see so many starters on the bench while Georgia was running up the score in the fourth quarter. I hope they enjoy it, though, as they lose a ton of starters after this season, and Florida will have a lot of payback in store for them next year.

Now, Tennessee, of all teams, is back in the driver's seat to win the SEC East, which makes this result suck even more. It looks like they are going to go back to Atlanta, while the Gators are looking at a trip to Orlando.

We'll see what the mental makeup is next week against Vanderbilt. I'm expecting a sloppy game against an out-manned opponent. This will be a real test for Spurrier and his staff getting players ready to play.

**Visor Flings, Week 9:**
**UF 20, Vanderbilt 7**

As expected, a rather feeble effort against an outclassed Commodore team on Saturday. The hangover from the loss against Georgia and the three straight tough SEC games have taken their toll physically and mentally on this Gator team.

The offense has lost its efficiency. The running game goes in fits and starts, and the passing game has barely completed fifty percent of its throws the past month – amazing. Maybe Spurrier is force-feeding the passing game to try and get them going, but it's hurting the team right now. As I've said before this year, it's time to feed Fred Taylor the ball and watch him roll.

Of course, it didn't help that the defense struggled to get Vandy off the field at times. Their depleted front seven gave up enough rushing yards to allow some time-consuming drives that, fortunately, did not lead to many points. Having this game at the Swamp helped give the defense enough juice to come up with the stops when necessary.

Hopefully, some of the injured defensive players will start coming back next week at South Carolina. Of course, establishing a solid running game helps across the board right now, and it would be nice to see.

**Visor Flings, Week 10:**
**UF 48, South Carolina 21**

Maybe I should be coaching this team after all!

Finally, Fred Taylor was unleashed, and he rolled to a huge day with over 150 yards and three TDs in a big win on the road. The O-line actually looked comfortable firing off the ball and knocking the Gamecock defense backwards. It certainly helped the QBs, who have been struggling for over a month, and it also gave the defense some much-needed rest, and allowed them to avoid another physical, close game, after building a big second half lead.

The lack of cohesion in the passing game, this late in the season, has to be a huge source of frustration for the Head Ball Coach, but maybe he's finally seen that sometimes (like using the shotgun in the Sugar Bowl last year), a change is necessary to give the offense it's best chance. The receivers, other than Quez Green, have simply not developed this year, and aren't providing the consistent play that Spurrier's offense generally requires.

South Carolina did most of their damage early, jumping out to an early lead and dominating time of possession in the first half. But once Taylor hit them with some big runs, it really seemed to surprise their entire team and take some steam out of them and their fans. Once the Gamecocks had to start passing to come from behind, they were doomed. They simply don't have the passing game to come back on a team as good as Florida. The pass defense has been the most consistent thing about this entire team this year, and the secondary had another big game, holding the Gamecocks to 12 for 34 passing.

Now, it's time to try and wreck the undefeated season and National Championship hopes (again) of F$U, as they come to the Swamp next week. I know the players will throw everything they have at the Seminoles, as, for the first time since 1991, there is no SEC Championship Game the following week to prepare for. The Swamp will be alive, and it should be a great atmosphere, as Florida will probably be a rare home underdog.

**Visor Flings, Week 11:**
**UF 32, F$U 29**

This had to be one of the greatest games ever at the Swamp.

I know that was the most exciting and intense game from start to finish I've ever witnessed. There was so much future NFL talent of the field, it was ridiculous. What a great way to ruin F$U's dreams of an undefeated season and a possible National Championship – on top of last year's Beatdown on the Bayou. The crowd was into it from the start, and not even some more terrible ACC officiating could take this one away from Florida.

The Head Ball Coach is still in the heads of the Seminoles and their coaches, especially after his brilliant handling of the rotating QB play. It really seemed to keep Doug Johnson and Noah Brindise calm and focused, and ready for what the F$U defense might throw at them. And Fred Taylor was a man. He and the O-line dominated the propped-up Seminole defense, after another walk through the All-Cupcake Conference. He has exploded the past few weeks, and will make himself a lot of money come NFL draft time.

The offense gets a lot of credit for not getting too down on themselves after the Gators fell behind 17-6 early in the second quarter (with the usual help from the ACC refs). Their two consecutive TD drives to take the lead at halftime sent the message that this would be a war throughout, and gave the Swamp crowd the sense that they could help determine the outcome. I love how Brindise was making plays with the passing game, while Taylor led the running game when Johnson was in – completely the opposite of what Mickey "the lizard" Andrews and Chuck "chesty" Amato expected. Travis McGriff was the complement Quez Green needed, and Taylor also showed his fine pass-catching ability to make some first downs out of short throws.

On defense, the Gators never could really stop Travis Minor, who looks to be a Warrick Dunn clone. The real players of the game were Fred Weary and Eli Williams, who did a fine job in slowing down the F$U receivers, especially Weary, who shut down Peter Warrick. The D-line got occasional pressure, and the linebacker corps tackled well in the open field, but it was the secondary that carried the day.

I love how the F$U staff choked on their next-to-last offensive drive, when they never threw the ball inside the five to try and get a clinching TD. And then the Polish fat boy, Janikowski, mocks the Swamp fans with a lame chomp – loser!

The way the Gators shocked the Noles on their last possession was awesome. The hitch-and-go pass to Green on the first play was a stunner. Then, a great call by Spurrier with the sprint draw to Taylor down to the one while the defense was reeling, then right back with no delay with a power off-tackle to Taylor to take the lead.

At that point, the Swamp was deafening. The defense then made three consecutive perfect plays to ice the game, the last when Duane Thomas intercepted Sad Busby to end it. That was the loudest explosion I've ever heard at Florida Field.

It is strange not to be going to Atlanta next week for the SEC Championship Game. We have been spoiled by an unprecedented run of success at Florida. But, a Citrus Bowl appearance against Penn St. in Orlando is a good consolation prize – almost as good as enjoying the Nole fans' meltdown.

**Visor Flings, Week 16:**
**UF 21, Penn St. 6**

We should all feel pretty good about that one. Granted, it can't make up for the key losses to LSU and Georgia this season, but at least we finish the year on a positive note.

So Spurrier is 1-0 in his meetings with the fabled Joe Paterno. I'll admit that the Nittany Lions were hampered by the absence of tailback Curtis Enis due to questionable dealings with an agent and the loss of Joe Jurevicius due to academic troubles, but our boys still seemed to be riding the crest of their great victory over F$U, even five weeks later. By contrast, Penn State, a preseason number-one pick, was blown out in their last regular-season game by Michigan State.

For now, it's onward to the recruiting season, spring practice, and then a new life. We've gotten past what I think is really one of the toughest sorts of seasons to get through – the one which follows a national championship, when expectations are high and everyone is gunning for you. Time for a much needed hibernation. See you all in 1998.

Very Truly Yours,
The Visor

# 1998
# Hard Knocks Up in Knoxville

We began the 1998 season with great hopes, and we were not entirely disappointed. I can't say yet that the sting has gone out of those losses to two of our fiercest rivals, Tennessee and FSU, but it is some solace to recall that those teams ended up playing for the National Championship that year.

And anyway, among the many things I have learned in my retirement is that this life is a learning journey. In the same way I see now that only a couple of small turns of fate kept us from another BCS title that year, I also see that most of us have gone on to the lives that were meant for us. For instance, Terry Jackson, one of my favorite Gators of all time, had an NFL career with the 49ers and has now returned to Gainesville to become Director of Player and Community Relations. His time as a student and athlete at UF showed us all that the "outstanding young man" still exists in this country. Terry was an Academic All-American, vice president of the student body, and one hell of a football player. And just as his father, Willie, did before him, he has come back home to serve his community.

It is with something like embarrassment now that I observe the inaccuracies of some of my observations in the 1998 journal. I guess my idea that Michigan should have gone with Drew Henson over Tom Brady now seems a little misguided, given Brady's accomplishments since then. Also, in noting that Stoops had "a tough job ahead of him" at the end of the season when he was hired away from Florida by the Oklahoma Sooners, I really just underestimated the guy. He has worked wonders there, especially in the 2000 campaign. Still, what do I know? After all, I am merely the Visor who rides atop one of the brilliant coaching minds of our time. No more, no less.

The most bittersweet memory I have of the 1998 season is undoubtedly that of Ed Chester, the promising senior defensive lineman whose football career ended with a knee injury against LSU in the Swamp. The venerable Dr. Pete Indelicato, a master orthopedic surgeon (whose career is a book unto itself), had to perform muscle transference to Ed's leg in order for him to walk again. The $1 million insurance policy Ed had reluctantly taken out before the season began set a trend amongst touted college players, and he, like Terry Jackson, returned to Gainesville to contribute, becoming deeply involved with the Boys and Girls Clubs there.

In any event, they can't all be championship seasons. Still, we came though it alright, some of us more intact than others. And I was there again to see it all.

**Visor Flings, Week 1:**
**Preview and Predictions**

Well, it's finally here. Should be another sellout at The Swamp, even though we're playing the lowly Citadel. Could Miami or F$U say that? Hah! They only sell out when they play us. How pathetic.

My only concern is injuries. Seems every time we play an option team, at least one defensive lineman goes down with knee injuries, especially with all the cut and chop blocking (some of it illegal) by the opposition. I'm almost resigned to the fact that it will happen again. Hope I'm wrong.

Actually, there's some good news on the injury front. Most of the offensive line seems ready, except for Ryan Kalich. I look for him to be hobbled all year with recurring problems (pessimistic, I know, but realistic -- remember Ed Chester last year?)

The only benefit we'll reap from this game will be some experience against option passing, something Tee Martin of Tennessee will do against us in Knoxville. I'm already looking forward to NE Louisiana giving the defense some semblance of a real offensive look next week.

Not much else to say right now, other than "HeeeeeeeeeeeeeeeeeRE come the GATORS!!!"

My predictions for this season's final Top 20:
1) Florida
2) Ohio St.
3) F$U
4) Nebraska
5) Michigan
6) UCLA
7) LSU
8) Kansas St.
9) Tennessee
10) Colorado St.
11) West Virginia
12) Penn St.
13) Syracuse
14) Arizona St.
15) Virginia
16) Notre Dame
17) Miami
18) Texas A&M
19) North Carolina
20) Alabama
Florida's final record will be 12-1 (probable loss at Tennessee).

**Visor Flings, Week 2:**
**UF 49, Citadel 10**

Well, game one was pretty much status quo for the Spurrier era: Dumb penalties, lazy run defense, and unfortunately, injuries! That always leads to a lot of air time for me.
Corey Yarborough out 4-6 weeks. Man! This sure gets old; time to re-shuffle the O-line once again.
Overall, Jesse Palmer and the receivers looked okay. It was nice to see Terry Jackson back, and he did all right. I really like what I see of Norwood and Gillespie. They're going to play more this season than many people imagined.
Northeast Louisiana will prove a tougher test. I'm sure the Head Ball Coach is "coaching them up" to improve on a so-so effort.
Observations from other games this past weekend: If I were a Syracuse fan, I'd string up Paul Pasqualoni. Third and goal from the 4, and he calls a dive play off-tackle, with the very mobile Donovan McNabb as his QB. Way to try and score the clinching TD, coach! What an idiot.
Speaking of which....
Michigan better hope their first-half fiasco against Notre Dame isn't repeated. Lloyd Carr better do a much better job of going for the knockout punch early. Tom Brady looked okay at quarterback, but I'd go ahead and throw in the Golden Boy, Drew Henson. I know this goes against conventional wisdom and is open to much criticism, but the kid is the real deal. Let him grow up this year.
Oh, yeah – Auburn better batten down the hatches; four wins will be a good year for them, given their play so far.
Tennessee looms. I'm still picking the Vols over the Gators. Unfortunate, but I am, after all, merely an impartial observer. I'm just there to keep the shade out of Coach's eyes. I get the feeling the young guys at QB and wide receiver are going to feel the pressure in front of 106,000+ fans. First we'll have to deal with Northeast Louisiana. See you next week.

**Visor Flings, Week 3:**
**UF 42, NE Louisiana 10**

Nice win, but preparation for the big game has begun, and I'm worried.
Jesse showed some flashes of brilliance this past Saturday, but too often exhibited poor judgment, forcing throws and not taking much underneath yardage. Doug Johnson may show up in Knoxville, after all.
Too many turnovers, some from the veteran players; this is very surprising and disturbing.
The defense will be ready. I just hope they're not too jacked up and start overrunning plays, especially early.
The Head Ball Coach really has his work cut out this week. Now don't get me wrong. From what I could hear, I'm sure there was some sandbagging going on in the play-calling and

game plan, and Coach Superior has improved his big-game planning. I just hope he coaches according to how THIS game develops, not according to his philosophy of throwing no matter what.
Should be exciting (actually, too exciting for me; I will likely be spending a lot of time in the grass).

**Visor Flings, Week 4:**
**Tennessee 28, Florida 17…Yikes!**

No need to belabor the importance of holding onto the football here. I only hope the flu bug that struck the offensive line was really a contributing factor, because they have been the most disappointing unit so far.
QB play was excellent, the defense was solid, and the special teams were dynamite (except for the lack of a field goal kicker - but unfortunately we all already knew that would be the case). Congrats to the Travis twins. I know they're heartbroken about the fumbles, but what a gutsy effort! We still should have utilized Nafis a little more...
I'm confident that we can still run the table from this point on.
What the offensive line lacks is an aggressive attitude. When are these guys going to run block with a mean streak? I'm sure many people will argue that it's because of the premium put on the passing game, and I'll agree up to a point. But, come on! Let's get tough, guys! Upon further reflection, though, this has been the trend for Coach Stephens' unit over the years, and maybe it will never change.
That said, I still was impressed by Jesse and Doug, and the pass blocking was solid. When you empty the backfield, you will give up some sacks. Hey - the QBs ate the ball instead of throwing interceptions, and with our defense, that's okay by me. My only thought on that matter is having a flat route or quick curl as a bail-out to possibly avoid taking a sack. That could be a wide receiver read that needs to be considered.

I was also impressed by the routes used by Spurrier and Dixon; I heard that they studied the BYU control passing game over the summer, and if so, this led to a terrific passing attack, especially in a loud, hostile environment with young skill-position players.

My initial post stated how much I respect Terry Jackson. I can only hope he bounces back; the last thing the ball coach and I expected was for him to be stripped of the ball once he had zeroed in on the end zone, and it was a devastating start to the game. If we're up even 10-0 at that point, game over.

I will not say it was Tennessee's time to win; I feel that's a defeatist attitude, and it was obvious that we gave the game away. Period.

Well, one step at a time. Stephens needs to get the offensive line on track beginning this week, and start building momentum.

**Visor Flings, Week 5:**
**UF 38, UK 17**

All in all, a pretty good performance against Kentucky. I know everyone was pulling their hair out because of the kickoff return against us, the interception return, and two long pass plays, but those things will be corrected. Plus, the Wildcats' Couch showed why he's the top QB in the country: accurate, mobile, and cool under pressure.

The running game still remains a concern for us, but it appears that opposing teams are now crowding the line of scrimmage with eight in the box, actually daring the Gators to throw. It is a strategy that has sometimes worked recently and will continue.

Unfortunately, it's painfully obvious now that TJ has lost a step. Before his knee injury and surgery last year, he could always hit the secondary faster and outrun them to the end zone. Ironically, though, I feel this could open up a great opportunity for the overall offense to actually improve. Now that Eugene McCaslin has returned, we can move TJ to fullback. This will (1) give you a terrific blocker who will crush blitzing linebackers, (2) get Gillespie more touches (this guy is very talented), and (3) allow McCaslin to shake off the rust and show whether he's really someone to count on next year or not.

On to Alabama – too bad Arkansas exposed them before we could embarrass them on TV. I wanted them to have a false sense of security before we disciplined them. I hope Gator Boosters can take the money left over from the "Keep Ray Goof" fund and apply it to the "Keep Mike Dumbose" fund.

Actually, any time a college team gets crushed like that, they usually come out tough the next week, especially at home. Plus, the injury list continues to grow:

Ian Skinner - out for the year with ACL tear
Bo Carroll - out 2-3 weeks with sprained knee
Reggie McGrew - doubtful with bad elbow (that was unexpected, and hurts)
Buck Gurley - knee scope; out 2 weeks
Cheston Blackshear - hand (doubtful)
Teako Brown - left shoulder (doubtful)
Travis Taylor - right shoulder (doubtful)
Tony George - left knee (doubtful)

Spurrier will probably hold everyone out that he can as required. Potentially the biggest game of the year (now that Tennessee is history) comes up next week at The Swamp. We need to beat LSU to have any hope of a place in the Bowl Challenge Series (BCS).

My prediction: Florida 31, Alabama 14

See you next week.

**Visor Flings, Week 6:**
**UF 16, Alabama 10**

Yecch!!!

It appears that this team lacks the weekly dedication and focus that the 1995-96 teams exhibited. I'm afraid that it's too late in the season to expect any great improvement, so let's get it on with what we've got.

Contrary to popular opinion, I do believe that we can punch it in more often on the ground. I think the Evil Genius is just trying to work on the execution (an apt term) of the passing game in the red zone. However, at this point I feel he's ready to run it on at least first and goal, and maybe second, before throwing. It's obvious that what we were wonderfully successful doing in past years just isn't cutting it right now.

So be it.

Anyway, I'm not going to crucify TJ for another fumble, but McCaslin may get some more playing time this week. And that bootleg call by the head ball coach was pretty dumb (and he admits it), and it led to the fumble by Doug Johnson.

Congratulations to the Georgia Pups for beating LSU, but really – why was there so much hype about LSU? This is practically the same team that rolled over at home to Ole Miss and Notre Dame last year, so it's not a shock.

I can't wait for Tigers' Herb Tyler and Kevin Faulk to get their whuppin' Saturday night. I really think the defense will rise to their best performance of the season, and the offense will do its part, too.

The only player I really fear on LSU is Anthony MacFarlane. He is apparently un-blockable in the college game. Look for TJ to stay in and help block.

Oh, yeah – I still want to see a few plays with TJ at fullback and McCaslin or Gillespie at tailback. I'm telling you, this is the way to get the best personnel on the field at the same time.

The Swamp will be rockin' on Saturday!

My prognostication: Gators 31 LSU 17

**Visor Flings, Week 7:**
**UF 22, LSU 10**

Ouch! A satisfying win, but at a large cost. With Jesse Palmer's shoulder injury, Doug Johnson is the man now. Hopefully the head ball coach will protect him by leaving more blockers in on pass plays and establishing the running game.

It's really a shame about Ed Chester. Devastating hit in the first half ruined his knee. The guy finally seemed to be free of nagging injuries and was having a fine season. Now, his career seems in jeopardy. I'm not sure of everything a dislocated kneecap entails, but it sounds like there could be either blood vessel and/or nerve damage involved. Tragic. I hope he can finish his degree and mentally recover. I'm sure Dr. Pete can help him recover physically as well as possible; it's the psychological part that would worry me more right now.

No more QB controversy either. Palmer may have been able to return for the F$U game if it were his non-throwing shoulder, but no such luck. Now, DJ has to make it happen. If he'll relax and throw the underneath stuff to his running backs and tight end more often, he'll be fine. He does seem to be better at audibles than Jesse. Coach Spurrier can help with better red zone play-calling. Please stop calling pass plays almost exclusively against a three-man defensive line...

I was encouraged by the offensive line's play on Saturday. If the wide receivers would quit holding 10-20 yards downfield, life (not to mention play-calling) would be much simpler. The line did a great job against MacFarland, limiting his impact better than any team that's played LSU so far.

Kudos to Derrick Chambers, Gerard Warren, and especially Tim Beauchamp. Wow - he finally showed some real emotion and fire on the field. I think Chester's injury finally got these guys to play angry.

Let's just keep the ball rolling (with no more injuries). It will be nice to spank Baby Bowden again, and then have two weeks of preparation to bitch-slap the Bullpups for laying down for the Vols. What a gutless performance! It makes me want revenge all the more.

What a great crowd at The Swamp this past weekend; it certainly helped shut up the smack-talking LSU fans. I wonder if anyone else heard the same crap from those guys that I heard down on the sideline. Big talk for not having done squat nationally for 10 or 15 years. I loved punking them on and off the field.

Next week, we're at home again against Auburn. Visor Vision predicts: Florida 41 Auburn 10

**Visor Flings, Week 8:**
**UF 24, Auburn 3**

Well, that was about as exciting as watching a Big Eleven game (I refuse to call it the Big Ten – those guys should learn to count!)

The second half sure was ugly, but I think the head ball coach just shut everything down in anticipation of whipping the Bullpups.

Johnson looked marginally better, but STILL throws into coverage. Oh, well, I'm used to seeing it by now. It'll never change, so Gator fans will have to deal with it. Unfortunately, he can still has the potential to lose a game for us.

There's not a doubt in my mind that Georgia coach Joe Kines will use the same scheme as last year: play zone and let the Gator offense beat itself. I'm sure there's a long list of Gator fans that want blood in Jacksonville, and not just because it will be Halloween.

Also, I'm sure Coach Stoops' boys are ready to get after Quincy Carter and make him wish he were playing Tennessee again.

Actually, it wouldn't surprise me to see Kentucky beat them in Lexington.
More to come next week on this game. The Cocktail Party awaits. Go Gators!

**Visor Flings, Week 9:**
**Off Week**

Well, well, well. It's that time again. The World's Largest Outdoor Cocktail Party. The Border War. Florida-Georgia.

The Gators will have some nice tricks for the Bullpups, and it won't be a treat for them. It's payback time for last year, especially with all the trash talk after they beat us, 37-17.

I remember how the Pups backed it up, losing AT HOME at Fred Sanford Stadium the following week to a mediocre Auburn team by 17 points. Then, when they could have done us both a favor (not to mention the rest of the country, which now will have to listen to the incessant whining of the Tennessee In-breds the rest of the season), they roll over and play dead AGAIN, AT HOME, scoring only three points against the Vols.

Boy – I can't wait to neuter and punish them! Can you tell The Visor wants this one real bad?

I really feel that the defense will play its finest game of the year to this point. And I think the head ball coach has a little extra motivation as well.

Quincy Carter, the Georgia quarterback, will make some plays with his speed, and Coach Champ Bailey will dictate some schemes on both sides of the ball, but that won't be enough to hold back an angry bunch of Gators.

Plus, we'll get to see (I hope) how Eugene McCaslin might fare as next year's starting tailback. This is his last real chance to make something of his star-crossed career at Florida – I just hope he grows up and plays hard.

Look for more short and medium-range stuff to the wide receivers and running backs as well. This will hopefully keep DJ from throwing away the game.

Visor Vision: Florida 31 Pups 14

**Visor Flings, Week 10:**
**UF 38, UGA 7**

Trick or Treat, Pups! Nothing like 38 rocks in your candy bag, huh?

A nice win. After thinking about the lack of sacks, I realized that Stoops probably was playing more of a containment scheme to keep Quincy Carter from scrambling for big yards and improvising big pass plays. Still, from my vantage point, I couldn't overhear his instructions to the defensive line. A lot of noise in that stadium. Georgia racked up some yards, but only seven points. Wonder who the Pups think is better -- UF or UT?

Actually, I'm sure the Pups feel like we've felt after a lot of games this year: lots of yardage, few points, turnovers. Too bad for them.

Well, it's on to the soft part of the schedule. Two easy wins coming up. Now the concern is being as healthy as possible for Nov. 21 vs. the Semi-holes.

I never like turf games, especially on that concrete called a field at Vanderbilt. Hurts a little more when I get flung. I think the Head Ball Coach will work the running game a little more with his running game coordinator, Stephens. Maybe this will work out. I like seeing McCaslin carry the load; time to get him sharp for the big game in three weeks, and it will be one more week TJ can rest his knee.

I predicted we'd lose to Tennessee and beat F$U, and I'm sticking to my story.

As for this week, Visor Vision sees Florida 31 Vanderbilt 7

**Visor Flings, Week 11:**
**UF 45, Vanderbilt 13**

Another solid victory. I really liked how the receivers performed. And how about Eugene McCaslin? Good, hard running, and his pick-ups on blitz protection were excellent. He really laid the lumber to some of the linebackers. He and Rob Roberts are the physical runningbacks needed to smash those F$U linebackers in the mouth a few times when they blitz.

Doug played well. The only thing he seems to be doing wrong now is being impatient when the blitz IS picked up, and he has extra time. He still throws the deep ball into double coverage when something else has to be available over the middle. Hope the QB coach helps him with this.

I really have only two concerns at this point:

1) staying healthy

2) not getting a false sense of security beating up on Vandy and the Lamecocks. The receivers better be aggressive against those overrated F$U defensive backs, and the O-line and running backs better be prepared for Mickey Andrews' blitz packages. Just like in 1995-1997, when the Gator QB has some time, he'll burn the Semi-hole secondary

I also enjoyed watching the play of Alex Brown, Andra Davis, and Keith Kelsey. As far as next year goes, a solid group of starting LBs. Actually, a defensive line, consisting of McGrew (hopefully), Warren, Chambers, and Gurley sounds good, too. Just need some depth developed in a hurry.

Well, time to hammer the last nail into Coach Brad Scott's coffin.

As I see it: Florida 48 Lamecocks 7

**Visor Flings, Week 12:**
**UF 33, South Carolina 14**

Another routine win, it seems.

As to other games on Saturday…Hoo, boy! This is what happens when you don't take care of your own business. What a bunch of BS!

Tennessee pulled one out against Arkansas. The great Nutt Job who coaches the Hogs went into an offensive shell, with the Vols defensive backs playing a soft zone in fear of being turned into more toast! Disgusting! By the way, I'm sick of hearing how good Dwayne Goodrich is. Did you see that punk celebrating? He knew what kind of BS had just pulled him out of the fire. What a joke!

Congrats to Kansas State on their victory over Nebraska, but as the ever watchful Visor who has seen many Gator players injured, I'd say please suspend that pathetic referee who watched the 'Husker QB almost get paralyzed. It may not have made a difference in the end, but let the players decide that, okay? First down at the 45 with 2 1/2 minutes left would have been interesting. Disgusting!

Now about this weekend's game for us...

Why does everyone fear F$U's defense? Please! Let both teams switch schedules each year, and we know what the results would be.

Let's see: R. Wilson, P. Boulware, A. Wadsworth, S. Cowart, D. Bush, etc. vs. T. Polley? L.Smith? J. Johnson? L. Green? I'm tired of the over-hyping of these guys. They're good, but not that good. I'll take our bunch against anyone. Period.

The Head Ball Coach knows how to beat these guys. Just keep burning them deep. Plus, look for McCaslin to get more calls, including screens. Just keep telling DJ to relax and not force things. Running Game Coordinator Stephens needs to tell his guys to smash a few people in the mouth, like Donnie Young. That'll slow down the rush. Tell the O-line to be the aggressors. All you have to do is watch last year's game again to see what damage the ENTIRE offense can do. Patience!

It will be nice to welcome back Reggie McGrew and Willie Cohens. Nice game from Gerard Warren, D. Chambers, J. Rutledge, and B. Alexander this past week.

I just hope Stoops tells the defensive backs (especially T. George) to stick with the receivers until the play is over, and quit peeking into the backfield. The LBs will take care of the Rooster. People who are familiar with the ESPN commercial that shows the Vikings' John Randle chasing the chicken with a Farve jersey on will know what I mean.

Just double Peter Warrick and prevent cutbacks by Travis Minor. Look for Jevon Kearse to play more as a down lineman to beef up the pass rush. That'll be fun to watch.

Too bad the Semi-hole fans will have the injured Weinke excuse to fall back on. Well, we've lost Palmer, Chester, and 12 other guys for various parts of the ENTIRE season. So, shut up and play.

I'll go with Florida 27 F$U 17

**Visor Flings, Week 13:**
**FSU 23, UF 12**

What a disappointment! I think many people expected more from this team, and it just hasn't really come together this season.

DEFENSE: In retrospect, the defense played well. The F$U offense did many different things, and ran the ball well. Unfortunately, Stoops had to play it conservatively with four freshmen (Cromartie, Norwood, Alexander, Manuel) playing most of the game due to physical injury (Graddy) and physical/mental injury (T. George). The young guys acquitted themselves well under a lot of pressure; we'll be fine there for years. McGrew played a gutsy game as well, making two big plays. Warren was active as well, and the linebackers were solid. It was tough having to play what was in actuality a new offense with little film to study.

OFFENSE: Well, now I know why the Head Ball Coach picked Jesse Palmer as his starter. Apparently Doug Johnson will never overcome his knack for forcing the ball into coverage and not throwing it away. Two critical interceptions that dramatically altered the pace of the game. The pass protection was fine. I expected some sacks, but Johnson had plenty of time to throw. McCaslin did all he could do. I'm not even shocked at the poor run blocking anymore; maybe it's time Coach Stephens starts all over with his schemes, because things aren't developing as they should. Injuries are not an excuse for this game. Coach Spurrier probably wishes he'd called more running plays against 6 and 7 defensive backs, even though the sledding was tough. But, he'll always pass first, so that's not a surprise either.

SPECIAL TEAMS: Wasiliewski was terrific! One bad punt out of way too many attempts. And, angling the kicks away from the returner with distance was impressive. Coverage was adequate, and Chandler made his one attempt (although he should have had more).

MISC.: What was wrong with Tony George? Sorry, no excuse – period. How foolish does he look? What a terrible call by the refs on the fumble recovery for a touchdown! Inexcusable. What about the pass call on third and goal from the five after the safety? Everyone was stunned, including the other side. Marquand Manuel probably felt sick dropping a sure interception that turned into a gift touchdown that changed the game. But, the offense never picked up the slack, and gets most of the blame for this loss.

Well, a bitter end to the regular season. My guess right now is that we'll play Michigan in the Citrus Bowl. Doesn't that sound exciting? Looks like we'll have three undefeated nationally ranked teams after all, and I think that's a good thing -- maybe it will speed up the realization of a playoff system in the future.

Time to get an early start on recruiting...

**Visor Flings, Weeks 14-16:**

Well, the Gators' defensive coordinator, Bob Stoops, is off to Oklahoma. Good luck to him and whomever on the coaching staff goes along - he has a tough job ahead of him.

Also, it looks like Carl Franks (and maybe Jim Collins) may go to Duke, Franks as head coach.

Yikes! We'll have maybe six coaches left for the bowl game.

Speaking of the bowl game, it looks like the Gators are the leaders for the Orange Bowl, surprisingly. This would be an unexpected windfall for the program, exposure-wise and monetarily. A BCS bowl carries much more weight than the Citrus, and the financial gain is roughly $550-$650K (after splitting 12 ways for the conference). The Visor is hoping for a trip to that old house of thrills, where many a classic game has been played. It would also raise our profile in South Florida for recruiting.

Recruiting!

This much instability in the coaching staff does not bode well. This is a critical year for filling needs at DL and LB, and we're lagging behind right now. The Gators are not on nearly enough blue-chip visit lists at present, and that has me scratching my head. Maybe we need some assistant coaches with some actual charisma who will aggressively pursue recruits. This has me nervous.

## Visor Flings, Weeks 17-18

Happy Holidays to everyone (except Noles, Vols, and Pups, of course).

The Visor is hoping for presents to put under the Gators' tree, especially new defensive linemen and linebackers.

Recruiting is starting to pick up. Five so far, four on offense. Look for several of the Jacksonville boys from Ed White and Raines to join the Holy forces for next year's Jihad (guess we've been watching too much bombing of Iraq around Coach's house .)

The trip to Miami should help raise our recruiting profile in South Florida, and we could pick up some unexpected benefits.

See you in January for my Inaugural Recruiting Analysis (IRA).

And make sure to check out my Bowl Picks. Challenge me if you dare!

Ho! Ho! Ho! (Chomp! Chomp! Chomp! to you non-Gators).

**Visor Flings, Weeks 17-19:**
**UF 31, Syracuse 10**

The Visor has been out on the recruiting trail, so there's a lot to catch up on.

A fine effort from the entire team in the Orange Bowl, especially the defense, given the coaching flux. Bob Sanders is to be commended for a nice job preparing for the Syracuse multiple attack, and the defensive players played hard. Big Money was terrific, despite his suspension for unsportsmanlike behavior. Hope his suspension will only be one or two games this fall.

The offense was solid. DJ played well, and Jesse was back from his injury and really came through, especially since he ought to have been cold after being out for 10 weeks. Unfortunately, Johnson was injured in the game, and this might lead to another QB soap opera this summer and fall. My opinion is that Jesse is the guy, but red-shirting him and going with Doug might be in the best interest of the team and the Head Ball Coach long-term.

Sorry, but there was no way I could pull for F$U in the Fiesta Bowl against Tennessee. Think about it – they will never, ever root for us, and if someone says so, don't believe him. Still, since the Vols won 23-16, thus capturing the National Championship, we now have to listen to and see the obnoxious TV ads for Tennessee. Well, we get our chance again at both of them in the Swamp this fall.

It was obvious that having a whole month to prepare for F$U's Marcus Outzen (along with double covering the speedy Warrick) was all the Vols really needed. Too bad we didn't have that luxury, or else I really believe we would have had that rematch we all wanted. Oh, well...

The Gators' coaching staff welcomes Jon Hoke. He comes highly recommended by Bob Stoops, and I believe Coach Spurrier has found someone to ensure continuity in the defense. He obviously has some big shoes to fill, and will be under pressure unlike anything else he's ever experienced professionally. Looks like he might double as special teams coach as well. He'll certainly be busy.

As far as recruiting, this upcoming weekend is huge for the Gators, with around 20 kids coming in. I'm sure Spurrier wanted a defensive coordinator in place by now, and we have one. It's no secret that we need a lot of help on the defensive line, then at linebacker. So far, the news has been less than scintillating. I hope that the big names on the Gators' board come into the fold soon, so we can gain some momentum before Signing Day (February 2nd).

Next year's defense will be very good, but very thin in the front seven. There will be a lot of youth backing up the starters and getting significant minutes early. That means some trouble ahead, especially early in the season. Unfortunately, I expect a return to the 1993-94 seasons in terms of having to outscore some teams, including Tennessee.

I guess that's it for the '98-99 season. We'll get the guys in the gym – can't let anybody get soft. It never ends, does it? Still, I think some nice wintertime sleep will do us all some good. And as for me, I'm due for a little shelf time.

Very Truly Yours,
The Visor

# 1999
# The Pothole at the End of the Road

Looking back at my journals for the 1999 season, I see that I fell into a trap. I pinned a lot of hope on a young team – too much, and I seemed to forget that many of these players were, after all, if not teenagers, then certainly young men with very little experience in high-pressure situations. So, you might say I was forced by circumstance to change my own perspective on things by the end of it all.

True, we came out with guns slinging, winning our first four games convincingly (and finding redemption against Tennessee), but the first split in the seams came against Alabama. After that, injuries, missteps, and a clash of egos between one quarterback and one coach gradually undid us.

Sadly, the three big games we lost to close out the season circumcised our fine streak of ten-win seasons, but as they say, all good things must end. To add to the bitterness was Florida State's victory over an out-manned Virginia Tech team in the National Championship.

I would say the greatest pluses for us came after it was all over and we had lost to Michigan State in the Citrus Bowl. The Gators had an excellent recruiting year in the spring of 2000, and the broad picture shows that many of those new players helped make for some very good football in the early going of the new millennium.

And Coach and I, what did we learn? Why, the same lesson we always did: patience.

**Visor Flings, Week 1:**
**Preview and Predictions**

Finally! The new season is here; enough pre-season talk. Time to put up or shut up (this means you, too, Arizona and Ohio St).

OFFENSE

Talk about put-up time.

Doug Johnson has the reigns -- no excuses. He's had by far his best fall practice, so let's see if he's learned to check-off to secondary receivers and avoid critical turnovers. Jesse Palmer is ready in the wings, and according to the Evil Genius, will play this year and not be red-shirted. He wants to play now, and you can't fault him for that. It's scary – our season rests with DJ and…

The offensive line. I have to admit I'm sick of seeing this much talent be out-of-shape and underachieving. They're two-deep, and have the additional coaching help of John Hunt. All they need is to average around 150 yards per game to really explode this year. Maybe seeing the young guys get some significant playing time the first two games will shake up the veterans.

The receiving prospects look very good right now. One star (Travis Taylor) and a group of solid athletes who will make things happen. Reche Caldwell could have the best natural ability of them all. Will the tight ends contribute other than as blockers and decoys? History says no, but they sure could ease the load on the QBs and receivers (I know – I'm probably fooling myself).

The running game is the mystery on this side of the ball. Earnest Graham gets first crack at solidifying this position. Practice reports are encouraging, but it's time to perform when it counts. Hopefully the Head Ball Coach will incorporate Robert Gillespie in the short passing game as well – this could really help take pressure off the QB (not to mention keep him healthy). Chuckie Marks could be the sleeper. Rod Frazier really needs to stay healthy all year – his blocking is often overlooked until he's out, and the running game sputters and the protection gets shakier.

DEFENSE

Wow! No returning starters...three or four true freshmen slated for lots of snaps...a thin line...not the best of situations, but it is what it is.

Surprising that this situation could develop at Florida, but it partly reinforces the Visor's opinion that our recruiting still isn't what it could be. Believe me, we get a great group each year, but always seem to miss out on guys at a needed position. Curious...

The defensive line is getting the most attention (and receiving the most concern). Lots of ability, and some proven studs like Gerard Warren and Derrick Chambers. But, lots of inexperience behind them at tackle and end. It's time for guys like Thad Bullard and Buck Gurley (maybe Alex Brown at end?) to perform consistently.

The linebacker corps seems to be ready. Keith Kelsey has his chance to shine in the middle; Andra Davis could be a run-stuffer, and Eugene McCaslin (yes, that Eugene McCaslin) is the most athletic of the bunch and has impressed in camp. Alex Brown is by far the best physical specimen, but his role seems undefined even now. I'm hoping the defensive staff doesn't waste his ability. Lots of young studs (Hardman, Farrior) will also get their chance to shine.

The secondary is young also, but could be the most exciting unit (and the best at he end of the year). At corner, Bennie Alexander is firmly entrenched right now, and Robert Cromartie is capitalizing on the experience gained under fire as a true freshman last year to start on the other side. What is surprising (and actually exciting) to the Visor is that Lito Sheppard is pushing so hard for significant time; this guy is the real deal. The safeties should be solid. Lester Norwood went through the same learning process as Cromartie last year, and

Marquand Manuel is the vocal leader of the entire defense. Todd Johnson and Dwight Jackson are solid second-teamers, and could push for lots of snaps this fall. Oh, forgot to mention Rod Graddy...NOT!! What a waste.

Overall, an athletic, fast, inexperienced group. Welcome to the SEC, Jon Hoke! Good Luck...

SPECIAL TEAMS

Yes, a not-so-special group (especially the kickers) since the departure of Judd Davis and Shane Edge in 1994.

Jeff Chandler is the starting place-kicker, and seems to at least be consistent from 40 yards in (I hope). I surely had enough Tennessee overtime experience to last a long time. David Wasiliewski finished strong last year, and looks ready to settle in as the punter for three more years.

The return group is what's exciting here. John Capel...Reche Caldwell...Bo Carroll…Lito Sheppard. Enough said.

OUTLOOK FOR 1999

There's a real chance that the Gators could match their home loss total in the Spurrier era this year. The Visor feels losses to both Tennessee and F$U are quite possible again. I hope the magic of the Swamp will help. Believe it or not, the game I want to win the most is against those Inbreds from Knoxville – anything to make up for that travesty last year.

However, the Vols have probably their best running game ever this year, and that could make for a real headache.

F$U still can't run the ball consistently, and that can always hurt you on the road. Their defense, though, picks up the slack and then some. Plus, a big-play receiver like Peter Warrick can never be overlooked (remember Peerless Price?).

The prediction: 9-2 regular season (7-1 in conference)

Can't wait for the team to prove me wrong and burn down Atlanta once again on their march to New Orleans – I'd gladly humble myself.

LET'S GET IT ON!!!!!

**Visor Flings, Week 2:**
**UF 55, Western Michigan 27**

Well, a rather lackluster showing Saturday despite the lopsided score. The offense looks improved, but the defense (especially the line) looked very shaky.

On offense, the running game looked much improved. Looks like Stephens and Hunt may have something going here this year, but the proof will come 9/18 vs. the Inbreds. Once again, though, an injury could haunt the line. If ZZ can't play against the Vols due to injury, that will be a major blow, despite what Yarborough may do – ZZ was named the starter. Earnest Graham did a nice job of setting up his blocks and making extra yardage after the first hit. However, Gillespie, Carroll, and Marks are a noticeable drop-off as far as rushing the ball. I get the feeling we'll throw to these guys in 2 weeks (at least I hope so – could be some real mismatches created here).

Doug Johnson looked better, but I'm still not sold on his supposed "great" improvement in the off-season. Still locked on to the primary receiver occasionally, and should have had his first TD pass picked (could have been the receiver's fault, though). He still needs to improve weekly for this to be a big year.

The receivers were very good. Travis Taylor looked fine, with smooth routes and aggressiveness toward the ball. After him though, I still don't see a reliable 2nd option. Maybe this will be spread around all year – I'd still like someone to step up. The young guys showed some flashes, especially Caldwell. His running ability after the catch is unquestionable; he could really do some damage this year, even in the big games.

The defense was okay, especially for a unit that combined for around 15 TOTAL career starts. The line was disappointing, however. No pass pressure (except for A. Brown) and little penetration. I'm sure a lot of this was due to showing only base defenses on film, but I'm still worried about the one-on-one play of the linemen. Thad Bullard looks like a bust to me – he should be moved to linebacker, where he can utilize his speed and agility – because he just doesn't get in the backfield. Derrick Chambers was a NON-FACTOR. The coaches better figure out if he's out of position or needs some extra motivation, because his performance was lousy. And the hope that some of the young guys like Campbell and Reynolds could contribute this year seems far-fetched right now. Looks like everything rides on Warren and Gurley staying healthy, which is usually a recipe for disaster, given injuries.

The linebackers were the most effective unit. McCaslin actually made some good pursuit plays, but he doesn't have the strength or aggressiveness to penetrate the backfield. Andra Davis looked quicker than I expected, but he and Kelsey need to learn how to drop into proper zones on pass plays. The middle was wide open all evening.

The safeties were OK. Poor Lester Norwood was chasing down "Toast" Cromartie's receiver all night, but he does come up too strong on the play fake occasionally. Todd Johnson looks like a real hustler and seems to be an aggressive tackler. Marquand Manuel was fine.

The cornerbacks were very disappointing. Is there a new scheme? Is Hoke hiding something and not playing press coverage much? Or did they regress? Part of it was the good play of Lester and his receivers no doubt, but I'm troubled.

I'm sure there will be improvement all around this week. The Head Ball Coach knows he's got his work cut out this year. Looks like UCF won't be overlooked...too bad for them. It could be ugly. I still don't see enough to pick us over the Inbreds right now.

**Visor Flings, Week 3:**
**UF 58, University of Central Florida 27**

Random thoughts:
1) Either this is a great con job by Hoke (remember "The Sting"?), or we'll need at least 35 points this coming Saturday night against Tennessee.
2) I've been going to the games since 1973 (Nat Moore was the first guy I was old enough to follow) and I just don't have a good vibe right now. It would be a real shame to lose at home to the Inbreds, especially after what happened last year.
3) It was good to see DJ come right back after the "Dilfer" on the first series, but I expect better from a senior quarterback in that situation. He'll be in it many times this Saturday. By the way, I'll bet Tony Dungy wishes he had Jesse Palmer to come in.
4) Hope the Offensive Line fires out and smashes some people so Graham can do his thing. A hundred yards rushing is a must.
5) We need both lines to play their best game of the season (at least until 11/20). Losing Ben Brown and Chris Reynolds doesn't help (especially Brown).
6) It was somewhat embarrassing and frustrating to sit and watch four quarters of defensive backs backpedaling 10-15 yards off the receivers. What is Hoke afraid of? Let 'em play! And what's up with the safeties? More bad angles on long passes and rushing up too quickly as the patterns develop. Ugly.
7) On the positive side, so far so good on the penalty front. A real improvement from last year. It's amazing how much easier managing the game is without stupid things holding you back. Just keep a clear head and perform the assignments this week; that's all you can ask.
8) I'm in a foul mood for Saturday night, prime-time, and the Inbreds will hear it as I watch the boys on in the Swamp. If the team performs as well as the Swamp Things cheer, we'll be okay.
9) Prediction: objectively speaking, UT 31 UF 24. Like I said last week, I will gladly humble myself if we do win and march on to Atlanta to burn it down.

**Visor Flings, Week 4:**
**UF 23, Tennessee 21**

Well, that was quite a game. A supreme effort by the defense – Alex Brown is the National Player of the Week, but every member of the defense contributed. Gerard Warren's impact was obvious. He clogged the middle sufficiently to free up the linebackers to run free and make plays.
The offense did a nice job of executing. The pass protection was very good, and the establishment of the running game in the second half was important.

Both units were able to dictate the flow of the game, especially important for a young unit like this defense. Looks like Jon Hoke was indeed holding back a lot from the Vols to look at the first two games, but the players made things work. Kudos to both.

The performance by Alex Brown reminded The Visor of a similar performance by a Gator player – Wilbur Marshall's destruction of USC in 1982. I suppose Tee Martin wasn't laughing in the face of this pass rush, and the vaunted Inbred offensive line took a beating. Jamal Lewis ran well, and should have had 30+ carries. Once again, however, Tennessee's Phil Foolmer showed his real colors as a game coach, especially against the Evil Genius. I have to laugh at all the accolades he received for his coaching acumen after last year's BS; any real follower of college football knows luck is what saved the Vols last year. I still remember the almost incredulous look on his face as he lifted the trophy last year (just like the look on many other Gator, Razorback, and Semen-hole faces). I don't think even he could believe that garbage! What a chump...

So, did the Gators win BECAUSE of, or DESPITE Doug Johnson? I'd say it's a wash. He did make some excellent throws, and checked off to many proper plays, blocking schemes, etc. But (seems like there's always a "but" with DJ), he needs to move around in the pocket or adjust himself before making more of those off-balance throws. Yikes! He's personally made Deon Grant all-SEC the past two years, and really made the game closer in score than in level of play. Overall, however, a good performance.

The crowd once again showed what makes the Swamp the toughest place to visit as an opponent. The noise level was equaled only by a few other games – F$U in '91 and '97, and Tennessee in '97. Don't those comments by the Inbreds about how "we'll shut the fans up" and "it's no different than Kentucky" sound stupid to their fans now? We (along with the rest of the country) already knew what awaited them.

So, now it's on the road to Kentucky. Beware – their offensive style will be especially difficult for the young defense, and the quick passing game will negate much pressure. Don't expect the big numbers by Brown, Gurley, et. al. this week. The LBs and DBs will really have to make the key plays in this one; they'll be under a lot of pressure. We'll need a solid passing AND rushing game from the offense to prevent the unthinkable. There will be a letdown after the Inbreds, so the Head Ball Coach and his staff must keep the player's attention. Here is where the seniors can step in and keep the team focused.

Looks like Buck Gurley might get limited snaps, which is a good sign. However, Travis Taylor will be out for 2-3 games, and will be missed, being as he is DJ's favorite receiver. Darrel Jackson did a terrific job of stepping into Taylor's role, and hopefully can keep it going the next few weeks. I'll admit I was unsure whether he could handle it, and he certainly did this time. We don't need any more injuries to the defensive linemen or receivers.

As I stated in previous posts, I would gladly humble myself if we beat the Inbreds on the way to burning down Atlanta. Consider me humbled.

**Visor Flings, Week 5:**
**UF 38, Kentucky 10**

A nice way to take care of the first road game of the season.

The offense did what it should have done, especially considering the mismatch of our offensive line to their defense. I'll admit I was disturbed watching Graham go out after the second play of the game, especially not knowing what exactly had happened. But Gillespie and Carroll filled in more than adequately. Looks like coach Teevens is doing a good job so far.

When will we throw to the backs more? Seems like the Head Ball Coach saves plays like that only for certain situations or games, instead of incorporating it into the weekly game plan. Curious.

I thought Bo Carroll would move to wide receiver more, especially with Taylor out for 3 - 4 weeks......

Doug wasn't as sharp as I would have liked, but did avoid turnovers and made a perfect throw in stride to Dwight Jackson. By the way, when Jackson came out, it was pretty gruesome-looking, with the blood gushing. He showed toughness coming back later. Nice catch by Haugabrook on the fade route in the end zone.

The defense did a great job of changing mind-sets from Tennessee's running to UK's throwing. I liked that Hoke inserted Manuel and Dixon at linebacker. I'd grown very tired of watching all that underneath stuff be open all game. Also, I enjoyed the heavy hits laid on the UK receivers and tight ends – funny how they didn't seem to run their routes as sharply as the game wore on. It was obvious that all we needed for pressure was our front four. It's amazing how much the entire defense benefits from a consistent, strong push from up front. Hope it continues.

It will be interesting to see how effective 'Bama's offense will be against us. I think they actually could prove more troubling than the Inbreds, although that will depend mainly on how their WRs play. For some reason, I'm not overly concerned about Alexander. He's good, yes; but not an explosive player like Jamal Lewis. He is a good receiver, though, and that could cause problems if the ends and linebackers aren't paying attention.

It's a shame seeing a talent like Freddie Milons wasted at 'Bama. I wonder if he regrets not coming to Florida? He must to some extent.

I think the Gators will continue their roll to Atlanta by 10 - 21 points.

**Visor Flings, Week 6:**
**Alabama 40, UF 39**

Isn't it ironic that on Doug Johnson's finest day as a Gator, we lose? I wonder if this is one of those star-crossed careers that never gets rewarded? I hope not.

It's obvious by the postings so far that most concur that the defensive scheme was "soft" and passive. At this point, I'd suggest letting the defensive backs have the chance of pressing in man-to-man coverage (at least 50% of the time) and seeing what happens. Hey, if they get burned, we'll at least get the ball back quicker. I know that sounds flippant, but it's worked in the past (remember when Anthone Lott was "Antoast" against UT and Miss. St. in 1993?). They need the experience, so give them a chance. They'll have no better group of receivers to practice against than their own teammates. And by the way, for any misguided fans out there, we should NOT put Lito Sheppard at safety! He's got the talent and guts to be terrific at CB, so leave him alone.

LSU and Auburn pose little threat this year, and Quincy Carter doesn't have enough help to really scare me, either. So, we still should head to Atlanta, which I think most fans would have gladly accepted before the season started. Right?

Other thoughts on the game:

I'm surprised no one has mentioned what I think was a terrible play called by the Head Ball Coach. Second quarter, 3rd and 4 around the UA 20-yd. line, and we line up 5-wide with no running back?! What the @#%* ? Doug gets pressured into an intentional grounding call, forcing Chandler to try (and miss) a 47-yard field goal. Insanity! Alabama wasn't stopping the run OR pass, so why not show both looks to keep the defense honest? I hate that formation in the red zone. Remember the tight end (Kirk Wells) did some damage? Haven't Bo Carroll and Robert Gillespie made some great plays on swing passes)? Is this ego from the HBC? Just wondering...

When Doug fumbled the snap, the play clock was almost at zero, and the snap was rushed. There's the time to take a time out, to save a precious possession near the red zone. Can't fault the players solely for that one.

Also, on the subject of wasted time-outs, why take one on 4th and 8 in the 4th period, then attempt the field goal (especially since trying the FG was the right call with around 9 minutes left anyway)? A waste!

That game was eerily like Auburn in 1994. I could feel it from early in the second quarter on. The fans were flat, the defense was soft, we were playing from behind, a fumbled snap in scoring position, a late turnover leading to the winning/tying score IN THE SAME PART OF THE SAME END ZONE! Yikes!!! What a sickening feeling...

Oh well, I'm off to Baton Rouge to see a real ass-whipping administered by an aggravated Gator team. This will be the first step of the rest of the journey to Atlanta, and I'll be there supporting the guys. I can only hope for a chance at payback to the pink elephants.

**Visor Fling, Week 7:**
**UF 31, LSU 10**

Nice to see the team respond with a solid effort after the travesty against the Pink Elephants.

The offense was somewhat sloppy, mainly due to the weather conditions (miserable), and lack of concentration in the second half. But it was obvious that they could turn it on if the situation warranted.

The defense looked very good, although LSU's offensive line helped us. Big Money was worth at least 25 cents, up from the nickel Coach Broadway calls him. Manuel was all over the field, Sims showed some flashes, and Dixon did a creditable job. However, it's obvious with young players that their weekly performance will lack consistency until they mature and gain experience, so I'm just hoping for improvement game-by-game for the rest of the season.

My, my – the Head Ball Coach was unhappy after the game and in subsequent interviews. I do agree with him that there are still too many undisciplined actions and mistakes that must be eliminated, but I also believe he's trying to motivate the young guys to stay focused and to deflect at least some pressure from the defense. I think the message will get through.

Also, the late hit by Alex Brown was dumb, but a dark part of my psyche liked to see a nasty streak. It does need to be controlled so it's not a detriment to the team, but a little fear in future opponents is fine by me.

Had a great time as always on this road trip, but the rain was pretty miserable – the Visor got soaked. I thought Josh Booty played well, considering he was running for his life. He showed a lot of courage.

We listened to the local call-in shows on our way out of town (always fun after a win), and everyone, including a lot of the hosts, was brutal towards Dinardo. I've got to believe he's hanging by a thread, and Joe Dean is on the s*** list too. Oh, well, at least it's one less tough opponent on the schedule, although it makes the SEC look weaker.

It will be interesting to see how Auburn responds to what was a devastating loss. Really no excuse for not putting that one away, but I'm not complaining if they're in emotional disarray when the Gators come callin'. It appears that we should be able to wear down their defense in the second half, and that our defense should not allow more than 14-17 points. I think only a slew of turnovers could give the Tigers/War Eagles/Plainsmen a chance. After all the BS that's occurred there over the years, I enjoy any spanking we can administer on their home field. Take no prisoners!

Prediction: Florida 30 Auburn 10

**Visor Flings, Week 8:**
**UF 32, Auburn 14**

Another solid road victory. It never gets old punking the (pick one) War Eagles/Tigers/Plainsmen in their crib. "Loveliest" Village on the Plain"? How about "Loneliest"? Has to be the second-worst place to road trip (after the aptly named Starkville, MS).

The defense stayed focused for most of the game, but it's obvious that until they're more experienced that any lapses will be capitalized on. It looked like Hoke tightened things up in the fourth quarter after some of the Alabama bugaboos resurfaced (15-20 yd. square-ins by the wide receiver, with the running back isolated on a slow linebacker). Obviously part of this was caused by rotating in many players, so I'm not too concerned anymore that those things will recur (unless he goes soft against F$U – a big mistake). Nice to see lots of guys getting some seasoning, although it's a shame more of them couldn't be red-shirted to provide depth in the future. WE NEED A BIG RECRUITING YEAR DEFENSIVELY! Hope the Head Ball Coach gets Broadway and Sanders to make something good happen..

The offense continues to improve, but no one should expect what we saw in 1995-96 again for a long time, if ever. I'd love it, but a lot of people need to be more realistic, especially with defenses adjusting over the years. That's okay – if we continue to average over 30 points a game, we'll be in the hunt every year. Carroll and Gillespie are doing a great job, but I'll still be a lot happier when Ernest Graham returns. I think people (not the close followers) are starting to forget the difference he makes; how his presence improves the performance of the entire offense. And Darrell Jackson! His play compares to that of any of the stars of the Spurrier Era. I'll be the first to admit I'm surprised at the high level of production – but it says a lot to continue to make plays when you're the obvious #1 guy, especially while Travis Taylor is out.

There sure is a lot of hand-wringing over Doug Johnson's relationship with Spurrier, and I suppose the potential is there for things to sour by the F$U and possible SECC games. But to me it's been pretty much the same since Doug got suspended in 1997, and it's possible (maybe probable) that two egos that size will never co-exist smoothly. Well, so be it. I know it sounds short-sighted, but I just want to see good quarterback play and decision-making the rest of the year, for the benefit of the entire team. Doug's going to make some glaring mistakes every game, so get used to it. He's doing fine. Personally, I'm getting tired of this subject, and I hope the media doesn't continue to dwell on it.

I get the feeling the Gators are going to neuter the Puppies this year, and without using anesthesia. And I'll enjoy every snip.

**Visor Flings, Week 9:**
**Off Week**

Looks like it will be an interesting finish to this season. Assuming the Puppies are neutered again this Saturday, it will be the Gators vs. either Alabama or Mississippi State in Atlanta for the SEC Championship. It would be nice to get the rematch, but now Alabama will have to beat MSU to get in. I still think the Pink Elephants will show up. The Puppies have some real injury concerns this week, especially where they can least afford it – on defense. Looks like Marcus Stroud, Terin Smith, and Will Witherspoon will all play hurt. With the way the Gators' offensive line is playing, that bodes well for the running game to keep some balance. The offense should be able to put up at least 24 points, which should be enough. Quincy

Carter doesn't have the help he's enjoyed the past two seasons. Terence Edwards is doing pretty well at wide-out, but Jasper Sanks and Patrick Pass haven't produced decent numbers against a quality opponent. Looks like Matt Stinchcomb is missed, also. The week off came at a good time, both for physical recovery and mental freshness. The team can now focus on putting their best effort into the next four games to finish strong. The defense should improve from here on out. The Puppies will be a good test to see how the young guys are progressing, and then they'll have three weeks to prepare for F$U. The most important things now are consistency from play-to-play and to stay injury-free. Of note will be to see if the Head Ball Coach and Doug have ironed out their "differences" and if Jesse Palmer will actually see action in each game between now and November 20. If the red shirt is looking unlikely, then there's no reason not to get Jesse some significant action so he's game-ready. Here's hoping that Travis Taylor and Ernest Graham are back and regain sharpness before the last two games. Solid play and significant contributions from these two will really make things difficult for F$U. Looking forward to "fixing" the Puppies.

**Visor Flings, Week 10:**
**UF 30, Georgia 14**

Another successful trip to Jacksonville. It never gets old whipping the Puppies and then hearing the whining begin. "If only Jasper Sanks hadn't fumbled"… "If only we had run the option more"… blah, blah, blah. Nothing beats looking at those hang-Dawg faces as they quietly file out of the stadium, beaten again. Hey – deal with it! The passing offense really struggled in the third quarter, but I loved watching the running game start to take over. I couldn't understand why after Graham had run three straight times for two first downs, Spurrier started chucking it around without mixing in the run. Well, I guess even Coach is starting to realize (based on some of his post-game comments) that we can do damage on the ground. Hey, I love the passing game, but I love successful, consistent drives even more. Doug looked sharp in the first half, and I'm not going to bash him for a bad quarter. His first interception was his worst throw of the game, on the fade route to Darrell Jackson. Surprising, actually, since he usually makes that throw nicely. Bo did a terrific job of running hard, and it's obvious what Ernest Graham can do. We need him ready for F$U, no doubt about it. I love what Bo has done, but I still think EG is the guy that can help establish longer and more consistent drives against the Criminoles. Also, Travis Taylor looked to be getting closer to 100%. IF we stay healthy, we certainly have a shot at winning out. Also loved the underneath route to Kinney that led to the go-ahead touchdown in the second quarter. That's another play that can really foul-up F$U and Alabama/Miss. St. As for the defense, they really slammed the door from the middle of the second quarter on. I know Donnan took a lot of heat for not calling the option more when they were inside our 30 at the start of the fourth quarter, but I seem to remember Quincy getting hammered on some keepers after his second touchdown. It was obvious the heavy hitting took its toll on him. But hey, that's the idea, right? He was the only guy that could beat us, and when he was slowed, it was over. Congrats to the D-Line, who really established physical superiority as the game wore on. However, the touchdown runs by Carter illustrate that our young defensive players still take improper angles and aren't sure tacklers yet. That should be something that Hoke can use to keep their attention. I enjoyed being in the Puppy section, listening to the bitching as our defense took over and they were helpless – especially them running the ball with six minutes left. HA! Talk about back to the future...sounds like most of the 70s and 80s, in reverse. I think I'm going to cry. It's nice to see that the Head Ball Coach is focusing the team on Vanderbilt, so that I can go ahead and look ahead to F$U and Alabama/Miss. St. It looks like we have destiny back in our hands now. Still, it will be a monumental task getting to 'Nawlins. Sure, I want the National Championship, but returning to our rightful place as SEC Champions will suffice. Believe me, though, I can't wait until 11/20.

**Visor Flings, Week 11:**
**UF 13, Vanderbilt 6**

What a week for rumors and speculation! If the effort against Vanderbilt wasn't frustrating enough, now Coach has suggested what many thought was an underlying theme since the LSU game – that Doug Johnson may lose his grip on the QB position.

Certainly the offense was sputtering all day. Kudos to Earnest Graham and the O-Line for having the only semblance of continuity, because the passing game was horrible. Bad reads by DJ, poor blitz pickups by the guards, and poor routes by the receivers – the blame lies everywhere. I know Spurrier has stated publicly (again) that he did a poor job of game-planning and called some bad plays, but I think most Gator fans have been reading between those lines for awhile now.

So, what will happen? Well, it's known that Jesse Palmer will play, maybe start; but his number of snaps is still unknown. What does this do to the psyche of Johnson, Palmer, Spurrier, and the entire team? I'm certainly not the one with the answers – we'll only know when the upcoming monster games are played. The Visor feels, though, that the positives outweigh the negatives at this time. DJ needs to watch some plays from the sideline to help clear his head and relax, as well as seeing from Coach's perspective what he's trying to accomplish (we all remember F$U in '97). Plus, Palmer needs some game reps, any kind of game reps, if Spurrier thinks he'll be needed on 11/20. Sure, it has to hurt DJ's ego somewhat, but that's why the Evil Genius rakes in the big money, right?

I'm really interested to see how the rest of the team reacts, on both sides of the ball. Does everyone else start pressing? Does dissension within the team begin? Hopefully no to both, but they are kids, right? I think those things won't be a worry.

By the way, has anyone seen Travis Taylor or Reche Caldwell? Or the swing pass to the tailback (see tapes of UF vs. Tennessee in '94 and '98 for examples)?

Wow, what a way to approach the stretch of games that will make or break our season. I can't remember things being like this, even during the crash and burn of Terry Dean's career.

You know, some would believe that the Gators could lose out, starting with the Criminoles, and finish 9-4. Yikes! What a nightmare that would be! That would be the horror film of all time, even scarier than *The Bone Collector*, or *I was a Teenage Chemist*, starring Dan Kendra. Hopefully this won't be Florida's "End of Days". Can you see this Millennium stuff has me ready for Armageddon-type scenarios?

I'll say one thing – I feel sorry for the Lamecocks, because I think the Gators are ready to show their stuff to the nation, starting Saturday. Says I: UF 38, USC 10.

**Visor Flings, Week 12:**
**UF 20, South Carolina 3**

Pretty good win. My thoughts on THE game next Saturday:
1) F$U will use quick drops and lots of shotgun for Weinke to keep the rush away and get their receivers open underneath. Could be a good plan. I'm shocked that no one is suggesting a 4-1-6 or 4-0-7 alignment to counteract hitting the middle of the field and/or swing passes to Minor. I think we may return the favor from last year to a large extent. I like Kelsey and Davis, but don't be surprised if they don't play a lot of snaps.
2) Our defense has to have its best tackling game; don't keep drives alive by trying to blow someone up. A few consecutive 3-and-outs will instill some frustration in their offense.
3) The skill-position guys just need to relax and play. I really feel they will be mentally sharp and motivated. A big play and/or successful long drive early will do a world of good for everyone.
4) From watching film, I've seen the tendency for the defensive ends to rush straight up field and occasionally swing wide around the pocket. I'd love for Hoke to have some twists and stunts where the ends loop inside the tackles for a new look.
5) I really think the zone blitz can affect Weinke. This is where McCaslin (maybe Davis) and/or additional defensive backs could disrupt timing and create a turnover or sack. Just another way to get the crowd going.
6) I'm very curious as to how patient the Coach will be with the running game. Obviously, the score can dictate much of the play-calling, but we have to have faith that the offensive line will perform. And if the Semen-holes start crowding the box and/or blitzing, I think either QB will hit a big play or two.
7) I noticed that F$U ran a play last week we used to have so much success with; the slot receiver running right down the hash inside the thirty (Warrick scored on this play). Look out – it could hurt us. On the flip side, I'd like to see us resurrect this play. I think both DJ and Palmer make this throw very nicely.

8) Fantasy play. Third or fourth and goal...4th quarter...down by 4...Reche lines up at QB....rolls right and appears to be running....pulls up, and hits Erron Kinney running against the flow in the left side of the end zone after falling down faking a block...crowd explodes, as does St. Booby's head.

It's strange – it's been a long time since I've struggled getting a feel for the team. Do we run the table, or (shocking!) lose out? Talk about the "End of Days."

**Visor Flings, Week 13:**
**FSU 30, UF 23**

What a disaster! Most of the bitching and moaning has been about critical penalties and mental lapses, and there is some merit to that argument. But as the Head Ball Coach has said all year, this team has not shown it can play smart for 60 minutes, and a very good (not great) team beat them.

Most of what's been said is redundant now. Personally, I wish Graham had had more touches and that Jesse had taken most of the second-half snaps. Hey, he wasn't that sharp, but it's painfully obvious that he has more "presence" and is a much cooler customer under pressure. Plus, he shows a knack for evading the rush and making plays outside the pocket. That's just the way it is. I remember stating before the season that I really believed there was a reason that Palmer was picked as the starter back in the middle of '98, and I think we've seen why. Too bad for DJ – he's tough, shows heart, and is very competitive. I still like him. Things just didn't develop as ALL of us would have liked. Time to move on. Maybe he'll still have a shining moment in the next two games.

It might be time for Spurrier to seriously consider shaking up the staff. He has shown tremendous loyalty to his assistants, but there seems to be something lacking in their preparing the team fundamentally, as well as some recruiting shortcomings.

The offensive staff in place seems okay. The O-Line improved significantly this year (maybe Coach knew that Stephens might be considered for a head coaching job of his own, thus bringing in Hunt). Teevens did a great job with the running backs; I just wish Coach involved them more in the passing game. Surprisingly, the receivers struggled at times this year, so Dixon has some work to do. I know he's come under some serious criticism for the first time this year, but his record speaks for itself. However, as we all know, our program is at the point now where it's "what have you done for me lately?" We need another playmaker here next year.

The defensive staff did a fair-to-good job this year, but nothing great. The D-Line was inconsistent, even with some spectacular individual performances at times. This group needs to show more fire next year (reflection on Broadway?). It also need an infusion of more quality depth. The LB play was adequate, especially with a converted running back (McCaslin) becoming a starter. But this group lacks overall speed, and Kelsey never really stood out like others predicted (because he played with too much weight, I believe). Davis was solid, but the young guys will really have to produce next year. The secondary really came on the second half of the season, but still needs to improve on cover skills (especially Cromartie – even though he played hurt against F$U). Hoke did pretty well overall, especially starting with a young unit. But again, there's plenty of room to improve, and this could be a dominant group next year. I want to see it on the field, though.

Well, it's off to Atlanta on December 4th, and we're at a crossroads. Does this team lose out, or right the ship? This will be one of the Head Ball Coach's toughest coaching jobs, getting the players ready for Alabama. He has directed some pointed criticism at the players themselves, and who knows how they will react. He is really catching heat for this from many people, but it's just another example of his perspective as (1) both a former player and (2) as somewhat of a fan, wanting the Gators to do well so badly. I suppose most people, especially outside the program, will never fully understand this. But at least he's honest and consistent. I think he'll have a lot to reflect on in the off-season personally, and will come back even better.

Revenge will help get the player's attention, but only so much. Achieving a real mental focus and fundamental play will be the real cures. As bad as it sucked losing to the Semen-holes, losing to Mike Dumbose (again) would be much worse. The team needs to really lay the wood to the Pink Elephants, both as payback and as a springboard to the bowl game and next year. No excuses!

I'm curious as to how the attendance will be split at Atlanta – probably 60/40 'Bama. We need to show something ourselves as fans and show up in force.

I'll preview the SEC Championship Game next week.

**Visor Flings, Week 14:**
**Off Week**

It's gut-check time for the Gators. I hope the players understand that the revenge factor only goes so far; they will still have to perform on the field.

I wouldn't be surprised to see Alabama play both their quarterbacks, in any possible sequence. They may decide that this could be the difference in a rematch. Plus, I'd look for some long passes early as a change from the first game, then a heavy dose of Shaun Alexander in the second half (obviously if they are close or ahead).

It will be interesting to see what they do on defense, as well. Remember, neither team was really stopped on offense in the first game, so there may be major differences in each team's philosophy this go-around. If they really are thin on the D-Line, expect more blitzing. And, if they only rush three, RUN THE BALL. It's time they were introduced to Earnest Graham.

I really enjoyed the success of the screen and dump-off passes to the running backs against F$U, and hope to see more this game. This tactic could really cause confusion and create big gains, as well as open up other facets of the offense. Looks like both DJ and

Palmer will share snaps again; I wonder if Coach will go with the hot hand in the second half instead of continuing the rotation.

A lot has been said about how our defense will attack this time. Well, I want to see it for myself. They need to make some big plays early to set the tempo and show both Alabama and themselves that they dictate the action. If they play with the anger the fans felt after the first game, look out. If not, then I see a lot of head-hanging and the need for the offense to win the game. The match-ups I'm looking forward to are Bennie Alexander/Freddie Milons and Alex Brown/Chris Samuels.

If I have to see Mike Dumbose hoist the trophy, I'll be nauseated and pissed off. We're the biggest reason he still has a job (along with Alexander and poor Auburn recruiting).

There's a lot at stake in this game for the Gators: an SEC title, respect, reassertion of conference dominance, a boost in confidence, a springboard to the bowl game and next season. I want this game badly, and want to show the Wolverines the SEC rules the country when the big boys play.

I'll call it Florida 31 Alabama 23

**Visor Flings, Week 15:**
**Alabama 34, UF 7**

The "End of Days" is upon us after all.

Unfortunately, my mention before the F$U game that the Gators might lose out may come true. It's hard to fathom how the offense could regress so badly in two weeks. Any progress and momentum gained against F$U evaporated.

Where are the running backs in the passing game?

Where are the patterns more 15 yards down the field?

What is going on in Travis Taylor's head?

Why did the offensive line not open holes for the running game?

Where was Bo Carroll?

How can Tyler Watts scramble on a quarterback draw for 20 yards from his own 5 on 3rd and 10?

I'm actually glad Alex Brown called out the offense after the game. Maybe it can help them get their heads out of their asses. I also noticed a lot of jawing between Spurrier and other coaches. Is it time to seriously consider a shake-up of the staff?

The defense played very well before finally caving in in the 4th quarter. I saw a lot of hustle, and the freshmen LBs really played a solid game, considering their lack of experience. But, they were out of position occasionally, allowing 'Bama to convert more long 3rd down plays. Some of that has to be expected, though, given the circumstances.

The only feeble complaint I have with the officials was the blatant downfield holding by 'Bama's receivers and linemen. Only one downfield call, when many more were apparent. Just like Alexander's overtime run in the Swamp.

Well, at least Jesse will now have an additional month of practice with the first unit to improve. And maybe all of the offensive players and coaches will summon some pride in the Citrus Bowl (I'm sick just having to mention that). We have a streak of top-ten finishes and 10-win seasons on the line.

Now we get to hear all the BS about how Va. Tech can beat the Criminoles. I'd love it, but please. Now we see the fruits of this season....one very good team playing one good team from two mediocre conferences. I can hardly stand the excitement. I can already sense the interest building across the country... NOT!!!

Looking forward to discussing recruiting the rest of December. If Saturday didn't show a huge need for playmakers, nothing will.

**Visor Flings, Week 16 and Beyond:**
**Michigan State 37, UF 34**

I've decided to change my attitude. Despite an irritating loss in the Citrus Bowl, I see now that this is not the End, but the Beginning. In the spirit of renewed hope, I'd like to focus here on the recruitment of high school players which came after the clouds lifted.

It was certainly an interesting recruiting season for the Gators. Coach Spurrier exhibited a willingness to personally recruit players more than ever before (Boldin, Maddox, Royal, LaFavor, and Dixon in particular). Obviously he wasn't successful with all, but no one ever is. I am impressed with the energy and excitement the newest assistants (Teevens and Hoke) brought to the process. I feel if they were on board sooner, we could have signed a few more of the guys we wanted – but it's a solid class anyway.

DEFENSE:

Linebackers. There has been much discussion on the number of linebacker types signed. This certainly fills a need. But more than that, I feel this group will add some much-needed speed and foster some great competition, thereby improving each player in the long run.

Farrior, Hardman and Royal look to be the best of the group, based on athleticism and speed seen on film. It will be interesting to see how Nattiel and Poitier fare. Nattiel obviously has some bloodlines (Ricky), and has good instincts. Poitier is the player that has the most intrigue – not highly recruited, not highly rated, but already the MVP of two South Florida post-season all-star games. This could the finest group of linebackers in one UF class, but only over the next 3-5 years can that be fully evaluated. Still, a terrific group.

Linemen. The Gators went in a slightly different direction this year, signing players not as big, but in keeping with a recurring theme. They're fast. I'm including in this group McCray and LaFavor to go along with Charles, Mitchell, Rolle, and Willliams.

Williams is probably the most accomplished technique-wise, but still has to attain a qualifying test score. If not, he will be the first partial-qualifier Florida has accepted since

1991 (and well worth it). Mitchell is another player with bloodlines (Jeff), and seems to be an instinctive tackler. He'll need some additional bulk to really make an impact, but looks like a fine defensive end. Charles and Rolle are not considered cream-of-the-crop by analysts, but are valued for their smarts as well as their ability. Both could have a future at tackle, especially Charles. McCray and LaFavor will be interesting...will they bulk up to play rush end, or play as stand-up outside linebackers? Both are great athletes, and Butch Davis really wanted LaFavor at Miami.

Backs. Florida signed three studs, with Sheppard everyone's top pick. He is really going to be fun to watch, with fine cover skills and the ability to run with the ball.

There are already rumors that he will eventually see time at WR, but for now, he needs to learn the defensive schemes first and become accomplished there. Anything else is icing on the cake. Dixon hails from New Smyrna Beach and is an interesting player. In addition to playing cornerback, he has some experience on offense and has a knack for blocking kicks. H e originally agreed verbally to attend Alabama before recanting and signing with Florida; maybe he felt overlooked early in the recruiting season. Jackson is the latest player from the fertile Belle Glade area that has supplied a steady stream of talent to the Gators historically. His build suggests he could project to strong safety, where he could see significant playing time early in his career.

OFFENSE:

Running backs. Ran Carthon was the only RB signed. Another player with bloodlines (dad Maurice played mostly for the NY Giants). He missed seven games his senior year with an injury, but is highly thought of by many analysts. The Gators jumped on him early, obviously feeling he will recover fully. Speculation has it he may develop into a great fullback like his dad, but the coaching staff probably will not make that decision until next year.

Quarterbacks. Coach Spurrier signed two good ones in Grossman and Stephens. Both have good size and mobility (assuming Stephens' knee recovers fully from surgery – doesn't sound serious). Right now it looks like Grossman could have a good chance of playing some next year (already enrolled for Spring semester and will participate in Spring drills). Film on both shows good arm strength, escape ability, and ability to read defenses. With Johnson a senior and Palmer a junior, these two will continue the line of fine QB play at Florida.

Wide receiver/tight ends. Florida signed five solid prospects. This group has the next best chance of seeing early playing time, behind the linebackers. Hicks seems to be the most highly thought of by the coaching staff. Very good routes and hands – only question is separation speed, in which opinions vary wildly. I'll trust Coach Dixon on this one. Jacobs and Ratliff appear to be similar in size and speed. Jacobs has experience at QB, while Ratliff played DB and WR – both good backgrounds for developing good receivers. Jabar Gaffney has the most recognizable name (father Derrick, uncle Don – both from the 70's). He is the most questioned WR prospect, mainly for his speed. However, Coach Spurrier seems to have the touch with guys like this (remember McGriff and Doering?). Schaap is the least-known prospect, playing tight end in a running offense. He had verbally committed to Clemson early, then switched to the Gators after the untimely departure of Dwight Edge. Has good blocking skills already, and played defensive line also. Seems like a good, tough player who might blossom.

Linemen. No linemen were signed, as much a reflection of the fact that Florida has 12-14 on scholarship already. Missed out on some outstanding ones, but the depth is there. Will be a need position next year.

SUMMARY/COMMENTS:

Florida signed a terrific class, one that met need and exhibits great overall speed. Recruiting services list this class around 8-10 nationally, only because of the lack of quantity of big names, but the coaching staff is very pleased. Once again, the new coaches seem to have infused some enthusiasm and excitement into the process, and perhaps Coach Spurrier will continue to personally become more involved. This development has to be a plus. Much has been made of the big names that got away, such as Anquan Boldin, Nick Maddox, Bryce Bishop, and Reggie Brown. Florida offered to each of these players and would have loved to have any of them. But, dealing with teenagers in a high-pressure situation such as recruiting leads to some crazy, sometimes disappointing events.

Maddox is by far the best running back prospect in the country, and Boldin was personally recruited by Spurrier. Maddox seems to have played the Gators all along, and apparently Bowden convinced Boldin he would have a legitimate shot at QB. Of course, the fact that both signed with F$U rubs salt in the wound, but sometimes we forget about the fine players already signed, as well as the returning players. Both positions are well-stocked now, as are WR (Brown -- Georgia) and OL (Bishop -- Ohio St.). My feelings are that Brown and Bishop signed with teams that actually had a larger need at those positions and will see a lot of early playing time. This is a strong attraction to young players.

Overall, a satisfying recruiting season and a fine group of players. My personal feeling is that recruiting in the future years looks more promising than ever. We'll see what the new season brings.

Very Truly Yours,
The Visor

# 2000
# Brawl on Bourbon Street

Well, all right, so the little scuffle between Florida and Miami players in downtown New Orleans before the Sugar Bowl was, perhaps, a bit overplayed by the press. Still, it showed that we were mired in the same bad karma which haunted us from time to time throughout the season. To be sure, we did win another SEC championship, our first in four seasons, but some of us will remember the days when the Gators seemed cursed when it came to achieving that much.

I think it also shows how far the program came throughout the nineties that other high-powered teams measured their own success with victories over UF. I mean, for gosh sakes, Miami even tried to lay claim to a share of the national title after they beat us in the Sugar Bowl.

As I look over my reports for the 2000 season, one recurring theme stands out to me, and that is the developing relationship between Rex Grossman and Jabar Gaffney, who would come to be ranked as one of UF's great passing combinations. Maybe they weren't up there with Wuerffel/Doering, or even Reeves/Alvarez, but each went on to more prominent professional careers than any of these others. Who could have guessed that within eight years, both would have competed in Super Bowls – Grossman for Chicago and Gaffney for New England?

The year 2000 – how time does fly, whether you're having fun or not. For most of it, though, it was fun. No, it was more than that: this was life back then.

On with the Visor's journals. Enjoy.

**Visor Flings, Week 1:**
**Preview and Predictions**

It's that time again...when people like me try to predict what a bunch of 18-22 year-olds will do. Crazy, huh?

OFFENSE

It's Jesse James Palmer's time to shine. In a way, he's one of the most inexperienced seniors in recent memory, which will make his performance sometimes inconsistent and perhaps leave him with fragile confidence.
However, I believe he will improve as the season progresses and will be the man. The talk of Rex Grossman and Brock Berlin is just that. Rex will probably be the back-up and Berlin will be red-shirted, barring injury or poor performance. Palmer's biggest challenge will be...

The offensive line. Once again, lots of potential and a handful of solid players, such as Mike Pearson and Kenyatta Walker. However, there are a startling lack of experience and lingering injuries (Zac Zedalis). The play of Leon Hires, Erik Strange, and converted defensive lineman Tommy Moody is critical. It does look like a couple of true freshmen will play this year, most likely Shannon Snell and Max Starks. Jimmy Ray Stephens and John Hunt will have their hands full forming a cohesive unit as the year progresses. This could lead to lots of pain for the QB and for...

The running game. Lots of talent and versatility here, but will they get a real chance to show it? Robert Gillespie begins as the starting tailback, with Earnest Graham and Bo Carroll seeing lots of time as well. All can run, and Gillespie and Carroll can create mismatches and big plays receiving. Rod Frazier will provide solid blocking. Probably the best offensive group this year, and hopefully they will ease the dependence on...

The receiving corp. Lots of talent, little experience, tons of pressure both to perform and ease the pressure on the QB. Reche Caldwell, Alex Willis, and Taylor Jacobs seem to be the lead guys, with Brian Haugabrook and Jabar Gaffney filling in. Kirk Wells at TE could be an X-factor, especially inside the red zone, but is a poor blocker. Unfortunately, lots of questions here. Can they catch consistently? Can they run precise routes in sync with the QB? Can they achieve separation? Looks like an up-and-down year for this group as they mature.

Overall, it appears to be a good (not great) unit that will show inconsistency at times. Is that enough to return to Atlanta and the SEC Championship?

DEFENSE

What a difference a year makes. Lots of returning starters, loads of experience, plenty of depth. This should be the team's strength this year, and hopefully can carry the offense through some anticipated rough times.

The line is in great shape. The tackle position has a nice rotation set with Gerard Warren, Buck Gurley, and Derrick Chambers. The ends will rotate Alex Brown, Tron LaFavor, Thad Bullard, and a host of others. The only question with this group is whether individuals will take plays off or stay aggressive? This group will set the tone for the entire team and, fair or not, will carry the hopes for a great season.

The linebackers are talented, but short on experience, especially the back-ups. Andra Davis was the lead guy in the middle, a true leader and run-stuffer. Now that he's gone for the season, Travis Carroll will have to perform at least at his Alabama level when he returns from suspension. Until then, true freshman Travis Harris and red-shirt freshman Matt Farrior carry the load – a scary thought heading into Knoxville. On the outside, Bam Hardmon has lots of potential on one side, while Daryl Owens and Marcus Oquendo-Johnson must step in at the other. Lots of athletic availability here, but will it translate into results?

The secondary looks solid. Lito Sheppard has stepped into a starting role opposite Bennie Alexander. Todd Johnson has moved ahead of Marquand Manuel at strong safety, while Daryl Dixon returns after his surprising performance as a true freshman last year. Plus, young talent such as Matt Jackson and Tre Orr has been added. This group needs to be more aggressive and take more chances this year and come up with big plays.

It's time for Jon Hoke to show confidence in these guys and let them blitz, go for interceptions, and fly around more this year. It would be a shame to waste this much talent and potential. This group will be asked to carry the team at times this year, and must meet the challenge. Turn them loose and see what happens.

SPECIAL TEAMS

Ouch! A rough start here. I have confidence in Jeff Chandler, however, and he is now a reliable place-kicker. Alan Rhine (and the long snapper) are too slow, however. The punting game is cause for real concern, and looks to be inconsistent. The question is whether it will screw up at the wrong time to lose a game. Field position is more critical this year than in the past due to the concerns about the offense.

Once again, the returners are exceptional. Bo Carroll, Lito Sheppard, Robert Gillespie, and Reche Caldwell are all explosive, and will provide above-average field position, with the ability to score almost any time. A real blessing here.

OUTLOOK FOR 2000

It doesn't appear that there will be 2 losses at home again this year, although there will be some touchy moments against LSU and Auburn. The real danger lies on the road. The inexperience on the offensive line and at receiver spells trouble in every road game, especially against quality teams in a loud environment (Tennessee, Miss. St., Georgia, F$U). Look for a potential loss at Tallahassee and possibly at one of the other three.

The Game at Knoxville may be more "interesting" than the Gators would like. If it were at the Swamp this year, I would be very confident. But funny things happen to inexperienced offensive players on the road.

After hearing all the talk out of the Puppies this summer, it would be especially nice to neuter them once again in Jacksonville.

My unbiased prediction: 9-2 regular season (7-1 in conference)

**Visor Flings, Week 2:**
**UF 40, Ball State 19**

Well, an unpleasant time in the Swamp to start the season.

Sloppy, uninspired play, along with the obvious unsettled situation on the offensive line, made for a dull effort against Ball State.

The offense was inconsistent, as predicted. Jesse was up and down, although he did make mostly good reads. He wasn't helped by shoddy pass protection and wrong routes by the receivers. Gillespie played well, making sharp cuts, good decisions (except running backwards for a safety). However, Graham looked so-so, maybe due to the inexperienced line he had blocking for him. Bo Carroll showed why he needs more touches this year. The offense won't put together many consistent drives, especially early in the season, so big plays are a must. The receivers were average – some good routes and catches offset by poor routes and drops. Caldwell looks like a legitimate deep threat, something lacking in recent years. Hopefully he (and the others) will continue to improve as the season progresses.

The defense was pretty good, not very good or great. The linemen looked disinterested and passive. The one lineman that played hard was Gerard Warren; Big Money looks leaner and quicker this year, and could make all-SEC. The linebackers were okay, but still look confused in coverage. The loss of Andra Davis is critical – he was the one real run-stuffer of the unit.

Too bad Travis Carroll won't be back until after Tennessee. The Gators now have to rely on two freshmen, Harris and Farrior, to help stop the Vol's running game. Could be trouble. The secondary was vanilla and soft, again. Why won't Jon Hoke turn these guys loose? This will hopefully change soon, before we're ball-controlled into having to throw every down late in a game.

The special teams weren't sharp. Chandler looked way off and Rhine has to quicken his steps on punts. This team isn't good enough to make up for critical mistakes like in the past.

Overall, an unsatisfying first game. I hope to see big improvement in all facets this week. It's time to start turning up the heat.

**Visor Flings, Week 3:**
**UF 55, Middle Tennessee State 0**

Observations from the MTSU game:

1) I think our offense will be as good as that of the '91, '95, and '96 teams in two years. By then either Rex or Brock will be surrounded by great talent that's EXPERIENCED.
2) The young defensive linemen look great! Scott, Parker, and Mills seem to have a feel for the game already.
3) Ran Carthon has the same number as Rhett (33), and looks like he knows how to read blocks and holes. If he can catch, he can start by 2002.
4) Will the real Jeff Chandler please stand up? He looks very shaky so far.
5) Keep working the running game; I like what I've seen so far, but don't abandon it now that we're into the SEC schedule.

Well, the more things change, the more they stay the same...

Looks like two QBs will play against the Inbreds. If the game were here, I think we'd win fairly easily. Up there, it's close. I hope the Head Ball Coach comes up with his best game plan since F$U in 1997.

I hope that this Saturday against Tennessee we have fewer turnovers and penalties for a change and make them earn it. If we generate even an average running game, we'll be in good shape. I expect a lot of blitzes from UT – I hope he guards and running backs pick up their respective responsibilities.

Prediction: Florida 20, Tennessee 17

**Visor Flings, Week 4:**
**UF 27, Tennessee 23**

Well, there's nothing like giving it to the Inbreds the way they like it, and in Rocky Top, no less!

Hopefully not lost in the glow of victory is the fact that the Gators have a serious problem in the middle of the O-Line and that Jon Hoke and the rest of the defensive coaches apparently do not understand the phrase "making adjustments at halftime."

It's obvious that Spurrier and the team have a lot of work to do. One great drive doesn't mask the fact that the running game isn't ready for prime-time, and that the defensive linemen should be ashamed of themselves. The loss of Andra Davis was sorely felt as well – where were the linebackers to fill the holes? Too much inexperience and lack of muscle here. I do feel, however, that they won't face a better running game or back the rest of the season.

Jesse Palmer showed why he is the man, and all the talk about Rex Grossman is just that – talk. Rex is the backup, and Berlin will be red-shirted. End of discussion. It appears that he's held up under the QB coach's scrutiny, and that he can handle any pressure on the field.

At least the wide receivers grew up in the second half and played hard and aggressively. All the drops in the first half could have discouraged Jesse, but he kept his composure and really showed some leadership. IF they remember to catch the ball with their hands and where to line up properly, it will be a solid group.

A lot has been made of the little impact Alex Brown had, but the press and many fans missed two critical points: (1) the Vols paid so much attention to him, the other linemen should have made plays, and (2) A.J. Suggs wasn't going to be allowed to go downfield; Lito Sheppard showed what would happen if that continued. It's a poor reflection on both the players and coaches that a young, inexperienced line that also lost its best player to injury for the second half could run the ball so well. I still maintain it may be time for the Head Ball Coach to remake the defensive staff – it seems as if a lot of talent is being wasted. Hey, Jon

Hoke – ever hear of a run blitz? Hey Rod Broadway – ever hear of changing technique and/or gap responsibility at halftime?

It's also disappointing that it took a freshman lucky to be on the team (Gaffney) to wake up the rest of the receiving corps. He really rose to the occasion and showed his bloodlines (he just needs to learn to secure the ball – I've noticed him either juggling it or having it stripped going out of bounds a handful of times). Caldwell and Willis made some fine plays and clutch catches, as well. This group seems to need a leader to follow, instead of taking responsibility themselves. It was obvious in the second half that the Tennessee defensive backs were outclassed and that the only hope they really had was to have the lead and stay in a zone, dropping six and seven into coverage. Hopefully this will serve as a stepping stone for improvement the rest of the season and supply a much-needed shot of confidence.

At least the pass protection was solid – I was very impressed. But the run blocking...not so much. No push from the interior; Jorgenson was outclassed, Hires was disappointing, and Moody needs more experience. The tight ends were pushed into the backfield all afternoon. We miss Erron Kinney at TE – he really was a player.

One positive: only one turnover (not Jesse's fault), and no critical penalties. That really helped in a tough situation Saturday. I hope Spurrier remembers to compliment the team on that.

So, it's on to Kentucky. They appear to have an okay offense, but haven't run the ball as well as the past two years. Jared Lorenzen is a moose, but has no mobility. It could be a long day for him, especially if our sleepwalking defensive coordinator decides to blitz occasionally.

On defense, they are still weak. There should be no problem scoring 35-45 points.

Visor's prognostication: Florida 45 Kentucky 20

**Visor Flings, Week 5:**
**UF 59, Kentucky 31**

Late last year and in the preseason this year, I have made some not-so-subtle references to my disappointment in both the defense and the coaches, and now it may be time to remove all subtlety. It's time for a change – I mean a completely fresh start. Funny thing – the Gators could still go anywhere from 11-2 to 13-0, but our offense and overall talent can't continually cover up the inadequacies of the defense's performance and the apparent lack of imaginative, aggressive coaching. Are we afraid that we can't recruit with new defensive coaches? I don' think Florida will ever have that trouble. I feel for those kids. Of course, I heard Coach's comments about how most teams have a lot of players that don't pan out, but it's hard to believe that a lot of the defensive players at Florida that were also recruited by F$U, Tennessee, etc. are poor players. I know Spurrier shows loyalty to his coaches, but it's time to make a professional decision and shake things up.

One more comment. Many people were critical of Bob Stoops' game plan against F$U back in 1998, but that guy almost always played an aggressive scheme and seemed to generate some real fire from his players. See any fiery emotion from this bunch? I wonder if the players are starting to hear whispers about the poor coaching, and if it could be affecting them? I hope not, but who knows?

Well, the offense certainly is improving. Still a ways to go, but the O-Line did well with more movement of personnel (Strange at guard, Hires at tackle, no Walker). Good hard running by Graham and some smart decisions by Palmer running with the ball. I still think that the RBs need to watch for blitzes up the middle more than from the corners – that still is causing problems. This weekend in Starkville, it will be interesting to see if the Head Ball Coach tries to slow MSU's rush and blitzing with swing passes and screens, and if the defensive line responds to the challenge of a big, physical O-Line. I feel we should win by at least 10 points – this MSU team is weaker than in the past few years, and the noise level (despite those stupid cowbells) is nothing like Knoxville.

I'll say Florida 27 MSU 17

**Visor Flings, Week 6:**
**MSU 47, UF 35**

Well, if I waited for the dust to settle before writing again, last week's article would have been the last one for 2000. There's a dust storm raging, and I can see the tumbleweeds bouncing across Jon Hoke's front yard.

Not the most enjoyable trip to Starkville. On offense, poor execution (execution being a very applicable word here) did in what could have been a 50-point afternoon. MSU's scheme was to put 7-9 men up front and pressure a weak middle of the O-Line and running game, forcing the Gators to pass. And pass they did (494 yards). The pass-blocking was OK the first half, terrific in the second. Receivers were free all over the field; too bad drops and poor defense prevented a better day.

The passes in the flats to the running backs were well-designed and worked all day (except for Frazier's drop on the initial drive of the game). Grossman and Berlin really played well under the circumstances; no problems at QB in the future.

Many people are complaining about the intentional safety to make it a 10-point game. I'm surprised that no one has thought that maybe Coach wanted to kick off from the 20 to force MSU to start farther away from the end zone, figuring he probably needed at least two more scores to either tie or win the game.

Oh, and the reason the Gators kicked off at the start of both halves? A brain cramp by the player rep, not the coach's decision. What a huge mistake!

The defensive problems are well-documented by now. Little penetration from the line and young, inexperienced linebackers are making many opponents on the schedule look like Nebraska. Is it all Jon Hoke's fault? No. However, the ENTIRE defensive staff is to blame somewhat. It appears that if Hoke is still on the staff next year, it will be as the secondary coach only, at which he seems to be doing a good job. But Spurrier may need to clean house of the others and start over. Maybe he can talk Bud Foster out of staying at Virginia Tech after all or hire Woody after he's fired at Vandy. Actually, I've heard Spurrier say he may elevate from within (Sanders?) Ugh. Please clean the slate – the current staff is stale and needs new blood and fire (Odom was a good start).

What a fine game from Todd Johnson and Lito Sheppard. Those two are all-SEC in my book. Johnson put the offense on the field at the MSU 30 twice, and Sheppard is being thrown at less and less, shrinking the field (but not stopping the run, though). And Lito broke another kickoff return only to have it called back. He really is a weapon anywhere on the field and a true playmaker.

Please, please – move either Ellis or Brown to middle linebacker. They both have some experience playing LB, and IT CAN'T GET ANY WORSE! At least try to salvage the defense this year, not next.

A thought: Georgia could be this year's Alabama...bad early loss, screaming for the coach's head, then run the table. Sad, but true.

Well, there's no more room for error if this team wants to return to Atlanta, starting with a rejuvenated LSU team this week. While they did beat Tennessee, they allowed a ton of passing yards and their QB was punished. I believe the Gators will bounce back and show some fire at home, and expect a small letdown from the Bengal Tigers. At this point, though, can the team regain its confidence to a level to win the next three games? The talent and skill are there; this week's performance could be the most important of the year...

Oktoberfest (LSU, Auburn, Georgia) will tell the tale of the 2000 Gator season. Hope it's a celebration, not a disaster.

My pick: Florida 34 LSU 24

**Visor Flings, Week 7:**
**UF 41, LSU 9**

A nice bounce-back win vs. LSU. I suspected that their win over Tennessee in Death Valley would leave them a little flat, and that the Gators were hungry to show what they could really do. Plus, it's obvious now that the Inbreds are nowhere near the team of the past 10 years.

Now, what to make of the QB situation? It appears thet Rex will start again vs. Auburn, and that Jesse is the back-up. I feel the Head Ball Coach is more comfortable doing this at home, where everything that could favor a young QB is in place. But, as usual, nothing would surprise me that happens Saturday. I still feel Jesse will make something big happen before the year is over.

There is an obvious parallel to Rex's performance so far, and that is the big-play performance of Jabar Gaffney. It's apparent that they have developed a rapport with each other based on practicing together last season. Is this the portent of another Wuerffel-to Doering connection? Possibly.

I'm still unconvinced about the run-blocking capability of this unit. LSU is weak on defense – this week will be a truer barometer of any progress. Establishing the run will be even more important against the Tigers/Plainsmen/War Eagles (WHATEVER!!), because they are stronger on offense and more balanced.

The defense showed some promise as well, but again, they need to show consistency before I'll become a believer.

The third-down pass defense is still shaky and needs major improvement. Of course, it would help if the officials wouldn't call holding against Alex Brown and Gerard Warren so much. Geez! Those guys really played well and were disruptive, but would have had even more to show for their effort if the officials would wake up. The defensive line and linebackers (including new starter Mike Nattiel) played well, but, like the running game, need to show consistency to lead to a possible return trip to Atlanta.

It will be another entertaining time in the Swamp. More excitement and intrigue, I'm sure, but I feel the team may be ready to make a big push up to the Georgia and F$U games. Stop Rudi Johnson, and the Gators win.
Pick: Florida 27 Auburn 17

**Visor Flings, Week 8:**
**UF 38, Auburn 7**

How 'bout them Gators!

Wow! It's certainly been a roller-coaster ride the past three weeks. Not surprising, when you realize how many young, inexperienced players are contributing significantly this year.

The performance against Auburn was a flashback to the winning formula of the past – accurate passing opening up the running game, a big early lead forcing the opponent out of its game plan, and big plays on defense. That's what the Head Ball Coach means by having some "fun" again.

The roll of Rex Grossman continues. His decision-making and ability to make plays has been impressive so far. Now for the disclaimer: the last two games have been at home against weaker opponents, and a neutral site war with the Puppies and their tough D-Line awaits. That will be a truer test of his mettle. Hopefully he'll pass that test and start preparing for finals (F$U, SECC). Plus, Brock Berlin should be getting more reps with the first team. I think a fine opportunity has been missed the past two weeks for him to gain more experience.

The O-line seems to be playing better as a unit with fewer mistakes. The pass blocking continues to be solid, though I'm still not sold on the chances of a consistent running game. I like what Gillespie has done lately, and I really feel Bo Carroll can be a difference-maker this week. The Puppies will be a challenge, especially Seymour, Grant (what a stud), and the traitor, Stroud. If the Gators win, I'd love for someone to run up to him and rip off that crappy Puppy shirt to reveal a Gator one underneath, just as payback for that Sports Illustrated cover shot of him when he backed out on us in 1997.

The defense is improving, showing more hustle and better gang-tackling. Alex Brown may be awakening from his season-long slumber; he really got the fans excited against the Tigers/Plainsmen/War Eagles (WHATEVER!). Big Money continues to be our best defensive player. He really disrupted a lot of plays and some blocking schemes. He, Todd Johnson, and Lito should be 1st Team All-SEC, without question. Hopefully the linebackers are ready to play a solid game and Lito is healthy enough to play cornerback full-time and return punts.

Well, most of the news out of the Puppies camp is bad. Quincy's still sore, Musa Smith is gone for the season (knee), many others are banged up pretty good. Hmm......sounds like we're being set up by Donnan for a fall (is really that smart? Nah...). At least the Mildcats put a scare into them and made them play hard the entire game. I can only hope that if for some reason Quincy struggles against Florida, the Gators don't turn another back-up into a hero as has happened too many times in the past. The only advantage gained from Phillips' playing is that the threat of him hurting the Gators by running is remote.

I wouldn't be surprised at this point if the Pups play two QBs, either because one is struggling or to improve their passing game.

I think SOS is ready to neuter the Pups again. The O-Line has to play their best game of the season to date to help Rex and the receivers get settled into the game early, apply pressure to the Pups defense, and DICTATE THE ACTION, instead of reacting.

I also think there will be less scoring than anticipated.

Florida 27 Georgia 17, I would say.

**Visor Flings, Week 9:**
**UF 34, Georgia 23**

Puppies Neutered Again! Read all about it!!

Well, it sure is quiet up in Athens now. After all that talk since the summer about "payback," about "this being the year," about "having the best talent," yada yada yada. You know what? NOT! Florida still rules the East, and will continue to set the pace. They were fortunate to beat Tennessee, or it really would have been the same story again.

It was an exciting game, for sure. Momentum swings, big plays, and eventually the desired result. I hope people realize how important Jesse Palmer was in our two biggest games of the year. Too bad he's hurt again, but hopefully he'll be ready if needed against South Carolina and F$U.

The offense did a nice job of neutralizing the strongest part of the Puppy defense, their D-Line. The O-Line once again pass-blocked very well, and there was enough of a running game to ward off constant blitzing. The efforts of Rod Frazier should not be overlooked, either. His leadership and pass-blocking have been crucial to the success of the passing game so far.

Gillespie looks like the starter for the rest of the season. He continues to run hard, make big plays, and provide the option of receiving out of the backfield. I had mentioned last week that Grossman would be facing his toughest test, and he did struggle. However, he showed resiliency by returning to play well after JP's ankle injury. He and Brock will need to carry the load at least for one game, maybe two. They'll do fine – the Head Ball Coach will make sure of it.

The defense continues to come up with timely plays and turnovers, offsetting a still-soft run defense. The Puppies really should have pounded away more between the tackles, especially after Quincy was reminded of last year's beating. They had success with Smith and Sanks, and didn't stay with it. Thanks again to Jim Donnan for a fine game plan; that guy is overrated as a coach. He does recruit well, but the coaching part has not been impressive.

Now the team travels to Nashville. I want to make my opinion very clear – I DON'T CARE IF THE GATORS JUST PLAYED AUBURN AND GEORGIA! WE ARE SUPERIOR ACROSS THE BOARD AND SHOULD POUND VANDERBILT! All the talk about the past struggles is not productive. I don't worry about Spurrier getting the team ready, so we will crush them. Don't forget the last visit there – a 30+ point whipping.

What matters now is: 1) staying healthy
2) staying healthy 3) staying healthy

Can't wait to cut off the (Game)Cocks.

For this Saturday: Florida 38 Vanderbilt 14

**Visor Flings, Week 10:**
**UF 43, Vanderbilt 20**

Overall, a solid win in Nashville. While the QB play struggled at times, the entire team stayed together and outclassed Vanderbilt, as they should have.

On offense, Rex discovered what a good defensive coordinator can do to your rhythm. The Head Ball Coach had the luxury of letting him work through his mistakes, however, and his performance improved as the game wore on. I did like the fact he dumped the ball off to his running backs over the middle when pressured. His progress under the circumstances has been great – but don't forget that the pass blocking of the O-Line and Rod Frazier have helped.

Once again, there was enough of a running threat to balance things out. Both Gillespie and Graham ran hard. Seemed like Graham was the red zone back, getting tough yards and breaking tackles around the goal line – a nice change-up from Gillespie.

Gaffney and Caldwell are way ahead of the other receivers at this point, which is good and bad. It's nice to have a threat on each side of the field, but no one else has stepped into what could be a fine situation of roaming underneath and in the dead spots in zones. The tight ends and running backs are in the mix, but can't provide big plays as consistently as a wide-out. This missing productivity separates this passing offense from prior years. Could spell trouble in two weeks.

The defense looked very good. The play of Warren and Brown is consistently effective, and the DBs continue to make plays. However, what a difference Travis Carroll makes! I hope people noticed how he shed blockers and moved down the line. He missed some tackles that I think were mostly due to being rusty. What surprised me the most was how effective he was in pass coverage – very active and athletic. This will be a bonus against F$U, where he can be left in on long yardage situations in case a draw play is run.

Well, I suppose I'm in the minority again this week. I mentioned before the Vandy game that I was tired of all the talk about how the Gators struggle in Nashville and that we should just go in and beat them across the board. Yes, it was 17-13 at the half, but Woody should be thankful he only lost by 23 instead of 30+, which easily could have happened if Spurrier hadn't dialed back the offense a little.

Now, for South Carolina. THE GATORS ARE THE BEST TEAM IN THE CONFERENCE, AT HOME, AND WILL POUND THEM! Enough of Lou Holtz and his magic. Hey, I'm happy for them, but that was then, this is now. We will exert our will and roll over them. This is the same team that lost to a mediocre 'Bama team on the road and lost at home to an average Tennessee team with a true freshman QB. So I say to the fans, "Come loud and come proud to the Swamp, and cheer the Gators to a BIG victory over USC!" It's Homecoming, to boot.

Stop the run, and you've stopped the Lamecocks.

Crystal ball says Florida 38 USC 14

**Visor Flings, Week 11:**
**UF 41, South Carolina 21**

A very satisfying win over the Lamecocks, especially after overcoming so much early difficulty.

It was obvious even through the first quarter that a successful game plan was in place, and that if the team didn't panic the Gators would win. Florida obviously had a huge edge in the match-ups between the WRs and DBs. Despite an 18-point deficit, the Gators continued to hit big plays downfield – maybe the worshiped Lou Holtz and Charlie Strong should take some heat for that.

The stats don't bear out what was obvious, especially to the Head Ball Coach. Rex was nervous, had trouble just getting the ball from center, made many throws off his back foot (a bad habit developed recently), and did not look underneath when pressured, instead making some dangerous throws. He is a freshman, after all, a fact too many overlooked earlier this season.

What you see is what you get with Jesse at this point. I honestly feel that his occasional wildness is a direct result of inconsistent playing time, going back to his injury against LSU in '98. Between injuries and bad luck, a promising career has been turned into a hit-or-miss proposition.

Gillespie and Graham continue to run hard and impress. Looks like Graham is the short-yardage and red zone back now, which is fine. I also enjoyed the use of them as well as Frazier in underneath routes; this kept many drives alive in the first half, and could be of real benefit against F$U.

Gaffney and Caldwell looked great. Gaffney is truly playing beyond his years, and Caldwell has shown an improvement in toughness through the season. Looks like Jacobs will only contribute on an occasional deep ball, and Haugabrook is doing some real damage over the middle on curl and crossing routes. The more diversity the better heading into Tallahassee. Also, the more Gaffney can be moved around in formation, the better the chance to isolate him in coverage and enable him to make a big play.

The defense and the game plan were solid. The Lamecocks never established a consistent ground game, and Petty was lucky to survive the pounding he took. This unit needs to keep their heads up Saturday, because they will give up some big plays and points. However, if they can generate some turnovers (especially interceptions by the safeties), they should hold up their end of the bargain.

It will really be interesting to see what develops against the Semen-holes. Injuries will affect their running game somewhat, but their strength is passing, so that isn't a big deal. What is a big deal is that the Gator defense needs to generate some three-and-outs, both to give themselves some rest and to put doubt in the minds of the F$U offense. They are too good to shut down, but slowing them down may be enough.

The key will be in the trenches on both sides of the ball. Can the Florida O-Line establish a semblance of a running game to show some balance, or will Jesse and/or Rex suffer a pounding? Can the D-Line control enough of the run and put pressure on Weinke without the need for constant blitzing? The more Hoke can mix-up blitzes and coverages, the better their chances of winning.

It will be interesting to see if the road wars at Tennessee and Miss. St. have seasoned the players for such a big battle. They certainly have had their share of adversity and handled it fairly well. Can F$U handle some real adversity and close competition? I feel the closer the game and the tougher the Gators play, the bigger the advantage into the second half and fourth quarter.

The bottom line is, I just want to see the players have fun, stay focused, and pump each other up after every play. Stay together no matter what – remember, there is another big (perhaps bigger) game after this.

My prediction: F$U 35 Florida 24. Hey, a prediction is a cold choice – I want nothing more than to beat half-ass U.

**Visor Flings, Week 12:**
**F$U 30, UF 7**

Disappointment at Doak.

Well, another sad trip to Tallahassee. Anytime a game this big is lost, many small things are magnified, sometimes too large. What really happened was this:

1) Once again, spotty QB play hampered the offense. A lot is being made of the lack of a running game, and I agree to a point. But, the Gators have always set up the run with the pass, and a consistent threat was never established. I actually liked the offensive game plan and how certain key plays were set up – tight end involvement, working the middle, moving Gaffney around – but the execution wasn't at the high level it needed to be. Jesse's development was interrupted too many times in his career, and Grossman was just short on experience. Palmer and now Berlin should have been red-shirted - questionable decisions that may have hurt the team now and for the future.
2) The O-Line's pass-blocking was again great, but where is the aggressiveness, the willingness to fire out, on running plays? Too many times a simple slant from a D-Lineman caused easy penetration. Stephens and Hunt have to correct this. I did enjoy Moody's obvious frustration and over-aggressiveness near the end – he's got some real fire, and will improve tremendously next season. Walker needs to return, and the strength and technique of the interior needs to improve as well. Graham again looked strong, and should have been used at least 15 times. And while Gillespie's style didn't fit against a speed defense, he did have success on straight draws between the guards. Spurrier needs to run straight ahead more against the Semen-holes in the future.
3) Gaffney impressed once again, and his presence did open up other receivers. However, once again Caldwell only did so much, and no one else contributed. Taylor Jacobs seems to have regressed, Haugabrook got fewer snaps/looks than anticipated, and Willis obviously wasn't being counted on. Two or three guys really need to step up next season – the opportunity is there to be very productive.
4) A major disappointment was the lack of a pass rush. It seems that Hoke was unwilling to take many chances blitzing, but apparently that didn't stop the deep ball. A major area of work in the off-season.
5) The run defense was fine – the line and linebackers flowed well to the ball. In fact, the pass coverage by the LBs was good also. So what happened......
6) ...the backs are the weakest link on the defense. Lito may have been hampered by a groin pull, but Alexander still continues to get burned deep. Scary as this sounds, but Cromartie looks like our best cover guy at the moment. He may have played his best game of his career, covering both the deep ball and the seam routes. Actually, while the safeties did take some bad angles on slant routes, I think if Lito had not pulled on some jerseys that some of those passes still would have been broken up. Of course, I'm only speaking from a live

perspective of being at the game, not watching any replays. Another area needing an upgrade next year – perhaps some red-shirts/re-signs (Orr, Carter) can help.
7) Some key sequences really influenced the outcome, some of which the Head Ball Coach gets the blame for:
First quarter, an effective drive capped by a TD pass, followed three plays later by a F$U bomb? Momentum crusher…Second quarter, third and a half yard at the F$U 39, and a delay hand-off!? Where was the easy sneak for the first down? And then a punt!?
Three-and-out by the Gator defense at the start of the third quarter, followed by starting at it's own 41. A stuffed run (again), followed by an overthrow to Jacobs, followed by a pass well short of the first down...

Yeesh! I know many fans are deeply disappointed by the result, including myself. However, I appreciated how hard the Gators played the entire game, and cannot fault the effort. This was a game where the Gators had to play at to the best of their ability and get some breaks to win, and that didn't happen. I was encouraged that Weinke was held to just over 50% passing, and some turnovers were generated. Now is the time when the coaches have to encourage the players to keep working hard, and the players themselves have to pump each other up. A BIG game awaits in Atlanta, and that would be a much worse disappointment for everyone. I'm sure we all remember last years' flame-out. THAT CANNOT BE ALLOWED TO HAPPEN! And it won't...this is still a fine team, and I'm excited about whipping Auburn again in the conference championship while burning down Atlanta.

GO GATORS!!!

**Visor Flings, Week 13**
**SEC Championship Game @ Atlanta**

A huge game for the Gators this Saturday. It's hard to believe, but it's now been four years since the last SEC title. Despite the disappointing effort at F$U, the team must be ready to play at or near their best against Auburn. The Tigers/Plainsmen/War Eagles (WHATEVER!) have a chance at redemption after getting waxed at the Swamp, so they will be sky-high emotionally for a shot at revenge.

Much is being made of Rex Grossman's comments after the first meeting. Of course, it's funny that they were largely ignored then, and suddenly being dredged up by Auburn as a rallying point. Fine, but maybe their real rallying point should be, "Let's not get embarrassed again." I think that's a more powerful motivator once the game begins. But we all know that the fishwraps need something to sell

In addition, a prevalent story line is how much better Auburn is playing as a team right now. Well, I put it to you that Florida is better now as well, despite the score at Tallahassee. The Gators are better than Auburn, even at a neutral site.

It will be interesting to see how much the Tigers/Plainsmen/War Eagles (WHATEVER!) will try to use Rudi Johnson early on. Will they just pound away at Florida's "soft" defense (as Clint Mitchell reminded us that those were Rudi's words after the first game), or try a lot of play-action to try and hit a big play or two, then go back to the run? Well, play-action usually doesn't work if you haven't already established a running game, or are behind early.

Also, I'm still not impressed with Auburn's secondary. I know their two senior cornerbacks were toasted the first meeting and want to show the country a better effort. The effort may very well turn out better, but in four years they should already be established. If the Gators execute their game plan efficiently, they will still move the ball effectively through the air. I wouldn't be surprised to see Auburn try the F$U approach of dropping seven or eight into coverage, and making T-Rex go with the underneath stuff and be patient. If he does this, then the Gators will have a lot more time-of-possession than usual, and the Tigers/Plainsmen/War Eagles (WHATEVER!) will go down to another bitter defeat.

I do have a feeling that Jesse will play significant minutes.

The only way Auburn wins this game is if their D-Line dominates with no help from blitzes.

It's also worth noting how much the Gators run the ball, especially in light of Coach's comments after the Disaster at Doak. Gillespie could definitely be effective on the turf, especially on short passes. It will be interesting to see who starts and plays the majority of the snaps. Graham has improved as the season has progressed; will he be rewarded this game?

And who will step up to take some of the attention away from Gaffney? I fully expect Auburn to double-team him, seeing if Caldwell and/or someone else fills the void – wouldn't you? This has been a sore spot for the passing game most of the season.

All this being said, there should be no lack of effort, focus, or intensity from the Gators Saturday. Everyone associated with the program knows the importance of assuming the role of SEC Champions again. Will the team and coaches be too tight for this one? It says here...NOT!

Florida 35 Auburn 21

**Visor Flings, Week 14:**
**UF 28, Auburn 6**

As expected, a superior Florida Gator team whipped Auburn on Saturday in the SEC Championship.

The keys to victory were the first-half takeaways (obviously), the efficiency and balance of the offense, and the dominant play of the defensive line.

Looks like the noise from the Auburn camp on Rex's comments was just that – noise. I didn't see much difference from the first game as far as their stopping the Gator offense or being able to pass effectively. Auburn did have two nice drives in the first half, but Travis Carroll stopped one and poor tackling helped the other (Heath Evans was made to look like Tommie Frazier on that swing pass – tackling has been shaky all season). The final score in both games could have been much worse had the Head Ball Coach not called off the dogs in the second half.

It certainly was nice to see the running game be so effective. It was a little surprising, because I felt the Auburn defense was pretty strong against the run. But once again, it seems that the Gator offense is that much better than the Auburn defense. Other than a silly fumble (lack of concentration), Graham looked very strong hitting the proper holes quickly and delivering some punishment to tacklers. When he plays with determination, he's a load. Maybe consistent focus is all he needs to have a huge season next year. If his pass blocking and catching improve, Gillespie could become more of a third-down back and lose some playing time. Just goes to show how valuable Errict Rhett was; very good at running, blocking, and catching.

Once again, Gaffney and Caldwell carried the load, with Aaron Walker continuing to improve and Haugabrook providing tough catches over the middle. It appears that the third- and fourth-receiver positions will be wide open competition this spring – Kight, Perez, and Jackson have a terrific opportunity to shine next season, IF they continue to work hard. Gaffney is very smooth; reminds me somewhat of Ike Hilliard in his route-running and running after the catch. And Caldwell displayed another glimpse of what the coaches only hope becomes more common – a big target that can break tackles and stretch defenses. IF he doesn't become lazy or satisfied, look out next year. He seems to have made big strides this season – let's hope it continues.

The defense really played well. I enjoyed the hustle and pursuit to the ball, even with the lapses in tackling. Man, Travis Carroll is big-time – a guy who plays the run AND pass and really plays sideline-to-sideline. Lito once again showed why the notice he's received is much-deserved. I hated to see that damn Astroturf aggravate Brown's and Warren's injuries, but at least they have a month to rehab. The big problem they'll have is that they may not be in shape to play their normal amount of plays – looks like Ellis, Scott, and others will see significant time against Miami on January 2nd.

At least the experience playing on that cursed stuff should prove beneficial in the Sugar Bowl.

The scUM fans are already clogging the airwaves with their smack. Typical – they're on the bandwagon again after the last one came apart five years ago. That's okay – they can overlook the Gators all they want. Spurrier will have them revved up in Nawlins, and we'll see if they're really a storm then or a bunch of blowhards. It's funny to hear about how they will run up the score on us to impress poll voters – we'll see about that.

I'll just have to go and see it for myself from the best spot in the house. Can't wait to renew the rivalry.

**Visor Flings, Week 15:**
**Random Thoughts**

Donnan's gone, and maybe Dooley, too, from Georgia. Actually, Vince's watch has been poor over their Athletic Dept. Most of their teams are pretty good to poor now, except women's basketball. No knock on the ladies, but they don't pay the freight. With the school president making the decision on Donnan, Vince might think of resigning now instead of getting axed. Hope he stays (heh heh heh).

There were some interesting comments made by the president indicating that some improprieties and the classic "philosophical differences" exist. Trouble on the horizon for the Puppies...no sympathy here – just another team weakened for us to dominate.

There are some fun bowl match-ups this year --
Nebraska - Northwestern
Kansas St. - Tennessee
Texas - Oregon
Oregon St. - Notre Dame
Va. Tech - Clemson
Oklahoma - F$U
and of course...Miami - Florida

Northwestern, Oklahoma, and yes, Florida, just might jump up and get someone.
Playoff musings: A 10-game regular season with only 7 conference games required opens up the possibility of more intersectional games 8 teams (7 games) or 16 teams (15 games), seeded based on BCS ratings all rounds except for Championship game at higher-seeded team – this gives teams a reason to try to still win as many games as possible and encourages more intersectional match-ups during the season (therefore tougher scheduling).

Championship Game at a neutral site. One sponsor pays for everything, such as the European corporation's bid to pay for everything a few years back. All NCAA 1-A teams get a piece of the pie, with the playoff participants getting a larger cut, but still equal among the 8 or 16 teams.

Other teams not in the playoff can still go to bowl games.

It really is simple. What a shame that politics and lining the pockets of Bowl committees holds it back. We need to keep the faith and keep campaigning.

**Visor Flings, Week 16-17**
**Pre-game Analysis**

Well, even after 13 years, the thugs from Miami continue to deserve their reputation. Hurricane players actually brawled with a few of the Gators on Bourbon Street the other night.

I'm amazed by how much credit Butch Davis receives for Miami becoming a winning program again. Sure, probation hurts (as the Gators know all too well), but with the talent level in this state, it should be expected that each major program field a winning team each season (especially in the perennially weak ACC and Big East conferences). I look at Butch Davis, and I see a smugness that is undeserved, especially for really winning only one big game in years, against F$U in October. This attitude, combined with the recruiting hijinks exposed during the Jonothan Colon fiasco, tell me he's two-faced and covers his messy tracks well.

Now, on to the game.

OFFENSE

Hopefully the Gator offense will channel their anger from the brawl into some aggressive blocking against the 'Canes. Yes, Damione Lewis is a stud, but there is a lack of depth here that can be exposed. It will be interesting to see how the Head Ball Coach schemes a way to neutralize the real strength of the Miami defense – the linebackers. Dan Morgan is the real deal, playing the run and pass effectively. Some semblance of a running game is key, plus the use of the middle of the field on pass plays. The Gators can really take advantage of the over-aggressiveness of the Miami defensive players.

Rex Grossman needs to establish himself right away, showing quick and accurate decision-making, or else he'll be in real trouble, and Jesse will be called upon to try and save the day. Plus, it's Earnest Graham's chance to establish himself as the man, not in just this game, but for next year as well. I know Kenyatta Walker is ready to blow open some holes and pay back the thugs for their disrespect on Bourbon Street.

I am worried about the "slight" knee injury reported to Jabar Gaffney. Many times these "minor" injuries turn out to be much more serious, and this would cripple the passing game. I think Aaron Walker can have a big impact, if Spurrier involves him in the game plan. The tight ends and running backs can be used to take advantage of over-aggressiveness, giving Miami a taste of their own medicine. And I know Reche Caldwell wants some payback, too. Hopefully the Gators can use their emotion in a positive way, instead of trying too hard and just making mistakes. The pass blocking has been solid all season, so I hope this isn't an area for concern.

DEFENSE

Well, since this looks to be Big Money's last game as a Gator, I can only hope his groin injury has healed well enough so that he can inflict some pain on the 'Cane runners and Dorsey. I haven't heard much about Brown's condition, and frankly, this worries me. I suspect his effectiveness may be limited to only certain situations, so the rest of the D-Line will need to play their best game of the season. Maybe Chambers, Ellis, and company will pick up the slack. Miami will definitely try to run the ball, and forcing Dorsey into long-yardage situations could generate some turnovers.

The linebackers will be tested both against the run and pass more than against any other opponent this season. Miami uses the tight end very effectively, and works the backs over the middle as well (see F$U tape). This is Travis Carroll's time to announce his presence on a national stage, and I think he's up to the challenge. I'm curious as to how Hoke decides to scheme the front seven. Does he gamble and bring up a safety (or substitute an extra DB for a LB) to offset the TE and make Dorsey look to Moss and Wayne (their best receiver, not Moss), or does he play a lot of zone, hoping quickness provides sufficient coverage? Sheppard, Alexander, and Cromartie are under the gun in this match-up. Time for Todd Johnson to save the day (again?) It won't take long to see how the defense is doing, so here's hoping Hoke has installed his best game plan of the season.

SPECIAL TEAMS

Big-time playmakers on both sides. Moss obviously is one of the best returning both punts and kick-offs, so it will be interesting to see if the Gators employ “directional” kicking, staying away from him when possible. May be a good idea.

And of course, Lito Sheppard can take it to the house as well, which I'm sure the 'Canes know by now. I just hope we see a lot of punt returns from him, instead of kick-off returns.

The Gators have a decided edge at both place kicker and punter. This may prove critical – any field-position advantage gained just takes that much more pressure off the defense, and limits the amount of gambling they would need to do.

OUTLOOK

Florida has less room for error than Miami, and will need it's best performance of the season to win. Based on past performances in big games by each head coach, I give the advantage to Coach. In comparing the defensive coordinators, the advantage goes to Chiano and the 'Canes. Each QB is under the gun this game, and right now that advantage goes to Dorsey. The Gators will have a huge edge in the fan base, from 2-1 to 3-1 in size.

A tough call, and a close one (only if Gaffney, Warren, Brown, etc. are healthy).

Florida 27 scUM 24

Bonus Pick: F$U 27 Oklahoma 17

**Visor Flings, Week 18**
**Miami 37, UF 20**

So, the wheels came off for good in the third quarter. A very dramatic game – lots of offense, lots of tough penalties, a 51-yard field goal by Chandler, several lead changes – but in the end we came up short.

The Head Ball Coach probably summarized it better than anyone: "We got basically what we deserved. Miami's a better team than we are. Better coached, more disciplined, they played with more purpose. We were embarrassed."

We'll take some satisfaction in our SEC championship and also in F$U's loss to national champs Oklahoma in the Orange Bowl, 13-2. All that hype and the Semi-holes can only manage a safety.

Now it's shelf time for the Visor. I'll see you all in August.

Very Truly Yours,
The Visor

# 2001
# Big Events, Big Changes

Looking back, this was a very emotional year, and a tragic one in many ways. Among the many aftershocks from the events of September 11 was the necessity for all of us to take a step back, to look at ourselves in new and different ways, and to remember the things we value most. In the larger picture, any single athletic competition is of very little consequence compared to matters such as the attacks on the Twin Towers, but in another and maybe even profound way, American sports can represent the things we love: spirit, loyalty, the opportunity to develop one's gifts to their highest level, and the chance to see what we are made of when it counts. The Visor believes in these things.

It also seems that sadness comes sometimes when you're not looking for it, and when Steve Spurrier retired from college coaching after the Orange Bowl Game, many people were left wondering: Now what?

But of course, as we now know, you couldn't keep the Head Ball Coach out of the game. He served a fairly unremarkable stint with the Washington Redskins, where he tried to team up once again with Heisman winner Danny Wuerffel, to little success. Some Glory Days are best left in the rearview mirror, it would seem. Still, a bit later, as we shall also see in these pages, the Gators would encounter the Head Ball Coach again – this time on the other sideline.

Also among the notable events for the Gators in 2001 was our devastating loss to Auburn in the sixth game of the season. The Visor wrote at the time, and I still believe, that this was one of the most dismal losses in UF history. It was clear that we had managed to lose to an inferior team, and hindsight shows that this probably derailed our hopes early on for another national championship.

Still, this year saw the ongoing development of Rex Grossman as a fine college quarterback, as well as many magical moments between him and his receiving corps, especially Gaffney. Some guys gave us hope for the future, something we would need a lot of in the post-Spurrier age.

## Visor Flings, Week 1

### Preview and Predictions

Once again a new season is upon us. And once again, expectations are very high; higher this year than since 1998. There is a lot to cover.

OFFENSE

This unit has the potential to be the Head Ball Coach's best since 1995-96. Experienced players such as left tackle Mike Pearson, center Zac Zedalis, running backs Earnest Graham and Robert Gillespie, and wide receivers Jabar Gaffney and Reche Caldwell provide a solid nucleus to surround the quarterback and support the young players stepping in to meaningful roles this year.

On the offensive line, Max Starks steps in for early departure Kenyatta Walker, Shannon Snell vies for the starting left guard spot, and freshmen Mo Mitchell and Jonathan Colon provide depth at the tackle positions. Normally the thought of freshmen at tackle would be extra cause for alarm, but this is not necessarily the case. Mitchell originally signed with Alabama in 1999 but never enrolled there and attended prep school in 2000. And the saga of Colon is well-documented by now. Fortunately he has stayed in shape and has not lost any eligibility. Erik Strange and David Jorgensen provide experienced back-up in the interior. This should be an effective unit this season.

The situation at running back is a good news/bad news one. The Gators are loaded at tailback with quality. Graham and Gillespie are proven performers; Graham especially has been underutilized and could be relied on heavily this year. Plus, quality depth in Ran Carthon and Willie Green awaits. Green especially shone in Spring drills, but once again will be slowed by more knee surgery until October. At fullback, the sad death of Eraste Autin will be felt. His efforts were being counted upon heavily for a true freshman, showing his promise. A real tragedy. Rob Roberts is a hard worker but still remains a mystery as to when he'll return to full strength following major knee surgery. Reid Fleming is moving over from linebacker and is a fine athlete with high school experience. Maybe he can perform like D.J. Williams did for Miami last year, then move back to linebacker when Travis Carroll and Andra Davis depart. The combination of these two along with another freshman, Ray Snell, and some support from Carthon will be adequate.

The unquestioned leader at wide receiver is Gaffney. His performance last year was sensational, showing speed, route-running capability, and toughness. Reche Caldwell improved dramatically from 1999, and still looks to improve his consistency and concentration. Once again, however, the third and fourth options remain a question mark. Is this finally the year Taylor Jacobs realizes the promise the coaches have for him? If not, it's time to look elsewhere. Sophomores Carlos Perez, Matt Jackson, and Kelvin Kight may need to fill the void, with freshman O.J. Small a possibility. These slots have remained mostly empty since Jacquez Green left, and this has hampered the effectiveness of the passing game. The health of Gaffney and Caldwell is critical.

The tight end position may contribute significantly in the passing game for the first time in many years. Aaron Walker appears to be the starter; he came on strong late last season and exhibits good hands. Ben Troupe is a good athlete with toughness coming from experience in high school on defense. Of course, the player who shows the best blocking ability may eventually take the lead, as Spurrier will always look to attack downfield with the receivers first.

Of course, most attention in the spring and fall has been focused on the QB battle between Rex Grossman and Brock Berlin. Despite the overzealous attention here, it's apparent Grossman leads, and I expect him to start against Marshall. What a waste that Berlin wasn't red-shirted last season. No matter who takes the snaps, however, the running game will be improved this season and will help balance the attack more to Coach's liking. The pass-catching ability of the backs and tight ends can also provide a safe outlet for either QB. Expect to see both play, though. Berlin needs significant game experience, as Ingle Martin, a true freshman, is the only other scholarship QB.

DEFENSE

It's now year three for Jon Hoke, and it's time for this unit to deliver a complete package: run defense, pass defense, and turnovers. The Gators led the nation in takeaways last year, which was fortunate because the yardage given up was unacceptable. The line underachieved, and the secondary was torched by F$U, much of which was plainly poor execution and only partly due to some unfortunate injuries.

As much as there is to discuss about new starters, the additions to the coaching staff deserves mention. The Visor has complained for the past few seasons about the staleness and lack of fire in this group. Ricky Hunley and Jerry Odom will certainly change this. Both men seem to have instilled some urgency into the players, reflecting their respective playing careers. This is a welcome and long-overdue upgrade.

The line will receive the most scrutiny this fall. While the coaches are optimistic about this group's potential, it has to be proven under fire. Ian Scott steps in for Gerard Warren, and has both the biggest shoes to fill and the most promising future. He showed glimpses of great play last season in limited duty; now the challenge is to start and compete for an entire season. Alex Brown is being asked to do two things – be the leader and be consistent. His athletic ability is unquestioned; his performance could key the entire unit's success. The coaches are high on Darrell Lee and Bobby McCray at defensive ends. They will need to be productive, especially with the loss for at least six games of Clint Mitchell due to suspension. Tron LaFavor and Juco transfer Bryan Savelio need to provide production at the other defensive spot opposite Scott and contribute to an effective rotation. The talent is adequate here; the quality of depth isn't.

At linebacker, there exists tremendous ability, experience, and depth. This could be the strongest group since 1998 (Rutledge, Peterson, Kearse) and be the best defensive unit this year. The return of Andra Davis in the middle to lead and plug the run is critical. This will free up Travis Carroll to either back-up several positions and also to play some situations simultaneously. The outside has a plethora of fine players. Byron Hardmon and Mike Nattiel are the starters, and there is only some drop-off to Matt Farrior, Travis Harris, and Marcus Oquendo-Johnson. All can run, and received a trial-by-fire last season. There is little to worry about here.

The secondary is strong and probably the most athletic group since the mid-90's. Of course, the standout is Lito Sheppard, who has the knack of making big plays at crucial times. The loss of Robert Cromartie to a torn pectoral muscle hurts, but hopefully Kiewan Ratliff can physically handle a starting role. Bennie Alexander provides senior leadership and quality depth. The mission for this group is to provide consistent coverage and avoid mental lapses that hurt at crucial times last year. At safety, Todd Johnson and Marquand Manuel are the leaders, while Gus Scott and Dwayne Dixon are effective back-ups. Scott may actually be a slightly better player than Manuel at this point. Look for Tre Orr to perhaps surprise as the season progresses. This unit just needs to play smarter, avoiding taking bad angles on long passes and taking unnecessary risks trying to make big hits. If this group improves it's consistency, it could provide a huge lift to the young linemen.

## SPECIAL TEAMS

Placekicking is in the valuable and capable hands of Jeff Chandler, Florida's all-time leading scorer. His field goal accuracy has improved, and he has also exhibited the ability of making clutch kicks in big games. His kick-offs have shown the most improvement in his career; rarely does an opponent start outside the 25-yard line. Hopefully his NCAA-mandated one-game sit-out will not prove costly against Marshall.

The punting seems to be in the hands of freshman Matt Leach right now. This is always a dicey situation in big game and pressure situations; the consistency just can't be expected yet. The coaches hope he can deliver on the promise he showed in high school.

Of course, the big-play man here is Lito Sheppard, who is one of the most dangerous return men in college football. It's obvious that he can turn any kick return into a score. It will be interesting to see how much opportunity he's given by opponents this season. Kiewan Ratliff has great speed, and showed flashes of providing big plays as well. No worries here.

## OUTLOOK FOR 2001

The Gators play eight bowl teams from 2000. The big games at home are Tennessee, Mississippi State, and F$U. The big road test seems to be LSU, with South Carolina a possible challenge.

Can the confidence of the Head Ball Coach and the new fire from Hunley and Odom steer a young team to a memorable season? The talent is obviously there...the consistency and mental toughness have to be proven.

The Visor has had a difficult time gauging where this team is right now and where it can wind up. The unusual question marks at RB for the Vols and at QB for F$U certainly provide hope for wins at the Swamp. Motivation after last year's embarrassment at Miss. St. isn't an issue. Nick Saban has things on the upswing at LSU, which never should have sunk to the depths it has seen the past decade. That could be a minefield no matter how well the Gators play that day, as the Tigers are both talented and unpredictable. Much is also made of the "Holtz magic" at S. Carolina. I don't believe that Spurrier will let his team sleepwalk into that game, though by then it has already been a long, physical season with F$U the following week.

PREDICTIONS

Regular Season 11-0 (8-0 SEC)
SEC Champions (win over LSU)
National Champions (win over Miami or Oklahoma)

For the first time, The Visor predicts an undefeated season. While the Gators certainly have questions, every team that has National Championship aspirations does as well. The defense will have to carry the day, and I believe they can do the job adequately. The schedule is also favorable (as favorable as an 8 bowl-team schedule can be). Talk about sticking your neck out, huh? It will be interesting and exciting no matter what unfolds.

The opener against Marshall is certainly the most competitive of the Spurrier era. The Thundering Herd are a quality team, owning wins over other 1-A "major" schools and winning the MAC Championship four years running.

Byron Leftwich and his corps of big receivers will cause some problems for the Gator secondary. Leftwich is a bona fide NFL prospect, with the size (6'4", 250 lb.) and arm strength scouts love. The NCAA suspensions handed down this week, however, will cost the offense a starting lineman and both starting running backs. That's a break for the defense. Still, the loss of Robert Cromartie will be felt this week. It will be interesting to see how Marquise Westbrook and Kiewan Ratliff fill in.

Marshall's defense will be hurt by the suspensions as well, losing their starting nose tackle. The Herd secondary is replacing two starters from a unit that was somewhat shaky last year. Rex Grossman and the receivers should have their way, with at least a 300-yard performance to be expected. It's the running game that will need development for Florida, though. It would be great to see a dominating effort, but with the new starters and youth, I'm not expecting too much yet.

I'm surprised that Coach Pruett has let his boys talk so much smack before the game. While building their confidence is all fine and good, those players will regret getting the attention of the Gators. I expect a solid performance from the entire team, unlike the uninspired, sloppy effort the fans are usually subjected to against weak opening opponents.

This is the first step in seeing whether Rex will put aside all talk of QB controversy and separate himself from Berlin. I expect him to play well, but also hope Brock gets to play at least one full quarter. The Tennessee game in two weeks may very well tell the tale of the QBs this year.

This should be an entertaining game. Hopefully the fans aren't expecting a blowout. Marshall will make some plays and provide a good challenge. The Gators, I believe, will come out ready to play and control the game for the majority of time.

Prediction: Florida 45 Marshall 17
See you next week.

**Visor Flings, Week 2**
**UF 49, Marshall 14**

Overall, the Gators put on an excellent performance in the opener. I guess the Marshall players' comments before the game got the attention of the Florida coaches and players.

The passing offense was especially sharp for a first game. The protection was adequate despite a good dose of blitzing, and the receivers ran good routes to get open, despite the presence of five or six defensive backs on most downs. Rex played a good game, but once again showed the inclination to lose mental focus at the start of the second half. The running backs played well, showing a nice mix of talents rushing and receiving. I'm still waiting, however, for a third receiver to become a consistent option.

The defense played hard and with emotion. It's about time Hoke started actually blitzing with some regularity. Despite rushing three men much of the night, the blitzers (especially Gus Scott) applied sufficient pressure. Alex Brown seemed to have his motor running most of the game. And it was great to have Andra Davis back. He certainly made some big plays early, especially in short yardage situations. It was interesting to see Kiewan Ratliff and Lito Sheppard lining up as safeties on many pass plays. Not a bad idea to let the guys with speed roam about looking to make a play occasionally.

As for this next "game," it is nothing but a glorified scrimmage. Of course, I'm mostly concerned about anybody getting hurt. This will be an opportunity for the young players to get more on-field experience, hopefully to improve the quality of depth as the season progresses. Berlin should see plenty of snaps.

Prediction: Florida 59 Louisiana-Monroe 7
See you next week...

**Visor Flings, Week 3**
**UF 55, Louisiana-Monroe 6**

*(The remarks below were drafted just before the events of 9/11/01. Obviously, The Visor just wished for a competitive, safe game, one that I still hoped the Gators would win. Still, the tragic attack on the Twin Towers and subsequent loss of life put sports and other leisure activities in perspective for all of us. We're all one nation, after all. Thanks.)*

The preliminaries are out of the way, and the real season begins...
After all the talk about remaining focused and playing hard no matter the opponent, the Gators once again started out slowly against an out-manned opponent. Oh, well, this has been the history of the Spurrier era, and once again, it repeats itself.

The best outcome of the game was NO MAJOR INJURIES. It was nice to see the playmakers do their thing. Robert Gillespie is really showing a valuable versatility, and his pass-catching prowess will be especially needed starting with the Inbreds. The defense was allowed again to blitz occasionally and take some chances. Will this be allowed against a tough opponent? The Visor hopes so. No need for Hoke and Co. to go into a shell now.

It will be interesting to see how wide-open the Head Ball Coach allows the offense to be at the start. Of course, field position can play a part, but historically this hasn't been a hindrance to the play-calling. It's time for the young boys on the O-Line to grow up and toughen up. The Inbred front seven is solid and will play aggressively, although I really don't expect to see Henderson at 100%, as a high ankle sprain can linger an entire season. Plus, Chavous knows his only consistent success against the Gator offense has been pressure and blitzing up the middle. The blocking of Zedalis, T. Moody, S. Snell, R. Snell, and the other guards and fullbacks is critical. I'd love to see some quick swing passes to the running backs and fades to the wide receivers to negate some of that pressure. It's time for Jimmy Ray to get his crew fired up and angry. I think a viewing of last year's poor performance and a good pep talk should get his guys ready. Just an average running game presence (100-130 yards) should be enough to allow Grossman to expose the Vol secondary (again!). Talk about a mental edge...that group has been torched annually, just like you can expect those raging wildfires in the West every year. If Rex starts using the middle of the field occasionally with the tight ends and a third or fourth receiver, watch out.

The Gator defense now has its opportunity to be accounted for. Yes, they've performed well so far, but it's time to contend with a quality O-Line. Phat Phil always has a solid group here, and the return of Fred Weary at center could spell trouble. Travis Stephens is a good player, and the freshmen backing him up have the athletic ability to make plays. However, their blocking is suspect, so it's obvious what the goal is here...make all-SEC QB Casey Clausen win the game. He's a good player, but come on! Let's see him lead a comeback against the Gators in the Swamp. I don't think so. The loss of Stallworth is unfortunate, but aren't you supposed to have a group of players, not just one? Could be big problems here for the Inbreds.

I'm also excited about the Gator special teams. Returns and coverage have been terrific, and the kickers are very good. Looks like the added emphasis in fall practice has paid off, and I suspect some big plays will come from this group Saturday.

Yes, it's Tennessee, and yes, they're ranked number eight, but I honestly see a real gap between the teams this year. Barring the great equalizer (poor weather may be likely) or a meltdown caused by turnovers (are you listening Rex?), the Gators should once again Rocky Top the Inbreds.

We will never know how Tuesday's tragedy will affect this game; I just hope each team plays the best and hardest it can.

Visor's forecast: Florida 34 Tennessee 17

**Visor Flings, Week 4**
**Game Postponed**

World events postponed last week's big game, and certainly put a new twist in the schedule and the balance of the season. Now, along with trying to coach and motivate college players, the coaches have to wonder about their mental make-up as well, even more so than usual.

I know Tennessee fans are glad they didn't have to visit the Swamp for their annual whipping. Now they can hang their false hopes on "being the better team at the end of the year," their usual lame motto. Now, they'll get their chance to prove it.

Kentucky is pretty much in shambles right now. They have scrapped their wide-open passing game for more ball-control, and the man-child Jared Lorenzen is now the second-string QB. I really question this strategy, especially against the Gators. I suspect something will be done to surprise them in Commonwealth Stadium, but it won't be enough.

The offense should have little trouble moving the ball and scoring at least 35 points. This will be another growing opportunity for the younger starters in their first road game of the season; some adversity will help them develop. No special game planning is necessary to ensure a comfortable win. Look for the running game to get a little more emphasis, and hopefully the blitz packages will be picked up effectively.

The defense should have plenty of opportunities to make big plays, especially with the Mildcats being forced into many third-and-long situations. I'm more interested in seeing the defensive line making some plays without the aid of blitzes. Alex Brown and Ian Scott are known assets; it's time for others to start making a name for themselves. This can be a confidence-builder for the young linemen, especially with a big, tough O-Line in Mississippi State as next week's opponent.

Barring a rash of injuries and/or inclement weather, everything points to another comfortable win in the Bluegrass State.

Visor Vision says: Florida 45 Kentucky 13

**Visor Flings, Week 5**
**UF 44, Kentucky 10**

Another successful trip to Lexington. The layoff and emotions of the day seemed to affect the Gators somewhat, but it was encouraging to see improvement in the second half. Once again Rex seemed to have some lapses in concentration, but Spurrier stuck with him through the start of the 4th quarter and he came around. Brock certainly made the most of his limited time. Robert Gillespie was the best player on the field, doing it all...running, catching, blocking. He's a great complement to Graham, who made a nice long TD run to extend the lead back to 20 points right after UK's last score.

The defense was solid as well. There were some missed tackles, especially on the QB, but that was probably a combination of the layoff and the running talent of Boyd. The line generated good pressure, and the coverage in the intermediate and long areas was solid. However, no takeaways once again...certainly not like last year. Hopefully this trend will reverse itself starting this week.

This looks like a revenge game for the Gators. Certainly that could enhance the motivation, but I believe that the Head Ball Coach just wants to have the players perform their assignments correctly, and let their talent and emotion do the rest. The trip to the aptly named "Starkville" last year was a bitter one, what with the poor performance of the team and the MSU fans after the game. It's payback time.

Already the news is that Dicenzo Miller, MSU's top tailback, may only see limited action due to a high-ankle injury. Well, the Gators lost Palmer to injury last year, so too bad. Will Wayne Madkin be able to lead their offense to 30+ points? No way. Lost in the ashes of last year's result is that the Gator pass offense was unstoppable against Joe Lee Dunn's defense, with turnovers and bad shotgun snaps killing scoring drives. I expect a fine performance out of the QBs and wide receivers Saturday, and I expect a little more balance provided by Graham and Gillespie. The Gator OL matches up size-wise much better this season, and should get some push at the line of scrimmage to take the pressure off the passing game. I'm sure Stephens and Teevens will have the line and RBs working on blitz protection. With any amount of time, a 300+ yard passing day is pretty much assured.

I love the passes to the backs and tight ends vs. the opposing linebackers. With Florida's athletes, there will be mismatches to exploit if Coach will allow it to happen. This has led to successful third down conversions that have kept many drives alive, and kept the defense off the field more often. You can't beat that combination. Nothing wrong with a little patience the frustrate and tire out the defense.

I have to expect Jackie Sherrill to ask Madkin to do whatever it takes to keep drives alive, so I expect a lot of option calls and QB draws to try and slow down the rush. I also expect a lot of long balls to try and hit the occasional big play. I just don't see the same MSU offense as last season, and I certainly don't see the same poor Gator defense as last season. I will point out that MSU always has great special teams play; Florida will need to continue it's fine play here to offset MSU's unit. No need for a major breakdown or two here to hand them easy points.

I did find the comments about Lito by Spurrier interesting. Perhaps he trying to motivate him for some reason...maybe he's somewhat in the doghouse right now? I think the Gators will be fine this week even if he doesn't play...there are bigger games down the road, and a groin injury can linger (see last year). Hopefully Alex Brown will play, but if he decides to be with his girlfriend if premature labor or a C-Section is required, I can't blame him.

Remember, "Revenge is a dish best served cold."

Stars show Florida 38 MSU 14

**Visor Flings, Week 6**
**UF 52, Mississippi State 0**

The real season kicked off in fine fashion Saturday. Talk about payback (and lots of it)! Things certainly went the Gators' way from start to finish, including no significant injuries. The players are to be commended for their effort, as well as the coaches for developing a good game plan. Now, the first real test of the season awaits...

I saw highlights of the LSU-Tennessee game, and I was struck by the poor coaching by the LSU staff. There is no reason the no-huddle shouldn't have been run the entire second half, and the defensive secondary strategy was horrible. Kelly Washington looks to me to be a real player, but come on...where is this "defensive genius" Nick Saban is supposed to bring to Baton Rouge? I believe he was made to look better by the mediocre offenses in the Big 11 than he really is. If there is any intelligence out there, look for a lot of no-huddle against Florida, but less blitzing than MSU. I believe the best chance LSU has on defense is to be patient, rely on crowd noise, and hope for poor execution by the Gator offensive players to slow them down. The LSU defensive coordinator is Gary Gibbs, who never showed much as the Oklahoma DC and then as head coach in the late '80s and early '90s, especially in the then still run-oriented Big 12. As bad as the Tiger defense played the fade routes, Spurrier has consistently carved them up over the years with crossing routes and deep curls in zones. I'm sure he'll have an effective game plan ready; let's hope the players (especially the QB) execute it smartly.

On offense, the Gators need to continue to utilize the entire field and all the skill positions. I believe defenses will still concentrate on Gaffney until Caldwell and Jacobs are established on the outside during the game and until the tight ends and running backs burn them consistently. No need to go into any shell here...using the ends and backs worked wonders against MSU's pressure, and will continue to ease the pressure on the QB and entire offense. I look for the running game to get a little more emphasis this week in the first half. I really like the inside duo of Trev Faulk and Bradie James at ILB for the Tigers, but Graham and Gillespie need to perform well to keep these guys honest instead of just dropping into pass defense. The bottom line for this unit is the O-Line. If Jimmy Ray Stephens and John Hunt continue to develop these young guys, give them schemes they can execute, and keep their confidence up, there's no reason the offense should bog down against anyone, home or away. One small complaint: the running backs need to pick up the blitzes a little better and more physically.

The defense played inspired ball against MSU, and I believe it was obvious after the game that even the presence of a healthy Dicenzo Miller would have only helped the Bulldogs avoid a shutout, not a blowout loss. The ability of Ian Scott is now becoming apparent to many, but also the need for his continued good health is vital to maintain a solid rotation at defensive tackle. The ends are really playing well. Brown and Ellis stood their ground against the run, and displayed smarts in rushing the passer while staying under control (especially Ellis). I hope this is a sign of more consistency from Kennard this season;

he really could be a key player as long as Alex continues to play hard and draw attention on his side of the field. I really am enjoying the camaraderie the defense is showing on the field...the guys are picking each other up and encouraging everyone to play hard. This attitude can really help on the road in a hostile environment against a quality team like LSU. This group is playing very well right now, and needs to continue to play smart this week against the scrambling ability of Rohan Davey. He is a big, strong player, and won't go down sometimes. However, he can be pressured into mistakes, and carries the ball far from his body while looking downfield, providing opportunities for fumbles. LaBrandon Toefield is playing hurt, so the Tigers may throw a lot (especially running a no-huddle offense) Saturday to try and pull off the upset

This will be a test, one that I believe the coaches will have the attention of the players for. Time for the seniors to really exhibit their leadership now.

Visor goes with Florida 31 LSU 21

**Visor Flings, Week 7:**
**UF 44, LSU 15**

Looks like the Gators were focused on the task at hand against LSU. It was quite a performance by the offense in all phases: QB play, receiving, running, and especially blocking. The players and coaches are to be commended for their preparation and execution, even more impressive coming on the road.

What more can be said about the play of Rex and the receivers? Everyone is sharp right now. And the Head Ball Coach looks to be sticking with spreading the throws out to the tight ends and running backs as well. The Visor certainly hopes this continues all season. Nothing wrong with keeping the defense honest to alleviate pressure on the QB and linemen. This should reduce the amount of blitzing seen in the coming games, and should allow the running game to continue to provide the balance necessary for perhaps a big year. Patience by the Head Ball Coach has always been a question, however.

The defense was again solid if unspectacular. The linemen continue to provide some penetration and are hustling to the ball. The LB play was only OK; lots of missed tackles, although Andra Davis had some excuse. This game was good in that it showed that the defensive backs (and much of the pass defense schemes) need more work. Too many third-and-long conversions, and poor drops by the linebackers and cornerbacks in zone coverage – the deep outs and seams were open many times. Bennie Alexander seems to have regressed from 1999 until now; his technique is spotty and he obviously lacks the confidence to play man defense effectively. Looks like the loss of Robert Cromartie will be especially felt against Georgia and F$U. Plus, the three-man rush basically sucks. Get after the QB in obvious passing situations!

Now it's time to once again smack down the Tigers/War Eagles/Plainsmen...WHATEVER! It's hard to believe they're in first place in the West, but so be it. Time for the Gators to help LSU and Alabama out by giving Auburn a reality check.

Much continues to be made of Tommy Tuberville's coaching acumen, but I fail to see it. He is definitely being helped by Alabama's pending probation woes, but if he doesn't take advantage of it recruiting-wise the next two years, he'll never establish a competitive superiority in the West Division.

Auburn's defense again looks solid, but seems to lack the depth to consistently slow down Florida's offense. I suspect they may lay back in zones to try and confuse the QB into some turnovers, so I feel Graham and Gillespie will be called upon the carry the load early. I did note that Saban said it was a mistake for LSU to play so much zone, so maybe Auburn will go all-out after the quarterback? Hmmmm...quite a dilemma for the defense, huh? Continued use of the tight ends and running backs can once again prove beneficial in negating this defensive tactic, as well. I don't expect such a big early scoring run this time, so the O-line will need to continue to execute and play physically. If this happens, 30+ points shouldn't be a problem.

The defense once again will face a big, mobile QB, but experience against Madkin and Davey will prove valuable. Auburn did run very effectively against MSU, and would be foolish to abandon this tactic Saturday. I actually feel they will have some success running, but not enough to need to put 8 men in the box regularly. Looks like the passing game will be screens and long passes down the sideline, hoping for a great catch or flag. I don't believe this will be a consistent enough attack to force a shoot-out.

Too much Gator firepower, too much Gator experience, too much Evil Genius.

Florida 38 Auburn 17

**Visor Flings, Week 8:**
**Auburn 23, UF 20**

Well, I've had 48 hours to cool off.

This has to be the most maddening and disturbing loss in the Spurrier Era, even more so than the home loss to Alabama in 1999 and the Choke at Doak.

When the Gators have lost, it was usually a combination of being on the road against a team with some actual talent and playmakers and/or and turnovers with shoddy special teams play.

This time Florida lost to a team with inferior talent and no real playmakers. That's right, Gator fans – Daniel Cobb(!?!) actually led that crew to a win over the Mighty Gators.

I don't want to hear that crap about the Auburn staff doing a great job. They played an ultra-conservative game plan, praying that Florida would choke. Tuberville basically said as much when interviewed by ESPN right before kickoff.

It's time to call out the Gator coaching staff for losing this one.

It was frustrating enough to endure the first half, but I figured adjustments would be made by (1) the offense against the twists and stunts Auburn's D-Line employed, and (2) by the defense against the underneath pass patterns and delayed handoffs out of the shotgun formation.

So, what do we see?

(1) The same twists and stunts stuffing a running scheme UNCHANGED for the second half, and

(2) The same underneath pass patterns and delayed handoffs out of the shotgun moving down the field in the 4th quarter against a scheme UNCHANGED for the second half

Conclusions:

1) The coaches showed a shocking lack of confidence in the players other than the top 22…Does that mean those players, who were very successful high school players and were recruited to PLAY at Florida, suddenly have no ability? No talent? No heart?

2) The coaches forgot that they have to COACH during a game at times, helping and encouraging a group of 18-21 year old guys needing a boost and some sideline leadership. At least you could see Spurrier staying calm with Rex, trying to coach him on the sidelines after a mistake; really an improvement in his demeanor from previous seasons.

3) The guy you have supported staunchly for so long, Jimmy Ray Stephens, showed me NOTHING during that game; the O-Line was pushed around by smaller players and showed no aggressiveness and explosion off the ball.

More thoughts:

Does Jon Hoke fear that a supposedly healthy Lito Sheppard can't cover any of the vaunted Auburn "deep threats" man-to-man, freeing up others to play underneath coverage? Does he feel Gus Scott or Bam Hardmon can't cover those "Kellen Winslow-like" Auburn tight ends? Do Lawson Holland and Buddy Teevins feel that Ran Carthon can't smash through Auburn's "Steel Curtain" D-Line for 3-5 yards on occasion, helping the QB out and resting Gillespie a little? Does Jimmy Ray Stephens feel his small, undersized O-Line can't push over a cardboard wall? What a waste of talent! Will it change the rest of the season?

Sure it's "just a game," and "isn't the most important thing in life," blah blah blah... Well, why do you, the Visor, the other readers/posters, the players, the coaches, and the fans, care? Because IT IS IMPORTANT TO US. If others can care so much for music, education, hobbies, and whatever else they truly enjoy, then I can be obsessive in my love of the Gators. Besides, given my vantage point atop the beleaguered cranium of the Head Ball Coach, what else do I have?

I honestly can't believe I'm so pissed off right now. That performance had to be the worst I've seen, especially given the quality of opponent. I'll get over it soon, and I'll be in Jacksonville to hopefully whip the Puppies again. But will the "coaches" be there, and will they have done their job in preparation before the game AND in making adjustments DURING the game? I'll have to see it to believe it.

Rex will learn from this, or will be on the bench if the Head Ball Coach sees that he hasn't learned. Rex showed good presence in the pocket, and stood in there to take some big hits to deliver the ball. Yes, he screwed up not throwing the ball away instead of towards the end zone in the 1st and 4th quarters – now he will show everyone whether he has learned and improved himself or not. At this point, I hope he plays the rest of the season and somehow Spurrier can convince Berlin to be red-shirted next season. Probably highly unlikely, but it would be such a shame never to see Brock given a complete chance to perform in Spurrier's system over an entire season, showing off his poise, mobility, and accuracy.

Aren't you glad I waited 48 hours to cool off?

Go Gators!

**Visor Flings, Week 9**
**Off Week**

If you read last week's diatribe about the Auburn game, you will no doubt understand the Visor's lack of confidence in the coaching staff right now, despite my precarious position. There's no sense even thinking about BCS standings right now; the Gators need to get their house in order and win this Saturday. Another SEC loss and it's time to pack the bags for Orlando or Tampa this bowl season.

The burden is on the offense this game, especially the O-line. Some semblance of a running game is almost mandatory to give Rex and the receivers time to exploit a weak Puppy secondary. Plenty of holes to run up 300+ yards, given time and some running balance. It's almost more a mind game than a physical one now – will the coaches have the team ready and inspired, or will they lay another egg? History says the Gators will be ready, since Coach has lost two consecutive SEC games only once, back in 1992, and that team was considerably weaker than this one.

Now the news comes out that Earnest Graham will play (at less than 100%, I suspect), and that Robert Gillespie is doubtful with a sprained foot. What the hell is going on with the running backs? It looks like poor personnel management to me. The coaches better have Ran Carthon ready to go, and to be a contributor, not just a token presence. If he's not ready as a red-shirt sophomore, then shame on the coaches. If he really can't execute his assignments correctly by now, then free up a scholarship after the season.

On defense, the jury is still out, in my opinion. Yes, the overall statistics look good, but cracks were seen against LSU, and they collapsed in the 4th quarter against Auburn. I've heard the argument about being tired, but it rings hollow with me. Where is the supposed quality depth? And where are the aggressive schemes, including actual blitzes, used up until Auburn? Once again, poor coaching by Hoke, who appears to not have confidence in 1) himself to manage a game and take chances, and 2) his secondary's man-to-man coverage ability. Oh, by the way, isn't he the secondary coach as well? Hmmm...

I believe there is enough leadership on this unit from Alex Brown, Andra Davis, and Todd Johnson to win this game. Plus, the return of Clint Mitchell should provide some spark, as his motor always is running. You would think his role would be limited this week, but given the good chance that the Puppies will have a hard time running, his pass rushing ability could be critical.

The media boys are beginning to play up the Richt F$U success vs. Florida angle, but it will have to be proven in the win/loss column first. He does have his offense playing with confidence right now, but with Musa Smith hurt, they appear one-dimensional to me. Of course, many are saying the same about the Gators. If that's true, then I'll give the edge to Rex, Jabar, Reche, Taylor, and our tight ends over David Greene, Fred Gibson, Robert Edwards, and Randy McMichael. Georgia has a good group, but not at Florida's level.

Unfortunately, a tougher game to call than I really expected this season, but I'll say…

Florida 30 Georgia 24

**Visor Flings, Week 10**
**UF 24, Georgia 10**

A solid win over the Puppies...AGAIN! Yes, it was sloppy and yes, the final margin should have been much greater, but overall it was a good performance.

It was refreshing to see some new passing schemes to the backs, and the wrinkles in the formations to help with both pass blocking and running the ball. I guess the coaches figured out a way to get Ran Carthon on the field... What a waste that this couldn't happen against Auburn. I especially enjoyed watching the O-Line fire off the ball and open holes for Graham to rumble through. The Puppies never stood a real chance in this one. It's about time Spurrier calls more running plays against three-man lines and actually sticks with it even on second and long or into the fourth quarter. Rex certainly was sharp...just one really poor decision on the day leading to another end-zone interception. His touch was right on and he seemed more relaxed moving around the pocket. If he just will take the five-yard dump-offs a little more, that's about all you could ask. Being at the game, you could see opportunities for short gains instead of throwaways.

The defense played a smart game. Not much blitzing, but enough pressure from the D-Line to free up the linebackers and safeties to shut down the dink-and dunk passes Greene uses so much. I was disappointed that the 10-15 yard post and seam route never was really covered; no adjustment seemed to be made. This was the only play that really ate up chunks of yardage (not counting phantom interference and holding calls – another subject already discussed by many). Players such Alex Brown and Lito Sheppard, respectively, showed good patience and discipline in their assignments, helping to hold the Pups to 10 points. A good overall scheme by Hoke this game.

There's really not much to say about this week's "game" against Vanderbilt. I know some will bring up close calls recently, but I maintain that solid QB play will make this a comfortable win. I just hope for the usual: lots of points, lots of players seeing action, NO INJURIES! It's about time to really step up to the plate against South Carolina and F$U back-to-back, and to start peaking mentally in preparation for those two games.

Visor Vision: Florida 41 Vanderbilt 10

**Visor Flings, Week 11**
**UF 71, Vanderbilt 13**

I hope everyone enjoyed the Homecoming scrimmage against Vanderbilt. Fortunately a lot of players saw action in the second half, and no major injuries were incurred. The result was somewhat surprising, even with the known offensive capability of the Gators. The best thing to take from the game was the good execution of assignments by both the offense and defense. The only real potential stumbling block now is the elimination of turnovers. Both Gaffney's bobble/interception and Jacobs' fumble are correctable – mainly concentration errors. But the team needs to play as mistake-free as possible to make their task easier.

Now, the stretch run begins. The usual bluster about how Lou Holtz prepares a team has started. Well, I believe the Gator coaching staff will quickly tire of hearing that and come up with an effective, winning plan (especially after that embarrassing job against Auburn). Unfortunately, it took that loss to re-focus the entire team on playing winning football. But, that should bode well for the mental preparation for another Saturday night SEC showdown. It's time to expose a USC team that is above-average at best. Of course, if the Gators lose, then they really are pretenders, not contenders. Harsh, yes, but given the talent level, there are no other excuses.

I'm sure Charlie Strong will have his defense ready, with Kalimba Edwards ready to roll. A few pre-emptive strikes early and deep will cool that unit off. Will Spurrier continue to pound Graham and not lose patience with a few short gains? Hopefully. Will the backs and tight ends be involved to slow down the pass rush and spread the field? Hopefully. Will Rex have another 300+ yard game? Definitely, given any sort of balance by the run game.

What I will be watching especially closely is whether Hoke takes an aggressive approach as long as the game is in doubt, or if the three-man rush, tight end crossing patterns, and soft flats remain evident, allowing another mediocre QB like Phil Petty to become all-SEC for a night, like the forgettable Daniel Cobb of Auburn (that still pisses me off; maybe it's pissed off the players and coaches, too). USC does have two big, strong running backs, very similar to what Jackie Sherrill had working for him last season. I would be pleasantly surprised to hold them to under 120 yards rushing, which would put their offense in an uncomfortable position. Also, Ryan Brewer has been kind of quiet this year. Hope it remains that way – he's the kind of gamer that comes up big in the clutch. It appears to me as if their pass offense is basically the fade/go route to their tall receivers (especially Brian Scott); the "jump-ball" offense. Low efficiency but hoping to catch a few big breaks. Time for the defensive backs to play tough, man-to-man coverage, to allow blitzes to disrupt an average unit.

Too bad about Ole Miss, but that shows you that they are a team not used to the pressure and not ready to rise up to the level needed to win an SEC division. Auburn is still in front, but Georgia should stomp them pretty good this week, and then Alabama and LSU have a good chance of beating them. LSU may wind up in Atlanta after all.

Prognosti-Visor sees: Florida 31 S. Carolina 17

**Visor Flings, Week 12:**
**UF 54, South Carolina 17**

Well, so much for "Black-Out Florida" night for USC. What a joke! These guys have been to how many bowl games in over 100 years of football... less than 10? And the Gators spotted them with a 21-3 lead last year and they got blown off the field 41-21? I have to laugh I loved the player's comments after the game. Even they knew the hype was stupid. Another sea of empty seats in the third quarter...does that mean the Gators parted the "Black" Sea?

Please, put the Lou Holtz motivation fear to rest! It's not going to happen up there. So we continue to enjoy beating the crap out of the Lamecocks (or is it the Blackened Chickens?)

Unfortunately, after more choking by the Puppies and F$U, Florida still hasn't beaten any team with fewer than three losses except Marshall. We are now #5 in the BCS, but still need tons of help. Have to hope Auburn wins out to make the SEC championship more valuable than just exacting some revenge.

There's not really much to add to what has been said about the USC game. Near flawless execution by the offense, solid if not spectacular defense, and a nice game plan by the coaches. Rex continues to improve his decision-making, but the real test remains against a quality opponent in a close game to truly set him apart. He gets his chance against F$U and the Vols to show his true mettle.

Actually, the USC offense did give the Gators something very important to work on. Chris Rix runs a lot of designed draws/sweeps out of the shotgun, and that hurt the defense (actually more than the running backs). Expect to see a lot of that to try to keep the Gators from eating him up in obvious passing downs. Plus, I think the F$U O-Line and Greg Jones will provide a stiffer challenge than USC. The loss of Brett Williams at tackle could be crucial, however. This may necessitate their blocking schemes be altered to help double-team Alex Brown, freeing up others to make plays. If he can wreak havoc, F$U is in deep trouble.

What will the Head Ball Coach devise for this game? Actually, I think he just needs to re-enforce what the QB and receivers are doing right now. F$U's secondary is their weakest in years, and even when they were strong Florida still managed to pass for 300+ yards most times. Just keep pounding away with Graham and Carthon, and let the Gator O-Line really lean on and beat up the F$U D-Line, another soft spot this season with little depth. Patience should once again be rewarded. Plus, continue to spread out the passes to the running backs and tight ends. Doesn't have to be often, just enough to confuse their defense even more.

Normally, I would expect Mickey Andrews to really try to rattle Grossman with blitzes and, of course, the "echo of the whistle" philosophy. This time, though, he and Coach Bowden, the elder, may decide to drag the Gators into an ugly game, playing zones and running the ball often, to try and make Spurrier become impatient and the Gators nervous if the game is close in the second half. I'm really interested in what they will attempt this year as opposed to the recent past, because their performance has, frankly, been lacking.

Of course, the fact that this is a rivalry game and that the pressure is off F$U just might play in their favor in this kind of game, especially with their youth and lack of experience. I believe two scenarios could play out in this one. Either it's an ugly, lower-scoring-than-expected affair, or the Gators blow them off the field with an early rush followed by a 4th quarter payback fest. I think Florida wins either one this year, especially at the Swamp.

Personally, I know the Gator Nation wants to pound the Semi-holes mercilessly, but a solid win with no major injuries is fine by me.

Eanie-meanie, Chili-beanie: Florida 38 F$U 21

**Visor Flings, Week 13:**
**UF 37, F$U 13**

There was much to enjoy against the Criminoles (time to break out the old name after the criminal intent of Darnell Dockett vs. Earnest Graham's knee – more on that later). It was a weird atmosphere...the usual deafening noise until the 14-0 lead, then the inevitability that the Head Ball Coach could name the final score.

Seems like many people are trying to talk up Rix's improvement, but the Half-Ass-U coaching staff has reined in his running too much. His premature slides cost them at least two first downs. Plus, his passing was fair at best – too bad the stats don't show four interceptions instead of just one. Most completions were the flat pass to the tailback and quick slants. Granted, he had some drops, but I'm not terribly impressed.

I was disappointed in the lack of a sustained pass rush by the Gators, but part of that was the scheme, which once again proved effective. Rix definitely gave the Gators many opportunities for turnovers, which was part of the plan. Injured or not, Jones and Maddox had little room to maneuver. Yes, their young line can pass block (although Florida didn't blitz much), but not having a running game will doom anyone (remember Auburn?)

All kidding aside, the lack of catching ability evidenced by the defensive back this year is a little disturbing. One suggestion – quit leaping while trying to catch the football, and use your hands and stay more balanced. No sense in giving a team numerous chances to continue a drive.

As for the newest Criminole – Dockett. Look, no one may ever really know what happened, but guys that have played the game that saw the replay strongly suspect something's up. There was some activity in the pile late. So now, unfortunately, two things result. One, a player is hurt, perhaps damaging Florida's chances vs. the Vols. Two, the specter of dirty play and bad blood flares up again. It's hard for a fan like me to not wish some retribution on F$U; imagine how hard it will be for the players in next year's game. Here's hoping what goes around comes around for Dockett and Mickey (thug) Andrews;

enough is enough. Plus, the media boys are already starting the Spurrier-bashing about whining. Look – he is, and always will be, a Gator player and head coach, and he will always say what he feels. Too bad people aren't smart enough to understand that. He's no fool – and isn't afraid to remind others of that fact.

Congratulations are in order for the entire team and coaching staff. Everyone has really improved their quality of play, and the team put aside perhaps the most perplexing, unfathomable loss in the Spurrier Era. Not to be overdramatic here, but that the Auburn game truly was a tragic loss, especially if it cost the Gators a shot at the Rose Bowl. Okay, I am being overdramatic, but if we didn't care about this stuff, I guess there wouldn't be message boards or opinion columns in the press, huh?

Hope everyone has a safe and happy Thanksgiving, especially in these difficult times. I get the feeling Spurrier and the boys will be ready to greet the Volunteers in two weeks in a most Swampy way!

I'll say… Florida 37 F$U 13 (HA! -- just checking to see if you're paying attention)

**Visor Flings, Week 14:**
**Off Week**

What an unbelievable turn of events in other games this week. I'm not surprised by Colorado defeating Nebraska, but I am by the manner in which it happened. However, what is even more stunning is watching Oklahoma choke away it's chances, especially to a 3-7 Oklahoma St. team – at home! It's strange...for years the general consensus was that SEC teams would knock each other off, leaving pretenders from the Big East, Pac-10, and Big 10+1 a shot at the BCS title game. Now, it seems the Gators are benefiting from a down year by the conference as a whole, while the PAC-10 and Big-12 teams derail each others' title hopes.

It certainly is a second chance unforeseen. Now, can Florida take advantage of it's good fortune?

First up are the Vols. This is actually Phat Phil's best team since his '96 and '97 teams (I'm not counting the '98 B.S. crew). Tennessee has developed a passing offense that they can rely on the road in crunch time. Of course, it's not in Florida's class, but their running game is always solid, unlike Florida's. Once again, it's the Vol defense that will make or break their chances in this game. It's obvious what caused the '98 debacle at Knoxville: turnovers. This year's Tennessee defense hasn't shown the ability that was expected, and it's pass defense still looks shaky, despite experienced players. At this point, it's all about confidence for them. Can they make big plays, get the lead, and pressure the Gators to make plays? The longer they hang around, the more dangerous they become.

Which leads me to...

The unit that will win or lose this game for Florida is the O-Line. Can they establish a semblance of a ground game? Can they convert short-yardage situations? Will they give Rex enough time to find his receivers consistently? I think the Vols will play Phat Phil's game...mount long drives, generate turnovers, play with the lead, shorten the game. Travis Stephens has proven he's for real, and the Gators are in real trouble if the Vols can apply the hammer with him in the second half. I am confident, however, that the Head Ball Coach is on a roll as far as devising effective game plans right now. I get the feeling a lot of names may play a part in the passing game that have been neglected recently – Troupe, Walker, Carthon, Gillespie. Anything that gives the Tennessee defense more to think about will really foul up their plans. They have historically struggled against the Gator pass offense, and I have to think 300+ yards and 2-3 TDs are in the offing, especially in the Swamp.

I am going to give the defense the benefit of the doubt at this point, and expect a good showing. They should continue to mix up the coverage and schemes, using that and the crowd noise to confuse Clausen and his receivers. They have used the quick slant and the fade extensively this year, which actually should help them in this game. Also, the tight end has played a large role on third down for them the second half of the season. Hopefully the defensive staff has used the off-week wisely, taking in all the film available. The key will be whether the pass rush will generate enough pressure to throw off the timing. If Hoke has to start blitzing regularly, then the Gators are in trouble.

I expect Tennessee to hit some big plays, both running and passing. Unfortunately, it appears that most of Florida's big plays will be relegated to the passing game only. I also expect that because of the stakes involved, it may turn into a tight affair affecting players on both sides. I'm looking for each team to try for the big play early, to set the tone and dictate the flow of the game. I think the Vols will open up their offense more in the first half, to try and get the Gators to play from behind and to then grind out yards in the second half if still in front. But Florida can respond with scores as well as anyone. That's why I give the edge to the home team, especially THIS home team.

Gotta love 'em: Florida 31 Tennessee 24

**Visor Flings, Week 15:**
**Tennessee 34, UF 32**

Well, as Judge Smails said in *Caddyshack*, "You'll get nothing and like it, Spalding!"

That's right Gator fans, nothing. Nada. Zero. What a waste, throwing away the entire season – twice.

What else can be said that everyone isn't already thinking? The defense completely collapsed...poor tackling, bad angles, physically dominated, passive scheme...just soft overall. This unit really let the entire team down, and will be weaker and thinner, depth-wise, next year. So, once again, Jon Hoke is on the hot seat. What is he afraid of, especially at home? That Tennessee will score 34 points? Unbelievable. It may not be fair, but it's the reality of college football. It's obvious that the past two or three lackluster years of recruiting defensive linemen came home to roost as well (not to mention Roy Williams, Santonio Thomas, etc.).

The one bright spot was the heroic play of Rex Grossman. Faced with the fact that the Tennessee defense knew the running game was no threat, he was the sole target of the Vol front seven. And he paid a physical price for it. Despite that, he made many clutch throws into tight spots under duress, and got up time after time to do it again. And, he led the team to a must-have TD. To those who say, "Well, he got away with some bad throws," I say, "Shut Up!" Look at the situation he was facing – the guy was terrific! Poised, tough, a real leader. The receivers were in a fight as well, and made some great catches, especially in traffic. As for the O-line, sure they would probably say to you that they could have performed better. Once again, however, with no hammer at running back, they weren't surprising Tennessee by having to pass-block continuously, often against blitzes.

I've heard criticism about the tight ends missing in the passing game. Well, if you want your QB to survive, you'd better leave them in to help pass block. The poor running game can be blamed for that. Please tell me that Ran Carthon is really that bad. And that Willie Green can't run tough and break some tackles in limited carries. Lawson Holland needs to come clean or get replaced. These guys have been there long enough to contribute something. Shameful.

There were some critical mental errors. False starts by Moody and Walker that turned 3rd-and-1 and 4th-and-1 into changes of possession. The late hit on Clausen to help make it 14-0. Plus, I have to question Coach on one item – why not call your last time-out to set up the two-point conversion? With 1:10 left, you know you'll have to onside-kick if you don't convert the 2-pointer, and making that is a lot easier than recovering an on-side kick. Puzzling. Plus, even the good ones like Jabar had some miscues...his drop of a catchable pass that could have tied the game at 14, and his overthrow of Carlos Perez on the replay of the 1994 SEC championship-game Doering-to-Aubrey Hill pass – Perez was all alone.

So, the cold reality is that when it came down to the 4th quarter, this team failed. Unfortunately, the pattern was already established – sluggish running game, unable to slow down a power-running team, the offense becoming one-dimensional. Will anything be done about it?

Ah, yes, the Head Ball Coach is in an uncomfortable position. Once again, his lead O-Line coach (Stephens) and Defensive Coordinator (Hoke) are hearing severe criticism. Will this game be looked back upon in five or ten years as the beginning of the decline of the Gators' SEC and national run? Or will Spurrier work even harder, working the recruiting trail harder than ever, perhaps even curtailing the loyalty he has shown to his assistants? An overreaction? Maybe. But five years of losing big games may necessitate making some hard, controversial decisions. Hoke may have to be demoted or let go. Don't laugh – Widenhofer has worked wonders occasionally with little talent at Vanderbilt, and while he sucked as a head coach at Notre Dame, Bob Davie is recognized as a very good defensive coordinator when he has some real material. I'm starting the "hire Bob Davie or Woody Widenhofer as DC" campaign right now.

Speaking of which...This coaching staff needs to recruit like never before the next 2-3 years. The Gators need real studs on the D-Line and at linebacker. No excuses. We may have some "nice" players, but how about some real stars? This is the chance for Ricky Hunley and Jerry Odom to make their respective marks. Plus, Buddy Teevins/Lawson Holland(?) need two great backs and Dwayne Dixon needs a few more quality receivers. After 2002, you'll have Carlos Perez (Sr.), Kelvin Kight (Sr.), and...and...

Get ready to deal with some shoot-outs the next few years in the big games. The defense will have trouble against Miami, F$U, and Tennessee, plus some other SEC games. Historically, that means at least one or two losses when trying to outscore quality teams. Even three losses are possible next year. We can't expect young players to come in at defensive line and linebacker and hold up their end. Plus, the Gators will need real luck with injuries as well. This past year was the healthiest in a long while. A rash of injuries could doom the team to an F$U-like drop-off.

Don't count on Tennessee losing to LSU. Yes, they had to play at a very high level to beat Florida, but LSU probably has nothing left in the tank after having to get up twice for Arkansas and Auburn. The Vols will win comfortably. Their confidence level will be at an all-time high.

Hopefully the seniors can go out with a big win, and should be thankful if they get a chance to do it in a BCS game, especially if it's in-state in the Orange Bowl. It may not mean much, but a win certainly would start the off-season and recruiting on a positive note.

Hey, look on the bright side...only nine months until we get a shot at Tennessee again! Boy, what a lousy off-season this will be. Only a huge recruiting year will cheer me up.

**Visor Flings, Weeks 16-18:**
**Orange Bowl Preview**

Florida is fortunate to get an invite to a BCS game, especially in-state. This should allow a partisan crowd to attend and try to get on with football life after the Tennessee game. Maryland will have around 20,000 fans there. This is their first major bowl in over 20 years, and they are anxious to come down to Miami and show what they've got.

The Terrapins responded better than anyone expected in Ralph Friedgen's first season. The offense was balanced, averaging 222 yards per game rushing and 219 yards per game passing, while scoring an average of 35.5 points per game. Quarterback Shaun Hill (Sr.) completed 59.9% of his passes, with 13 TDs. This team played F$U evenly for more than three quarters in Tallahassee before falling, so they are for real. After the terrible defensive performance turned in by the Gators against the Vols, nothing should be taken for granted.

Maryland's defense is led by Butkus Award finalist E.J. Henderson (Jr.). He was recognized for playing both the run and pass effectively and received much acclaim, especially playing on a team that before this season was off the national radar. The unit as a whole allowed an average of 19.1 points per game. However, they were pushed around occasionally, especially in giving up 52 pts. to F$U. They have not seen anything like the

Florida offense, and could be in real trouble, especially matching up in the secondary against Gaffney, Caldwell, and Jacobs.

I won't get into much detail about the Florida offense and defense. At this point, most fans know what the team and players have done by now. What's more important will be how the team handles the rumors about early departures, transfers, possible significant coaching changes, etc. (even I don't know what's going on the Head Ball Coach's head right now. Combine this with a one-month layoff, and you can see how highly-ranked teams will sometimes lay a big egg in their bowl game.

Spurrier will have his hands full trying to keep the players' focus on the game. Judging by the media stories so far, everything but the game and the opponent are getting attention.

Aside from the confidence they have in winning the ACC, the Maryland players will say they still have little respect, judging by the fact they are 16-point underdogs. Well, that may jack them up emotionally before kickoff, but that's what you get when you haven't done anything of national significance in 25 years. Look for Fat Friedgen (the guy makes Phat Phil look like Ichabod Crane) to throw everything at the Gators early, to try and get an early lead and rattle them. After that, the superior team should start taking command.

It should be an entertaining game. I think Coach will have the boys ready to go, and make some turtle soup out of the Terps.

Visor predicts: Florida 38 Maryland 21

**Visor Flings, Week 19:**
**UF 56, Maryland 23**
**…And the End of an Era**

The Gators defeated the Terps handily on January 2nd in Miami, but what really shook the whole college football world was the following statement issued by the Head Ball Coach only two days later:

"I'm announcing my retirement today, Jan. 4, 2002, as head football coach at the University of Florida. I simply believe that 12 years as head coach at a major university in the SEC is long enough.

I thank all the players, assistant coaches, support staff people and the greatest football fans in the world for the success we have shared the last 12 years.

I also personally thank all the Gators that went to the Orange Bowl to support our team last Wednesday night in my final game.

I believe Jeremy Foley, who has a reputation of hiring outstanding coaches, will bring a coach to Florida that will do just as well or better in the years to come. I believe I'm certainly not the only coach to be able to win consistently at Florida.

Our football program is in excellent shape and the next coach will inherit a very talented team, just like I did from Galen Hall's program in 1990.

I've had a wonderful working relationship with all my bosses over the past 12 years. I thank Bob Bryan for hiring me, and I thank Bill Arnsparger, Jeremy Foley, President John Lombardi and President Chuck Young for allowing me to run the football program.

I'm not burned out, stressed out or mentally fatigued from coaching. I just feel my career as a college head coach after 15 years is complete and if the opportunity and challenge of coaching a NFL team happens it is something I would like to pursue.

I believe that the University of Florida is the best place for a high school football player to get an education and play football in the best stadium, The Swamp, before the best football fans in the world.

Again, I thank the Gator Nation for the overwhelming support of our teams for 12 years. The seven SEC championships and the 1996 national championship are memories of a lifetime that we will all share together.

I'm a Gator and will be for the rest of my life."

Well, the news was not a complete surprise, but stunning nonetheless. I am as close to Coach (literally) as anybody, and even I wasn't certain what would happen. Steven Orr Spurrier is leaving Gainesville once again, and the First Golden Age of Florida football possibly leaves with him.

All the superlatives apply to his accomplishments and his placing of Florida at the top level of college football. No need here to recount his style and methods, which were always controversial and disliked by many, mostly outside the Gator family. His coaching career is marked by tremendous success, unprecedented fan and booster following, and respect from the rest of college football (not to mention a healthy dislike from many other teams, coaches, and media boys).

No one will ever really know his reasons for leaving, unless you take the man completely at his word. However, instead of trying to understand the decision, it is better to thank him for all he's done and to wish him well.

It will be quite difficult this fall to try and turn the page and move on, not being with the Head Ball Coach stalking the sidelines, pouring his heart and emotion into each game. It would serve every fan and player, though, to try and do just that, and hopefully enjoy some of the same successes in the future. All Gators, while thankful for the good times Spurrier brought us, need to move forward and encourage the future coaches and players, and hopefully see new faces reach those same lofty goals.

If the NFL is his next employer, all the best to him. It's a completely different world surrounding the pro game, including agents, the salary cap, and runaway egos. Don't forget though, that there is still a game that's played on the field, and Coach Spurrier has few peers as to preparing a game plan. Here's hoping he benefits from a strong organization, able assistants, has some talent to work with, and that he enjoys success at least for a while; the NFL environment really doesn't allow for continued winning over a long stretch anymore.

As for me, I really don't know what will become of the Visor. Will I be shelved? Thrown out with the trash? It's too early for me to tell right now, so I'll just say, So long,

Coach Spurrier, and all the best! I hope to see you someday back in Gainesville, at least so everyone can say hello and thank you once again in the future for all you've done for the Florida Gators. Thanks for all the excitement, all the wins, all the championships, and for establishing the foundation for continued success in the future. And a special thanks for the statement that, “They may call us a lot of things, but they can't call us losers anymore!” I've really enjoyed the looks on the faces of the other teams fans, knowing they've been beaten by the best.

One more sad note after the 2001-2002 season: I never met Jim Finch. Didn't even know his name until recently, when news of his death made the sports page.

But I knew his voice, as did all Gators since 1966.

Here's the only clue you need: “Heeeeeeeeeeeeeere come the Gators!”

I first heard that voice in 1973, when Nat Moore was the star tailback, before he gained fame as a wide receiver for the Miami Dolphins and now as the Sunshine Network color man for Gator football game replays.

I don't have any real input as to who his replacement will be or if his distinctive introduction will be copied or replayed by tape (my hope). My real wish is that whoever replaces him as P.A. announcer at the Swamp will at least emulate his understated style of showing no favoritism and not becoming overly emotional, like the droning, grating guys at F$U or Tennessee. Gator fans don't need any artificial stimulus to get excited by the action on the field.

"Heeeeeeeeeeeeeere come the Gators!"

There's no better, more exciting introduction in college football.

# 2002
# Zooking When They Should Have Zagged

I don't believe any Gators fan with any sense really blames Ron Zook for what happened during the Ron Zook years. After all, since he left us, he has single-handedly resuscitated the Illinois football program, and was named the Big Ten Coach of the Year in 2007. And after all, he was 23-14 at Florida.

But after the glory of the Spurrier Era, second or third place was no longer good enough for the Gator constituency. From the very beginning, the karma was all wrong for Zook in Gainesville. The mythology says that the very day he took over the program, the infamous fireronzook.com website went up on the internet. He became the victim of the same voracious hunger for championships which grips big-time sports, especially in an environment such as UF, where that hunger was sharpened by going 51 years without winning the Southeastern Conference. Their first national championship, the culmination of Spurrier's genius, didn't come until 1996 – ninety years after varsity football arrived at UF. Just ask Doug Dickey or Charley Pell (well, maybe not Pell – he's deceased): the Gator Nation can be brutal on a coach who doesn't meet the expectation, with no more sentimental attachment than one might have to a toilet seat.

Still, like many others who felt closely attached to the old Head Ball Coach (and no one was more closely attached than the Visor), I tried to reserve judgment. Oh, yes, the Visor is still on the sidelines for all the Florida games… I'm just riding on a different scalp these days. Happily, an old crony of Spurrier's, someone who remains in the inner circle, found me "hanging around" after the office was cleaned out, and he adopted me. Seems SOS has opted for Washington Redskins colors. I am pledged not to reveal my rescuer's name, but believe me when I say that he is close to the action. And that's where I'll be, too, for the foreseeable future.

That's my story, and I'm sticking to it.

**Visor Flings, Week 1:**
**Preview and Predictions**

A new season and a new era begin in Gainesville this fall. Expectations and opinions vary wildly, especially because of the new leadership and new schemes. There is quite a bit to discuss.

OFFENSE

The former offensive coordinator and quarterback coach is now in the NFL, so Ed Zaunbrecher steps in, bringing his (hopefully) productive and high-scoring scheme with him from Marshall. Leaders this fall should include quarterback Rex Grossman, running back Earnest Graham, wide receiver Taylor Jacobs, and offensive linemen Matt Starks and Shannon Snell.

The quarterback situation is clearly defined – Rex Grossman is one of the best in the country and will be counted upon heavily to grasp the new offense and remain productive. His leadership and toughness were proven last season, and should prove critical when the Gators encounter some rough stretches throughout the season. Ingle Martin showed flashes of promise in the spring, especially when exhibiting athleticism outside the pocket and scrambling. Obviously, losing Grossman for any extended length of time would be costly, but Martin showed enough that he could surprise in short intervals, as needed. Freshmen Gavin Dickey and Patrick Dosh show potential, but hopefully both will be red shirted and get their chance to shine in 2003.

At running back, Earnest Graham is expected to carry the biggest load, and should have a very nice season, barring the ever-present chance of injury. The only real worry with him is whether he has cured his occasional fumble problems; his toughness and ability to get extra yards after contact are proven. Ran Carthon proved a pleasant surprise in the spring, exhibiting a nice burst to go with good pass-catching ability. For his sake, the new staff and scheme seem to have revived his career. Willie Green will hopefully get the chance to spell these two occasionally and provide some big-play capability as a nice change-of-pace. The fullback position in the new offense is almost non-existent. Ray Snell will get some chances, but mainly as a blocker in short-yardage and goal-line situations. Freshmen DeShawn Wynn, Jimtavis Walker, and Ciatrick Fason are all quite impressive, and one of them could see action this fall. Fason may the quickest and most gifted athlete – the possibility remains he could be moved to cornerback, unless of course he proves to be special at tailback.

The wide receiver situation is somewhat unsettled right now. Taylor Jacobs is the unquestioned leader of this group, coming off his MVP performance in the Orange Bowl. However, he is now the number-one option, and it remains to be seen if he can produce in this role and take pressure off the others. The leading candidates for spots two and three right now are Carlos Perez and Kelvin Kight, who also happen to be the most experienced of the others. There is no questioning their ability at this point; the question is productivity and consistency in a starting role. The loss of Reggie Vickers to an ACL injury (in an off-season workout, no less) could prove troublesome. He began to show off the athleticism and open-field running that could have set him apart from everyone else, but now someone from among the group of Dallas Baker, Matt Jackson, OJ Small, or even incoming freshman Kenneth Tookes will need to step into the rotation. Baker, a 2001 signee (if ruled eligible), shows the most promise.

The offensive line is talented, and huge, but has little experienced depth. Health is the main concern for this group as the season progresses. The starting unit going into the fall is (from left to right) Max Starks, Shannon Snell, Mike Degory, Jonothan Colon, and Mo Mitchell. This group has excellent size and athletic ability, but Degory is a red-shirt freshman, and both Colon and Mitchell saw only limited playing time last year. That being said, Degory could be the best center at Florida since Jeff Mitchell, finally settling a position that, quite frankly, has struggled since 1996. The positioning of Colon and Mitchell is curious as well. Colon seems to have the height and long arms necessary for better pass protection off the edge, while Mitchell exhibits better drive blocking for the running game. If Mitchell struggles early, the coaches need to seriously consider a switch, and quickly. David Jorgensen will provide senior leadership at center and guard. Ronald Dowdy, Lance Butler, and Bobby Williams are inexperienced, have much to learn, and have to get up to speed quickly. At this time, true freshman Randy Hand has shown enough to the coaches in fall drills to be seriously considered in the rotation. Injuries among this group could spell disaster for the entire offense.

Unlike most of the past 12 years, the tight end position is actually a central part of the new passing scheme, and the Gators are blessed with two fine players. Aaron Walker is penciled in as the starter, and has shown excellent catching ability; consistency and improved blocking are his goals. Ben Troupe is the better blocker, but also shows toughness over the middle. Both have the size and experience to thrive in the new offense, and really help ease the pressure on the QB and receivers.

DEFENSE

Once again, a new coordinator and scheme are in place, as with the offense. However, this unit, despite the loss of experienced starters, may be a pleasant surprise this fall. It certainly won't reflect the vanilla, passive, and too-conservative philosophy of Jon Joke, who thankfully is far, far away from the Swamp. He arguably is the worst hire of the Spurrier era, and will always receive most of the blame for the disappointment of 2001 in the Visor’s opinion. John Thompson comes from Arkansas with a reputation for aggressive and unpredictable defense – a breath of fresh air and a welcome change.

The defensive line has received much attention in the off-season from both fans and the media. But as the depth chart has clarified, this unit should be solid, if unspectacular, in 2002. Ian Scott is the star of this group at tackle, with help from Tron LaFavor, Sylvester McGrew, and hopefully Kenny Parker in the interior. The ends should provide a good pass rush and make some big plays. Big expectations await Bobby McCray, Darrell Lee, Arpedge Rolle, and Clint Mitchell. Once again, a solid group, but thin depth-wise. An injury to Scott could cripple this unit. There is a lot of pressure on this group to produce, especially to help protect the inside linebackers.

The linebacking corps is the weak link this fall. True, seniors Bam Hardmon and Mike Nattiel are solid players and leaders on the outside. However, the loss of Andra Davis and Travis Carroll in the middle will be felt. Todd McCullough and Matt Farrior step in to the breach, with Reid Fleming backing them up. Unfortunately, an unproven and thin group. Travis Harris will be counted on to provide depth both inside and out. Because of inexperience and injury, he remains a question mark as well. Somehow this unit will have to elevate its play and also stay healthy for the entire defense to be productive and bail out the offense when it struggles.

The strength of the defense is in the secondary, despite the early departure of Lito Sheppard. Robert Cromartie returns from a lost 2001 campaign due to injury to re-gain his starting role at cornerback, while Keiwan Ratliff takes over Sheppard's spot. Cromartie should be solid, while Ratliff may provide the big plays from this group, being the fastest of the group. Marquise Westbrook and Tre Orr are solid back-ups, while Deshawn Carter and Cory Bailey could show signs of being future starters. The safeties are among the best in the country. Todd Johnson is an all-SEC choice at free safety, while Guss Scott takes over from Marquand Manuel at strong safety. Both are smart, and sure tacklers. They are backed up by Daryl Dixon, Lester Norwood, and Larry Kendrick, another solid group. Hopefully the coverage and run support provided by this unit will assist the front seven, and I expect some big plays on interception returns as well.

## SPECIAL TEAMS

This group will probably most reflect the new leadership of Coach Zook this fall. His prior experience and success in coaching this group at both Florida and in the NFL should prove invaluable. A new field goal kicker is the largest hole to fill, with the departure of dependable Jeff Chandler. Matt Leach appears to have the inside track right now, with Brendt Talcott pushing him. Matt Piotrowicz does a good job of pinning down opponents on kickoffs. Sean Morton may take over for Leach at punter. He performed very well in the Spring game, putting 3 kicks inside the 20; however, walk-on Jason Hunter may have passed Morton in fall drills. Ratliff and Vernell Brown could be explosive on returns, showing the quickness and speed necessary to improve field position. The attitude of this unit should provide excitement not seen in many years at the Swamp.

## OUTLOOK FOR 2002

The Gators play seven bowl teams from 2001. The big games at home are Miami, LSU, Auburn, and South Carolina. Huge road tests are Tennessee and F$U, with Georgia at Jacksonville. Ole Miss is also capable of surprising the Gators in Oxford. The toughest and most challenging schedule in recent memory faces Ron Zook, an almost entirely new staff, and new schemes on offense and defense.

The Gators are fortunate that the game against Miami is early and at the Swamp; the emotion and home field could swing the day in their favor. Tennessee, despite a re-built defensive line and questions at running back, could prove too difficult on Rocky Top. Losses in both those games could damage the team's confidence heading into Oxford, but I doubt Coach Zook's intensity will allow that. There will be no lack of motivation facing LSU (the defending SEC Champion – that's still hard to fathom) or seeking revenge against Auburn at home. The media has fallen in love with Georgia's Puppies, but most shrewd observers remain skeptical of that squad until the season progresses, especially with the psychological edge the Gators enjoy. South Carolina believes it can win the East, but with questions at QB and a weak offense overall, I seriously doubt they will win at Gainesville. Then the Gators travel to Tallahassee to try and win there for the first time since 1986 (still difficult to believe).

There are so many potential mine fields that, despite the intensity and aggressiveness of the new coaching staff, this team can lose two to four games. Hopefully Coach Zook won't burn the team out emotionally in September, and they will show consistency and fire throughout the balance of the schedule. I do believe that John Thompson won't allow the defense to fall on it's face and allow offenses to dictate the action, and perhaps this group can steal a big win and prevent an upset loss. Ed Zaunbrecher's offense looks a lot like F$U's old "fast-break" – effective, yes, but it struggled scoring touchdowns in the red zone against quality opponents, something the old Head Ball Coach's teams excelled at.

One fact that can't be overlooked is we will miss the confidence and play-calling of Steve Spurrier, neither of which may ever be totally replaced.

The prediction:
For the opener: Florida 41, UAB 14
Regular Season 9-3 (6-2 SEC); losses at Tennessee, at F$U, and either Ole Miss/Georgia
No SEC Championship Game
Citrus or Outback Bowl berth

The Visor predicts an exciting, unpredictable ride of a season. The Gators have more questions going into 2002 since a decade ago, when they finished 9-4 after a 1-2 start. We will see very soon how those questions are answered by both the players and coaches.

**Visor Flings, Week 1:**
**UF 51, University of Alabama-Birmingham 3**

Overall, an excellent performance for an opener, especially given the changes in coaching, schemes, and personnel from last season.

On offense, Rex certainly looked sharp, displaying good accuracy and calling audibles when necessary. The only negative with his performance was his continued penchant for overthrowing the seam route to the tight end, which he was guilty of last year, as well. Seems as if he drops sidearm a little, making the pass float high. Hope that doesn't show up this week. The running backs looked very good, both running and blocking. The blitz pick-ups were solid as well. The power-I formation in short-yardage and goal-line situations certainly gives the 'Canes something to work on in practice. Graham will get 1000+ yards this season if he stays healthy, and the back-ups look good. I'm still searching for a dependable second and third option in the wide receiver group; perhaps someone will break out this week. The only group that still appears shaky is the O-Line. Mo Mitchell needs to get his mind right; he whiffed on edge rushes, which will get Rex killed. I hope Colon starts at RT, with Jorgensen at RG – this seems to be the most effective unit right now. Starks and Snell on the left side looked very good, and I'm very encouraged my the play of Degory at center. I've said it many times: we've struggled at this position since Jeff Mitchell's graduation in '96 – solid play from Degory will make this line (and the entire offense) much more effective.

The defense played well for an opener, but even given the weakness of UAB's offense, still exhibits some problems.

The pass pressure was okay, but I still see little consistent push from anyone other than Ian Scott or Bobby McCray. I'm not concerned about the QB scrambling yards; Dorsey will not hurt Florida that way. However, there still were some gaping holes opened, especially when running right at MoJo. The play of the inside linebackers wasn't noteworthy, either. Still some missed tackles, and no real field presence exhibited by Farrior, McCullough, or Fleming. Unfortunately, this group will be exploited by Miami this week, both vs. the run and pass. The secondary did not need to show great coverage against UAB, but impressed me with their closing speed and hitting ability, especially Gus Scott and Johnson breaking up some passes. This group needs to play their A game this Saturday to help out the front seven.

Special teams were only okay. Petro's kickoffs were terrific, as always, but the punting game has the Gator Nation worried. Any time there is a freshman punter, bad things occasionally happen; it's when they do that can affect a season. Hopefully Coach Zook and Coach Odom can get Hunter's confidence back up. Matt Leach looked good on his 44-yard field goal, but let's see his performance under pressure. Here's hoping that Jeff Chandler isn't missed too much this year.

Upcoming Miami is certainly a confident team, despite the loss of a stellar class last season. There is talent upon talent there thanks to Butch Davis, but experience still counts, especially on the road against a quality opponent. Inexperience could affect the pass-blocking vs. the blitz, especially the pick-ups by the young running backs and the "hot" reads by the wide receivers. Coach Thompson can give the Gators an advantage here if he can confuse the blockers somewhat, because Dorsey reads defenses very well. Andre Johnson is the go-to guy at wide receiver, and his size (6'3", 225 lb.) gives him an advantage over every Gator cornerback. Also, the 'Canes tight ends are always very evident in the passing game, and historically the Gators have struggled in this matchup. Kellen Winslow Jr. is not at Jeremy Shockey's level, but the difference is not great. The Miami running attack will win the game if it shows it can control the clock and give Dorsey short-yardage situations. Clinton Portis and Najeh Davenport are missed, even with the ability of Jason Geathers. Injuries to Frank Gore, Jarrett Payton, and Kyle Cobia have hurt continuity as well. Unfortunately, Miami has one of the best O-Line coaches in America in Art Kehoe, and I don't expect much fall-off from this group.

The Hurricane defense has a terrific front seven; athletic, strong, and fast. This may be Florida's toughest match up the entire season for the O-Line, and the pressure is squarely on this unit and Coach Wickline to play at a level it has not achieved yet. The announced starters include Jorgensen at right guard and Colon at right tackle; this appears to be the best unit, with the depth being very thin. I believe there will be some two-tight-end alignments to help with protection, the running game, and ball-control passes, but the only real way to pressure the young and inexperienced UM secondary is to send four receivers out and see what happens – probably some big plays, and some sacks as well. A worthwhile trade-off (hopefully).

The key defensive positions for the Gators will be defensive end and inside linebacker. No edge pressure against the pass and poor run stopping/tackling will greatly diminish Florida's chances of winning. On offense, the O-Line, second and third options at wide receiver, and some catches by the tight ends are the best way to keep momentum during the game. I know the Gators have the QB to play catch-up, but I really feel playing from behind with this group is conducive to losing, even at home. An even score or lead in the second half will keep the Swamp in a frenzy, an experience like nothing any of the 'Canes (other than Brock Berlin - Ha!) has ever experienced.

Visor's prediction: Florida 28 Miami 24

**Visor Flings, Week 2:**
**Miami 41, UF 16**

The Miami game was certainly an eye-opener. I believe I put too much faith in the team picking up the new schemes so rapidly, and did not give the Hurricanes enough credit for their talent level overcoming the Swamp factor. It's good that the players can go out and play this week instead of reliving the mistakes for two whole weeks leading up to another huge game, the SEC opener at Tennessee.

At the expense of rehashing the all-too-obvious mistakes against the 'Canes, I'll list some random thoughts:

1) The defensive line is average, at best, and somehow the coaches and players will have to come up with a strategy to improve the performance as the season progresses. The tackles never provided much of a push into the backfield, and did not consistently neutralize the Miami O-Line. Give credit the to the talent of the 'Canes and to Art Kehoe, perhaps the best O-Line coach in the college game.

2) Unfortunately, the linebackers are what they are, which is below average right now. This is what the coaches have to work with, so somehow they need to instill some confidence in this group and/or make personnel changes. If personnel changes are made, make them this week, not the week of Tennessee, when mistakes will once again be magnified. James Bates was pretty critical after the game, and rightly so.

3) The offensive line played about as well as I could have expected. The running game was as good as I had hoped for – around 160 yards against Miami's front seven is a fine effort.

However, the lack of quickness and experience, especially on the right side, was painfully obvious (and painful to Rex, as well) in the passing game. This just exacerbated the other major problems.
4) The poor performance of the receiving corps was disturbing. Even given the talent level of the 'Cane linebackers and defensive backs, the lack of separation and willingness to fight to get off the ball and run routes was disappointing. This isn't the Spurrier system now, so these boys had better get their butts in gear. Looks Like Dallas Baker may get into the mix very quickly, and a true freshman may be asked to step into the breach. I don't want to burn a red-shirt like that, but there may not be an alternative unless the game performance improves dramatically.
5) The special teams did generate a huge punt block, but that was offset by another kind of block (mental) incurred by Hunter the punter – talk about a brain cramp. Matt Leach may only have the next two games to establish himself, or else the bench will be his place. Harsh, but true. The return game still is below expectation, while the coverage has been pretty good. Time for this group to play with more fire, or else shuffle the players out as necessary.
6) Very disappointing play-calling by Zaunbrecher after the blocked punt, and especially on first-and-goal at the 6 late in the 3rd quarter. Yes, the first play after the blocked punt was a delay-of-game penalty, but I can't believe something wasn't ready to implement inside the red zone to take advantage of a golden opportunity. Also, Earnest Graham mysteriously disappeared for that entire sequence. What a waste! What pissed me off even more, however, was the goal-line sequence. Hard to believe, but even James Jones was pointedly critical (just as I was, as I saw the last, best chance of winning evaporate) that the supposed "commitment to running the ball" was abandoned. There was no better opportunity than that to try and establish a mind set for the rest of the season than right there. Pretty disgusting.
7) I think even Mr. Grossman realizes he needs to improve. I feel for him, as he had to run for his life occasionally, but he is throwing off his back foot and sailing some passes over the middle high – still. He'll be okay, but he needs to play better.
8) I have to say that Ken Dorsey is a nice college QB, and a good caretaker of the offense, but I remain unimpressed by his arm strength and accuracy. Believe it or not, I feel the 'Canes will be better next year, when they see what a guy with a better arm, accuracy, and mobility will do for them. Unfortunately, we will get to see Brock Berlin evidence that at the Gators' expense in the Orange Bowl, where another loss will be very possible.
9) That was the most talented group of linemen ever to play in the Swamp, and perhaps ever to play the Gators, period. That's what Florida needs to aspire to in recruiting to get to where everyone is used to being.

The defensive line and linebacker areas are Coach Zook's biggest concern the next two recruiting seasons (talk about understatement). It will take time to fill the pipeline with better talent, and the Gators' performance may very well suffer for it in the big games the next few years.

All that being said, this team has time to get better and start to exhibit improvement each week. It's good they have a game this Saturday so they can get their focus off the poor performance of last week and make some corrections before the trip to Knoxville. That game is still winnable, but continued mistakes cannot be overcome by this team (unlike past years). A nine or ten-win season is still very much achievable, and many goals can be reached. The coaching staff's biggest challenge now is to build up confidence and improve the level of play, which I think they'll do.

I feel sorry for Ohio, who comes to town this weekend. The Bobcats lost at home, 31-0, to a division 1-AA team last week. I don't care if they run the option or not, they will get crushed this week, as the Gators flush away last week and prepare for Tennessee.

Expect a route: Florida 62 Ohio 7

**Visor Flings, Week 3:**
**UF 34, Ohio University 6**

Well, I said last week it was good to play another game and not have to relive the Miami debacle for two weeks. That being said, it was still a shockingly lackluster effort against Ohio.

The weather is no excuse. A team with superior talent should get even more of an advantage in bad weather, especially if it has a decent passing offense. The entire offense seemed confused, with the QB and right side of the line still thinking too much and not “playing” enough. Yeesh – it’s getting old real fast. Now, there is no time left. The alarm clock is sounding, and it's off to Knoxville to either wake up or hit the snooze button for 2002.

Sad to say, but I'd almost accept a “moral victory” – just a solid effort from all three units and let's see what happens. It's time to settle on a right guard and right tackle on offense and let them go to work. It's bad enough to rotate players at a position, but to rotate them at MULTIPLE positions? No continuity develops, and the results were obvious. The Gators will almost have to “out-Tennessee” the Vols, with a solid running game and occasional deep strikes. I hope to at least see a tight end on the right side for most plays, if not a two-tight-end, two-wide-receiver, one-running-back set for most of the game. I have to believe Florida will have some success running the ball, but will Zaunbrecher exhibit patience when necessary? Expect another heavy dose of the “Cover-2” defensive scheme from the Vols, until the Gators show they have the pass offense/running game to beat/change it. The off week really helped Tennessee get new players ready on the defensive line, but I can only hope the Gators show enough toughness and confidence to rattle the new players and take the game to the Vols’ defense.

A statement I made before the season still holds true. The effectiveness of this offense vs. the Head Ball Coach's will be determined in the red zone: settling for field goal attempts, turnovers, and a low touchdown percentage will doom this year's team – period.

On defense, I unfortunately have to take a “show me” attitude right now. Lots of talk, lots of personnel changes, but where are the results in stopping the run? The Vols will always have a quality running attack, so slowing them down would be a huge lift to the confidence of the Gator front seven, not to mention improve the chances of winning the game dramatically. I'm curious as to whether Coach Thompson will let the cornerbacks actually challenge the Vol wide receivers, trying to disrupt their timing and routes. It sure would be a nice change, for once. Historically his defenses at Arkansas gave Tennessee trouble – I can only hope this trend continues.

The coaching staff has mentioned a lack of discipline by the defensive ends, rushing straight up field and not honoring their run responsibilities. In addition, there has been mention of the linebackers not playing their respective assignments against the run. Well, that's all very nice to hear, but where are the improvements? Is it coaching, or talent level? So far, I'm afraid the blame is shared by both. Can the front seven rise to the occasion and actually make some big plays to give the offense a chance to win the game? Once again – show me.

It is interesting to note that many fans were curious to see how Zook would act/react on the sidelines during the game, especially with his wild ways from his previous Gator stint. Seems like he is making a conscious effort to stay cool, especially given the fragile emotional state of the team in general and some players in particular. Given the performance so far, it may be time to see him start to get a little crazy and loud on the sideline this week – maybe that will get the team focused.

Until I see evidence of the aforementioned improvements in both the offense and defense, I'm afraid the Gators start 0-1 in SEC play.

Sadly, I'll say Tennessee 31 Florida 17.

**Visor Flings, Week 4:**
**UF 30, Tennessee 13**

Well, I said, "Show me," and they did.

Believe me, I'm as happy as any Gator fan with the win. This should prove to be a huge boost to the team and coaches. As the game progressed, you could see the confidence of the players grow, seeing for the first time against a quality opponent that the new systems on offense and defense could work.

That being said, I'm afraid I have to temper my enthusiasm with the following observations:

1) The O-Line is still a work-in-progress. I'm encouraged that some of the blitz and stunt packages were picked up more effectively as the game progressed, but Rex still took a pounding. That will wear on a QB as the season goes on, and must be addressed. I've said it many times – this unit has needed a quality center since Jeff Mitchell left, and Mike Degory is the real deal. He's a pleasure to watch; strong, quick feet, intelligent.

2) Yes, some other receivers such as Perez and Kight made some plays, but it still appears to me that these mostly came as a result of Rex somehow escaping a sack and the coverage breaking down. I still don't see much separation on the routes. Maybe some of it is just confidence, and their production will start to improve.

3) Rex improved during the game, but he has to stop throwing off the back foot when he's not pressured. Yeah, I know, I'm not being chased and pummeled by the defense, but it seems to have become a habit, even when he's not under duress. Hopefully he'll work it out.
4) The D-Line and linebackers played much better, but there's still a lot of work to do with these units. No, I mean NO, pressure on the QB. I'm afraid it is what it is at this point, however, and can only hope their shortcomings can be helped by good schemes from Coach Thompson. It does look like Bam is the man at middle linebacker now.
5) The special teams are showing signs of life. It looks like Ratliff is settling in as the punt returner, and he definitely can score from anywhere. Our own punting game is scary, though. Sean Morton can't remain the punter – he's incredibly slow getting the ball off, and should have had at least one blocked by the Vols. On the plus side, the Gators should have had at least one or two blocks themselves – it appears they have something going with the punt-block unit.
6) Maybe it was the weather, but the secondary still continues to play too far off the wide receivers. I can't believe guys like Ratliff and Cromartie aren't allowed to play more press coverage. The limited time they did against Tennessee, Clausen wasn't nearly as effective.
7) On an individual basis, Grossman, Jacobs, Perez, Carthon, I. Scott, Hardmon, and Johnson stood out. Corey Bailey is a player – I think his block was legal on the punt return, and he plays a physical game. He wasn't afraid to go tackle Jason Witten, who's a load.
8) As for Tennessee, their performance wasn't based solely on the Gator's performance. They did not play well at all on offense, and Coach Foolmer, the Great Pumpkin, really cost his team a chance of winning by not just pounding ahead with Jabari Davis. That guy was rumbling and breaking tackles, and should have had 25-30 carries – screw the rotation. Tony Brown could have really helped the passing game, but didn't impress. Jason Witten is NFL material, and should have seen the ball even more. I know everyone's All-American, Kelley Washington, certainly showed his ass before the game. But, let's face facts – he still caught 7 passes for 102 yards, and was out of game shape and playing hurt. The Gators caught a major break there, and fans shouldn't lose sight of that fact.

It's still obvious that the Gators need to make some "corrections," as Coach Zook so often says. And he's right – corrections and improvements. I don't believe the coaching staff will let the players start to think that they are over the hump, and all is smooth sailing from here on out. Plus, I believe some of the guys like Grossman, Jacobs, Hardmon, and Johnson can really exhibit their leadership and keep the team motivated and focused on improving and not relaxing too much.

Now, the undefeated Kentucky Wildcats come to the Swamp.

Jared Lorenzen is back as the starter this season, perhaps Guy Morris's best decision. Plus, Artose Pinner leads the SEC in rushing. Granted, this comes against a less-than-stellar schedule so far, but this team is playing with confidence right now, which should get (and hopefully keep) the Gators' attention. The UK defense still leaves a lot to be desired, though, and doesn't have the depth to hold an improving Florida offense down.

This could be a closer game than in past seasons, especially with the Jekyll-and-Hyde Gator performance so far. Until Florida establishes some consistency from week-to-week, I can't anticipate a blowout win. However, the Gators are still the superior team, and should win comfortably.

The Visor's forecast: Florida 38 Kentucky 21

**Visor Flings, Week 5:**
**UF 41, Kentucky 34**

The final score against the Wildcats certainly wasn't indicative of how well the Gators handled them. Just when the offense and defense are beginning to show some continuity, the not-so-special teams play taints an otherwise solid performance.

On offense, it appears as if the O-Line is learning to pass-block better, especially against the blitz. Rex still took some hits, but far less often, especially with a back left in to help out. The running game wore down the UK defensive line in the second half, and helped the Gators re-take the lead without resorting to a pass-only attack. Graham and Carthon both ran well, and the blocking of Mo Mitchell was a pleasant surprise. He definitely looks more comfortable at guard, where he can use his strength more often and rely on help in pass-blocking, if necessary. Grossman still looks to Jacobs too often. He had the tight end in the middle zones and backs in the flats available to him, but he often ignored them. The toughness displayed by Carlos Perez should encourage Rex to spread the ball around a little more. Of course, his accuracy and Jacobs' hands lead him to take more chances than most QBs. However, the offense really won't take another step forward until more receivers touch the ball.

The defense really played well against the Kentucky spread offense. The scheme employed by Coach Thompson was light-years ahead of Jon Joke's. No 10-plus play drives all day and 400-plus passing yards. The only real glaring need is a better pass rush (still). The return of Darrell Lee could be a huge lift to the entire defense, providing quality depth and perhaps an improved pass rush. It appears to me that the Gators won't get many sacks at this point, and will need to rely on solid coverage and confusing the opposing QB into mistakes. Keiwan Ratliff is a stud, and the entire group of defensive backs is as good as any in the country. Mike Nattiel and Bam Hardmon really seem more comfortable in their LB positions, and are making big plays more frequently.

Of course, no discussion would be complete without a few comments on perhaps the worst exhibition of special teams play ever seen. I still believe that Jason Hunter should be the punter. Sean Morton is much too slow, poor blocking or not. That's not to forgive the blocking, however, either on punts or field goals. Both areas need vast improvement, and fast. It may require Coach Odom and Coach Zook to juggle and/or replace personnel, again. I'm sure they realize that bigger games down the road will be closer in score throughout the game, and that key mistakes will cause a loss (or losses). There is a lot of talk that Ingle Martin will get a close look. That could prove beneficial on pooch kicks and/or short-yardage situations on 4th down, helping to slow the rush, but I'd be surprised if he becomes the regular punter. The performance of Matt Leach is puzzling. Leg strength is not an issue – his timing to the ball and the elevation are the problems. Perhaps Petro should handle extra points – a two-step approach as a straight-on kicker should be very simple. As for the return coverage, the root causes seem to be a lack of discipline in staying in the respective lanes and overrunning/taking bad angles (duh). Talk about stating the obvious...these guys have to perform better. I can't believe someone of Zook's ability won't get this corrected, though.

An interesting road game awaits the Gators this week. Ole Miss is becoming a more consistent and dangerous team under David Cutcliffe. The offense isn't all about Eli Manning, with a solid running game averaging over five yards a carry and nine touchdowns so far. Cutcliffe developed some excellent offenses at Tennessee, with the running game dictating the flow of the game. Manning will pose problems for the Gator defense, especially with his ability to read defenses. I expect Coach Thompson to take more chances and disguise more coverages than against any other QB except Ken Dorsey.

The Rebel defense is still the soft spot for this team. Florida should be able to move the ball effectively running or passing. Barring a spate of turnovers by the Gators, they should prevail. Hopefully they won't expect an easier time than at Knoxville, though. Ole Miss will play their best game of the season, and I'm sure will have many surprises ready to spring on the Gators.

Visor Vision looks like: Florida 38 Mississippi 24

**Visor Flings, Week 6:**
**Ole Miss 17, UF 14**

Man, I certainly didn't expect a performance reminiscent of last year's Auburn game, but there it was for all to see. You can rationalize all you wish to about the players and coaches right now, but it's apparent something is seriously wrong at the foundation. It's time for Gator fans to look up the word "disillusioned" and understand that that's where the program has led us, for now.

After five games, it "appeared" that the O-Line was starting to come around and play more physically. Then against Ole Miss, they revert to human turnstiles. Plus, Wickline can't develop at least two solid backups from Mitchell/Jorgenson/Hand? I excuse Hand, but Jorgenson has sucked since he started playing, and never remotely approached his press clippings out of high school. If Mitchell dedicates himself, he will be a fine guard – not yet though. The talent pool is awfully shallow here – hard to fathom. Maybe Wickline gets a little slack here.

Coach Zaunbrecher's stay in Gainesville won't last beyond 2003 if he can't exhibit any type of second half adjustments to help out his QB and use all the skill positions (remember the tight ends?). That was Jon Joke-like in lousy performance. It "appears" that he may not be "ready-for-prime-time" yet. A shockingly poor effort. Hey, Coach Z – ever hear of the 2-WR, 2-TE, 1-back offense? It sometimes helps control the ball, get some first downs, and can keep your quarterback alive. Oh yeah, ever hear of maybe throwing a deep ball on second-and one?

Poor Kelvin Kight. Yes, he's great in open space – but the guy just can't get separation in his routes. He just looks like someone to occupy one defensive back, unless Coach Dixon miraculously turns this guy around. Carlos Perez is really starting to tap into his potential, and his toughness is unquestioned. However, if Jacobs and Perez are both covered by double-teams, then SOMEONE ELSE IS OPEN.

Rex' performance is a combination of things at this point. He hasn't been "coached up" well during games, he simply hasn't played as well as he can, and the punishment is starting to take its toll. How hard is it to hit Jacobs or Perez on 2nd-and-one when the defensive back is eight yards off? Low marks for the QB and the offensive coordinator there. It's time for a true "gamer" like Ingle Martin to get some snaps each game to give the opponent a different look (what a concept!). Yeah, it would have taken some balls to put him in on short yardage situations in the fourth quarter, but his toughness and running ability, in my mind, would have kept the sticks moving. Look, Rex is still the guy, but he needs coaching and play-calling help right now – no shame in that. But Rex won't be there forever, either. Perhaps they both would be helped by...

The supposed "COMMITTMENT TO THE RUNNING GAME." Sure, he did a fine job in the second half. Don't feed me the line about 'the great play of the Ole Miss defense.' That unit is average, and the loss of one lineman (the Showstopper) certainly stopped the offensive show by the Gators. There's simply no reason for such an anemic second-half output. The running game was fine in the first half – it only needed to be okay in the second to pull out a win. If you need one yard and decide to call a running play, ditch that deep, delayed, counter-handoff and blast straight ahead on a quick hitter. Let those big, wide, fat uglies deal out some punishment.

Looks like the star of this staff is John Thompson. He's already getting more production out of the D-Line than I expected, and the entire defense sure showed some fire and guts all afternoon. Eli Manning was fortunate he didn't play from behind in the second half, because he would have taken a beating similar to what Rex gets each week (let alone what Peyton received at Tennessee). His familiarity with the West Division teams is a great bonus. Hopefully his group can pull out wins the next two games against LSU and Auburn, so we can put all of our eggs into the Georgia basket.

There are some injuries that we aren't hearing about, because of the new school policy of not disclosing injury status during games and the Coach Zook policy. If Snell's shoulder was just "dinged," he should have come back at some point, right? Rex is beaten up, and I think Graham has a slight leg problem he's trying to play through – he's lost his explosiveness getting through the hole and breaking tackles. Time for Ciatrick Fason to get some meaningful carries, to help out this season AND next.

It's stunning, really – the Gators could be headed for the Outback or Peach bowls before they even get to Jacksonville. The Swamp will have to pull them through the next two weeks, because there has to be a lack of confidence developing now. I only hope the players pull together instead of fracturing apart at this point – it could happen.

Low marks for Coach Zook, as well, for the 4th quarter decision to go for a first down on 4th-and-12. Look, if you have decided in your mind that you won't attempt a field goal outside of 35 or 40 yards, then tell the offensive coordinator to call plays that can get you 10 yards in 4 downs, not just 3. There was a lot of time left at that point, and it was obvious that Cutcliffe wasn't going to let Eli lose the game. Twelve yards is too much – punt the ball and play for field position.

And yes, those two penalties killed the last drive in Rebel territory, but it really didn't need to come to that, did it? Did it?

Well, at least we have a punter in reserve quarterback Ingle Martin, who was a very good kicker in high school. He will have to work on his form – you can't get away with dropping the ball so much before the punt – you will shank more that way and a strong wind affects the drop more. But the guy is a great team player, and I like having a "Slash" player on the Gators. Looks like Zook will have some extra scholarships available, if Morton, Hunter, or Leach are even on one right now. Jorgenson certainly won't be missed as a senior, for sure.

Get ready for a big dose of Domanick Davis this week. LSU suffered a huge blow losing LaBrandon Toefield to a broken arm, but Davis is one tough competitor. Plus, no Josh Reed or Rohan Davey anymore. I can't believe that Mike Mauck can pass the Tigers to a win. Look for a power running game, a few attempts at the deep ball, QB roll-outs and scrambles, the option, and a conservative approach on defense from Nick Saban, hoping the Gators continue to implode, especially with the added pressure of playing at home and having no room to spare in trying to get to Atlanta.

Florida cannot get in to the mindset of trying to make big plays happen at this point, or they will just help LSU and Auburn succeed in getting into their heads. The Gators had better exhibit a lot of pride and guts the next two weeks, or it will get even uglier.

All that being said, I still believe that Rex, Taylor, and the defense have too much character, talent, and pride to not win these upcoming games. I'm just hoping that the Bullpuppies will still need to fear the Gators, knowing that the winner of that game in all likelihood will go to Atlanta.

The Gator Nation needs to support this team. I will be at the Swamp Saturday, of course, in my capacity as a secret analyst. A trip to Atlanta and/or a New Year's Day bowl game would still be a tremendous accomplishment for this team, and they can still do those things. Motivation, whether it be from inside or outside, should not be a problem.

Optimistically: Florida 27 LSU 17

**Visor Flings, Week 7:**
**LSU 36, UF 7**

After only seven games, it's come to an almost "desperation" time for this year's team and coaching staff. Fair or not, the culture of business and of society's small attention span and "what have you done for me lately" mentality has crept into sports, and a team's affairs seem to be treated as such.

What these players and coaches need right now is a win – simplistic, yes, but absolutely true. Especially with a bye week after Auburn. A three-game losing streak followed by two more weeks of bitching and moaning by the entire Gator Nation will almost certainly cause the rest of the season to unravel (and yes, I know many believe it's already begun).

It's painfully obvious that these players do not know how to handle real adversity, and that the offensive coaching staff and head coach are not providing adequate leadership at this time. Perhaps there is a NFL parallel – the St. Louis Rams had things quickly come apart after great success, and started 0-5 before finally getting that first win. You can't tell me that doesn't make doing the work and practicing easier. Of course, I'm not blind to the fact that the game plan, coaching, and halftime adjustments are, quite frankly, very poor right now.

It's interesting to watch how Coach Zook has chosen to handle his QB, trying to weigh the less-than-expected performance against the new scheme and shuffled O-Line, while trying to keep the confidence level up. What's unfortunate to me is that a lack of guts and foresight has been evidenced by not establishing right at the beginning of spring practice that certain "packages" of plays could be set up for Ingle Martin to run, giving him invaluable experience, and also laying down the edict that Rex, while still The Man, would get some help within the framework of helping the entire team. I can't believe Grossman couldn't have accepted that.

LSU was a hungry bunch Saturday night, and can you blame them? The Gators' struggles aside, the Tigers have been embarrassed for years by Florida (as have many others), and made a stand. The fine line between putting doubt in their minds (Rex hitting Jacobs for a TD on the first possession) and opening the door to a true belief that the Gators were ready to be beaten was that thin. Add in a blown fake field goal, a dropped pass near midfield during the two-minute drill at the end of the first half, some remarkably poor play-calling by Zaunbrecher on the first drive of the second half (along with the QB making a very poor check-off), continued poor coordinating by the offensive coordinator, and a tiring defense, and the walls came crumbling down. LSU didn't have to do a damn thing differently, leaving them in their "comfort zone" the entire game. You can bet Nick Saban was glad he didn't need Mauck to pass them to victory.

My feelings quickly went from frustration to anger to resignation as this developed, something I thought I'd not feel again after 1979. It can happen so fast...but can also be so unnecessary.

So, what happens now, starting with the Auburn game? It sure doesn't hurt that Auburn was embarrassed themselves, letting Arkansas bounce back from a crushing six-overtime loss at Tennessee by running wild over the Tigers. Maybe their front seven isn't as good as advertised, huh? Yeah, some will say they'll be as desperate as the Gators now, but so what? Tommy Tuberville hasn't shown much, and he's been there four years. Good defense, decent running game, no passing game, every year. Oops – that's what many were saying about LSU last week. Well, at least LSU showed some guts and kicked Tennessee's ass last year in the SEC championship game instead of lying down like the Vols did.

There's no doubt you'll see a lot of "Cadillac" Williams, because Daniel Cobb and Jason Campbell both are poor QBs. Campbell can at least run – hopefully Tuberville doesn't get a good idea and play him. Hmm...wonder if the Gators will fall prey to the same tight-end-in-the-flat, wheel-route-to-the-back, bend-but-don't break defense, and other ploys of last year? Auburn would be foolish not to keep that philosophy, especially with the rock-bottom confidence level of the Gator offense right now.

I can only hope Zaunbrecher starts to tailor the play-calling to the strengths of his personnel. Ditch the rollouts, which shrink the filed for the pass defense. Run Graham and Carthon hard between the tackles. Set up a package of plays for Ingle Martin to run and pass from. It's not that difficult! Could pride be getting in the way of progress at this point? Maybe becoming more of a conservative, running team should be the identity of this year's team. At least Kight can run block, and Perez is great at it. It sure worked for F$U against the 'Canes.

I also hope Thompson unleashes the blitz, run and pass variety, against Auburn. Maybe the defense will have to take control of the rest of this season, and dictate the action. What's the worst that can happen – lose at home by 29 points?

By the way, whoever keeps saying that Kelvin Kight and other receivers are getting open (other than Jacobs or occasionally Perez) is full of it. It ain't happening, folks! It's stunning that the Gators are running four-receiver sets with Ingle Martin and Vernell Brown. I'm not knocking Martin and Brown, but really, think about it. Here's hoping Dallas Baker is the real deal, and Reggie Vickers can at least approach his form of the Spring Game.

I'll leave many, many other thoughts and issues for the bye week, including red-shirting (or lack of it), the performance of some coaches (and players), and other juicy subjects. For this week at least, I'm still concentrating on trying to win one single game, to pull this team back from the brink.

Imploringly: Florida 24 Auburn 20

**Visor Flings, Week 8:**
**UF 30, Auburn 23 (OT)**

A classic case of "snatching defeat from the jaws of victory," except in this case two great players made a great play that may have salvaged the season. Rex Grossman and Taylor Jacobs did what we've come to expect at the most opportune time imaginable.

Where do you begin in reviewing this game? The first half was the most complete effort of the season to-date, including the win over Tennessee. A solid running game, combined with spreading the ball around to many receivers, led to a dominating performance. The defense certainly benefited as well, being well-rested and allowing only five first downs and seven points. Ingle Martin impressed, looking composed and confident leading the second TD drive both running and throwing. The return of Shannon Snell obviously improved the overall play of the O-Line, as well. Graham and Carthon ran hard, getting some extra yards after the first hit. It was also a boost to the entire team seeing Matt Leach hit some nice kicks on field goal attempts. The only negative was four(!) illegal-formation penalties, not because of the wide receivers, but from the tackles playing too far off the line. Poor coaching...make the adjustment after the first infraction!

Then it all went terribly wrong. Penalties on two Ran Carthon TD runs that would have iced the game. Atrocious tackling, both at the point of attack and in the secondary. Being physically manhandled at both lines-of-scrimmage. Poor adjustments by the offensive coordinator (again), failing to stretch the field and allowing the Auburn defense to slowly squeeze the field down the entire second half, and especially in the fourth quarter when a few first downs and a field goal would still secure the win. I also have to find some fault with Coach Thompson playing so soft against Jason Campbell on both two-point conversions – crash down from both corners and make the guy make a decision, instead of allowing him to do what he does best – roll out or QB draw and run. To Thompson's credit, he did start employing some corner blitzes late in the game that messed up some Tiger plays.

Then, the coup-de-grace. Ron Zook voluntarily placed his head on the guillotine by going for the first down at his own 43, with less than 4 minutes remaining and with Ronnie Brown rolling downhill for the Auburn running game. Unbelievable! Look, the decision was bad enough on its own. But I guess he was watching a different game, because that bunched-up, two-TE, three-RB alignment just allows Auburn to stuff the run. Either have Ingle Martin in there to add the roll-out pass/run option (because he's a great runner and Rex was really limping by then), or do what the Head Ball Coach used to do – spread the field with four receivers, so at least the O-Line has a better chance to create a small crease that additional linebackers or defensive backs can't quickly fill in. Horrible call, and bad formation.

Some thoughts:
1) I'm still looking for evidence that wide receivers other than Jacobs and Perez get any separation on their routes. The only time Kight seemed to get in space was on the quick swing pass. Brown, Jackson, and Small were no factor whatsoever.
2) Our defense is alarmingly less strong, both at the lineman and linebacker positions, than most opponents. Yes, Ian Scott is an all-conference-caliber player, but the others get pushed back too often on straight ahead or zone blocking. Not a good game for either Hardmon or Nattiel either, especially Bam. I counted at least four plays where he was actually in position in the hole to make a play, and either grabbed a bunch of grass or got knocked backward.

3) Yes, the Gators got a much-needed win, but, to paraphrase Jeremy Foley, "what may happen eventually must be taken care of immediately." The win masked many basic ills still befalling this team. The offensive game planning in the second half of games is horrible. The defense must be stretched vertically – when is the last time the Gators threw a bomb? Post-corner? Seam route to the slot receiver? Both times the Gators were inside the ten in the third quarter, Zaunbrecher goes to the shotgun with six(!) defenders lined up in two lines of three at the five yard line and goal line. Where's the "commitment to the run?" The tackling is still awful. Too much stripping of the ball, too little wrapping up and tackling. Gus Scott gets a pass on the strip that caused a fumble 50 yards downfield, because no one was within 10 yards of the guy when the catch was made.
4) About Rex: on fourth and one, some people have wondered why Rex didn't sneak it, but it's hard to drive forward with a bum knee/leg. Rex played a smart game, but still had a tight end breaking free towards the South end zone on third-and-goal in the third quarter – he never looked at him. Rex made some amazing recoveries to throw the ball away once out of the pocket, especially after he took a dumb seven-yard loss earlier in the game. He learned from that mistake, which is encouraging. It really seems such a waste that a guy with such a great arm and touch is restricted to curls, quick slants, and swing passes, but, unfortunately, the combination of the offensive coordinator and the lack of talent at receiver is killing the downfield passing game. Grossman's courage should never be questioned, however, especially when he must feel frustration at the performance of the pass-blocking and route-running.
5) There were definitely some "phantom" calls by the officials, but the offense still could have overcome them with at least one more touchdown instead of a field goal. Too much excuse-making there.
6) Isn't the defense allowed to sack the QB? Neither Auburn QB can read defenses well – I'm surprised Coach Thompson didn't blitz more often to rattle them more, especially Cobb.
7) It sure would be nice to intercept some passes, but maybe that's not allowed either?

Well, at least the mindset is more positive entering the off-week, and perhaps the confidence level is rising. A lot of healing and work needs to be done before the trip to Jax. Maybe the Gators will surprise us (this time in a good way) against the Puppies.

Also, it would be nice to see UK play the Puppies tough for a change, instead of playing Florida tough and lying down for Georgia.

**Visor Flings, Week 9:**
**Off Week**

Georgia Preview:

It's time for the Visor to make his annual pilgrimage to Jacksonville for the Georgia game. There is certainly a different feel to the upcoming trip, what with so many questions surrounding the play of the Gators, while the Puppies are in the driver's seat for the SEC

Championship Game. Georgia will be favored more strongly than since 1992, and the late '80s before that.

So much for the Mildcats putting up a 60-minute fight. Typical – they fight until the end against the Gators, but roll over for Georgia.

Overall, the Puppies have the advantage on offense, especially with a strong O-Line and running game. If healthy, expect a lot of Musa Smith early to soften up the Florida front seven, followed by slants and go routes to Terrence Edwards, Fred Gibson, and others. The tight end is prominently displayed as well, especially on flat routes and seam routes down the middle. I expect a lot of David Greene – D.J. Shockley will show up early only to shake up a slow start or because (unfortunately) the Gators are behind ten-plus points by the second quarter. The Georgia O-Line has a distinct size advantage, and are playing very well right now. The return of Jon Stinchcomb is only a plus.

The advantage is smaller for Georgia on defense, with the Gator secondary perhaps the best in the SEC. However, David Pollack, Boss Bailey, and the rest are just playing better (and probably are simply better, period), than the Gator front seven. Their defensive coordinator finally got smart and used his superior talent to blitz in the second half, and it was all over for Jared (Subway) Lorenzen and the Mildcat offense. Too bad they got away from pounding Pinner at the Puppy D-Line, because that guy was doing some damage.

Mark Richt has the Puppies believing now, as their second-half performance proved. No panic, just keep executing the game plan and pull away. I sincerely hope the Gator fans and players aren't pinning too much hope on Georgia's injury problems, because their strong O-Line just makes everyone better, and they have a lot of depth. The only way to change this is to make a strong early showing and try to start having doubt creep into their minds concerning Florida's dominance since 1990.

If we lose, Georgia wins the East and goes to Atlanta. No need to hold anything back now, and it will be interesting to see how Ron Zook has the Gators prepared after his first off-week. Much has been made of the good timing as far as resting injuries and preparing for the biggest SEC game of the season, but the proof won't come until Saturday.

Expect the same "Cover-two" look from Georgia's defense. Florida must establish the run, and stay with it this time if successful. If Earnest Graham is still slowed, then Ran Carthon must hit the holes hard and fast, and a few carries by Willie Green and Ciatrick Fason could help. Rex must continue to improve upon his performance against Auburn, but I hope Coach Zaunbrecher call some long passes, because Kentucky exposed the Georgia secondary. I get the feeling that Taylor Jacobs will make some big plays, but he needs help from Perez and Kight. It would be a welcome sight to see the tight ends used for ball-control passing, instead of the occasional try at a big play. Both Walker and Troupe can get open and keep the Georgia front seven honest, giving Rex a chance to show what he can do in a big game.

I feel Coach Thompson will have a great game plan in place, and that the defense will be flying around early. Now would be a wonderful time to generate some turnovers and make timely plays, because I can't see the Gators holding Georgia's offense to less then 350 yards total offense – too many weapons, and too many good ones.

Unfortunately, unless the Gators force some turnovers and get points off of them, they will be hard pressed to win. This appears to me to be the best Georgia team since 1997, and we know what happened against Mike Bobo, Robert Edwards, Hines Ward, Marcus Stroud, Champ Bailey, and company. The quality depth they have this season, both in ability and performance, greatly outweighs Florida's. I'm afraid it's their year.

Prediction: Georgia 34 Florida 24

**Visor Flings, Week 10**
**UF 20, Georgia 13**

Then again...maybe it's not Georgia's year, at least to beat Florida.

A really gutsy performance turned in by the Gators against the Puppies, who once again have been neutered, this time by Dr. Zook. At least for one evening, the better team was Florida, and it's fortunate they deservedly won.

What an incredibly exciting and frustrating first half, which served as a microcosm for the entire season to date. Spurts of fine offense, sharp passing, little running game (especially between the tackles), iffy play-calling in the red zone, bad luck with turnovers (including Rex's only poor decision, forcing a pass intercepted by Pollack), horrific kicking game. Yep, that about covers it, all in one half of football.

1) The coaching staff should be commended for putting together a fine game plan, offensively and defensively, to give the players the best chance to win. The dink-and-dunk swing passes wound up being the best strategy, especially with the loss of Jacobs on the first series, and the inability of the O-Line to hold out any stunts or blitzes by the linebackers. The plays set up for passing to the tight end were timely, and showed off perhaps the best pair of tight ends in the country. Aaron Walker had a nice game, and Ben Troupe was a monster, breaking tackles and firing up the entire offense. The young receivers were thrown to the wolves, and acquitted themselves well. Perez is really a fine blocker, and Kight showed his toughness. Matt Jackson looks like the number-three wide receiver the rest of the year. Looks like Brown, Small, and even Sharpe will get even more experience with the first unit than they expected.

2) The running game was a big disappointment to me. It seems this area is regressing, and Earnest Graham is not performing at the level he's capable of due to injury. This is a real predicament – perhaps it's time for Green and Fason to get the opportunity to help out. However, it seems these two aren't even on the radar screen, except for Green in that lousy bunched-up, short yardage set. Why did it take until the fourth quarter for Coach Zaunbrecher to finally ditch that crap and spread the field some, to provide some room for the run and also present an opportunity for a short throw to a running back or tight end?

Amazingly poor coaching and execution – Coach Wickline still hasn't shown me any improvement, and I can't believe the starting five are that bad.
3) Once again, Coach Zook voluntarily placed his head on the chopping block and went for a fourth down at mid-field, with half of the fourth quarter remaining, and a defense that was playing exceptionally well. Unbelievable.
The defense put together by Coach Thompson was largely effective, even though the Puppies did have some success running the ball. Other than a low percentage of completions, some including significant chunks of yardage, Greene and Shockley were ineffective, and never allowed to become comfortable with the plays they are best at. D.J. sure got a rude welcome to the rivalry, and looked as nervous as he played. The memory of Gus Scott running by him into the end zone for a TD will stay with him for a long time. Great effort by the D-Line in staying after the rush, especially with the fine coverage of the secondary allowing them to record four sacks. Savelio and Mitchell hustled all over the field, and Ian Scott was solid in the middle, again. Nattiel and Hardmon played perhaps their best game as well, breaking up passes and rushing the QB.
(4) Only one real breakdown, and damn if it didn't allow Georgia to tie the game with around three minutes left. I almost passed out when I saw Terrence Edwards break free on the post right towards me, with Todd Johnson nowhere in sight. Thank goodness he broke a cardinal rule for receivers in catching the ball – he jumped for the catch instead of running through the ball, and his timing was off just enough. Actually, many of Georgia's receivers were guilty of that mistake. It's hard to believe Georgia was 0 for 13 on 3rd down – completely unacceptable for any offense.
5) I'm still puzzled by some of the personnel usage in key situations. I saw Sharpe as the slot receiver in the 2nd quarter inside the 10; saw Brown and Small a lot in the red zone. I suppose it was a combination of Jacobs' injury, the receiver rotation, and the formation for the particular play called. Still, perhaps a more experienced group or package in that critical area would benefit in a game of that magnitude. I sure would like to see a 2 WR, 2 TE, 1 RB set inside the 10 more often. Also, I expect little change in the passing philosophy from here on out. With Jacobs out, it appears that the deep ball will be very rare. Curls, square-ins, and post routes will be utilized from max protection formations, unless the O-Line is actually protecting the passer with just five or six guys.
6) Very curious play-calling by Richt, which, frankly, helped Florida win the game. Musa Smith was underused; he seemed to be running well. However, he was ignored inside the red zone except on the one-yard line. TD run in the third quarter called back by penalty. Also, Richt should have continued to use the flats until the Gators firmed up that coverage area. There were big chunks of yardage available much of the game. If memory serves me correctly, Georgia threw only one pass into the end zone, for their first score. Very, very conservative. It certainly kept Florida in the game, especially within one score of the lead, where the offensive play-calling could remain virtually unchanged.
7) As for the Special-Ed teams, where can you go from here? I'd say let Matt Leach do all the place-kicking – he has the best leg, and maybe will get some confidence going. If the

coaches don't like him, then let Petrowicz give it a shot. Talcott appears no better than Leach, with a weaker leg. I'd stick with Martin as the punter – at least he doesn't fumble the ball and doesn't let the opponent have at least a 50% chance of blocking every punt. I think Morton is done as a punter, especially given Coach Zook's comments yesterday about how Morton did not perform as he was coached during the week.

Well, what can we expect this week on the 2002 roller-coaster ride? I hope the opportunity to still win the East will help offset any letdown. Plus, the loss of Jacobs, while disheartening, means others will get their chance.

Vanderbilt's offense is actually improved this season, and shows some balance. Even the occasional big pass play has happened this season. However, the defense has been shredded by the run and pass, so Florida should be okay throughout the game on the scoreboard, even with a struggling running game. The weather is always iffy in Nashville this time of year, but I don't think it will affect Rex much, if any.

Nothing should be taken for granted by this team, and hopefully another solid effort by the players and coaches is in store this coming Saturday.

I'll go out on a limb: Florida 31 Vanderbilt 14

**Visor Flings, Week 11:**
**UF 21, Vanderbilt 17**

I am so tired of the "Vanderbilt always plays the Gators tough" refrain. Look, those guys stink, and we barely got by, because the offense pretty much sucked the entire second half. It's too late in the season to expect much else, so I'm prepared to be in a struggle with South Carolina this week and to get whipped by F$U on 11/30.

Don't be fooled by the running performance; the Commodores are very weak on defense. Once again, the second half adjustments were nonexistent and the defense was called on to save the day. For a while I thought the offensive struggles were a mirage, and now it appears that a win over a quality team like F$U will be just that – a mirage. That oasis known as the Gator defense is going to dry up at some point.

The pass blocking, including the pick-ups of blitzes, is disgraceful. I'd love for Rex to come back next season, but Zook is going to have to sell him (again) on how productive the offense under Coach Zaunbrecher can be.

Hey folks – we're ten games into the season. I'll say it again: we are what we are, whether it's because of poor play, less-than-expected talent level, or poor coaching. I'm starting to believe it's a combination of all three. This is incredibly disappointing – while the defense has settled into a consistent weekly effort, the offensive production is poor.

Man, the O-line looks fat and slow. I saw that Randy Hand got more snaps at right tackle than Colon; frankly, Colon's performance this season warrants it. Wickline had better learn how to improve the footwork of all the linemen, or else update his resume.

Thank goodness Snell walked off his injury, but losing Ben Troupe to a high ankle sprain could be devastating. That's an injury that can linger for many weeks – it certainly messed up John Henderson of the Vols last year. The Gators need the monster back for F$U. I'd prefer he not play this week.

Another solid effort by the defense. Thompson and the players did a fine job, allowing only one real TD drive all day. I still can't fathom how Hardmon and Nattiel seem to run themselves out of position so often against the run. Maybe the option is an excuse for this past week.

Cory Bailey can be a star next year, if he continues to practice hard and stay motivated. I know he's been the nickel back most of the season, but he sure looks like a great replacement for Todd Johnson right now. Maybe DeShawn Carter will show that much improvement next season, giving the Gators another fine secondary.

I am so tired of the "illegal Formation" penalty. Poor coaching and poor discipline – no excuses. Yes, the officials were mandated to call this penalty more often, but shame on both the coaches and players for not phasing this mistake out as the season has progressed. This game would have been effectively over if that penalty didn't cost Aaron Walker a TD for a 28-10 lead just before the half.

In other games the Mildcats played nice defense by against LSU. You absolutely have to have a guy behind everyone else to make the tackle, especially when the pass only gets to the 20-yard line. What a crushing way to lose. Bad karma for the Gators, as well. That loss would have set up Auburn to win the West. Now, they'll still need help, even if they beat the Puppies this week. No Edwards for Georgia this week, and probably no Boss Bailey. Still, if the Puppies make Jason Campbell have to make plays to win the game, they're in good shape. Auburn will have to generate turnovers and make Georgia play from behind.

Oh – have I mentioned how much I hate needing help from other teams? Another reason to get sick over the choke against Ole Miss – how unnecessary! Once again, I get the feeling of bad karma, as far as Auburn winning.

Unfortunately, the offense could turn the upcoming game against South Carolina into one of those ugly, boring affairs that Lou Holtz loves, and seems to get his team ready for. That's one thing I really liked about SOS – he didn't buy into that "Lou Holtz Magic" crap, and didn't let his players get sucked into that mental black hole either. He'd go out and bomb poor ol' Lou into submission, and the steam would go completely out of their sails by the 2nd quarter.

Looks like Coach Zook may need to get into a lot of faces during the game this week, to keep the players focused and playing hard, especially if this turns into a low-scoring affair. I'd love to be wrong, but I don't see much evidence to the contrary. Hope the defense is ready...again!

Hocus-pocus: Florida 20, USC 13

**Visor Flings, Week 12:
UF 28, South Carolina 7**

A bittersweet win for the Gators, against the backdrop of the Puppies stealing a win from Auburn and the East title. There isn't much to say at this point; the loss to Ole Miss was unacceptable and cost the Gators a chance at a great season, and, anytime you need another team to help your own cause, your chances aren't very good.

Florida's effort was perhaps their most complete of the season. Granted, USC is down this year, but the dominance of the running game, the four-touchdown performance by Grossman, and the solid play of the defense and special teams was overlong in coming.

Congratulations are in order to the players and coaches in keeping their focus on the game at hand even after the results from Auburn were known. Despite what most would say, that game was in the thoughts of all even after the second half had begun, and to still come out and play sharply was impressive.

The running game improved upon the previous week's effort against Vanderbilt, and it appears the O-line is finally beginning to come together. The pass protection was improved, but still has some leaks. Graham looked healthier than since the first half of the Tennessee game. The receivers did a fine job overcoming the season-ending loss of Perez, the only real downer to come from the game. It will be critical that Troupe can play some in two weeks, and perhaps Jacobs can contribute a little. The passing game will really be under a lot of strain to produce the last two games, as the level of competition increases significantly.

The defense continues to impress, especially with its consistency from game-to-game. The front seven is playing the run better, and seems to have eliminated a lot of the mental mistakes committed during most of the season. It is still physically out-manned, especially at linebacker, but intelligent play and hustle can overcome some of that. The secondary hasn't been challenged in a while, and must prepare to play it's best games against F$U and in a bowl. Not many big plays allowed by this unit all year – I can only hope this trend continues. Coach Thompson should get recognized nationally as one of the best

Coach Zook and the rest of the staff did a fine job coming off of the last off week to prepare for (and defeat) a very good team. It will be interesting to see what they can develop for the in-state rival. Two more weeks to heal up are critical for Troupe and Jacobs, and should allow plenty of time to let go of the disappointment of losing the SEC East and prepare to defeat the Semiholes. Unfortunately, F$U is playing its best ball of the season right now, and appears to have found a QB that won't screw up too badly. This will be another huge test. At least the players will have lots of practice time, knowing exactly what (and who) they will have at Tallahassee.

The build-up to this game is unlike any seen in many years. F$U has four losses, Florida three; neither team is in the top ten for the first time since 1986; no real national importance on the result. No matter – this is a huge game for the Gators, in terms of continuing the momentum gained the second half of the year, and especially leading into Coach Zook's first real recruiting season.

The state of the Semihole union is not good right now. The suspension/dismissal of McPherson, the injuries at running back and O-line, the erratic play, and the failure of the defense to get opponents off the field quickly has led to much internal questioning and doubt among the players. Actually, these occurrences in a rivalry game can seem to pull a team together for a great effort, especially at home. Also, I feel the reinstatement of Chris Rix as the starting QB will help the F$U offense – It's unfortunate that Coach Thompson could not unleash his many schemes against an inexperienced QB. Rix' running ability, while criticized by many, will probably serve him well this game. The 'Holes are also fortunate that a great freshman talent like Leon Washington is available. He's easily more dangerous than Nick Maddox, and has also been terrific on punt returns. I expect him to see double-duty Saturday. The play of Boldin, Gardner, and Morgan at WR is puzzling. I still feel these guys have great athletic ability, and can only hope their penchant for dropping passes and losing their mental focus continues. I'm still of the opinion that the outcome of the game rests with this unit. If they rise to the occasion, it could be a long night for the Gator secondary. The play of the 'Hole defense is less curious – this group just doesn't have the sheer number of playmakers as past seasons

It will be very interesting to see if patience is still the credo of the Gator offense. Will Zook and Zaunbrecher stick with the run if it struggles early? Will the chuck-and suck still be the method for ball-control, even with the hopeful return of Taylor Jacobs and Ben Troupe? The loss of Carlos Perez, the Gator's best blocking WR, especially hurts this philosophy. It would be a shame to see perhaps the best deep-ball thrower in the college game not allowed to attack downfield, giving Jacobs and Kight a chance for the big play. Of course, if he's on his ass because the O-line blows assignments, that's a moot point. It will also be of interest to see how Coach Thompson attacks Rix, especially with the blitz. It's obvious that by now Rix will most likely tuck-and-run under any real pressure. Will the linebackers be in position to contain him?

You have to believe that, deep down, Earnest Graham and the O-line really want to punish Darnell Dockett, and get the opportunity to run hard and often. As much as I would like to see it, too, hopefully Coach Zook (and the entire coaching staff) can get the players to focus more on the task at hand. The success of Graham and Carthon will probably dictate the Gator's fortune. A win is the sweetest revenge of all, saving the trash-talking for after the game, if Florida is fortunate enough to win.

Coach Zook and the rest of the staff did a fine job coming off of the last off week to prepare for (and defeat) a very good team. It will be interesting to see what they can develop for the in-state rival. It's been way too long since the last win there, in the rain in 1986. Against my better judgment, which says stick with the historical trend until proven otherwise, I'm picking the Gators to break the streak, and predicting…Florida 24, F$U 20

**Visor Flings, Week 13:**
**F$U 31, UF 14**

I've waited a few days before trying to review what was a very disappointing effort, but it's still difficult to understand how the team seemed to regress after finally getting on a roll. Perhaps the week off was a bad thing, letting too much emotion affect the performance. Perhaps a false sense of security settled in, given the troubles in Tallahassee leading up to the game. No matter – every unit was outplayed Saturday night, especially the defense.

Despite some heavy criticism leveled at the offense, I was very impressed with the ability to move the ball the entire first half, and even on the TD drive in the third quarter. Rex was sharp, the O-line seemed to pass block better than the entire season, and Earnest Graham finally looked healthy, breaking off some big, tough runs. What defined this game (and really, the entire season) was poor red-zone efficiency. I stated before the season started that what would really define the success (or lack thereof) for this offense would be whether it maintained a high touchdown percentage. Unfortunately, the 2002 Gator offense receives a poor grade, as turnovers, poor blocking, questionable play-calling, and a general lack of execution at most positions (QB included) undermined any good work done between the 20's.

Too bad the game didn't remain manageable on the scoreboard, because the run blocking was generally effective. Of course, the drops by Aaron Walker didn't help, but he's been plagued by them the past two years. And Mo Mitchell may have run out of second chances, especially ending drives with two personal foul calls. I don't like saying it, but perhaps his dismissal from the team would be addition by subtraction. Of course, given the extremely thin depth on the O-line, maybe he'll have spring practice as a final chance to turn his career around. The receivers played okay, and O.J. Small seems to have secured more playing time for next season.

The defensive performance really disappointed me. It's hard to say the scheme wasn't effective, because it sure looked like the D-line was in the backfield a lot, and Rix was scrambling for his life many times. What angered me was the fact that, either because of poor discipline or too-slow adjustments, Rix wasn't contained inside the pocket, and we let him escape the rush to make positive yardage by the run or pass much too often. Also, it was painfully apparent that F$U's senior-laden O-line was too much for Florida to handle in the running game. Too bad Nick Maddox wasn’t allowed to dance around and get punished, as Jeff Bowden and Daryl Dickey realized that Leon Washington is a much better back, and he certainly showed it.

What else can be said about the special teams? How about abysmal, stunningly poor, ineffective? Zook and Odom deserve criticism for sticking with Martin on punts – if Leach's field goals are affected by pulling double-duty, tough. Field position was a huge factor in determining the outcome. Also, when is a kickoff or punt going to be returned for big yardage, injecting some life into the team? An incredibly poor unit all season, and there's no excuse except for poor coaching if this isn't rectified in 2003.

Without belaboring it much further, it was a bitter way to end the regular season, and even a solid effort in a bowl game can't erase the pain of this lackluster overall effort. At least the coaches will be hitting the recruiting trail hard, and have an extra few weeks of practice to evaluate players for next season. There will be a lot of analysis ahead, through Signing Day and spring practice, and plenty to talk about before 2003 begins.

**Visor Flings, Week 19:**
**Michigan 38, UF 30**

Once again the Gators emerge with all the better numbers in all the right columns, except for penalties and turnovers, and except for the most important one: points.

Grossman's accomplishment – 323 yards passing, his $17^{th}$ 300-yard game and a school record – must be acknowledged, and there's talk that he may declare for the NFL. Otherwise, not an uplifting night in the Outback Bowl.

I've waited a while to let the frustration wear off, but as far as that #$%@*ed up call at the end of the game is concerned, shame on Zaunbrecher for even thinking to call it, and shame on Zook for allowing it to happen anyway. He's the HEAD coach! Unbelievable!

Good luck to Rex in the NFL– a great Gator. Good or bad, this cleans the slate as far as the remaining image of the Head Ball Coach at Florida. He will be okay in the NFL, IF he can get into a decent coaching and scheme situation. Best wishes.

Ian Scott?!? Man, best wishes to him too, but, based on his optimism about his possible draft status, something is terribly wrong for him at Florida. Good Luck.

Clint Mitchell?!? Well, maybe we are lucky we even got some contribution out of him at all. He was always walking on the edge, so, unfortunately, maybe it's best he leaves. Just a thought: he may be better off trying outside linebacker or tight end in the NFL – no way he makes it as a defensive lineman. Good luck.

Yes, it's a relief in a way that this season is over, but I'll always get a bittersweet feeling about 2002, because this team still should have accomplished more. Seems like so many things were working against this group.

Good news about most of the other guys coming to their senses and returning for 2003. Yes, they were disappointed in the season and the bowl game, and yes, watching Willis McGahee's horrific injury was chilling, but they need to stay if they really want to improve their stock.

Zook had better hope Chris Leak's announcement starts a domino effect, because he will be up against it in 2003-2004, especially depth-wise. Hard to believe, but the Gators are really deficient, talent-wise, compared to what is required to be a consistent top-ten team. Antonio Cromartie and Andre Caldwell would certainly be well-served to choose Florida. Also, Zook and Charlie Strong need to start landing big-time talents on defense, and begin a steady pipeline on that side of the ball. If not, forget championships. Hope Ernie Sims and all those DL prospects decide to step up and be recognized as the group that put the Gators back on the road to greatness.

Man, what pressure Zook and his staff are under. Best wishes to all Gators for 2003!

Very Truly Yours,
The Visor

# 2003
# Sweating It Out

Okay, so these were some lean years, but not the leanest. The 2003 and 2004 seasons mirrored one another, with 8-5 records for Florida, but one only needed to go back to 1989 to find the Gators wrapping up the season at 7-5. And go back another ten years, and you'll see something amazing: a goose egg in the win column…that's right – zero victories.

But we don't want to go there. All of this is to say that whether we liked it or not, '02 through '04 would be the proverbial "rebuilding" years. If there was one thing Zook did with great success, it was recruiting. You may talk about players such as Ben Troupe (one of the Visor's favorites) and Ciatrick Fason, who did suffer through those seasons and were to a great extent under-utilized, but we have to acknowledge the fortuitous arrival of a player such as Chris Leak, who would become a four-year starter and would most certainly have his day in the sun.

Oddly enough, another freshman from the 2003 season stands out in my mind, for somewhat odd reasons: Channing Crowder, who now plays for the Miami Dolphins. Granted, he got into a bit of trouble with the law in the off-season, but he was also the one at the end of the season who led the charge in Gainesville when the Florida $tate players walked on the Gators' logo at the Swamp that year – a real no-no in college football tradition. Let's just say that Crowder and some of the other Florida guys reminded F$U of their manners.

To me, that incident showed that despite "the troubles," the old spark was still there. A loss here and there merely becomes a number, but honor is forever.

**Visor Flings, Week 1:**
**Preview and Predictions**

An outstanding class of recruits, and more of the same is needed for at least the next two years. This is probably the most balanced class, in terms of numbers at ALL positions, since 2000. Hopefully this way of thinking will continue in the future, precluding little or no depth (experienced or not) at any particular position.

It appears that Zook and his staff are willing to play some true freshmen this season, especially quarterback Chris Leak, wide receiver Andre Caldwell, wide receiver Chad Jackson, defensive lineman Marcus Thomas, and cornerback Demetrice Webb. Most of the attention will obviously be on Leak. The Gators will still need a ton of linemen on both sides of the ball the next few years.

The offense, and especially the defense, need to find cohesion, and quick. Ingle Martin was far ahead of the rest of the QBs in the Spring; actually I thought Patrick Dosh looked much more promising than Gavin Dickey. I think Dickey (barring injuries at QB) will be better suited to change positions by 2004. He is elusive, but has little accuracy, which will absolutely kill an offense. Leak's performance in fall practice is very encouraging so far, and has pretty much separated him and Martin from Dickey and Justin Midgett. The O-Line still needs a lot of work, especially after the starting five. The recent move of Max Starks to right guard will certainly shore up the middle, which killed the Gators last season. IF the combination of Randy Hand/Lance Butler at right tackle and Jonothan Colon/Ryan Carter/Tavares Washington (JC) at left tackle somehow plays adequately, this unit could carry the Gators farther than many expect this year. Running back looks solid with DeShawn Wynn seemingly in front, followed by Ran Carthon and Ciatrick Fason. Wynn could be the hammer Zaunbrecher needs to provide room for a promising WR corps to explode. Great senior leadership with Kelvin Kight and Carlos Perez (who seems fully recovered from his broken fibula), followed by a combination of athleticism and speed from the likes of Dallas Baker (finally this guy sees the field), Jemalle Cornelius, O.J. Small, Caldwell, Jackson, and others. Plus, we have a potential All-American candidate in tight end Ben Troupe, who has been underutilized his entire career. The defense has lots of athletic ability, but is sorely lacking in experience and is as yet unproven. You can hope all you want, but actual game experience will be the only way to get a real idea of what lies in store for this unit in 2003. The fall practice performance of Channing Crowder, Brian Crum, Taurean Charles, and Todd McCullough at linebacker, as well as Webb, Reynaldo Hill (JC), Keiwan Ratliff, and Matt Jackson at cornerback, seems to portend improved pass defense. However, the situation on the D-Line is worrisome. I don't care how good Kenny Parker looks right now; all the comments about “watching the number of reps” he sees tells me he should only be counted on for 20%-30% of the snaps per game. I am hearing good things about Darrell Lee and Bobby McCray, but until I see consistency in their play, I remain skeptical. Eric Holcombe (JC) and Mo Mitchell must provide bulk and run-stuffing ability, but are untested. Ronald Dowdy? Steven Harris? Ray McDonald? So many question marks, literally. Hope Charlie Strong can scheme a way to get something out of this group without sacrificing too much from the LBs and DBs.

Finally, the kicking game. Can place kicker Matt Leach regain his confidence for field goals? Is true freshman Eric Wilbur ready to be a consistent punter? Like the D-Line, only on-field performance will tell this tale. Thankfully, Matt Piotrowicz will provide two more years of great kickoffs and coverage. Here's hoping that the return game is put in the hands of true return-style players, and guys like Carthon can concentrate on the tailback position. Ratliff and Vernell Brown appear to be the punt return men right now, while Caldwell and Jackson lined up as kick returners in the latest scrimmage. It's always scary with true freshmen in the kicking game, but the Gators need to put the best players available at all positions.

Anyone who really follows what goes on in this state should not be surprised by anything related to T$U (not even F for Felony $tate University anymore – T for Teflon, since absolutely nothing sticks there). The athletic-director is an absolute joke, the administration is gutless, and I'm hoping against hope that their football fortunes continue to struggle. Anyone, if they want to, can wish them success, but I'll never be counted in that group. Winning football games is the only shallow thing that school can hang its hat on, and I certainly hope that changes soon. The new T$U President, Wetherell, sure is a pillar of integrity, continuing their now long-running Modus-Operandi of cover-up and undermining the legal system.

Gator player transgressions: looks like two of the three guys involved in an assault case (Crowder and Charles) are okay in terms of eligibility to play immediately, and perhaps Steven Harris will get a lesser punishment once the final story comes out. Mo Mitchell and Jonathan Colon are down to their final chances. Mo has a great opportunity to really help this team by playing at defensive lineman, and Colon can work to establish himself on the offensive line. They may be friends, but some "friends" either need to be avoided or changed.

The 2003 Season still looks to be a struggle to me, and another 8-4 record may be an accomplishment for this group. Even with a first season under their belts, Z & Z have a different cast to work with, the loss of a lot of solid senior leadership, and another difficult schedule, and a new defensive coordinator (again!). Here's hoping Leak and Martin perform as well as they exude leadership, that Charlie Strong develops the front seven like he's done at other schools, and that injuries aren't too numerous or at key positions (especially QB, OL, and DL). Already, LB Brian Crum could miss significant time with a stress fracture in his foot, while Colon and Anthony Guerrero have knee injuries that could keep them out a month or so. I know there are a lot of potential players at OL, DL, and LB, but I get nervous every time I look at that depth chart and the lack of quality experience. For now, I foresee road losses at Miami and LSU, and at least one loss between Arkansas (road), Georgia (Jax), Tennessee (home), and T$U (home). I'll forecast a cautiously optimistic 9-3 (6-2 SEC East) record, with little hope of better and a decent chance of worse.

**Visor Flings, Week 2:**
**UF 65, San Jose State 3**

A rather surprising outcome against the Spartans. Very few observers expected as complete a victory in all phases of the game; obviously the players were more focused than expected, given this week's opponent.

On offense, the running game was sluggish at times, and wasn't as dominant as predicted. Tavares Washington looked lost at times at left tackle, and needs to improve considerably. Ran Carthon ran hard, and displayed his usual burst of speed – too bad he doesn't have the ability to break tackles like Deshawn Wynn or Ciatrick Fason. Wynn really struggled, hopefully only due to first-game jitters. C-4 actually impressed me the most. Too bad – it appears Skyler Thornton will not be red-shirted this season to create separation with Fason and Wynn – puzzling.

Ingle Martin and Chris Leak played fairly well, although they both had some shaky moments. Martin HAS to step into all his throws to stop short-hopping receivers (two balls to Ben Troupe in particular). Leak took some unnecessary shots in the pocket because of some indecision, but that has to be expected in his first playing time. The receivers made some nice yardage, but it's time to open up the downfield play-calling in anticipation of the Miami Hurricanes.

On defense, the line surprised with its penetration and quickness to the ball. Kudos to Darrell Lee for containing the bootleg roll-outs, while Ray McDonald really looks like he could develop into a disruptive force. Hopefully Marcus Thomas won't get manhandled too badly this week; he needs to keep his confidence up, because he is the real deal. The snaps I watched Mo Mitchell on, he had no problem plugging the middle, and displayed a lot of exuberance. He and Kenny Parker will be up against it this week, and have to stand their ground to give the young linebackers a chance. Todd McCullough played well, although it's hard to gauge his performance (and, in reality, the entire defense's) on such an outmatched opponent. The return of Channing Crowder and Taurean Charles is a boost, but I'm afraid that, in their excitement, they will overrun some plays or bite on play-action too easily early on. That is not to downplay the hustle and solid open-field tackling, two items sorely missed last year.

The secondary was solid, as usual. Guss Scott showed again why he should be all-SEC with his all-around game. Johnny Lamar impressed me with his ability to cover a lot of the field to make tackles; his experience on special teams makes him the surest tackler of the group. It will be interesting to see if he can cover the big-time wide receivers, though, starting with Miami. I didn't notice a lot of Reynaldo Hill; looking for him to get his chance to shine this week.

The special teams, at least for one game, sure looked like a well-coached, cohesive bunch. The blocked punt (G. Scott, of course), fine punt returns by Keiwan Ratliff, solid kick coverage, and good kicking by Matt leach and Eric Wilbur all will certainly make the entire game much more manageable for the coaches.

As for the Miami game, this will be an entirely different scenario from game one, from the quality of the opponent to the venue (the Orange Bowl - that old house of thrills) to the talking between the teams before and during the game. It's obvious that Zaunbrecher will have to open up the playbook and try to stay ahead of Miami Defensive Coordinator Randy Shannon in the guessing game. Of course, all things will be better off if the running game can control things, but I'm not sold on this year's group just yet. Martin and Leak will have to spread the filed and hit some 15-yards-plus plays to keep things honest, or it will be a l-o-o-ong night. The raw ability is there on offense, but can it be transferred into a huge performance on the field this quickly? That's an iffy proposition.

Miami's defense has some real studs in Wilfork and Harris on the D-Line, and Vilma and Williams at linebacker. Plus, that secondary is obscene. Jennings and Rolle are solid cornerbacks, and strong safety Sykes is good, but free safety Sean Taylor is one of the top five players, at any position, in the country, and his presence holds it all together. Yes, the

Gators have loads of receiving talent and senior leadership, but it's hard to envision a consistent passing game against this bunch. Any big plays that are made almost will have to go the distance to help win the game.

Perhaps the hype and pressure will force Brock Berlin, who transferred to Miami from Florida, into some bad decisions, but the Gator defense had better generate its own pressure, or things could snowball downhill in the second half. Ryan Moore looks scary good, Winslow is double tough, and, while Gore is nowhere near to McGahee, that doesn't mean he isn't still a top running back. Having that ability spread around the entire offense is a hard thing to stop. If the 'Cane O-Line performs well, it probably won't matter how well the Gator offense plays.

It was obvious last season that even in a close fourth quarter game, Dorsey, McGahee, and the other guys now departed kept their composure and confidence in pulling out a win. This year's Miami group has to prove that, and I'd love to see Florida put them in that position. The 'Canes, though, still have quite a few players from the past two seasons that have been through that type of pressure, and, unfortunately, I feel they have a big mental edge over the Gators in that respect. Can Florida win? Of course! Can I predict a Gator victory? Of course! But will I predict a Gator victory? Unfortunately, not this year.

Resignedly: Miami 30 Florida 20

**Visor Flings, Week 3:**
**Miami 38, UF 33**

What a tough loss to take. What looked for so long like a possible watershed victory for Ron Zook and the Gators turned into a bitter disappointment.

The offense played at close to maximum efficiency for most of the game. Despite settling for a few field goals in the red zone, the O-Line was terrific, opening running lanes and providing mostly solid pass protection. The play of Martin, Leak, and even Dickey was excellent under the circumstances. Each QB did some of the things each is capable of very well, and all three maintained their composure nicely. That was the toughest running from Carthon in his career, while Wynn shook off his first-game jitters and showed his big-play ability. Ben Troupe showed why he should be the all-SEC tight end, and the receivers caught well and ran hard after the catch.

With the news that Martin suffered a concussion, it certainly explained the appearance of Dickey and the extended playing time for Leak. Yes, no points were scored when either was QB in the second half, but both still acquitted themselves well. Leak will improve as far as spreading the wealth to all the wide receivers; it's just natural that he looked for Dallas Baker a lot at the end. If Baker becomes a factor on routes not just down the sideline, he will be nearly unstoppable. It seems Zaunbrecher went into somewhat of a play-calling shell as far as passes downfield, and that, in retrospect, could have cost the Gators the victory. His greatest mistake, however, was not using his dominant O-Line on third-and-short in some critical situations, especially after UM scored to make it 33-18. A few first downs on the ensuing drive could have made a world of difference. Still, a very good game plan was in place and executed well.

Obviously, the defensive collapse after the score became 33-10 was the biggest disappointment. Yes, the D-Line and linebackers did not pressure Berlin the last 20 minutes of the game, and I'm afraid Charlie Strong and Zook have to shoulder a lot of that responsibility. Many are bemoaning the lack of pass rush and, while that was painfully true, the lack of a better secondary coverage (perhaps a Cover-2) certainly would have helped. Both of Kevin Beard's TD catches may have been prevented by a safety playing more of a centerfield responsibility. Or, just keep blitzing the hell out of Berlin. What's the worst that could happen? Twenty-eight points and 200-plus passing yards in 20 minutes to lose the game? Again, the coaches have to take a lot of the heat for this. The play of Crowder and Charles at linebacker was very encouraging, especially with the less-than-stellar play at that position the past few seasons. I really do believe McDonald and Lee at defensive ends were gassed the entire fourth quarter; they are too good to be controlled as easily as they were. I was disappointed that the DE (I think Lee) didn't stay at home on the fourth down bootleg to kill Miami's last drive. Maybe the coaches could have yelled an alert, or perhaps he should have known better. It was gratifying to see the defensive backs again make some big plays. Dixon and Ratliff were alert on their runbacks. It was interesting that Guss Scott's name wasn't mentioned a lot. Did he not blitz? Perhaps Miami schemed to take him away from a lot of the action? He was strangely quiet.

There's not much to say about the special team's kickoff coverage in the first quarter. They did not seem to stay in their lanes on the first runback, but give Devin Hester a lot of credit - he's a big-time playmaker. The second runback, by Taylor, was embarrassing. Terrible tackling, but the guy is a tremendous player - a man among boys on the college level. Leach looks very confident and controlled on his field goals, and Wilbur is a very good punter - his pooch kicking needs some work, but give the kid a chance to get some experience. Nothing wrong with the punt coverage so far, either.

Unfortunately for the Gators, the big lead put Berlin in his most comfortable position, throwing out of the shotgun on most downs. His play completely changed, and his confidence soared. I guess the old Head Ball Coach does know something about QBs, huh? If Miami can stop being so stubborn running its usual offense with the QB under center more often than not, look out. F$U may be the only thing between them and the Sugar Bowl.

This week's game against FAMU will probably have some sloppy moments, especially with us looking ahead to Tennessee (and don't believe the players aren't already thinking some about the Vols). I can't see any real problems with the Rattlers, although Coach Billy Joe has had a high-flying passing game the past few years, so it will be somewhat entertaining. The real key is, and everyone say it with me, hopefully no one gets seriously hurt.

By the way, why is Jarvis Moss losing his red-shirt year to play sparingly as a rush defensive end? And Joe Cohen will be wasted at fullback - that guy can help the team better at tight end, middle linebacker, or defensive tackle. Very questionable decisions...seems like very little return-on-investment.

Kreskin foresees: Florida 48 FAMU 14

**Visor Flings, Week 4:**
**UF 63, Florida A&M 3**

A workmanlike victory over the out-manned, overmatched Rattlers. Other than fine-tuning the running game somewhat for Tennessee, not much can be taken from this win.

The offense was efficient in pushing around the smallish FAMU D-Line, running the ball at will. The passing game did not get much work to help against the Vols.

The defensive front seven still had some lapses, exhibiting some poor tackling and less-than-100% hustle at times. Obviously a lot of that can be attributed to the letdown after the Miami game, and some of it to the youthfulness and inexperience of many players.

Now the real season starts – the quest for an East Division title and a berth in the SEC Championship Game. First up are the Volunteers at the Swamp, which will be perhaps the toughest challenge for the Gator defense this season. The Vols, once again, appear to be at their best employing a powerful running game, led by an experienced, quality O-line and two fine running backs in Jabari Davis and Cedric Houston. Based on Tennessee's last visit to the Swamp, in which Travis Stephens ran wild against a supposedly tough and experienced Gator front seven, you have to believe Phil Fulmer will rely heavily on that formula again. Helping the Vols is the fact that their QB is senior Casey Clausen, who has loads of big-game experience, as well as a win at Florida, under his belt.

It will be very interesting to see if Zook and Zaunbrecher will copy the usual Tennessee plan of using the running game and defense to dictate the outcome. Unfortunately, fat Phil has lots more experience using (and sticking with) that philosophy. If that strategy is employed at the start and things go poorly for the Gators, is the offense poised enough to keep their heads, especially if Z & Z change gears and go to the air? The O-line has acquitted itself very well so far, and Florida should have some success with the running game. It's critical that Martin and Leak efficiently handle the passing game, especially to wear down Tennessee's defense on what should be a hot day (a noon start, the first in a long while at the Swamp). This is definitely a game where all positions will need to play at a peak level to aid in winning, but at least the Miami game is evidence that this group can achieve it.

Charlie Strong's defense is really up against it, dealing with a tough running game. Even Miami had success, especially in the second half, running Frank Gore either off tackle or on sweeps. The combo of Davis and Houston is at least as good, and I don't see them being slowed down completely. Of course, in the Head Ball Coach's days, the Gators could negate that advantage by building up an early lead, but Zook has not shown a proclivity to follow that same philosophy. This may be the game that defines whether the secondary is indeed the strength of this unit or is overrated, especially if the Gators commit seven or eight men 'in the box' a majority of the time. The play of Mo Mitchell and Kenny Parker at defensive tackles is critical. Plus, the linebacking crew has to stay disciplined and fill the gaps properly. Hopefully they won't over commit to counter-action in their excitedness. Plus, the Vols kill teams with the naked QB bootleg on short yardage plays at critical times in a game. Will the defensive coaches have the ends ready for this?

You don't want to put too much emphasis on one game, but the outcome of Saturday's match-up could determine not just Florida's chances at a division title, but the mental makeup of the squad for the balance of the season. The main motivation many players have repeatedly stated this year is the lack of respect from the media and other teams. A 2-2 record after playing the Vols only will confirm what many in the media and most of the rest of the nation feel about this year's Gator team: that it is (1) too young, (2) not as well-coached under Ron Zook, and (3) missing the mystique built up during the Spurrier Era. Of course, those are harsh and rather unfair statements, but perception goes a long ways these days.

The makeup of this team is very interesting – a handful of strong senior leaders with a ton of young guys trying to make significant contributions. A loss to Tennessee could cause a schism between these two levels of experience, not to mention the wrath of the fans towards the coaches. Yes, a loss could really do some harm to the balance of the season.

The coaching staff is really under the gun to provide both a winning game plan and ensuring its execution against a quality opponent and with a bunch of youngsters on the roster that still haven't produced a big and meaningful win (I'm counting last year's win over Georgia as big but not that meaningful, given the fact the Puppies still won the division). There are so many variables going into this week's game that I believe it is very difficult to handicap and try to predict a winner. It's obvious most Gator fans don't really have a feel for what to expect against Tennessee, including myself. Maybe this is truly one time that the fans and the Swamp factor could be the difference in the outcome, because the Vols' strength vs. the Gators' weakness is a decided advantage for the visitors. This one could fall directly on the shoulders of either Martin or Leak to pull out a victory, for which, unfortunately, neither has the experience of yet.

Prediction: Florida 30 Tennessee 27

**Visor Flings, Week 5:**
**Tennessee 24, UF 10**

Disaster strikes! And to go down with such an anemic offensive performance! Just as John McKay once said, “Our team's execution? I'm all for it!”

This loss goes well beyond just X’s and O’s. There is something seriously wrong with the direction the offensive game planning and play-calling are going, and the culprit needs to look himself in the mirror and admit it. I just have to hope that whoever is really at the bottom of this mess either straightens himself out or goes, and soon!

The amazing thing about Saturday's outcome is that, no matter what kind of fan watched it, old or young, occasional or obsessed, emotional or calm, most of the same themes are common, and that, my friends, leaves little doubt that the sand in Ron Zook's Gator coaching hourglass has found a larger opening sooner than many could have imagined. Not counting, of course, those who railed against his hiring from the start.

Stunning, really, that it's come to this, so fast. I've not really made any statements about Zook's abilities, pro or con, choosing to judge the team's performance and his game-day decisions. Well, no more waiting. He's quite possibly out of a job after this year if he doesn't admit to himself he's not getting the job done. His strategy about the end of the first half was ill-conceived, and to say after the game that there are positives to be seen insults the intelligence of most fans. He needs to publicly take some blame for the results so far. Hey, perhaps he'll demote himself to Special Teams Coach and let Zaunbrecher and Strong actually coordinate their respective units the rest of the season. Maybe Spurrier knew exactly what he was doing demoting Zook back in '94.

There's really not much to say about the offensive ineptitude that already has been bitched about *ad nauseum*. It's painful to think of these kids going through such a tough time, a lot of which has been brought about by coaching. Maybe the only thing that will hold the young guys together is their inexperience and youth, because the older guys who played for the Head Ball Coach must be dying inside. It will take a tremendous effort by the coaches (and an unbelievable amount of leadership by some members of the team, whoever that may turn out to be) to prevent this season from unraveling. A dire and perhaps excessive statement? Perhaps. But a carefully thought-out one.

The defense does look pretty good, but even Charlie Strong has made some major gaffes as far as third-down defense is concerned, both against Miami and Tennessee. Hard to believe that the Vols could run the same 3rd-and-long slant or square-in pattern, and keep getting away with it. The coaches need to get the cornerbacks to start jumping a few routes occasionally. Plus, poor idea to remove Mo Mitchell as Tennessee got inside the 20 on their last TD drive. Marcus Thomas did play well, but Mo really blew up a lot of plays. His play so far is really encouraging.

This next statement needs to be taken in the proper context, because it's not just an emotional rant. This week's game against Kentucky starts the most critical stretch of Gator football since the pre-Spurrier days. It appears that Zook has realized that Chris Leak is the only guy that can save his job, and I'm ready to see the young guy take the reins the rest of the season to try and help salvage the pride (and bowl possibilities) of this team.

All this being said, there is no doubt that the Gators out-talent Kentucky easily. However, a lack of confidence and poor coaching can even out almost any playing field. I do think the team will be energized by Leak being the starting QB, but that only lasts so long. Only some first half TD drives will turn this team's thoughts in a positive direction. No room for error now. Put-up or shut-up time for everyone starts this Saturday.

The Visor envisions: Florida 34 Kentucky 20

**Visor Flings, Week 6:**
**UF 24, Kentucky 21**

From the edge of disaster to a big relief. Truly a maddening, surprising, and exciting effort. This win was very big for the sake of not just the players and coaches, but for the collective Gator Nation hopefully backing off on all the negativity pouring out after the Tennessee game (some of which I contributed to).

The offensive performance for most of the first half was indeed offensive, until some of the silly mistakes finally went away and some consistency was achieved. Chris Leak showed a lot of poise in fighting through the turnovers and penalties and leading the offense on its fourth quarter comeback. The running game was a major disappointment; both the blocking and the running were below par. Too many missed holes and impatient decisions by the running backs (especially DeShawn Wynn), and too much penetration allowed for the Kentucky defensive ends (Max Starks was especially at fault, but maybe his injury is more serious than anyone knows). Even the receivers were sloppy for much of the game, both in route-running and concentrating on the ball. Just a mediocre effort all around. However...the Gators still pulled out a big win.

What has to be especially frustrating for most Gator fans is knowing the playmaking ability of the running backs and wide receivers, yet not seeing those opportunities presented to them on a regular basis. Perhaps this will improve, using the momentum gained in the second half against the Wildcats. The position coaches, especially, need to get the skill guys playing at full speed all of the time.

The defensive effort was also frustrating, especially the third down conversions allowed. Granted, that whale Lorenzen contributed by completing some throws with guys hanging on him, but the fact that he of all people could break containment consistently and scramble for first downs shows a lack of discipline by the defensive ends. Fortunately, Darrell Lee and Bobby McCray made up for those lapses by constantly applying pressure on pass plays and getting some timely pressures and sacks. The play of Channing Crowder was fun to watch. That guy is a playmaker and a disruptive force...when he's healthy. Johnny Lamar continues to impress, both with his sure tackling and nose for the football. The secondary continues to be the best-performing defensive unit to date.

The special teams showed some cracks against Derek Abney, but I have to give them a partial pass, because that guy has been burning teams for four years now. Credit is due to Kentucky's return units. The Gators' coverage did improve in the second half. Eric Wilbur continues to impress me as one of the best punters I've seen in the country so far. He hit more long ones last Saturday, including a 50-plus yarder down to the UK five-yard line. Matt Leach did hook one of his field goal attempts, but he's hit all of his PATs and drilled a 42-yarder earlier. He really has come back from the depths of both confidence and performance from last season.

Now come the Rebels. Forget payback Just try continue to improve and hope that the backups for guys like Kenny Parker, Crowder, and Todd McCullough play well in their absence. I just want to see a solid win, and I hope to see a big passing day from Leak and the receivers against one of the poorest secondaries in Division 1-A. Yes, a big win would alleviate some of the bad taste from last year's debacle at Oxford, but this team needs to concern itself with building some momentum going in to back-to-back wars with LSU and Arkansas. With all of the developing concerns with the defensive front seven, the offense has to start playing at it's highest level to give the team it's best chance at winning those games. The defense will have to try and hold on until all the regulars return (hopefully by the Georgia game). The time starts now for the third down defense to stand up, and for generating turnovers to give the offense some opportunities on a shorter field.

In a way, the loss of the aforementioned defensive players is offset somewhat this week by the necessity of playing more nickel and dime coverages. Yes, The Rebels will probably try to hit some big runs more than usual, but Manning's performance is still the only real shot they have of winning. Unfortunately, it seems that program peaked against Florida last year (gee, seems to happen a lot). Boy, it's difficult to imagine either the running or passing game for the Gators not being successful this week, but, sad to say, that sometimes seems to be when the strangest things (and play calls) begin to happen. Perhaps those strange things and plays will finally start disappearing.

Prediction: Florida 38 Ole Miss 21

**Visor Flings, Week 7:**
**Ole Miss 20, UF 17**

As difficult as it may be, the season goes on, and I will try to concentrate on the upcoming opponent as opposed to the turmoil surrounding Ron Zook and the coaching staff. It's obvious to most at this point that something is seriously wrong with the preparation by this staff, and the lack of halftime adjustments. Can they keep the spirit up and get these players to compete?

The performance against Mississippi was both promising (first half and some big second half plays) and extremely disappointing. It's stunning that a team with some terrific playmakers and senior leadership can't find a way to put an opponent away. A lot of blame lies with the coaching philosophy, but the players themselves have to accept some blame for losing to the mediocre Rebels.

The lack of a consistent running game this far into the season points to both the lack of quality depth and, quite frankly, ineffective development of this unit by Joe Wickline. Some big plays were made, but too often the Rebel D-Line was able to get penetration with just a four-man rush. DeShawn Wynn seems to have lost either some confidence, aggresiveness, or both. Maybe he's hiding an injury. And these “games” being played with Ciatrick Fason are too mysterious. What's the problem there? Just explain it clearly to the fans and media. At least Ran Carthon is playing the best ball of his career right now.

Chris Leak and the passing game showed some promise once again, but the lack of halftime adjustments and poor management of personnel put him into some difficult situations with less chance of succeeding in the second half. He may be a great talent, but he's still learning his way by on-the-job training, and needs help from all those around him. I need to see more accountability shown by each player for his own performance. Ben Troupe once again showed why he will be playing in the NFL, but the wide receiver play is too inconsistent and passive. Why haven't seniors Perez and Kight been given a majority of the snaps? There also doesn't seem to be much development of the younger, inexperienced players like Caldwell, Baker, and Jackson (who should have been red-shirted). Vernell Brown seeing plays over these guys? Obviously they just aren't getting it to lose snaps to him.

The defense is pretty much a mess in the front seven right now. Mo Mitchell is great for run-stopping and in a 3-4 player rotation, but he can't do as much as he's being asked to do right now. The linebacker play was very poor. Yes, Farrior made an interception, but, other than Fleming, there is no consistent run-stopper and sure tackler. An especially frustrating thing is that the defensive backs are not allowed to take chances by jumping routes (like that damn slant route that EVERY team uses effectively each week) and getting to play some bump-and-run. Sure, you can give up some big plays that way, but you will also get more three-and-outs from the opponent's offense and get the defense off of the field more often.

The offense will have to carry the load this week, to dictate the flow of the game and to keep a weak defensive front seven off the field for long stretches. They must be aggressive on first down, mixing run and pass, and definitely need to score at least 24 points to give the team a chance at victory. On defense, it's time to load up against Mike Mauck and the Tigers on first down to try and force second- and third-and-long situations. Time for a risk-and-reward style on both sides of the ball for the rest of the season. That's the only way to make the big plays necessary to re-instill the confidence this team is sorely lacking right now. Yes, this is a good LSU team, but I don't see it being better than the 2001-2002 versions, and they can be beaten, even at home. The Puppies showed how to move the ball on offense, and lost the game only by self-destructing.

Unfortunately, until I see for myself from the coaching staff that they can actually install a game plan to achieve this, I can't forecast a Gator victory.

Sadly: LSU 31 Florida 20

**Visor Flings, Week 8:**
**UF 19, LSU 7**

The roller-coaster ride continues. Are the Gators at the top of another rise, ready to plummet? Tune in this week to find out.

An uplifting win against the Bengal Tigers, for all of the Gator players, coaches and fans. There could be signs that the team is starting to gel on both sides of the ball, and that the coaching staff is beginning to strategize better. Unfortunately, given the performance of both the players and coaches so far, one game doesn't signify any type of trend. This kind of performance must become more the norm to restore the confidence of all concerned.

The offense showed signs of diversity in its attack, but the inconsistent O-Line play has to improve to save Chris Leak's health and help this team win. The loss of Max Starks was felt somewhat in the pass protection, and Leak took a pounding, but his decision-making is improving, and his poise and toughness are without question. The play of the running backs was very good, especially Fason's return from the MIA list. He might get the bulk of the carries this week if Wynn's mysterious struggles continue and Carthon is slowed by his injury. The wide receiver play is impossible to figure right now, as Kight and Perez still don't get a majority of the snaps. I've pretty much given up on trying to understand the on-again-off-again involvement of the tight end

The defense rose to the occasion, and the bonus of the return of Crowder cannot be understated. The front seven can't make any more excuses, and must persevere despite any injury or depth concerns. The challenges are only going to increase the rest of the way. The play of the secondary was outstanding, and here's hoping that Coach Strong turns these guys loose to play aggressively the rest of the season. There's too much talent there to waste on mostly passive schemes.

A lot has been made of LSU taking the Gators lightly, but I'm not so sure that their players and fans weren't suckered into thinking they were that good after beating the Puppies. I think some selective memories might have kicked in (also known as Volsheimer's disease), especially when by rights they should have lost that game by 14-21 points. Too bad for them, huh? And, I'm really starting to think Saban might be in the Mack Brown group of coaches; he sure has lost a lot of big games at both Michigan St. and LSU, even with great recruiting classes. At least he's won a conference title, unlike that clown Brown (hey - that rhymes!).

On to the Razorbacks. Probably an even more physical bunch than LSU, and coming off a tough loss to Auburn (including some officiating controversy). Don't be fooled by their losing – Auburn is playing better, and Arkansas did move the ball on the ground well. That, once again, will be their modus operandi of attack, with perhaps a few deep balls thrown in by Matt Jones. Hopefully the coaches will employ a "spy" on him, perhaps Fleming or Crowder, because most of his big plays come when he's scrambling for extra time to throw or to take off downfield. The Hogs have a big-time running back in Cedric Cobbs and their usual hard-hitting defense to contend with.

However, Florida has a passing game dimension that Auburn is nowhere near – one that must be employed with effectiveness to give the Gators a chance to win. Both the O-line and D-line will have to at least earn a stalemate Saturday in order for the Florida skill players on both sides of the ball to make the difference. Perhaps playing on the road, after the embarrassing losses to Tennessee and Mississippi, was the only thing that could bring the team together with a common purpose and focus. Here's a shaky vote of confidence that this will continue.

Cautious prediction: Florida 23 Arkansas 20

**Visor Flings, Week 9:**
**UF 33, Arkansas 28**

Maybe this can be regarded as a trend after all. This game was really closer than it should have been.

The offense continues to take shape around the play of Leak and Ciatrick Fason. Overall protection for Leak was quite good, but the defensive line once again did not come up to the level of play they will need against the Bullpups in two weeks.

After an off week, the Gators will jump right back into the heart of their schedule. Georgia is certainly beatable, as they have had several close calls this season. Many people are attributing this to the "look-ahead" syndrome, but I'm not buying it. I believe Mark Richt when he says they are vulnerable right now. And I don't agree with all of the worshipping of the Puppies' talent, either, at least not on offense. There is NO WAY they approach last year's group. The defensive back seven is very good, but the D-Line and the O-Line don't measure up to last season. Florida should have the offensive ability to get some effective running and help put Chris Leak in advantageous down-and-distance situations. I don't expect David Greene to leave the pocket much, unless the game is in doubt in the 4th quarter. If he goes down, their season goes with it, especially with no experienced backup available after D.J. Shockley's knee surgery.

We'll see, but for now the Gators will have two much needed weeks to get ready for their annual sojourn to Jacksonville.

**Visor Flings, Week 10:**
**Off Week**

I'm looking forward to some hard running from all three Gator backs, and I can only hope that the added threat of the screen pass to them helps open up things downfield for Troupe and the wide receivers. Florida has to take some deep shots this week, each quarter. The opportunity is there to hit a few of these to lead to scores. Plus, the O-Line is healthy with Max Starks back at full strength, and the recent play of Randy Hand and Lance Butler is encouraging.

It's really incumbent on the Gator defense (and Coach Strong) to get after the QB and play the receivers aggressively, as much of Greene's game is based on timing. I don't fear his arm strength too much, either, so I hope to see some man-to-man coverage mixed into the schemes Saturday. The Puppy running game doesn't look overpowering, with no dominant back to rely on. This unit needs to play more of a risk-and-reward style this week to make some good things happen. A passive approach plays right into Georgia's offensive philosophy. Mo Mitchell and Marcus Thomas must play very well this week to stuff the run. I think Darrell Lee and Bobby McCray can get some pressure off the edges against the Puppy offensive tackles. A big game from Channing Crowder and Reid Fleming would bode well for Florida, also. The secondary seems to be improving, but Johnny Lamar will be the focus of a lot of passes this week. He needs to play up on the receivers more, or he will get eaten alive underneath. I don't expect too much activity in Kiewan Ratliff's area.

Of course, this Gator football team, unlike the past editions under the old Head Ball Coach, doesn't carry the swagger (or offensive philosophy and firepower, at least yet) to go in and take apart a weakened Georgia team. And the coaching decisions during the game are still suspect, so Richt can still pull out a win and end any SEC East hopes for Florida. It's fun to try and project what will happen from here on out, especially with the Vols struggling mightily at Alabama, but the Gators have once again put themselves in a position where they need outside help. Unfortunately, there are very few (except maybe the players themselves) that really believe Zook can pull it off this year. I do think, though, that the timing is right for the Gators to win this game and make things very interesting the rest of the way.

Visor Vision says: Florida 23 Georgia 20

**Visor Flings, Week 11:**
**UF 16, Georgia 13**

Gators beat Puppies...AGAIN!

Another fine win for this team, continuing a great turnaround from a 3-3 start and after spiraling down to a possible losing season. Once again, the offensive coaching staff (and perhaps the Head Coach) faltered, leaving the door open for Georgia to perhaps pull out the win. Incredibly poor and unimaginative play-calling inside the 10-yard line. No rollouts, no two or three-receiver formations to spread the defense out, no play-action passes, no sweeps. Nothing. Despite that, the Gators won a tough game against a weakened but dangerous opponent.

Chris Leak continues to keep the offense running somewhat smoothly, limiting turnovers and striking for big gains (225 yards on only 13 completions). It continues to be painful to watch guys like Perez and Kight turned into possession receivers who run screens, curls, and hitches, but that will apparently not change the rest of this season. The running game struggled until the fourth quarter, which continues to puzzle me. Perhaps the predictability of the play-calling on first and second down is the culprit, because I can't believe this O-Line and stable of running backs can't run for 120-plus yards each week. The pass protection was again solid, as I don't recall more than one sack, which came early in the game. It was obvious that Carthon wasn't 100%, and I'm disappointed that Wynn didn't get more touches, especially trying more sweeps, which were very effective when run. Ben Troupe once again showed his big-play ability to the nation, and it will be a crime if he isn't at least First-Team All-SEC and an Honorable Mention All-American.

The defense proved to be stingy when it counted most, inside the 20, and made a huge stand in the 4th quarter to limit the score to 13-13. I was not impressed by the play of the Puppy receivers, as they continue to drop passes. Greene played okay, but his arm strength prevents their passing attack from threatening deep, which has to hurt their chances against tougher opponents. The 200-plus rushing yards by Georgia were unexpected and somewhat troublesome. Farrior was no factor all game and was usually out of position or simply blown off the ball; sorry, but he won't be missed next year, as this position will definitely be upgraded. Fleming at least made some big plays in the red zone, while Crowder continues to prove that he, along with Leak, should be freshman All-Americans this year. Another big game by the secondary, as Ratliff continued his interception streak, while Scott and Dixon played big against the run. Of course, they had to with the poor LB play. Both guys were playing hurt in the fourth quarter, but hung in there when the situation was critical. A gutsy performance. Still – when will the linebackers and defensive backs learn how to stop the 15-yard slant route? This play has killed the Gators all season.

And congratulations are in order for Matt Leach, who has rebounded nicely from a horrific 2002. I'm glad I didn't see the last kick on TV, because that sucker hooked pretty hard before straightening out. His missed 47-yard attempt was solid, too – just bad luck. Yes, Wilbur had perhaps his poorest game to date, but no blocks, no 10 yard shanks, and a HUGE 60-yarder in the first quarter when the Gators were forced to punt from their own 20. Piotrowicz was solid, and the coverage was good. The only concern I still have is how the freshmen, especially Everett, continue to overrun the returner, when just by breaking down five yards from him will pretty much prevent a big return. But at least the special teams performance has improved dramatically from last season.

Florida is finally home again this week, against Vanderbilt. Hopefully the team will perform at least as well as the past three games away from the Swamp. Now is not the time to relax – this team is not so good as to sleepwalk through games. Hopefully they saw how other teams allowed themselves to fall behind at home, and how difficult it can be to come back. The Commodores are weak again this year, although I'm sure the coaches will point to their strong performance against Georgia to get the players' attention. Jay Cutler has done some nice things with the passing game this year, but the Gators have way too much for Vandy to overcome. Actually, this could be another typical ugly Vanderbilt game, especially given the conservative nature of Coach Zook. It would be nice for a change, however, to get a big early lead and let the backups (including Ingle Martin) get some snaps before the big games ahead.

Prediction: Florida 31 Vanderbilt 10

## Visor Flings, Week 12:
## UF 35, Vanderbilt 17

And indeed it was another typical ugly win over Vanderbilt. It's really a shame that the starters couldn't get more rest before a tough game at South Carolina, but that's been a rare occurrence the past 12 years.

The offense was really clicking the first half, with a good mix of run and pass. Funny how Troupe seems to get more open than Perez or Kight, and seems to get more deep opportunities. The completion to O.J. Small on the seam route was nice – too bad that isn't used more, either. The running game was strong, with all three backs having a good day. No worries about Carthon being gone in 2004, with Wynn and Fason around. It looked like Colon got a lot more reps, helping to develop some depth on the O-line.

The second-half performance should give Leak and the passing game something to concentrate on. He stared down both receivers on the interceptions, something that can't become habit. Some people are criticizing the pass call on 1st down after the lead was cut to 28-17, but I liked it a lot – just poor execution. Hope that doesn't put the coaches back into a shell.

The defense was okay, but certainly lacked the focus of recent weeks. A lot of missed tackles and arm tackling, and a surprising lack of a consistent pass rush. Hopefully this was a result of a vanilla scheme. However, a lot of the option, roll-out, and misdirection in the passing game is what you can expect from Lou Holtz and his linebacker that plays QB, Pinkins. It was especially nice to see Dixon actually hold on to a couple of interceptions, and for Ratliff to get that 8th one and take it to the house...AGAIN. It was also good to see Taurean Charles get some work at linebacker. That guy can be a big contributor next year, if he's not in trouble.

The Gators catch a big break if Summers actually does not play Saturday, but Turman is a load as well, and South Carolina has their usual huge O-Line, which will probably give Florida trouble. Obviously, the passing game for them is hit-or-miss, as it seems they hit the 20-plus yard completion or nothing. Once again, the formula of getting the lead in the first half on the road is crucial for this team, especially so against the Gamecocks, who do not have the comeback ability of a LSU or Arkansas.

This is definitely a weird team for Holtz this year. Some actual signs of a big-play offense, offset by some major meltdowns on defense. If they put it together for the Gators (and who would really be surprised at that?), it could be a tough road through Columbia. Right now, though, I'll go with the team that is actually showing more consistency, especially at QB.

As I see it: Florida 24 USC 20

**Visor Flings, Week 13:**
**UF 24, South Carolina 22**

I'd say Ciatrick Fason has truly proven himself to be a big-play guy. He was the difference against the Lamecocks, rushing for a career-high 190 yards and helping us to rally from a 16-7 halftime deficit.

Leak did not have his best game passing, but showed some cool when it counted with the touchdown run and then the short toss to Ben Troupe in the end zone, although Troupe dropping that sure touchdown pass two series later will not contribute to his All-American chances.

Everybody will remember Kiewan Ratlifff's interception near the end of the game, but this was probably one of his best overall performances so far this year. Wish I could say the same for our punt coverage. That long return by South Carolina's Donnings certainly does not bode well.

With it looking like the Gators are probably out of the running for the SEC championship, this weekend's game against the Criminoles will be the biggest for Florida this season. Of course, this is two years in a row that Florida has no one but themselves to blame for this scenario, one that I personally dislike tremendously.

Obviously, there's no reason to play things too close to the vest, and perhaps the coaching staff will open things up on offense to the fans' liking.

The Gators must throw more on first down than they have to date. Not every first down, mind you, but enough to keep the F$U defense guessing. All three running backs and Troupe should get some action on first down to loosen the defense up. Historically, the deep ball for the Gators has been effective in this game. Time for some pump-and-go, out-and-up, and post routes, and perhaps a little "trickeration" to liven things up. Perez, Kight, and Troupe have the size and strength to create physical mismatches in the secondary. Even Clemson as able to go over the top for some long gains, so the chances should be there for Leak.

All that being said about the passing game, it's still incumbent on the O-Line to use their size to establish some semblance of a running game. If the Gators can get a lineman or fullback on the smaller F$U linebackers, Fason, Wynn, and Carthon should be able to net 100-plus yards rushing to keep the defense from tiring early. Look for the blocking of Perez and Kight on the outside to help break some big runs. If Florida tries to "chuck-and suck" it down the field, they will get eaten alive.

Coach Strong can't be afraid to blitz Rix occasionally. If most ACC teams plus Miami can generate turnovers, then hopefully Florida can do the same. Right? Right?? And when the Gators don't blitz on passing downs, PLEASE GET BETTER DROPS FROM THE LINEBACKERS TO SLOW DOWN THE SLANT ROUTES THAT HAVE KILLED FLORIDA ALL SEASON! Unfortunately, I believe F$U will have success running the ball if they stick with it. Leon Washington appears to be the 2002-2005 version of little Ricky Williams of 1980-1982, for you older Gator fans. I'm not forgetting Greg Jones either, as he will simply run over any Gator linebacker except maybe Crowder. I don't expect to see much of Booker unless F$U is comfortably ahead. This is probably the key match-up if Florida has any real chance of winning, barring a slew of F$U turnovers. Possible, but after making Rix look like a Heisman candidate last year, I'm not counting on it.

Going only by the common opponent, Miami, it would appear that Florida has a real chance in this game. Of course, this is the same team that made Brock Berlin look like Dan Marino. The blueprint for beating the Criminoles was laid out by the 'Canes, though. Tough, consistent running; screen passes in the red zone; relentless pursuit of the QB. The Gators have shown they can do the first 2 things, but can they achieve the third to get the win?

Sorry, but the "Old Testament" in me is hoping that Dockett gets hit by a good crackback or blindside hit. The Gators have to establish the tone and flow of the action, tackle well, and punish any F$U ball carrier. I don't see the Gators winning the game without winning the turnover battle.

Will Florida and Ron Zook reverse last year's two losses to end the season? Going by the play of the Gators at home the past two seasons, this game will be a challenge. So much rides on the outcome: in-state recruiting momentum, quieting the Zook critics, re-establishing the mystique of the Swamp. This pick is definitely from the heart, not the head:

Florida 23 F$U 20

**Visor Flings, Week 14:**
**Florida State 38, UF 34**

Words can't describe how painful and bitter this "loss" is, given the deplorable officiating and the collapse of the defense on the last two F$U plays. It is way too simplistic and naive to just say, "All the Gators had to do was make a stop on 4th-and-14, and the rest of that crap wouldn't have mattered." That may be the public face being put on by Ron Zook and Jeremy Foley, but no one I know, including long-time and knowledgeable fans, as well as many neutral observers, is letting it go at that.

Yes, this is just one of tens of thousands rants, probably deemed silly, stupid, misguided, etc., by fans of other teams that hate the Gators or people that just don't really care about college football, and that's okay. I just so happen to care, along with uncounted others, and that's OK, too. I can't remember seeing players on the field so upset and demonstrative with the officials. Sure, the rivalry game environment is already a volatile emotional situation for 18-21 year-old kids, not to mention the fans and supposed "adults" that love this atmosphere and competition that get overly emotional, as well. But to be in the battle and to have great plays and tremendous hustle wiped away by not just bad, but egregious errors, MANY TIMES OVER, justified the outward demonstration of frustration.

As long as we're going down this emotional path of saying things you can't take back (nor will I ever, really), I LOVED the fact that Channing Crowder led the charge to get the Criminoles off of the logo at the center of the field. That crap has been cultivated by the permissive coaching staff and athletic department at F$U for years, and hopefully it takes an ugly incident led by pissed-off players to end that garbage.

I'll say this about the actual game-planning and performance of the Gators: the fact that really only two situations were questionable, those being (1) the play-calling on first and goal in the fourth quarter after getting a new set of downs and (2) the poor decision of sitting back on defense on 4th-and-14, points out how well the team and players did their jobs. Any big game magnifies certain situations and plays, and for only these two to stand out is a remarkably low number. The offense performed very well, considering they racked up 445 yards, 34 points and only punted twice. It's too bad that Fason was hobbled and Wynn didn't play, because the usual running back rotation has been very effective, and the passes to Fason and physical running by Wynn were missed, especially in the first half. Chris Leak was terrific, as was the real All-American tight end, Ben Troupe. The wide receivers made some tough catches and blocked well, and the O-Line was solid.

The defense did what it needed to do to get the win, generating "turnovers" to offset a weak effort by the D-Line. Anyone who understands the game and who isn't biased would agree that the "supposed" turnovers, if granted, especially those at the F$U 30- and 11-yard lines, were true momentum swings and game-changers. Once again, however, the fourth quarter defensive collapse happened, pointedly indicating that if Florida is to truly return to elite status, the defense has to be improved significantly, both in talent level and schemes. The Gators will not win championships again until they have multiple difference-makers on the D-Line and at LB. What a shame for Guss Scott, but he did the same thing against Tennessee, getting turned around and losing sight of a ball that he easily could have knocked down. Too bad that since the coaches decided to sit back on 4th-and-14, they didn't put Keiwan Ratliff in the middle of the field to look for that certain-to-come slant or square-in route that NEVER WAS DEFENDED PROPERLY ALL SEASON.

Special teams play was both good and bad. Leach had a fine game, but the kickoff coverage was horrible, AGAIN. Too many freshman and "soft" types on that unit. Zook needs more linebacker and safety types at least to improve the tackling and toughness.

At the risk of sounding contradictory to the theme of this writing, once everyone gets this off of their chests, the best thing to do is to try and move on to thinking about vigorously supporting the team in their bowl game, and hoping for another banner recruiting year. I do feel that the result of the F$U game won't necessarily affect recruiting right now, but another bowl loss could be more damning to Ron Zook's chances of "filling the cupboard" again.

I'm looking forward to a return trip to Tampa for the Outback Bowl, making it a little easier logistically on the coaching staff as they hit the recruiting trail even while making bowl game preparations. Nothing like a big win in the last game to start washing away the stench from Saturday.

Now that the coaching vacancy at Mississippi State has been filled, perhaps Charlie Strong will show some love back to Florida and stick around a while longer to help build the defense up to a higher level.

Congratulations are in order to the team and coaches for a tremendous effort. That feeling of working that hard and effectively must be maintained despite the terribly disappointing "loss." Now the key is to carry over that effort into the bowl game and then for the returning players for next season to continue the work ethic into spring practice.

**Visor Flings, Week 19:**
**Iowa 37, UF 17**

Difficult as it is to say, I guess the loss in the Outback Bowl puts a proper perspective on the season and indicates the work we have ahead of us in rebuilding.

Iowa tailback Fred Russell made our linebackers look as if they were standing still, and special teams play reeked. The best new of all, though, is that Chris Leak will be around for a long time. In an otherwise unremarkable game for us, he did break Danny Wuerffel's record for passing yardage in a single season, and the kid is only a freshman.

Incredible that Iowa went to the locker room at the half with a 14-point lead and did not score a touchdown on offense. These things are all symptomatic of some intrinsic problems…but I'll let the media continue to explore those issues.

Sure, Florida played a very tough schedule this season, with seven nationally ranked opponents, but this is life among the best programs, and it will continue to be so. I am confident that in the long run the Gators will benefit from it. In the meantime, it's time for some much needed rest for the Visor. Good luck, Coaches, with the recruiting season.

Very Truly Yours,
The Visor

# 2004
# Eight Is Enough, But Seven Sends You Packing

Eight. Word on the street at the start of the 2004 season was it would take eight wins for Zook to remain as head coach at UF. He won seven.

Such is the harshness of life in Division One. Now, for all that, the Gators have always played a notoriously tough schedule, and this season was no exception. Even the most diehard fan, after some reflux, can eventually swallow losses to teams such as Tennessee, LSU, and Georgia…but Mississippi State? In the aftermath of that game, in sports bars and dens up and down the Gator Nation, there seemed to be unanimity on one issue: Ron Zook's head was on the chopping block.

And off it went, midway through the season, and we looked blindly into the void. But other things were brewing in '04 the import of which we couldn't quite see clearly at the time: the ongoing development of Chris Leak at quarterback was obvious, but who knew what that would really mean for the very near future? And there were other names coming up more frequently, too – Dallas Baker and Andre Caldwell, for example – names we would ultimately hear a lot.

First all of us, including a lame-duck coach, would have to stagger through the remainder of the '04 season (and a resounding loss in the Peach Bowl) in anticipation of the announcement that Urban Meyer would become the next coach of the Florida Gators. So it was that a despairing nation would turn its lonely eyes on him.

**Visor Flings, Week 1:**
**Preview and Predictions**

The 2004 season begins Saturday with possibly as many doubts as there are certainties. The most-heard buzz around Florida football this year is whether Ron Zook will keep his job. Fans, writers, and national media have all chimed in with their opinions, the consensus being that eight wins will probably be enough to earn a fourth year as head coach. This observer has his own take on what he feels is necessary for Zook to keep his job, and it's not entirely based on wins and losses. I'll touch upon many themes in my analysis.

The coach receiving the most scrutiny is Zook, and rightly so. Outstanding recruiting, endless energy, and a positive rapport with the players are certainly important and desired. However, wins and perceived improvement in areas including position play and in-game decision-making will ultimately decide not just his fate, but that of the entire team.

Question marks still abound on both lines, the receiving corps is unproven, the secondary is very inexperienced, and the depth at linebacker is shockingly thin. Joe Wickline has to find serviceable play at both tackle positions, especially left tackle, to ensure Chris Leak survives the season as well as helping to establish a consistent passing game.

Larry Fedora steps into the role of offensive coordinator, with promises of more downfield passing and less-predictable play-calling. The youth of the wide receivers, the loss of Ben Troupe, and the still-unproven play of Jonathan Colon and others at left tackle could severely hamper this hoped-for explosiveness, though. A huge season is needed from Chris Leak and the running backs for the Gators to make national noise, but the offensive unit overall is not quite at that level yet.

Here's hoping that somehow Dwayne Dixon is allowed to help with the wide receivers more, because there has been a marked decline in performance from this group since his move to "Inside Receivers" coach. What a waste of coaching talent!

Dan Disch steps into a minefield in the secondary, replacing four experienced players, along with making the step up from the high school ranks (Jacksonville Ed White). Uncertainty abounds at cornerback, with no projected starter garnering raves in the off-season. The only starter with significant experience is Cory Bailey at safety. Athletic ability abounds, and the coaching staff is excited by more speed and size, but inexperience is critical, and this area is a major concern.

Bill Miller has potentially a nationally noteworthy group of starters at linebacker, but an incredible lack of quality depth, as well as the very likely possibility that some true freshmen will be counted on to spell the starters at times. Injuries in this unit would cripple the entire defense.

Red Anderson has the deepest unit at defensive line, with quality tackles and a large-enough group of ends to establish a nice rotation this fall. Once again, though, depth is a concern at tackle, and the ends are athletic and quick but have little experience.

Charlie Strong has a lot of question marks from which to provide some defensive answers. The past two seasons have seen a marked decline in the overall quality of the entire defense and an alarming trend of second-half collapses. Also, the tendency to lay back has killed the defense on third-down conversions. This is a coaching philosophy that will be closely watched all season. This unit does not appear to be of league title ability this year.

OFFENSE

The offense is without a doubt led by Chris Leak. His potential for an outstanding career was glimpsed last year when he was a true freshman, and that experience will pay dividends this fall as he leads a unit with the potential for more big plays than the past two seasons.

Running backs Ciatrick Fason and Deshawn Wynn are one of the best duos in the country. The receivers have potential, but are mostly unproven. O.J. Small is a senior leader with good hands, but the much-anticipated breakout of Dallas Baker, as well as some game-breaking plays from Andre Caldwell and perhaps Chad Jackson, are all needed to balance out the offense.

The offensive line is led by Mike Degory at center, with solid players such as Steve Rissler and Randy Hand, and veterans like Ronald Dowdy and Mo Mitchell. However, there are still many questions within this group. Dowdy and Mitchell have switched from defense, the tackle position is unsettled, and some players have not yet shown what was expected of them. Jonathan Colon, Lance Butler, and others must provide serviceable play, or the pre-season excitement could be dashed early.

The big-play ability of Ben Troupe will be sorely missed at tight end. David Kenner and Markell Thompson are expected to provide improved run-blocking, which may be critical if the play of the O-line is inconsistent.

## DEFENSE

This unit will very likely carry the hopes of the Gators challenging for a SEC title this year, and mostly for the wrong reasons. Legitimate worries exist about consistent run-stopping ability, quality and experienced depth at linebacker behind a potentially outstanding group of starters is limited, and the secondary is painfully inexperienced, despite the hope for improved athletic ability, speed, and size.

Defensive tackles Ray McDonald and Marcus Thomas are critical to the success of the defense. The ability is there, but these two must stay healthy and fresh throughout the season. Kenny Parker is the leading backup, but his back is a concern on every snap. Steven Harris, Joe Cohen, Tree Morant, and cast of thousands have potential at defensive end, but there is a bevy of unproven talent right now.

Channing Crowder and Earl Everett are the top-heavy duo leading the linebacker corps this fall. Todd McCollough must stay healthy, and a few players from a group that includes Taurean Charles (if eligible), Steven Harris, and promising freshmen Brandon Siler and Javier Estopinan must make contributions. A scarily thin group.

The secondary is led by senior Cory Bailey at safety, but has no returning starters or other significant experience. Jarvis Herring appears to have the other safety position for now. Terrence Holmes moves over from receiver and showed promise during spring practice. The cornerback situation is uncertain, though. Reynaldo Hill has not progressed as hoped, Dee Webb has ability but no real experience, and Vernell Brown is a hard worker but terribly undersized. Freshmen DaWayne Grace and Tony Joiner may see a lot of time this fall, good or bad. Not a comfortable situation for the coaching staff.

## SPECIAL TEAMS

The kicking situation is the best it's been under Ron Zook. Matt Piotrowicz is terrific at kickoffs and coverage, while Matt Leach really came into his own last year for field goals. If Eric Wilbur can find himself after a puzzling slump in the spring as punter, this could be one of the top units in the country.

Kickoff returns may be shared, but Andre Caldwell shows the potential to be a premier SEC returner. Vernell Brown should handle punt returns, and also has the quickness to make tacklers miss and help the field-position battle.

Coach Zook has to get solid kick coverage out of this unit. Last year was horrendous and contributed greatly to the losses to Miami and F$U. No more excuses.

## OUTLOOK

While there are more athletes and speed in this, Ron Zook's third season, too many questions concerning depth, experience, and top quality play at key positions such as offensive tackle, wide receiver, linebacker, and cornerback exist to project a huge season. The youth and inexperience usually leads to some great highs, but also some unexpected lows, and the current coaching staff still has not proven itself in critical game situations. Much of this will hopefully change and/or improve as the season progresses, but too many unknowns exist right now.

In addition, quality opponents such as defending national co-champion LSU, Georgia, and Tennessee provide stiff SEC competition, while the Gators have not won in Tallahassee since 1986 (unbelievable).

The 2004 season finally kicks off Saturday against Eastern Michigan. I'm sure the players are ready to finally stop hitting each other and burn off some anxiety. EMU comes off a 37-34 win last week and shows some signs of offense. Obviously, though, this is a major step up in competition and the Gators shouldn't be seriously threatened. The most important thing for Florida in this game is to shake off the rust, get in to a normal game week mode, and, most of all, NOT HAVE ANY MAJOR INJURIES! It's unfortunate that this will be little more than a glorified scrimmage, not the best preparation for the huge SEC opener in Knoxville next week. There are too many young and/or inexperienced players that will see significant time this year, and one game isn't enough experience to comfort the coaches or fans.

On offense, look for the Gators to work on the timing of the running game, which will be a huge factor against Tennessee next week. The O-line needs as much continuity as possible. I'm expecting a vanilla passing scheme, just keeping the chains moving when necessary, with maybe a long pass or two thrown in to give the Vols something to see on film.

The defense should have little problem showing it's superior athletic ability. Once again, you should see vanilla schemes in both rush and pass defense, so as not to tip off any special schemes developed for Tennessee. This should not be a competitive game, but the Gators actually need to put forth a solid effort to get ready for the big game next week.

My projection for the season: 8-3 overall, 6-2 SEC East. I see less possibility for better and more for worse, but I feel this to be a fair and somewhat optimistic guess.

Let the games begin! Heeeeeeeeere come the GATORS!!!

**Visor Flings, Week 2:**
**UF 49, Eastern Michigan 10**

Well, the Gators' one preseason scrimmage is over with, and now it's time to jump into the deep end of the pool. Tennessee should prove to be a major test this Saturday night. Once again the Vols have a solid running game to rely on, and both of their true freshman QBs are obviously talented. Even with the potential loss of Cedric Houston, the other running backs, especially Riggs and Davis, will be a load. It appears that both QBs will play just like last week, and I'm sure Phat Phil has scripted certain plays that best suit their respective abilities and are dependent upon the game situation. It is vitally important to Florida to dictate down-and-distance situations to these young players. It was obvious looking at UT's game plan against UNLV that both Vol QBs were given max-protection if at all possible, and threw safe passes such as fade patterns and go routes to minimize the chances for turnovers. UT has some big receivers that supply safe targets as well, but can they stretch the field? It will be very interesting to see how aggressive Charlie Strong calls defenses, to see if he takes a "prove it to me" approach to Tennessee's down field passing game. The X-factor is Schaeffer's running ability, and may require a linebacker, perhaps Everett or Crowder, to spy him while he's in the game. Hopefully it won't come to that, as the rest of Florida's defense isn't that talented and/or experienced yet to handle that scheme. If either offense has to become one-dimensional by passing, at least Florida enjoys a big advantage there.

Tennessee's defense looks solid, but unspectacular. Hmm…sort of like Florida's. A pretty good D-Line and linebackers, and a secondary with decent size and experience. It's year three, and it's time for Joe Wickline's O-Line to step up and lead the way for the Gators. Hopefully Larry Fedora will have a balanced game plan ready, with plenty of formations to keep UT guessing. Chris Leak will need to play much better than in the opener, where a lot of his passes seemed to sail high. I look for the running backs to be involved in the passing game this week after a vanilla approach last week. Fason and Wynn have to make plays to give Florida a chance, at least until the wide receivers show the ability to get open against a quality defense and make big plays of their own. Perhaps the tight ends will get a few throws early to try and loosen up the Vols defense and prevent what happened last year, as they dared the Gators to stretch the field. That was a bitter pill to swallow for all Gator fans after enjoying how the old Head Ball Coach dictated to all opponents.

Is this young Gator team ready for a tough early-season road game? History, in terms of Ron Zook's first two years, says no. I'm hard-pressed to see where the playmaking ability can turn the game Florida's way, especially defensively. The Gators must exploit the inexperience of Tennessee's QBs, and the Gator running game must come up huge, or it will be another disappointing early loss. Right now, I just don't see that happening.

Realistically: Tennessee 27, Florida 20

**Visor Flings, Week 3:**
**Tennessee 30, UF 28**

Fool me once (Miami 2003), shame on you. Fool me twice (Arkansas 2003), shame on me. Fool me three times (F$U 2003), just shameful. Fool me again (Tennessee 2004), and I call BS!

If Zook can't see it for himself, Foley and Bernie will have to do it for him. It's stunning to see how lost guys like Everett, Bailey, and Webb look on defense. When guys play like that, you have to just turn them loose. Less thinking, more attacking. Period.

Charlie Strong is going to lose whatever reputation he had as a rising star. Plummeting meteor is more accurate right now.

Congrats to Terrence Holmes, who did actually contribute defensively.

It's terrible to start living in the past, but can you imagine what Spurrier would have done with Chris Leak and these receivers? And what he would have done to UT's defense? Blowout city!

Is it too early to start a list of potential new head coaches?
In no particular order:
Steve Spurrier (duh!)
Bob Stoops (duh! unlikely, but a man can wish sometimes)
Jeff Tedford (still don't know if he can assemble a defensive staff though)
Randy Shannon (dark horse with no head coaching experience, but, damn it, he can assemble a defense)
Urban Meyer (talk about a cool offense and disciplined team)

Third down and three. Hmm...eight guys in the box...how about something original, like a QB bootleg at least to give Leak a chance to win the game? Nope. Dive play.

Yes, another brutal call by the official looking at both Dallas Baker and the UT cornerback. Doesn't matter. Fifteen yards closer to a miracle, and the clock stops.

And the coup de grace...Ron Zook and Charlie Strong are made someone's bitches again by sitting back and letting a true freshman pick them apart...over the middle...again....and again...and again...

Well, a lot of high rollers in the Booster Club will start the buyout fund this week. Zook has zero room for error now. The Gators have to win eight of their last nine to save his ass as far as I'm concerned. In the tiny, fan-crazed world of Gator football, this really is a tragedy.

Great job by Leak, good running by Fason, okay running by Wynn, nice possession receiving by Small. Some young wide receivers made some plays...finally.

Lousy defense. You know what? The coaches do deserve the blame, but Florida has practically no playmaking ability on defense. When will a scheme be established to help try and help these guys out? Something. Anything! Hey! Maybe Zook can get this "corrected." Maybe this team will improve after this. Prove it to me...especially the coaches.

Anyone (are you listening Ron? Or is there too much "noise in the machine"?) who says the 99% of fans comments since Saturday night are wrong can stick it! We aren't stupid, no matter what some coaches and analysts say about over-zealous fans. This many people can't be wrong, can they? I don't think so.

What a crying shame that our fans are now suffering from Ray Goof syndrome! What a crime. Please find us a head coach that understands the immediacy of the moment and how critical EACH AND EVERY GAME is in a college season. Sounds like more of that NFL (No Fun League) Kool-aid. Let me tell you something. If lead assistant coaches aren't at least suggesting something to give Chris Leak a chance to win the game (Fedora), or trying to pressure a true freshman QB (Strong), then they shouldn't have the job. Ergo, if they DID make those suggestions and they fell on deaf ears (Zook), then he should be gone. Period. What is this great fear that is gripping the coaching staff? It has to start at the top. This is sickening.

By the way, the O-Line looked good, and I pray they are that good, but I still think the UT defense sucks worse than Florida's right now. No way UT comes close to running the table. No way! Looks like UGA vs. Auburn/LSU in Atlanta, unless there are a rash of injuries to those teams.

If the D-Line can't apply pressure right now, try actually doing something about it! Time to put Mo (as some others have suggested) back at tackle and move McDonald to end. He's the only interior guy actually getting some penetration. Marcus Thomas is getting better, but isn't there yet. Maybe he's out of position as well. If this is an attempt to copy Miami's (the 'Canes, not the sorry Dolphins) concept, it isn't working. Actually, not much is. I hope (there's that word again) that Red Anderson can improve this group. He's had some good ones before -- maybe he can get something out of this unit. Yeah, I don't know what the hell I'm talking about, right? Just another stupid fan.

Zook says, "we lost as a team." Bullshit! The coaches didn't give the players every chance to win. Take the blame, coach, and do something to really, REALLY, "correct it."

Oh, yeah. There is a game this Saturday, against Kentucky. Another crappy Wildcat team, another Gator win. Not much to say about this one. As far as predictions go, starting this week I will have two for each Florida game: one for what really should happen; one for what Zook will allow to happen.

Florida 45, Kentucky 14
(Visor prediction - what should happen)
Florida 31, Kentucky 17
(Zook prediction - what will happen)

**Visor Flings, Week 4:**
**UF 20, Kentucky 3**

Another desultory effort against Kentucky, which has usually been the case for the last 20 years except for blowouts under Spurrier. It seemed that the hangover from the debacle at Tennessee was still being felt, and the outcome was unfortunately not decided until late on the scoreboard.

There still seem to be a lot of timing problems between Leak and his receivers. I'm not very impressed with the route-running, and there are still too many pass plays where two receivers are in the same area, drawing extra defenders. It was actually the poorest performance by Leak since the second half of last year's Mississippi game. He is still floating some passes with too much touch, and was late a handful of times delivering the ball on corner and seam routes.

The running game was solid, given the opponent. Fason ran well and hard, and it was nice to get a short look at Thornton. He definitely has quickness and appears to have some strength in that smaller frame. The real question was, "Where was DeShawn Wynn?" Is he in Zook's doghouse again? If he's just feeling down because Zook has named C-4 the clear starter, he needs to change his attitude. He could be thrust into a starting role himself because of injury, and has to be ready.

The defense played very hard, and the tackling seems to be improving. Once again, there was a slow start in the first quarter followed by improved play thereafter. Jerome Mincey and Travis Harris made some plays on the outside. Brandon Siler showed a glimpse of what athletic ability and speed he brings to the table. However, still a sub par effort from the down linemen, with little penetration. Perhaps it was the UK scheme with a running QB, but it is worrisome.

The secondary is still playing soft, and Boyd would have had much more yardage if he were more accurate of a passer. Still a lot of opponent's wide receivers running loose in space, with no one seemingly covering them. Troubling.

This week the competition stiffens with the return of Houston Nutt's Arkansas team to the Swamp. Despite the loss of 17 starters from last year's club, they have been very competitive so far this year, and gave Texas all they wanted two weeks ago. Matt Jones is a slippery runner and scrambler, and their pass offense is much-improved from last year, which could be a big worry for the Gators. Nutt still wants to run the ball first, but seems to have adapted to his personnel, which is the sign of a very good coach. The Razorbacks' best defender is defensive end Huckaby, who reminds me a lot of Clint Mitchell from a few seasons back. High motor, relentless, good pass rusher.

Florida has more firepower overall, and more balance on offense. This will be tested against Arkansas, and the continued solid performance of Fason and Co. should determine this week's outcome.

Unfortunately, Zook seems to have no clue as how to put a decent team away in the Swamp, and until I see proof of that changing, look for another too-close-for-comfort fourth quarter game.

Florida 31, Arkansas 17
(Visor prediction - what should happen)
Florida 27, Arkansas 24
(Zook prediction - what will happen)

**Visor Flings, Week 5:**
**UF 45, Arkansas 30**

Great performance by Leak and the receivers against Arkansas. Better throws, better timing good runs after the catch. However, there are still timing issues, especially on routes run near the sideline, and I'm still unimpressed with how the receivers work to get open if Leak has to scramble. Believe me, he will be scrambling some this week against LSU.

The O-Line did a pretty good job of picking up blitzes, but this was not a vintage Razorback defense, especially because of their inexperienced secondary. Big step up in competition this week, despite the results in Athens.

Another puzzling performance by the defense. They did a good job of containing Jones when he tried to scramble on passing downs, but when he ran run/pass option plays, they were terrible. Some of the credit for that does go to Jones, because he is one slippery customer. But the pursuit, angles, and tackling were shoddy in the second half. If Houston Nutt had turned Matt Jones loose the entire game instead of playing it safe to first half, this could have been even uglier.

Looks like Herring and Holmes are the best safeties by far. Bailey just doesn't seem to have the knack for coverage. Dee Webb is a good tackler, and his coverage is improving. Reynaldo Hill's performance is still very shaky; he never seems to cover anyone closely. Nice interception, but after the outcome was decided.

The coaching staff as a total group still gets no higher than a C+. When will this team put together a complete performance for four quarters? Still too many shaky moments, and NO KILLER INSTINCT. It's just doesn't seem to be in Zook's of Strong's make-up. Hope I'm proven wrong, but I'm getting tired of beating my head against that wall...seems as if is the wall is winning.

A lot of people are going to take LSU more lightly than they should this week, and that's a big mistake. This team has had its pride hurt, and that spells danger. There is too much talent on the Tigers for them not to bounce back, and Florida had better be ready for an angry, inspired effort. Just thinking that being in the Swamp will make the difference would be misguided, especially given the Gators' penchant for not putting teams away under Zook's watch -- home or away.

Nick Saban has two QBs who are mobile, and I'm afraid he might do the smart thing and let them run a scramble offense like Matt Jones. I think at this point that it's obvious that

JeMarcus Russell should be the starter, and he could pose problems for the Gator defense. They will need to play smart as far as rush lanes are concerned. If they can get him to throw while being pressured, he will throw some passes up for grabs.

Hopefully Skyler Green is still not 100%. I think that fact has been lost on a lot of analysts this year. He would have helped both QBs out immensely.

Despite the 45 points, LSU's defense was victimized only by one type pf play, really – the long fade route against man-to-man coverage. Don't look for their aggressive defense and man-to-man coverage to change. Leak and the receivers will be severely challenged this week, and have to play perhaps their best game of the season so far to get a win.

Finally, I'm afraid that LSU's QBs will be given enough time by a poor pass rush and soft coverage to make some plays. I hope that changes, but I foresee a very close game in doubt deep into the fourth quarter.

Visor Vision: Florida 20, LSU 16

**Visor Flings, Week 5:**
**LSU 24, UF 21**

The Day After the Day After Tomorrow. Nothing changes. I have the unfortunate experience of having been on the sidelines during the Spurrier years and now wondering if it's "Back To The Future." Lots of movie references... Then again, "Panic Room" could apply, huh? I have to tell you something – when it got to 14-0, I said to myself, "LSU has us right where they want us." And they did. What a &#*!... travesty!

It's humiliating to look at the opponent's fans mocking you in your own house, over and over, knowing the head coach is the main reason this is happening. I haven't watched any replays this year, and refuse to listen to Zook's show or post-game comments any more. Why, when you can read them from early in 2002 and know what was said? This is such a critical juncture for the Gator football program. It can slip into years of mediocrity, with players turned off from coming to Gainesville in the future and talented coaches seeing what a difficult environment is being cultivated.

There is one obvious choice to lead the program back from the brink of the abyss. Shame on Foley and Machen if they don't make that choice. Really – shame on them! Of course, if he really wants to. I have to believe, knowing what a true Gator Spurrier is, that the current state of affairs is killing him. I really think that he is planning on coming back to the college game in 2005, with the Dolphin job a very slight chance. Actually, I think that he probably believed that the Florida job was unlikely, but now with Zook's continued very public failures, he really could come back to Gainesville once more. I can only hope, because The Head Ball Coach is truly a unique talent with his own style, and once again may be the only person to unite the Gator Nation, which is starting to fracture as far as football is concerned. Of course, I could be wrong.

Disinterest is the worst thing that can happen, and it's already starting. Coming a close second is squandering the potential of tremendous talent. I really feel Chris Leak's struggles are from regressing as the season goes on, and can only hope and pray that a real QB coach like Spurrier can transform him into what everyone, but especially Chris himself, wants and expects. Two years could be enough to turn the results back to where they should be for him and the entire team. What a shame if it doesn't happen.

If Spurrier doesn't return, then Stoops has to be Option One. I don't care what the backroom politics were that kept him in Oklahoma in 2002. Foley has to up the ante and make a bold stroke, and quit backing down from taking a stand – public or private. You don't think a lot of fans and alumni still seethe with losing Stoops, the Dockett affair, etc.?

Tedford could be a possibility. His background is very interesting – a tremendously difficult and humbling childhood and early adulthood, which he's risen above quite nicely. Situations a lot of recruits can share and understand.

Other than those two, it's probably someone who hasn't been discussed, but hopefully shows a real penchant for coaching to win and has the proper experience.

As far as the game is concerned, folks, that was one real beating administered by LSU, and, really, they were the far better team that night, especially for the last 50 minutes. Other than two bad throws by JeMarcus Russell (whose performance surprised me, as I thought he was the proper choice to go with by Saban), the Gators were whipped on offense and defense, badly.

The defense is not close to championship caliber, and people need to realize it. The talent is okay in places, but the D-Line is still two ends playing tackle, the linebackers out of position on many pass plays, and a secondary that, while it showed some big-play capability last night, is being held back by youth and conservative coaching. Dee Webb is really starting to come on; Hill is physical enough, but still needs to improve his cover skills; Herring and Holmes look pretty good but still lack consistency; and poor Cory Bailey is still out of position too often, especially on the 15-yard slants and square-ins, which Charlie Strong hasn't stopped in two years.

Those guys played pretty heroically, knowing that the offense was going nowhere, but were physically manhandled the entire second half and finally collapsed at the end. Tragic, really, but all too predictable with Zook and Strong.

The offense has gone backwards since the second quarter of the Arkansas game. Zook gets the blame for second half of that game – all the offensive coaches get a D grade for the LSU effort. The only reason it isn't an F is that LSU does have a very good defense, despite what a lot of fans may think, with a head coach in Saban that does know defense – not like Zook, apparently. Unfortunately, just another painfully obvious reason why a guy like Spurrier and his offense are so unique, fun, and sorely missed. So much for those who complained about his "poor running game." Those people don't appreciate what they had, but I think that iceberg has finally started to melt as well, huh?

One complaint is not going with the one horse that was running, and that was C-4. Fason had a too-small workload, especially from the middle of the second quarter on. Where was he on those two 3rd-and-4 or -5 calls late in the third quarter, when another field goal in either drive would have probably guaranteed overtime? The other area that needs work is that the wide receivers need better coaching on how to work loose into open areas when the QB can't hit the first option or has to scramble and improvise.

Oh yeah, I have to take Chris to task for not toughing out a first down on his last scramble. Yes, another case of the coaches probably telling him not to set himself up for a big hit, but he really wouldn't have had to in this instance – just cut inside to get across the 13-yard line and get a fresh set of downs. I think he would agree, especially after seeing the tapes today.

Well, enjoy the Kool-Aid the rest of 2004. If the players can rally after such a devastating loss, they still could upset Georgia or F$U. It kills me to say this, but I'm getting the feeling that a big loss to the Puppies is on the horizon, and if that happens, every last vestige of the Spurrier Era will have been torn down. Maybe that's what it will take to rebuild, a complete demolition. It's stunning, really, to think it's come to this. Disheartening, too.

Oh yeah, there is a game Saturday. Poor team; probably a Gator blowout. But, then again, that's the pattern, isn't it? Not much else to say.

Common sense would say: Florida 48, Middle Tennessee St. 17

**Visor Flings, Week 6:**
**UF 52, Middle Tennessee State 16**

Hard to gauge much from this game, except that the Visor's predictions are getting more and more accurate. I guess that ll those years on the sidelines are paying off. Overall, a nice display of the Gators offense old-school. Now if we an only play like this against the big guns.

Next week at Mississippi State should be another good warm-up for the Pups, although the trip to Starkville is always a little unsettling.

Prediction: Florida 35, Mississippi State 3

**Visor Flings, Week 7:**
**Mississippi State 38, UF 31**

I will address the coaching situation at Florida a little later on in this column.

What an embarrassing effort, especially by the defense. The kind that can get a coach fired. Oh, yeah – that already happened.

What can be said? A lack of intensity, tackling, and effective schemes from the defense. Against the LOWEST-SCORING offense in Division 1-A. If that isn't a damning indictment of the coaching staff, nothing is.

The offense was pretty good, but still suffered lapses in concentration, especially on the O-Line. Leak was scrambling way too often. C-4 and Wynn looked very good running and receiving. It's a shame that that a combination of the wind and Leak having to throw on the run led to 2 or 3 under throws on sure TDs that would have iced this one early. The wide receivers played well for the most part.

Talk about highs and lows on special teams. Leach makes a 50-yarder into the wind, and MSU gets a 74-yard punt return TD. Awful.

It's too disturbing to address that game any further. It was all there on TV for everyone to see for themselves.

On to the Puppies. There is practically no way to foresee how players and coaches form both teams will react to the current emotional firestorm. Georgia has a ton of reasons to turn around the 1-13 record since 1990. The Gator players have reasons to play for the coaches and themselves beyond the usual ones. What a mess.

Mark Richt has a team almost as complete as his 2002 squad. Solid, balanced offense; attacking defense led by Pollack, Thurman, Jones, and Blue; adequate special teams. Punt returns have been the only consistent weakness for Georgia, as they have yet to find a dependable return man.

Georgia's running game is very good right now; however, Danny Ware may not be at full strength or have his carries limited. That would help the Gator defense, which is defenseless right now. Fred Gibson and Tony Brown have been a nice receiver combo this year. Gibson has actually stayed healthy this year. The Florida secondary must play physical with him, making him pay after the catch to try and throw off his concentration. David Greene has not been as consistent this season, and that could be a ray of hope. However, the defense has to find a way to pressure him, or it will be another long, miserable day.

Florida's offense should find some success during the game, but must get decent yardage from C-4 and Wynn to give Leak a chance to hit some big pass plays. Fedora's play-calling must challenge Georgia down the field to open up all possible avenues. The Puppies have a load of experienced defenders that will be hard to score against.

The Puppies have plenty of motivation looking at that 1-13 record to help them concentrate on the job at hand and put aside the situation at Florida. Can the Gator players focus completely on this game? Will the Florida coaches on defense turn loose all sorts of blitzes, let the DBs actually play some man-to-man, and devise an aggressive scheme for the entire game? Please, Gator coaches, don't hold anything back.

As hopeful as I could possibly be, I don't see that being enough to sustain for four quarters.

Dead Man Coaching…and correcting, and looking at film, and....looking for a new job after Thanksgiving. Amazing that such a dark hour for the program can do two things: bring out so much anger and frustration, but also show that fans care and pretty much share a consensus of opinion.

I suppose that the video played before the Gators run out of the tunnel at the Swamp should be shelved the rest of the season – no need to look at the opposing fans laughing out loud at it.

Looks like public opinion has it narrowed down to 4 candidates: SOS (Spurrier), Stoops, Meyer, and Tedford. Right now, I'm leaning towards the real HBC, because of the damage control his returning would help. Not just damage to the fan base, but to the confidence of a lot of good young players that really can win given the leadership they need. I still think guys like Degory, Fason, and Crowder would return for him.

Stoops is a very close number two, for many obvious reasons. The only drawback there is waiting for OU to finish their season after Jan. 1, while recruiting suffers.

Is Urban a myth or legend? We may find out around Dec. 1, if Foley swoops in to try and pry him away before their bowl game, which certainly looks like it will be a lot closer to Jan. 1 than for the Gators (if at all).

Tedford could be in the mix, especially if Cal wins out and possibly goes to the Rose Bowl. Unless the Urban scenario described above plays out.

Unfortunately, unless SOS was to come back soon, it appears Florida will have to suffer through the throes of very public discussion and speculation until after the F$U game.

If Spurrier was somehow to come back before the season ended, it would give him a great amount of time to evaluate his players and talent level for what he wants to do, sort of like the extra time coaches say they like to have before a bowl game. It doesn't look like there will be much of that this year right now.

And what a cattle prod to the ass of every Gator opponent's coaches and fans! Once again, for those who so short-sightedly either dismissed or criticized his Gator teams from 1997-2001, let's review:

Wins by year -- 10, 10, 9, 10, 10
SEC Championship Games -- 1999, 2000
SEC Titles -- 2000
BCS bowl games -- 1998, 2000, 2001 (with two Citrus Bowls in the "bad" years)
Bowl Record -- 3 and 2

He really fell off the end of the earth, huh? Defenses must have figured out his offense......NOT! How many other teams had that kind of success over those same five seasons? Maybe five?

The only thing that may swing the balances to Stoops would be for his defensive prowess, which the Gators have NONE of. What a travesty! Maybe some posters have it right on how this defensive staff was assembled. Pretty shaky stuff, to be kind.
Funny, Zook's supposed strengths (defense, special teams) have cost him the most. What does that say, in summary?

I'm writing this now as much for myself as anything. Kind of a self-analysis, to see how my initial reactions compare to what really happens after a new coach is hired. Probably will give me (and others) a reason to laugh at myself, but, so what?

1) Coaches to keep -- Fedora (RBs); Locksley (Recruiting Coordinator); Dixon (WRs - where he belongs).
2) Coaches on the fence -- Miller (LBs); Wickline (OL), Anderson (DL). I think Anderson is working with guys who just aren't DTs.
3) Coaches who are gone -- the rest.
4) I really don't want to see Zook on the sidelines the rest of the season. That is such an uncomfortable and unnecessary situation. He's fired. Go away quietly and with some dignity - now. Nobody fired where I work keeps his desk another month. Let Fedora have some fun, with Zaunbrecher in the booth.
5) Yes, recruiting could take a hit. However, a lot of kids considering Florida will ALWAYS consider Florida -- no matter what. People need to remember that.
6) There is only one guy who could step in before December or January -- the real HBC. It would be a thunderstroke that would shake up the state and the SEC, and I would love it. May not happen, though. Too bad.
7) As relieved as I am, what will get me pissed off all over again is to see that same vanilla, crappy defensive scheme the rest of the year. Go crazy. THE RESULTS COULD NOT BE WORSE! We may actually learn more about the defensive talent for next year.
8) There are too many guys either out of position, or that have not earned a starting job, or are out of position due to necessity.
   a) McDonald and Thomas should be DEs. Put Parker/Hill/Big Mo in as the DT rotation.
   b) Put McCollough at MLB, with Crowder and Siler outside.
   c) Move Everett to SS -- he just doesn't have the tangibles to be a LB -- out of position and out-muscled way too often.
   d) Speaking of "out of position"...sorry Cory Bailey, but Holmes needs to start NOW. Give Kyle Jackson a lot of reps the rest of the season, too.
   e) Start playing Trautwein at RT and move Hand to LT. I won't miss Colon and his penalties and injuries, or Guerrero/Washington at any position.
9) Much is being made of the lack of rushes by C-4, and some of that is justified. He does get a lot of passes thrown his way, though. Actually, if you include those touches, I liked the mix that C-4 and Wynn shared against MSU. Wynn can make some nice plays in the passing game, as well.

Well, we have to sit and wait now, which is sometimes harder than anything else. I have to reiterate that there is no real "added value" to having Zook around. The players need to move on starting now, because, "he's already gone...not feeling Strong (pun intended), and not singing this victory song," as The Eagles sung so well years ago. Boy, I kill myself...I'll be here all week, folks.

Stick together in all sorts of weather, Gator fans! Better days are ahead. Go Gators!!
Visor Vision: Georgia 31, UF 23

**Visor Flings, Week 8:**
**Georgia 31, UF 24**

It was a stirring effort in the second half against Georgia, but, at the end, the same painful result under Ron Zook that's become all-to-familiar to Gator fans.

Once again the offense played very well, out-gaining the Puppies overall and running the ball effectively. C-4, Wynn (when healthy) and Thornton all had success inside and outside. Thornton's performance especially was a pleasant one, and bodes well for the future.

There was a nice mix of pass plays, ranging from screen to the WRs and RBs to some nice work in the middle of the field. Georgia never solved the various screens. Caldwell made a great play on his long touchdown, and O.J. Small really sold out on runs after the catch. Still, the bugaboo of throwaway passes continues, really hampering the offense at key times in the second half, stopping some promising drives. Leak had chance to check down to his running backs in the flat, and missed some opportunities to keep drives alive with short gains. Hopefully he will learn to do this after watching the film. He did do some nice scrambling and rollout action, which really helped give him time to make plays.

Penalties by the O-Line really killed some drives as well. This area seems be to worsening as the season progresses and must improve immediately. Then again, what will change by the ninth game?

The defensive performance in the first half was atrocious, and wasn't helped by the possible season-ending injury to Crowder on the second series of the game. Again, poor tackling, little to no penetration by the D-Line, and soft coverage by the defensive backs. This story has gotten too old and is ridiculous to watch. Brandon Siler filled in reasonably well at MLB, especially given his experience. The secondary actually played a little better in the second half, and it was good to see Kyle Jackson lay the wood to Brown. Of course, Cory Bailey once again failed to make a big play when it was right in front of him, taking a poor angle on Gibson's TD that was the difference at the end. Jarvis Herring played poorly as well, and has played progressively worse as the season has gone on.

The safeties have been the weakest part of a mediocre defense all season, and must be upgraded in 2005. Why aren't Tony Joiner, Terrence Holmes, and Jackson getting more playing time? It can't get any worse, and they need the experience.

Special teams weren't against the Puppies. A ton of missed tackles on both kickoff and punt returns, and another missed short field goal by Leach. Maybe he was distracted after all his talk to the press about how poorly the Zook situation was handled. He needs to handle his own performance right now. Plus, a stupid personal foul by the punter(?!) Unbelievable.

I suppose that looking back at the body of work this team has created this year, on top of the coaching situation, led to predictable results. It's stunning to realize that the Gators may not qualify for a bowl game in 2004. Ridiculous! More damning evidence against Zook and the entire coaching staff. However, the players have contributed their share to the 4 losses, and must be held accountable. Perhaps accountability is lacking in the program right now, contributing to the myriad of problems on the field and off.

Now – a must win game against Vanderbilt this week. I can't believe I just typed that. At this point it's nearly impossible to get a read on the Gators from week to week. Perhaps this will lead to an easy triumph in Nashville, unlike most past games against them. The Commodores haven't shown much on offense or defense this year, and it actually has been a disappointing season for them. Join the crowd.

With eyes wide shut: Florida 31, Vanderbilt 17

**Visor Flings, Week 9:**
**UF 34, Vanderbilt 17**

I guess with the patented win over Vandy, hell hasn't frozen over quite yet.

Still, who wants to be the HBC?

I'd like to offer a few more thoughts:

1) Anyone who thinks SOS was too burned out to continue at UF in 2002 just doesn't get it. If you believe that all there was to the story was his being ready to leave, you are naive.

2) Foley and Machen have already burned so many bridges with Gator fans that no matter who comes in, there will be some that never, ever forgive them for not making at least a public offer to SOS.

3) Speaking of replacements...unless someone comes in and improves the defense DRAMATICALLY, the Gators will continue to relive the painful past of wasted talent and missed opportunities - pre-SOS. Florida's defense STINKS, and injuries aren't the main culprit. If you can't see this fact, then you are suffering from a "fog of war" that will never clear up.

4) Good job to those who are writing to Foley and Machen. That's better than just venting at this site or bitching and moaning to yourself. Of course, most politicians seem to ignore the wishes of their constituencies – I guess Bernie can do the same.

5) If Bernie really put SOS off and wanted an interview, then he should have already hopped aboard Foley Airlines and met the man face-to-face. What a travesty! Unconscionable. Maybe SOS isn't completely innocent in this scenario, but give me a #@$%ing break! Are Bernie and Jeremy too busy? Please! I wrote you on this weeks ago -- EGO IS THE ONLY THING THAT COULD KEEP SOS AWAY. If anyone is buying the spin-doctoring by Bernie, I feel sorry for you.

6) Yes, Urban Myer's offense looks good, but if he comes to Gainesville and Chris Leak is still the QB, then either the offense gets changed some or Chris transfers. He would get killed in that offense.

7) If Tedford gets the job, he has the offensive pedigree, but would need major help with the defense. Does he have the ego to get a coordinator in who, really, would be more important to the Gator's future success?
8) I hope Fedora stays in his current capacity, because I find little to fault in the offense this year. Yes, a few too many dinks and throwaway plays, but a great balance.
9) Here's hoping that leaders like Fason and Degory talk the others into sticking around, because transferring is very unlikely to help their respective careers. Not many schools can match Florida in terms of facilities, resources, and education. Time to grow up in a hurry, Gators!

That's all – for now.
This weekend: Florida 28, USC 24

**Visor Flings, Week 10:**
**UF 48, South Carolina 14**

An inspired effort against the Gamecocks resulted in Florida's biggest scoring margin in an SEC game since Ron Zook took over in 2002. It's a shame that it took his firing to seemingly loosen the bonds he kept on this team, especially the defense.

It was enjoyable to watch all of the stunts, slants, and games the D-Line employed, while turning Brandon Siler loose to just go get the ball. It looks like Kyle Jackson has the athleticism and nose for the ball that Cory Bailey never showed. The 4-2-5 scheme that put Bailey near the line of scrimmage seems to suit him well. Jerome Mincey looks like a solid SEC DE for next year. It was also good to see Thomas and McDonald allowed to use their quickness to shoot gaps whenever possible to try and disrupt the USC running game. It sure makes more sense than to let them try to just hold their position for the LBs, allowing them to be manhandled like they were most of the season.

A nice decision by Fedora to go mostly with the passing game. Hey, if USC wants to load up to stop C-4, then Bombs Away! And they kept doing it! This is one fine group of WRs that hopefully will keep working hard towards a possible huge 2005 season. Fason was nicked up most of the game, so it was good to see him not be overworked with the huge game coming up. Thornton got some valuable work and experience, and he will need to contribute against F$U, as it appears Wynn's groin injury will make him doubtful.

It was obvious that Florida was a jacked-up team, and I agree with Lou Holtz' assertion that, "this was not the same Florida team we saw on film." True, but also sad in many ways. Coach Zook would probably not be looking for a new job next year if he had just trusted the players and assistants more.

All that being said, it's on to Tallahassee to face the Criminoles. Maybe it will take the strange circumstances of the last month to end an interminably-long losing streak there that dates to 1986.

The offensive pieces and talent are in place to score 20+ points against a very good F$U defense. The running balance, as well as the size and athleticism of O-Line, give the

Gators a chance of winning. Of course, the inexplicable rash of false-start penalties has to stop. Perhaps having to go to a silent count on the road will help. Keep working C-4, even if he struggles for gains at times. Stay the course. Stay calm. Keep using some screens to the receivers and running backs to slow the pass rush and keep F$U's defense honest. And please – take a lot of shots deep!

What will ultimately determine the outcome of this game is most likely the performance of the defense, which has been a huge disappointment all season. I hope Charlie Strong employs most of the same schemes he used against USC. Let the defense use it's quickness to offset the decided size advantage the Semihole O-Line enjoys. That group, while large, doesn't appear to be as quick and athletic this season, and the Gators have to take advantage of that to try and force negative plays and rushed passes. Yes, F$U will hit some big plays running and passing, but so what? That will be no different than most of this year, but it's no reason to play safe and conservative. I feel that if Sexton plays most of the game, his lack of mobility compared to Rix will be a huge benefit to Florida. Of course, the Gators have a painful history of making marginal QBs look like All-Americans. Here's hoping that Crowder can play effectively, even if he has to play limited snaps. Having both him and Siler on the field at the same time really allows the other players to play their own assignments and to play aggressively.

I also think that the Gator special teams will have some "trickeration" ready for the right circumstances. Perhaps last week's punt block indicates another may be in the works. Leach has made some big FGs this last month, most of them long as well. Piotrowicz kicked off as well as ever last week. Maybe the failed fake FG attempt from the 2002 LSU game wil be dusted off. That play was wide open, and only Leach overthrowing a wide-open receiver by ten yards prevented a touchdown.

I'm looking forward to an exciting game at Joke Crumble Stadium Saturday, and wouldn't it be great to enjoy a win on "Booby Bowden Field"? Will it happen? I'm going to side with history, because you have to pick with your head, not your heart. But…

F$U 31, Florida 21

**Visor Flings, Week 11:**
**Florida 20, F$U 13**

Tough running by C-4. Even though he wasn't 100%, he ran hard and gave the offense the hammer it needed to balance the offense and keep the LBs from crowding the LOS.

The O-Line thoroughly outplayed FSU's D-Line. I'm sure those guys would say the Gators had the best line they've faced all year. A very good performance, despite more stupid penalties (just less than usual). Little discipline. Speaking of which, shame on Mo for that forearm to the helmet.

The receivers played well and ran well. I started to think I was seeing Kirk Kirkpatrick at tight end when Casey had his receptions.

Memo to Latsko – hold onto the ball, or sit down. He's fumbled too many times in limited touches the past two seasons. Terribly stupid unsportsmanlike conduct penalty as well. He was lucky to get bailed out by the pass interference call later.

Leak was solid, but I wonder if that hit on his 2nd quarter fumble affected him the second half. He was WAY off in the third quarter, but he's a gamer, and played well in the fourth. Still – he has to make some quicker reads and not throw so late. It cost him a TD in the second quarter on that corner route that would have made the score 17-0.

Defense: Great play by the front seven. It's a shame that they were treated like square pegs being forced into round holes until the last two games. Thomas and McDonald need to shoot gaps, not get pushed around. The team speed is enough that, while you may give up some big plays, few of them will turn into TDs, and you can stop the offense the next play. Siler was terrific chasing down ball carriers.

Hey! Hill and Webb can actually play some defense! Amazing what can happen if you give those guys some responsibility, freeing up the rest of the defense to do it's thing. Kyle Jackson played well, and Herring was actually in position on some deep throws. Boy, was Bailey out of position at SS all year – he plays much better closer to the line.

Special Teams: Leach made his field goals, unlike F$U. Eric Wilbur was an unsung hero. His punt out of the end zone was the best of his career, and he saved a TD by tackling Willie Reid. The coverage was great! Oh, and for those who are ripping Baker for his facemask penalty, get over it. It surely wasn't intentional, and unfortunately that jerk Cromartie made a good run. Just poor containment on the corner.

Coaching: Fedora gets a B. It would have been an A, but he apparently fell asleep the entire third quarter, with some horrendous play-calling. C-4 wasn't going to get yardage on sweeps, and the WR and RB screens already hadn't worked the entire first half, especially against a fast defense. He finally got aggressive again in the fourth quarter, and made the call of the game – running a draw on third-and-goal for the winning TD. I was screaming for it, especially with FSU lining up five defensive backs across the goal line. Attack them!

Strong once again had a good plan. It really wasn't much different than the USC plan, except he was actually more aggressive with blitzes, trusting the cornerbacks. Good call.

Worst call of the night goes to Zook. Going for it on fourth down instead of kicking a field goal to go up 10-0 in the second quarter was monumentally dumb. He got VERY lucky that Casey's penalty gave them a second chance for the field goal.

I will give credit where it is due. Zook made the right call on fourth-and-inches in the fourth quarter to force F$U to use all its remaining time outs.

Officiating: I LOVED IT, watching the Criminole fans pulling their hair out about the "bad SEC crew." Hey, those pass interference calls against Cromartie and Stovall were subjective, but nothing like the egregious non-calls on multiple obvious fumbles by an inept, shady ACC crew. Overall, their effort seemed very solid to me.

Hey Booby – CHOP THIS! Nice to see you're 0-1 on "Ron Zook Field." Did you hear his post-game comments on Sunshine? The usual smart-ass attitude when he loses, and crying about "a few plays here and there." Shut up. His act is so tired, as I'm sure he is most of the time, anyway.

I have plenty to discuss about other items later. Right now, I'm enjoying rubbing the F$U fans' noses in this one. 18 years of garbage is over! JUSTICE IS SERVED! Man, they are the worst, rudest, most classless fans anywhere. Losers.

Go Gators!

**Visor Flings, Week 16:**
**Miami 27, UF 10**

Just got back from the Peach Bowl in Atlanta. Disgraceful performance, especially by the offensive coaches, and some of the players, too.

This team sorely needs DIRECTION and LEADERSHIP. I can only hope Urban Meyer can provide it from the top and have it filter down.

What a crapy game plan from Fedora. Good riddance.

What a tremendous waste of talent in letting Fason touch the ball so little.

I will be so happy to see those roll-outs gone. All they do is cut the field in half and squeeze so many potential playmakers into a smaller space.

Line up and RUN THE FOOTBALL at Miami. Ridiculous play calling. Scared coaching.

Enough of the cutesy delayed screens, sweeps, and reverses against a quick defense, as well as more QB sacks because of poor coaching that doesn't get Leak to throw to the running back as an outlet. Good riddance to all that and Wickline, too. Thank goodness Chris finally started doing it in the second half – I think he discovered that the running backs in space on safe passes can lead to many good things! Plus, no sack or wasted down! An incredible amount of wasted downs the past two years.

The defense played well enough to win. They got more discouraged than worn down, seeing the inept offensive play calling.

Siler is a man.

Hey Channing – get your #*%* together and come back for at least one more year. I can only hope his dad has the sense to get his son to quit screwing around and grow up.

Love Kyle Jackson. Great safety prospect.

The Gators desperately need help with QUALITY depth on both lines.

Sorry, but I can only hope not to see guys like Brown and McCollum returning kicks ever again. We need to put the playmakers on kickoff and punt returns at ALL times. Those guys are simply not top-level players needed against top competition.

Please, please, let Urban Meyer provide direction and leadership immediately. Look at what Utah is doing to Pitt. Too bad they couldn't put a scare into one of the top 3 teams in a bowl, because they would. What a finely coached team!

New Year's wish for Florida football: DIRECTION, LEADERSHIP, and CONFIDENCE. All three are desperately needed! Go Gators in 2005!

# 2005
# Urban Renewal

He rode in from the West, out of the dust of an undefeated season as coach of the Utah Utes. Notre Dame wanted him, too, but UF outbid the Irish and corralled Urban Meyer with a seven-year, $14 million contract. Still, this wasn't Utah anymore, and Meyer would have to earn his stripes in the country's toughest conference. In the end, though, it was a familiar face which gazed upon the fall of the Gators and disallowed a shot at an SEC championship in 2005.

Losing to Steve Spurrier at South Carolina – to our own old Head Ball Coach, whose hairline the Visor had graced for so many years – was one of the bitterest pills I ever had to swallow; it was right up there with the 2003 "loss" to F$U and the battering by Nebraska back in the 1995 Fiesta Bowl. Nonetheless, time has clarified a few things, and now I see that it was a necessary moment in the life of Steve Spurrier rather than a dark alley in the journey of Florida football history. I still think SOS was sincere when he said that he would be a Gator for the rest of his life. But he's also a competitor, and none of us would have it any other way.

There were still many bright days for the Gators, and many more to come. Leak's brilliance continued to emerge, and the fine recruiting season under Meyer's guidance helped give us the boost we needed going into '06. Linebacker Todd McCullough deserves special mention, too – he put together a great career at UF despite battling numerous injuries, and he also distinguished himself in the classroom.

Besides, for every great chapter in every great book, there has to be the chapter just beforehand, right?

**Visor Flings, Week 1:**
**Preview and Predictions**

Another new era of Gator Football begins Saturday. Unfortunately, the Gators have experienced what most programs that lose a great coach do – the failure of at least one coach who follows to continue that level of excellence and to be fired.

Out of the ashes of the Ron Zook regime a new order comes about, led by the firm hand and steely leadership of Urban Meyer. From the first day he officially took over in January, Coach Meyer has rallied players, coaches, students, and fans alike to a common purpose – restoring Gator Football to the level it enjoyed during the brilliant run of the Head Ball Coach, Steve Spurrier.

The attention and scrutiny Meyer and his program have received is unprecedented. Finally, everyone gets to see the start of Gator Football under his leadership and the start of a new journey. That start leads to great excitement, but a number of questions remain unanswered until this season (and hopefully many more to come) reveals the short-and long-term results.

## OFFENSE

This is the area that most people are waiting to see. The spread option that Meyer has brought to Florida is being copied around the country, and imitation is the sincerest form of flattery. That being said, Coach Meyer has repeatedly stressed that his philosophy adapts to his personnel, starting at quarterback.

Chris Leak has been pushed to become a more vocal leader on and off the field. Also, his running ability, while underrated, does not match Meyer's former QB at Utah, overall #1 NFL pick Alex Smith. However, no one questions Leak's work ethic, and by sheer force of will, he should become more comfortable as the season progresses and push the offense to success. The backup situation however, as is the case at most positions, is filled with inexperience, youth, and questions. Josh Portis, who enrolled out of high school in January from California, seems to be #2, and his athletic ability is obvious. A true freshman at QB is usually a recipe for trouble, though Leak certainly was the exception to the rule. Gavin Dickey may be the guy who Meyer would trust more, but for now he is being a true team guy and taking snaps at wide receiver to help with the depth at that position, as well as to get his running ability on the field.

The offensive line has the luxury of starting four seniors, led by Mike Degory at center. It's hard to find a better leader. Randy Hand, Lance Butler, and Tavares Washington should be solid, and all of them will help freshman Jim Tartt pull his weight at guard. Once again, depth and experience is thin at this position, and only a few injuries could spell trouble.

The running back situation is a mystery. Neither Deshawn Wynn, Skyler Thornton, or Markus Manson separated himself from the others, and even true freshman Kestahn Moore will get some snaps early. As a group, this position should prove adequate, but having someone take charge would be preferable.

The wide receiver position has garnered most of the pre-season accolades, and rightly so. The group of Chad Jackson, Dallas Baker, Andre Caldwell, and Jemalle Cornelius is one of best in the country, and hopefully Leak and the other QBs will get these guys involved and let them strike fear in opponents. Especially interesting will be to see Jackson in the "H-Back" position, which asks a receiver to line up in the slot, go in motion, be a pitch man on option plays, as well as perform as a conventional receiver. Should be fun to watch.

The tight end position is the weakest of all. Tate Casey is a capable receiver, but lacks the bulk to be an effective run blocker. With the transfer of Dane Guthrie to Arizona State, this position looks to be similar to most of Spurrier's teams, where the tight end was not prominently featured. Casey does show the knack for getting open underneath and is a reliable red-zone target, so perhaps that will balance out the glaring lack of depth.

Overall, the offense will get a lot of attention early, and must develop quickly before Tennessee comes a-callin' on September 17. Here's hoping that Offensive Coordinator Dan Mullen will not hesitate to not just spread the field, but consistently strike downfield to truly make defenses hesitant to crowd the line of scrimmage.

DEFENSE

This unit is where I believe the hopes of a big season rest for the Gators. While so much attention has been focused on implementing a new offense, this group has been the reason for many late season losses under Ron Zook.

Coach Meyer has entrusted Charlie Strong and Greg Mattison to work together as co-defensive coordinators this year, with the emphasis on a more aggressive approach in both rushing the QB and in more man-to man coverage. By default this philosophical change should help the confidence level of the players. Hopefully the talent level is sufficient to maintain the strategy the entire season.

The defensive line has shown more promise than recent seasons that it can become a solid unit with adequate depth. Changes implemented in fall practice have Ray McDonald moving to defensive end and Steven Harris inside to defensive tackle. Along with Marcus Thomas and Jeremy Mincey, this is a solid front four. Mincey especially was effective last year, but his progress was overlooked in the late-game collapses. The depth is unproven, however, and a rotation that Mattison can trust has to develop.

The linebacking unit is the weakest on the entire team this fall. Even with a great player like Brandon Siler leading the way and a very good one in Earl Everett as well, after those two there is absolutely no proven depth or experience. Todd McCullough has just this season to finally contribute, while there will have to be contributions from true freshmen such as Jon Demps and Darryl Gresham, Jr. Any injuries here, and the defense could collapse like a house of cards. Here's hoping that the offense will establish plenty of significant leads during the year to allow Coach Strong to rest Siler and Everett and develop some experience in the young guys quickly.

The secondary was feared to be a weakness coming into the fall, but all indications form Coaches Meyer and Chuck Heater are that this is going to be an exciting group. Dee Webb leads the way at CB, a reliable cover guy. Opposite him Vernell Brown gets first crack, someone surprising because of his small size. However, the coaches were impressed with his tenacity and quickness, and hope he can provide adequate coverage and not become a regular target for opposing QBs. The depth at cornerback, while untested, is very athletic. Newcomer Reggie Nelson, fresh from the junior college ranks, looks like a real player for the future. Converted wide receiver Reggie Lewis has looked good in fall drills, and true freshman Avery Atkins will get significant playing time all season. The safety position is one of strength. Kyle Jackson and Jarvis Herring are one of best pairs in the SEC. Quality depth exists in Tony Joiner, Terrence Holmes, Nick Brooks, and even true freshman Dorian

Munroe. This group should be able to cover for some inexperience and mistakes in the other defensive units.

SPECIAL TEAMS

This area was no-so-special under Ron Zook, and must improve for any chance of a big season. Coach Meyer has spent a lot of time in both spring and fall practice evaluating which players he can trust to improve both kick coverage and returns. He has not hesitated to put his playmakers at the return positions (hallelujah!). Jackson, Caldwell, Webb, and some mix of the running backs will get their chances, and incoming freshmen like Atkins could help here, too. Punting is in good shape with Eric Wilbur, but the kickoff and field-goal duties are a mystery. No one has looked especially good coming into fall camp, and freshman Jonathan Phillips, who came in with a lot of hype, has struggled. It appears either Chris Hetland or Eric Nappy will get a shot, in some sort of combination of duties. This is a shaky situation that will hurt the Gators sometime during the season. Hopefully they can overcome it, but poor kicking can bring down any team.

OUTLOOK

Despite all of the hype and excitement, Urban Meyer knows he hasn't done a single thing yet on the field. So do I. Of course, uniting everyone involved with Gator Football can certainly eliminate distractions and make the job a little easier – the "path of least resistance" Meyer has referenced constantly. The players, especially, seem focused, motivated, and ready to prove something not just to the coaches and fans, but to themselves as well.

It is very difficult to have immediate success, with a new coach and system, especially as the level of competition increase. It is no tougher than in the SEC. That being said, at least Meyer has accomplished that feat at his previous stops, which can only help the players' confidence.

As usual, the schedule is very tough. After Tennessee, the Gators have road games with an improved Alabama team, a loaded LSU squad, and that little affair against the Head Ball Coach at South Carolina. That is one game I am not going to enjoy, and it has nothing to do with the talent level of his players. I will never enjoy having to compete against one of Florida's favorite sons, and even a win will be bittersweet. Of course, allegiance to a former leader doesn't outweigh rooting for the Gators first and always. The Cocktail Party at Jacksonville will be very interesting, because of the coaching turnover at Florida and the significant player turnover at Georgia. Then there is the finale against Florida State. The crap that school and its coaches and players have pulled has made this an especially big game for me.

Too many pitfalls here to see any run to the Rose Bowl, or perhaps even to Atlanta. There is too much unproven depth and inexperience at many positions. I believe a trip to the

SEC Championship Game would be a great accomplishment for this team, because these players haven't proven they can do it yet. That step is often the most difficult of all.

The crystal ball says: 9-2 overall
6-2 SEC (losses at LSU and to Tennessee)
Heeeeeeeere come the Gators!

**Visor Flings, Week 2:**
**UF 32, Wyoming 14**

The Gators put forth a solid effort against Wyoming, especially for the first game of the season. Of course, as with any first game, there were plenty of mistakes, especially offensively, only magnified by still learning a new system.

There was plenty of excitement for the fans, anticipating Coach Meyer's debut, the new Gator Walk, and moving on from the mediocrity of the past 3 seasons.

The offensive line was surprisingly shaky, allowing four sacks and struggling to establish running lanes in the first half. Wyoming deserves some credit, because they were both familiar with Meyer's offense at Utah and had all summer to practice for it. That being said, the O-linemen and Coach Hevesy would all agree there were still too many missed assignments, and even Mike Degory had some bad snaps. Lots of work to do and improvement needed here.

The receivers played very well. Chad Jackson is an All-SEC caliber player, with Caldwell and Baker contributing as well. Good running after the catch, and no drops. This group still needs to improve its run-blocking, though.

Chris leak was sharp as usual in the passing game, but it was obvious he has a long way to go until he's comfortable with the run option reads in this offense. He has to eliminate his tentativeness to really balance the offense out and make this scheme work to maximum efficiency. There's no way he will be the runner Alex Smith was, but he doesn't have to be, either. Meyer will emphasize the passing game more with Leak – he's no fool.

The defense carried the day. The D-Line applied more pressure by itself than in recent memory. The linebackers, led by Brandon Siler, were effective when blitzing and were solid in open-field tackling. The secondary had little trouble covering the Cowboy receivers. Vernell Brown continues to impress, but I'm still not convinced he can handle himself against top-shelf SEC competition. I won't mind being proven wrong. Dee Webb was solid as usual, but needs to hang on to potential interceptions.

Special teams were okay. Meyer will change the holder on placekicks after two extra point snaps were dropped. Chris Hetland did well on his two field goals, an area of major concern coming into the fall. The kickoff coverage is still a concern, and improvement must be made. The kickoff returns are is good hands with Caldwell, but I hope Webb is healthy enough to take over on punt returns. Brown is quick, but goes down way too easily.

Overall, a nice win, but this team has many areas it can improve upon.

It's hard to guess how the Louisiana Tech Bulldogs from Ruston will react to this week's game, considering their campus is one of hundreds of evacuation sites for refugees of Hurricane Katrina. I hope they can focus for few hours on the game and play well, but I would expect their effort to be less focused than usual.

Coach Bicknell will feature a wide-open, four and five-receiver attack to spread the field, but the Gator defense has been practicing against similar looks for months now. Tech may actually run the ball less than Wyoming did, but this scheme is probably their best hope for success.

The Florida offense will want to show improvement, especially the O-line, and I expect to see that, even against an outmanned unit. I also expect to see more of the backups, especially Josh Portis at QB. His continued development is critical, both for the team's sake and also to have future opponents spend more practice time against a different look. It sounds like Deshawn Wynn will finally see the field. No one running back has stood out to Coaches Meyer and Drayton yet, and they want someone to take charge. However, I don't see that happening until later in the season, if at all.

As usual with a game like this, the number one priority is that NO ONE GETS INJURED. Hopefully the backups get some more experience and can develop some much-needed depth, especially at linebacker and offensive line.

Prediction: Florida 48, La. Tech 14

**Visor Flings, Week 3:**
**UF 41, Louisiana Tech 3**

As I suspected, the La. Tech players seemed distracted, but I guess that's understandable when one third of your home state is underwater.

The Gators look ahead to Tennessee, and just as with every season, will have to muster their best game to repeat, especially in a "rebuilding" season. The defense will have to prove that it is as good as anticipated, and a good offensive effort will depend on Leak's willingness to rely on his mobility.

In the meantime, no calamitous missteps so far by the new coaching regime.

Visor pick: UF 21, Tennessee 14

**Visor Flings, Week 4:**
**UF 16, Tennessee 7**

What a tough performance by the defense last Saturday! And tough by the offense, too (in a bad way).

I can't tell you how hard I was screaming to turn the blitz loose in the fourth quarter and crush Ainge. For a while there it was looking like Zook ball, but Strong and Mattison put an end to that!

Is it the offensive scheme, or the O-line? Maybe some of both, but this isn't going to cut it for the rest of the season. What WILL happen is that the defense will break down eventually from exhaustion.

Unless Chris Leak embraces keeping the ball on the edge and actually running the option and pitches occasionally, I'm afraid this offense will never approach what we all want. Where is Portis for a change of pace for a few plays? I have to say I'm a little disappointed on how safe the play-calling was.

The penalties HAVE TO BE "CORRECTED." Please tell Tate Casey to slow down and wait for the snap before turning up. He personally killed two great runs by Wynn by himself. I know Meyer questioned the officials, but I'm afraid it doesn't matter. And the O-line was shaky.

It looks like the tight end will need to become a blocker, because the tackles were burned off the edge most of the game. Leak almost got killed a few times. We have some terrific defenses still coming up (Alabama, LSU, F$U).

If the TE is taken out of the passing game, then Meyer and Mullin may need to tweak the entire scheme.

What a shame that we became a chuck-and suck passing offense most of the second half, only going downfield on third and long. Big mistake. I can't believe the Gator receivers weren't better than the Vol secondary.

It was heartbreaking seeing McDonald and Caldwell on the ground. It appears Ray Mac has a chance to return in six weeks, but even then his effectiveness has to be limited. If possible, I hope the coaches decide to medically red-shirt him, just like they have already done to Caldwell. And Bubba was done as soon as the air splint came out. I knew when I saw him lying on the field that his leg was likely broken and he was done until next fall.

The Gators are getting razor-thin on the D-line. Cohen played very well, and he and Harvey will have to carry a big load the rest of the season. Another example of Zook's spotty D-Line recruiting that could bite Florida in the ass. I'm not counting on Jarvis Moss for much.

Hopefully Dickey or someone else picks up the slack for Caldwell. Looks like one of the freshmen will get a chance.

Florida's next test is its first road game under Urban Meyer – a trip to the bluegrass of Kentucky to face the Wildcats. UK has struggled mightily their past two games, after an inspired effort against Louisville in their opener. Their offense has had trouble running the ball, which should play right into Florida's hands. The UK QB and receivers have not done anything of real note, either.

Kentucky's defense, especially against the run, has been porous. They allowed over 300 yards to Indiana last week, which is unacceptable. It appears this group just doesn't have any real playmakers to make a difference, especially against stronger opponents.

There has been a ton of talk from the Florida coaches and players on the offensive side that changes and improvements need to made, but is it too late in game #4 to start? Coach Hevesy has stated he will go back to emphasizing blocking technique this week, feeling that the O-line is thinking too much about the new assignments in the spread offense and forgetting the basics. There may be a few new faces in the starting lineup as well. Tavares Washington has a hyper-extended elbow, and it looks like Jim Tartt will finally get his chance to shine after struggling with off-season shoulder surgery. Steve Rissler will also get more reps, perhaps starting over Drew Miller.

Jemalle Cornelius steps into Caldwell's WR role, while Gavin Dickey and perhaps some combination of freshman such as Louis Murphy or Nyan Boateng fill in at slot #4. Time to pick up the slack as well as possible and move on.

Chris Leak and the running backs will get plenty of chances to work on the running game. It's time for Chris to actually probe the edges on the option occasionally. I look for Josh Portis to get meaningful reps, because he needs them and because his continued development is critical to either spell Leak or to take over in case of (shudder) injury.

There's not really much to say about the defense. This week will be a test of their mental strength, to see if they let down after dominating Tennessee, and to see if the coaches' talk of "being invested" each week has really taken hold. Joe Cohen steps into McDonald's spot at defensive end, and red-shirt freshman Derrick Harvey will get lots of snaps as well. Lutrell Alford and Clint McMillan will need to provide depth at defensive tackle after Cohen's move to full-time defensive end. Unless the Gator offense goes on a turnover binge, I can't see UK scoring more than 14-17 points, on a good day.

Well, let's hope the Gators can win somewhat comfortably against Kentucky, because Alabama will be a real test on the road. Meyer and the rest of coaches had better figure out how to protect Leak and stretch the defense down the field much better, or Florida will lose some games.

I hope everyone enjoyed the Tennessee game – I know 80,000 Gator fans (including me) sure did!

Prediction: Florida 38 Kentucky 13

**Visor Flings, Week 5:**
**UF 49, Kentucky 28**

A tale of two halves, to be sure. That was quite a performance by the Gators in the first 30 minutes against the Mildcats, even though Kentucky is WAY down this season. The blocked punt certainly seemed to get the team's attention, and from there on until halftime it was total domination.

It was gratifying to see Chris Leak actually run all three phases of the running part of the spread option. He read the defensive end much better, and both ran and pitched to the running back or wide receiver as necessary. Alabama will be a much sterner test physically, but you have to show the willingness to run these phases to open up the entire offense and keep the opposing defense honest.

The O-line had a huge physical advantage, but at least they took advantage of it and seemed focused on reducing the pre-snap penalties that killed them against Tennessee. Anything they can do to make the skill players' jobs easier against the Tide is a huge plus.

Deshawn Wynn has proven he is the #1 running back, but it was great to see Thornton and Manson finally get some reps and provide a change-of-pace. True to his word, Coach Meyer made those guys pay their dues in practice as far as ball-protection before getting playing time.

Leak and the receivers were lights-out and very sharp, but I just can't read too much into it, because the Mildcats were overmatched physically and became demoralized as the touchdowns just kept on coming. Good work for Jemalle Cornelius in the #2 slot, giving him some confidence going into a huge road game.

The defense toyed with UK the entire first half and completely shut them down. Good to see the opportunistic takeaways and the hustle to the ball. Great pressure by the D-line the entire game.

There is a lot of Gator fans' hand-wringing about the second half performance, but this was a great opportunity to get the twos and threes some valuable experience for an extended stretch. Some of these guys have to fill in occasionally down the road, and the experience and coaching they will receive from this is invaluable. Great to see Derrick Harvey and Jarvis Moss making plays at defensive end, and Jon Demps playing a ton of snaps at linebacker. Avery Atkins and Reggie Nelson are continuing to improve, and are making the nickel and dime packages very effective.

This week's trip to Tuscaloosa could actually be a sterner test than Tennessee was. A very hostile environment against an undefeated team with many upperclassmen.

Brodie Croyle has stayed healthy at QB for the Tide, and they have shown better balance then the past two seasons. Their bread and butter is still the running game, led by Kenneth Darby, and it will be a challenge for Florida's defense to slow this phase down and try to make Alabama one-dimensional. There's a lot of talk about the Crimson Tide wide receivers – we'll see how they like the Gators' press coverage and hitting.

The Tide defense is once again solid and physical. Most of the starters have played for two or three years, and don't make many mistakes. Florida's O-line has to give Leak a little extra time to make his reads, so the field gets stretched and Wynn and Co. can get some critical first downs. It will be interesting to see if Leak continues to keep the ball and/or pitch it, because the Tide defense will lay some hits on him Saturday. Will this get him out of his normal game? That could perhaps be the deciding factor of all.

A tough match-up against a solid, veteran team. This will be a huge test for Florida, and the coaching staff will earn its money both in preparation for the game and making in-game adjustments, which will be necessary. If the Gator defense has to stay on the field for long stretches in the second half, that will be the telling sign as to Florida's chances. I'm going to go with Chris Leak's leadership to pull out a close, hard-fought win.

Prediction - Florida 20, Alabama 17

**Visor Flings, Week 6:**
**Alabama 31, UF 3**

Not much to review from this debacle.

The O-line was embarrassed, against a weak line. No running lanes, no push. Stuffed at the goal line. Decent pass-blocking, which seems to be the only thing they can do consistently. I honestly don't know if this group has what it takes. The situation at guard is especially troubling.

The receivers looked tentative and short-armed many balls. Dallas Baker was the only guy who played tough throughout. They did not help out the QB much at all.

Chris Leak didn't have much help, but even he looked skittish, and didn't set his feet all that well. He missed many short throws that are usually money.

Can't really fault the running backs, as they has little to work with.

The defense was shockingly ineffective, and played on it's heels all day. The safeties took many bad angles, helping with many big plays. Puzzling. Vernell Brown was finally exposed, and even Dee Webb had a poor effort.

The D-line got little penetration against an inexperienced Bama O-line, which shows how much the loss of Ray McDonald hurt, as well as the weakness at defensive tackle after Marcus Thomas. Little pressure from the ends as well.

The coaching staff gets a failing grade. The Gators were out-prepared, and any in-game adjustments were completely ineffective. I can't believe the defense could not get in the backfield consistently, and the play-calling by Mullen was strangely conservative.

Truly a team effort in this loss. Burn the film and forget about it, because this was a disaster in every way.

At least this week's opponent, Mississippi State, while having a poor record (again), will get the Gators' attention after the embarrassing loss in Starkville last season.

It will be very interesting to see how the coaching staff gets the players to put the Alabama game behind them and move forward. There may be more tinkering with the schemes and the players, because it just seems that there are a lot of square pegs being forced into round holes right now. The team's development has been halted, and that doesn't bode well with games against LSU and Georgia still to play this month.

Miss. St. should not prove to be a special threat on offense, as they still lack the playmakers and speed required to win on the road. They will try to win the running game battle first, but I think that the Gator defense's pride won't allow that to happen. The Bulldog passing game is nothing to worry about.

This week will be all about the mental aspects – rebounding from a crushing loss, and taking personal pride in picking up yourself and the team. I believe this coaching staff can do that.

Prediction Florida 30, Miss. St. 10

**Visor Flings, Week 7:**
**UF 35, Mississippi State 9**

Just when things were looking even worse than against Alabama, the offense seemed to wake up in the second half. I suppose the announcement that Leak and Wynn did not practice all week before the game explains their respective performances somewhat.

It was a painful first half to watch. It appeared the effects of the hangover from the debacle at Tuscaloosa lingered for a while. Penalties, bad reads by Leak, poor throws, hit-or-miss blocking by the O-line. Even poor ball security by Chad Jackson, ending a TD drive by copying the NFL habit of stretching the ball out to the pylon, and fumbling away a scoring opportunity. You could see the frustration showing even on the faces of the coaches, searching for anything positive.

Then, the shovel pass started to work. Markus Manson provided some burst into the hole. Dallas Baker picked up the receiving corp. The defense pummeled both MSU QBs, and scored two safeties. Then the avalanche in the second half of big plays on offense and defense, including a special teams touchdown. Finally some positives to give the team some confidence going into a critical game at LSU.

If Florida has any hope of winning the Eastern division, it has to win at LSU this week. This will be an interesting game in terms of watching the confidence level of the team in a hostile environment, one in which they have already failed miserably in. There will be no better opportunity to prove to themselves, the coaches and the fans that this team is indeed tougher then previous seasons.

The Gators must contain the LSU running game and force QB JeMarcus Russell to read defenses and make good decisions all game long. He has not shown that ability so far this season. If Joseph Addai and Justin Vincent can be slowed, the Gators have the chance to force some turnovers to help the offense score points.

Skyler Green is the most dangerous receiver and kick return man, and burned the Gators on a punt return two years ago. The special teams play has been inconsistent at best all year, and he must be contained by both the defense and kick return units to make Russell take the Tigers on long offensive series.

Surprisingly, LSU's secondary has played somewhat soft this year, and has given up some big plays. Coach Mullen must be willing to let Baker and Jackson challenge them downfield. Hopefully Jemalle Cornelius will be able to contribute after sitting out this past week.

Once again, the hopes of a win fall primarily on the shoulders of the O-line. This unit must protect well and eliminate the senseless penalties, or even a great performance by the defense could be wasted.

Finally, there are a lot of walking wounded, especially on offense. It's time to throw a lot of eggs into this basket and try to tough out a victory. I believe some of LSU's troubles against Tennessee were caused by the aftermath of Hurricane Katrina, and that they are just now beginning to settle into the rhythm of football season.

This should be a close, hard-fought affair. However, until the Gator offense proves itself on the road against a tough opponent, I can't favor them yet.

Prediction LSU 24 Florida 17

**Visor Flings, Week 8:**
**LSU 21, UF 17**

It is obvious that most people close to the Gator football program knew exactly what the game against LSU would be like: defense-oriented, good special teams, and which offense would make the most plays. And, most observers thought that until the Gator offense proved itself against a quality defense, they would probably lose, especially on the road.

Unbelievably, despite the defense getting five turnovers and three sacks, and despite 12 LSU penalties, the Gator offense could muster only 206 total yards. What a travesty. No excuses here, despite an injured wide receiver corps and struggling O-line. Florida football has enough players to generate a better performance than that.

It is now time for Urban Meyer to exercise his leadership more so than ever in his coaching career. A decision has to be made in fairness to these players who have bought in to his system and beliefs: for the remainder of this season, do you scrap the spread offense and go to a traditional two-wide receiver set to protect Chris Leak and let him throw the ball with confidence, or do you embrace the spread option and insert Josh Portis to run it?

It was an emotional Coach Meyer and Chris leak after the LSU game, and that showed how truly disappointed each was in his own way by what transpired. Leak is a true Gator, and has to be devastated by what has developed. And Coach Meyer showed that he does care deeply for his players, and can see how the struggles of the offense have affected Chris and the rest of the offensive players.

The Gators have a much-needed week off to rest, get some players healthy (Chad Jackson, Jemalle Cornelius, Mike Degory, Ray McDonald), and to plan an attack for the rest of the season, starting with Georgia in Jacksonville.

Tough decisions have to be made, from Dan Mullen's play-calling to the style of offense. I like the fact that Mullen moved to the coaches' booth two weeks ago to see the field better, but he is not giving the players the best and fairest chance of being successful. I do believe that he has tried to tailor the offense to help fit Leak's skills, but more radical changes may be necessary now. If Florida only has two or three healthy receivers, then stop using the four and five-wide sets. Especially since the O-line has not pass-blocked at all in those sets. Establish what running plays Deshawn Wynn is best at and emphasize them.

Coach Hevesy of the O-line and WR coach Gonzales are at fault as well. All three coaches supposedly confer before each offensive series as to what plays they would like to run. Well, the receivers are not breaking off routes when the blitz comes, and the O-line is still allowing too much pressure to come off the corners. I am not impressed at all with the performance of the coaches as far as making in-game adjustments.

The defensive performance does not grade an "A", because they allowed the Gators to get into a 14-point hole in the first quarter. The performance after that was an "A". Marcus Thomas was a beast in the middle, disrupting the run and pass game. Jarvis Moss and Jeremy Mincey were effective pass rushers, and Mincey continues to show good pursuit and tackling skills.

What was most disappointing about the defense was the run defense. While Brandon Siler continues wreak havoc, he repeatedly ran himself out of position to stop the run, rushing up too close to the line of scrimmage instead of staying a few yards back to prevent the draws from working. More film work needed.

Dee Webb had a rough game in coverage before settling down, giving up on the second LSU TD pass and getting out of position in the end zone. And the safety play was again spotty. Tony Joiner and Jarvis Herring did a poor job on the first TD pass, where if either had played proper technique, that pass would have been knocked down. And Kyle Jackson continues to get out of tackling position in the run game, allowing Joseph Addai to juke him numerous times for extra yards.

Eric Wilbur was terrific punting, both the directional and straight-away style. The past two weeks he has played as an All-SEC and All-American candidate. Coverage teams play was very good as well.

Vernell Brown has been a failure at punt returner. He incurred a penalty running after a fair catch signal, caught a long punt at the five-yard line instead of letting it bounce into the end zone, and he simply cannot break tackles. The coaching staff is doing a disservice to this team by not making a change here. While VB has played great at cornerback, this area needs an immediate upgrade.

This is critical off-week for the coaches. They must exhibit leadership in making changes that benefit the players and put then in position to win games. I'll be back next week with a Georgia preview.

**Visor Flings, Week 9:**
**Off Week**

This game has taken on an entirely new complexion with the absence of DJ Shockley from the Bulldog lineup this week due to injury. Unknown backup Jim Tereshinski takes over and tries to keep the UGA season perfect, and the Gators have an unknown element to deal with.

Georgia's O-line may be the best in the NCAA this season. Four senior starters, led by Max Jean-Gilles, controlled the Tennessee D-line, which no one else has come close to doing this year. Unless the Florida D-line can somehow achieve a stalemate at the line of scrimmage, it won't matter who the UGA QB is.

Georgia's running game has led the way all year, led by Thomas Brown and Danny Ware. These guys run hard and tough and don't go down easily. More importantly, tight end Leonard Pope is a huge target at 6'9", and has been there to bail out the QB all season. The Gator defense will probably need to assign a particular defender to him all game, even if it's a fifth defensive back.

The Bulldog defense has been just as good as last year, despite the loss of David Pollack, Odell Thurman, and Thomas Davis to the NFL. What may be a real loss, however, is Kendrick Golston to a knee injury. He was a load at defensive tackle, and his absence could help Florida's running game have some success. The overall defensive unit is still fast and tackles well, led by safety Greg Blue and nose guard Gerald Anderson. Mike Degory must contain his penetration all afternoon.

Florida's offensive output is the key to victory, no matter how well the defense and special teams perform. That was made painfully obvious against LSU. The offensive coaches, especially OC Mullen, O-line coach Hevesy, and WR coach Gonzales, have failed the players in putting them in positions to be successful, and have especially failed to make halftime adjustments to help the offense out. Unless the receivers read blitzes and break off routes to help Chris Leak out, he will get punished again. The O-line has to come around, even if it means simplifying the blocking schemes to protect the QB. They have been a turnstile all season, allowing many plays no chance for success. It will also be interesting to see how many carries Deshawn Wynn gets this week. He performed well at LSU, and has to be the force that provides balance to any passing game.

Florida's defense can probably afford to play the UGA wide receivers man-to-man, as they lack a true home run threat. This will allow them to assign someone the tight ends, and keep 6-7 men in to try and slow down Georgia's running game. Third and long will be especially difficult for UGA, with the threat of the QB breaking off long runs gone. It will be interesting to see if Coaches Strong and Mattison have the D-line slant or shoot gaps to try and disrupt things, because they will get overpowered playing straight up.

It's do-or-die time as far as the Gators' chance of getting to Atlanta are concerned. They have endured a ton of criticism the past two weeks, and also have last year's game to serve as motivation. If the offense can sustain a few long scoring drives, that may be all Florida needs to pull out the win. However, until I see evidence of this on the filed, I can't predict a win.

Prediction: Georgia 20 Florida 17

**Visor Flings, Week 10:**
**UF 14, Georgia 10**

Florida got back on track in the SEC East race with a big win over the Puppies last Saturday in Jacksonville. Even after a fast start in the first quarter, though, the defense and special teams were called upon repeatedly to hold onto the win, after the coaching staff went conservative the second half with the lead.

That was a beautiful first quarter by the offense, easily its best of the entire season. A nice mix of run and pass, with many receivers, including the tight end, in the mix. Georgia's defense was confused and off-balance the entire first half. The coaching staff apparently has removed most of the option part of the spread option for now, trying to do what it takes with the current personnel to get wins and move on. Unfortunately it took tough losses at Alabama and LSU to come to this realization.

Chris Leak was asked to be efficient, and he came through. However, he still had a handful of opportunities to keep drives going by taking five yards or so on short runs, and continued not to do so. After his leap into the end zone for the first score, I can't understand why he refuses to consistently pick up small gains. Those decisions stopped the Gators from possibly scoring 3-10 more points. The loss of Dallas Baker to an ankle injury once again exposed the lack of depth at wide receiver, and his absence severely impacted the effectiveness of the passing game the second half.

The O-line had its best day as well, establishing a good run offense against a solid defense. The pass protection was better, as the jail breaks that have snowed Leak under did not materialize. Part of that, though, was attributed to Georgia's seeming unwillingness to blitz more often, a curious decision.

The Florida defense was solid again, allowing only 10 points and stiffening repeatedly when Georgia crossed midfield. Jeremy Mincey continues his All-SEC play, Marcus Thomas was solid in the middle, and the young defensive ends got enough pressure on the QB to keep him from becoming completely comfortable.

The move of Reggie Nelson to free safety paid dividends with his interception and ability to prevent anything from getting behind him. Hopefully, Kyle Jackson will come back a better player after watching this. Brandon Siler played well, especially since he wasn't 100% with a bad ankle.

Once again Eric Wilbur looked like an All-SEC punter, with four inside the 20 and a run after a fake for a first down to slow down Georgia's momentum late in the third quarter. The coverage teams were very good, and, shockingly, Vernell Brown actually broke some long punt returns, the first of which set up the second Florida TD. That phase of the kicking game has been sorely lacking all season, and I can only hope it will now continue.

Overall, this was a win that can hopefully be the catalyst to a strong finish. The SEC East remains a possibility, but I'm more concerned with the continued improvement of the offense and gaining momentum for the F$U game in the Swamp on Nov. 26.

Coming up Saturday is Vandy, and this is the best Commodore team in many years, led by gutsy senior QB Jay Cutler. After a fast start they have stumbled lately, but not for a lack of effort, even against teams like LSU and Georgia. Coach Bobby Johnson has been able to get his team to play hard every game, and I wouldn't be surprised to see Vandy stay close at least through the first half against Florida, especially if there is an emotional letdown for the Gators after beating UGA. However, given the struggles of the Gators offense all season, I don't see the coaches having much difficulty keeping the players focused, and having them sharp from the opening kickoff on.

Vandy's defense is quick and opportunistic, and never quits. That being said, their stronger opponents have been able to stay with a power running game and wear them down in the second half. Opponents have also had lots of success blitzing repeatedly, and I look for the Gators to play a more aggressive scheme this week. The Florida run defense has been able to put most teams in poor down-and-distance situations this year, and I see that continuing this week.

Prediction: Florida 31, Vanderbilt 14

**Visor Flings, Week 11:**
**UF 49, Vanderbilt 42**

The Great Escape. Florida avoided disaster by piecing together two clutch overtime TD drives and finding a way to make one play in the defensive secondary. Yes, a terrific effort by Vandy, but some questionable coaching decisions, combined with some serious brain cramps by the players, led to nearly throwing the SEC season away.

The Gator offense was efficient, led by a running game that the Commodores could never stop all night. The loss of DeShawn Wynn was offset by a strong performance by Markus Manson and Kestahn Moore, and the surprising option runs by Chris Leak. The downfield passing game remains painfully unproductive, though. Yes, the absence of Dallas Baker hurt, but I find it hard to believe that a school like Florida cannot find a way to stretch the field, especially an overmatched defense like Vandy's. This spells major trouble against S. Carolina and F$U.

The defensive backfield never seemed to adjust to covering the middle of the field, especially the 15- to 18-yard square-ins and slants. This area has historically been a soft spot of Charlie Strong defenses, and once again a good QB exposed this weakness. Now it appears that Vernell Brown could miss the rest of the season with a broken ankle. At least on this night, his replacement, Reggie Lewis, was repeatedly abused, getting caught for numerous holding penalties and giving up big pass plays. Coach Heater has to coach up Lewis and the other defensive backs for the next two opponents, or the Gators will lose.

This week and game will remain my least favorite as long as Steve Spurrier is the coach at South Carolina. It's terrible to think that, along with his coaching ability, his team can derail the SEC hopes of his alma mater every year. This entire situation is distasteful for me.

USC's offense has had its struggles this year, mainly due to its O-line suffering from a combination of injuries, inexperience, and unfamiliarity with the passing game. The Gamecocks have never established an efficient running game all season, and Florida has to continue this trend. If Coaches Strong and Mattison can put the burden of the entire offense on the shoulders of Blake Mitchell, the defense should have enough success to give the Florida offense the chance to win the game. The season-ending loss of wide receiver Syvelle Newton really hurt USC's offense.

The Gamecock defense is a funky mish-mash of sets and blitzes, coached by SEC veteran John Thompson. The Gator O-line will see a myriad of fronts, but must remain focused on establishing the running game to take as much pressure off of the receivers as possible. Knowing how much the old HBC wants to stick it to Meyer and Bernie Machen, the offense has to be prepared to put up a lot of points if necessary, especially if the secondary struggles again. The training staff has to get Wynn back onto the field, and Chad Jackson and Jemalle Cornelius need to make plays downfield to loosen up USC's defense. Looks like Dallas Baker is very doubtful for this game.

This will be an uncomfortable experience for all Gators, and potentially a disastrous one. SOS will do everything he can to ruin Florida's season, and has the offensive mind to pull it off. Look for comments this week as well to get under the skin of the Gator coaches and fans, and possibly the players. Given the tremendous struggles of Florida's passing game, every decent-to-better opponent has a legitimate shot at winning. Losing this one would be a bitter pill for Gators everywhere to swallow.

Here's hoping that Urban Meyer and this year's group of Gators continue to “find a way” to win, but the margin for error is now razor-thin.

Prediction: Florida 24, S. Carolina 23

**Visor Flings, Week 12**
**South Carolina 30, UF 22**

Steve Spurrier...PARIAH?

Okay, it's the off-season.

SOS is visiting or vacationing in Florida.

Some Gator fans will grovel before his feet and say they wish he had come back (that should make him happy, or would it really?)

Gator-Haters will slap him on the back and thank him for crushing Florida's hope of an SEC title (that should make him happy, or would it really?)

Some Gator fans will turn their backs, and/or make an angry remark (that should make him happy, or would it really?)

The Greatest Gator…PARIAH?

Might be.

Another chapter in the brutal, dark part of Florida football history.

This sucks. Spin it however you want. This absolutely sucks.

Negative serendipity.

UGA screws UF on fourth down in 2002 (against Auburn).

UF screws itself in 2005.

Auburn returns the favor to UGA in 2005.

Good job everyone.

One of the DARKEST DAYS in Florida Football history.

I'm still stunned at the lack of intensity and urgency by the defense. Unbelievably, USC was successful running the ball, especially in short-yardage situations. Yes, only one big pass play, but a crushing one, as Dee Webb and Kyle Jackson missed the tackle to set up a USC touchdown. One tackle for Brandon Siler. ONE! Completely unacceptable.

The offensive performance was so close to excellent, but until big plays are made (and the chances were there), and crippling penalties are eliminated, nothing the coaches do will solve the scoring problems in SEC play. The running game is finally where Coach Meyer wants it, but the downfield passing game just has never come around. Leak and Chad Jackson has a long TD pass set up beautifully, but neither executed. The pass patterns failed to pick up necessary first down yardage, and the fourth-quarter offense showed no hope of running a two-minute drill. Incredibly frustrating.

And now, the Gator Nation has its worst nightmare realized. All the SOS-backers have their evidence, as many people who worried whether Coach Meyer can coach in the SEC are now claiming the sky is falling, and players and fans have to live with the bitter truth that an SEC East title was blown.

The hand-wringing and frustration have now started to turn the Gator Nation upon itself. Only a solid win over F$U can calm the masses and turn the thoughts more positively to recruiting and the off-season. It's unfair, but some of the good will and positive outlook engendered by Coach Meyer starting last spring was lost.

Florida has one last chance to salvage some pride from this season Saturday against Florida $t. No SEC East title, embarrassing road losses at Alabama and South Carolina, injuries, and the ongoing struggles of the offense have made 2005 a tough year for the Gator Nation. This game is very important for carrying some momentum into 2006 and for recruiting, as the Gators have many highly-rated players still on the board at most positions.

Once again, establishing the run will be huge, given the pass-blocking problems of the Gators and F$U's good D-line. The tailback rotation seems to be set nicely, and I'm hoping the running backs are involved in the passing game as well. The swing passes have been good gainers all season, and will serve to slow the $eminole pass rush. The Gator O-line should be able to establish a decent ground game against a weakened front seven of F$U, despite the fact that the $eminoles have a great linebacking corps of Nicholson, Davis, and the thug, Sims.

Chris Leak continues to take unnecessary sacks, and that has to stop this week. The receiver corps looks okay, as Jemalle Cornelius and Chad Jackson seem to be close to 100%, while Dallas Baker will apparently start as well. These guys have to make a few things happen downfield this week. Once again it would appear that given the experience and quality of the Florida WRs against an average F$U secondary, that some big pass plays can be executed, but that has been an all-to-infrequent occurrence all year.

The F$U O-line is decimated by injuries, and the Gator D-line should have some success against the run and pass. It is very important that the front four are able to control the line of scrimmage. If you see a lot of blitzing, that bodes ill for the pass defense, as the $emiholes have a talented group of receivers that will have a physical edge against the Gator defensive backs. Brandon Siler will want to bounce back from the one-tackle disaster against USC, while Dee Webb needs to put an entire game together and not lose focus as he has done all year. F$U's running game has regressed this year, but Leon Washington is back from injury, and has had success against Florida in the past. This game being in the Swamp is a huge advantage. The noise level will be tough on freshman QB Drew Weatherford, and should provide a boost to the entire Gator team, which certainly needs it after it's last game.

Another close game seems to be in the offing, even with the $emiholes struggles and the game at the Swamp. I believe the confidence of the Gator team is somewhat shaken right now. If Florida can make F$U play from behind, they should be fine. If Florida has to pass its way back from a deficit, though, it could be an ugly end to the regular season, and turn up the volume of discontent until 2006.

The Visor's Prediction: Florida 19, F$U 17

**Visor Flings, Week 13:**
**Florida 34, F$U 7**

It was a stirring win over the $emiholes, uplifting the sprits of the fans, players, and coaches after a disappointing SEC season, especially coming off the loss at S. Carolina.

Despite the statistical advantage gained by F$U at the end, most of those yards were in garbage time after the score ballooned to 34-0 in the 4th quarter. The Gator offense wasn't spectacular against a solid defense, but were efficient and opportunistic, especially after getting great field position after the defense generated three turnovers in F$U territory. Too bad that wasn't the case earlier this season against LSU.

The play of the game was undoubtedly Marcus Thomas's block of a field goal in the second quarter, scooped up and returned for a TD by Reggie Lewis for a 14-0 lead. The confidence of the entire team after that was sky-high, and the Nole$ never seriously threatened again.

The defensive performance was dominant. Drew Weatherford was punished all afternoon, the $emihole running game was contained, and the defense caused four turnovers and applied hard hits all day. The defensive line terrorized F$U, enjoying a huge advantage in experience and talent. The linebackers were solid in tackling and pass coverage, and the secondary made key plays, including causing two fumbles by stripping receivers, and Jarvis Herring's interception at the goal line in the third quarter, effectively ending the competitive phase of the game.

Recruiting has seen a huge bump as well, as the Gators racked up seven commitments within a week of the game and have recently continued a stellar run, now up to 24 as of 12/18. That is more than the Gators have ever had this early before National Signing Day, and the class so far is filled by an incredible amount of highly-rated players at most positions.

I'm looking forward to watching how Coach Meyer approaches the bowl game preparations. He has stated this will be a big game, and I know many fans are tired of seeing the last game of the season end in an embarrassing loss. I look for a solid effort against Iowa.

**Visor Flings, Week 19:**
**UF 31, Iowa 24**

Well, it's great to beat a Big 10 team anytime, despite the big letdown against the Hawkeyes in the fourth quarter of the Outback Bowl, but I'm satisfied.

The Leak-to-Dallas-Baker connection didn't really start clicking until late in the first half…In fact, unbelievably, Iowa had more passing yardage than the Gators for the game overall.

It's hard to explain the letdown in the fourth quarter. To give up 17 points in the season's final period of play is not exactly how you want to go out, but all in all, it was a successful effort. I'd say Urban Meyer has written his ticket for at least one more season, anyway.

Here's to the continuation of what has been a great recruiting season for the Gators so far. I'll see everyone in September.

Very Truly Yours,
The Visor

# 2006
# No Room for Error

The very idea that a team can take a loss early on, regroup, win the rest of their games, and then come into the BCS as an underdog but completely dominate the game on offense and defense – it all reflects the complexity and unpredictability of modern college football.

Still, some of us had a feeling about 2006. Then numbers seemed to line up: 100 years of Gator football, 20 seniors on the team, 10 years since the National Championship…and if you look back at the '05 run-up, with the exception of the loss to South Carolina and Spurrier, what you really see is a team shaping its own destiny. Other things came together, too; for instance, Tim Tebow, who had his own destiny as the Heisman winner the following year, played a very special role for the Gators in '06, emotionally and in the playbook. Who knows – had we not lost to Auburn, perhaps we would have grown complacent late in the season. All in all, with national championships coming for both the UF basketball and football programs, 2006 was one for the scrapbooks.

The Visor tries to take a hard, sometimes cold look at the reality of any football situation (after all, I learned from the best), but I have to say that seeing the smiles on the faces of Urban Meyer, Chris Leak, Reggie Nelson and all the rest of the boys put a lump in my throat. They were the smiles of winners, and no matter what troubles lay behind or ahead, those moments can't be taken away. And now, the Visor has the great privilege to say:

It happened just like this…

**Visor Flings, Week 1:**
**Preview and Predictions**

Time to celebrate the 100th year of Florida Football! It's "something old and something new" for the 2006 edition.

The old is the 20 seniors on the roster trying to win a championship of any kind in their last go-around. Sad to actually have to say that. Contributors such as Chris Leak, Dallas Baker, Steve Rissler, Ray McDonald, Marcus Thomas, Earl Everett, and Eric Wilbur have one last chance to leave a lasting legacy at Florida, and it will be interesting to see if they can respond to that pressure from both the fans and within.

The new is the infusion of freshman talent coming in with this staff's first full recruiting class, rated in the top two in the nation. Potential future stars like Percy Harvin, Jarred Fayson, Riley Cooper, Tim Tebow, Maurice Hurt, Marcus Gilbert, Brandon Antwine, Brandon Spikes, Dustin Doe, and Markihe Anderson will be counted on to play in a significant capacity right away. Brandon James and Bryan Thomas will have a chance to contribute as well, after recovering from minor knee surgeries by October.

It will be fun to watch how this kind of dynamic plays out over the course of a very tough schedule this fall.

OFFENSE

It's year two for the Gator version of the spread offense, one that has been tailored to fit Leak's skills better, meaning more rollouts and less option plays. Coach Meyer and Leak have been hounded all off-season about how the QB will perform this year, and I hope Chris takes it as a personal challenge and excels. Of course, behind him on the depth chart is all-everything recruit Tebow, who already enjoys a cult status of sorts on campus and with the fans. A special package of plays will be established to suit his skills in the offense when he plays this year. I know he's very capable of excelling, but here's hoping he isn't thrust into a starting role, meaning Leak has been injured or failed to move the offense consistently. I don't believe that will be the case.

The unit that has the most pressure on it actually is the offensive line. Four senior starters have gone, but it's funny in a way that the coaching staff and players don't seem terribly concerned. Coaches Hevesy and Addazio have worked overtime to create a new rotation of players. For all of spring practice and a few weeks into fall camp, this unit struggled. However, the past few weeks have seen marked improvement and at least a part of that credit goes to the very impressive defensive talent they are practicing against daily. Rissler will lead the unit at center, taking over from four-year starter Mike Degory. He's the most experienced returning player and has adapted well. A mix of upperclassmen and freshmen will mix-and-match at the guard and tackle positions. Phil Trautwein and Carlton Medder get the first crack at tackle. "Trout" has looked good in practice, while Medder has more to prove, inheriting the starting position after Drew Miller was moved to guard until Ronnie Wilson (who the staff really likes) returns in October from a broken ankle. Miller should be solid at either position. The other guard spot starts with Jim Tartt. The staff knows he can be a star for them, but his chronically-injured shoulders have hampered all his attempts so far to get significant playing time. If he can stay healthy, the running game should see improvement in both consistency and output this season. Hurt and Gilbert will see action as well, and have received praise from the staff this fall.

The wide receiver corps is loaded. Baker leads a talented group that includes Jemalle Cornelius, Andre Caldwell (returning from the broken leg suffered against Tennessee last year), rising star Cornelius Ingram at tight end, and the much-hyped freshmen Harvin, Fayson, and Cooper. Injuries and a lack of quality depth really hampered the offense's effectiveness last year, but enough talent is in place now to overcome that. The mix of talent and abilities should cover all phases of the passing game – long, intermediate, short, and quick. This group should be one of the top units in the entire country, and will be fun to watch.

Finally, the much-maligned running back group gets its chance to prove the doubters wrong. It's the last chance for DeShawn Wynn to outgrow the "body by Tarzan, game by Jane" rap. He has to play hard every snap and play though small hurts that have sidelined him previously. If not, Kestahn Moore will get the majority of carries. He isn't the fastest or the biggest running back, but has proven to be consistent and a hard runner, qualities that Coach Drayton has been searching for from the entire group. Markus Manson looks to be number three right now, and will have to wait for his opportunity and then seize it, or he will be just a bit player. Out of the freshman class, little Brandon James has impressed the most. It looks like he won't be red-shirted even after missing the first few games with a knee injury, because he seems to have picked up the playbook faster. He could be a significant contributor as a special teams kick returner as the season progresses.

DEFENSE

This is the group that is getting the most hype nationally, and once again will have to carry the hopes for the season, especially early.

The defensive line could be scary good this year. The tackle rotation of Thomas, Joe Cohen, and Steven Harris will be tough for opposing O-lines to handle, with Thomas getting some all-SEC recognition in the pre-season. The group of ends, led by Jarvis Moss, is just as dangerous. Moss is expected to be a terror rushing the passer, with Derrick Harvey and RayMac wreaking their own havoc. If this group can play to it's potential all year, it should be recognized as one the country's best.

The linebacking corps is solid at the top, but scary thin in terms of experienced backups. Leader Brandon Siler is back, along with Earl Everett. Both players should earn some sort of all-SEC recognition this year. The third spot goes to senior Brian Crum, another "Tarzan/Jane" type that has to turn in a solid performance. With the season-ending knee injury to Jon Demps, the backups that will probably see a lot of time are true freshmen Spikes behind Siler and Doe behind Everett. Unfortunately, an injury to Siler or Everett could be disastrous. I expect to see a lot of 4-2-5 looks to help mask the thin depth at this position.

The secondary was the most worrisome unit coming out of the spring, especially after the drama surrounding the eventual dismissal of cornerback Avery Atkins. The staff had already decided to move Reggie "The Predator" Nelson to the spot opposite Reggie Lewis, but a fortuitous new NCAA rule (imagine that) enables a former Utah player under Coach Meyer and Heater, Ryan Smith, to transfer and enroll immediately after completing his undergraduate degree this summer. He has apparently earned a starting spot, enabling Nelson to move back to safety, where he can stay deep or blitz, both of which he does effectively. Depth at cornerback comes from Tremaine McCollum and freshmen Anderson and Jacques Rickerson. The safety position is solidified by Nelson's return. Tony Joiner gets the first shot at strong safety ahead of Kyle Jackson, and could fill the spot left by one less linebacker in the 4-2-5 alignment. Red-shirt freshman Dorian Munroe had his moments in fall practice, while another member of the stellar recruiting class, Bryan Thomas (coming off of minor knee surgery), excited the coaches in practice.

SPECIAL TEAMS

This group made a dramatic improvement in 2005, playing a huge role in wins over Tennessee, F$U, and Iowa. Punter Eric Wilbur and PK Chris Hetland are solid seniors, and form one of the better pairs in the country. The punt and kickoff coverage was one of the best in the country last year. But the real excitement could come from a combination of true freshmen and a few upperclassmen in the return game. Harvin and James should see work this fall, while Nelson will also do some punt returning. There are some electric athletes available to give the Gators a chance (finally) of instilling some real excitement into the return game again.

PREDICTIONS

The Gators can beat any opponent on this year's schedule. There's no doubt in my mind. However, the consistent quality of opponents, I believe, will catch up to Florida down the line. Along with Southern Miss. and UCF, two bowl teams, to start the season, the Gators face Tennessee on the road, followed by a stretch later of Alabama, LSU (Homecoming), Auburn, and Georgia (after an off-week). Plus a trip to Tallahassee to end the regular season. I think the two losses come in SEC play. There are still too many unanswered questions with he new O-line and lack of depth at linebacker and in the secondary to allow me to predict a zero- or one-loss season. I will say this team goes 10-2 in the regular season (which I say is a very nice accomplishment, given the schedule), and gets to Atlanta for the SEC Championship.

As for this weekend, the USM defense has historically been good, but has lost its leading two tacklers from last season. The D-line is okay, but lacks bulk. The Gator running game should prove effective as the evening wears on.

The Gator offense has to make some sort of positive statement right out of the box this game to establish momentum for the year. I really believe the wide receiver corps will be very difficult to defend, and Chris Leak should have better protection to get the ball down the field. It would be nice to see DeShawn Wynn establish himself as the leading man this fall, but I have to take a wait-and-see attitude for now.

It will be very nice to see the 1996 National Championship team honored before the game. That should be enough to get both the players and fans ready to start the season with a big win.

Visor Vision: Florida 38, USM 13

**Visor Flings, Week 2:**
**UF 34, Southern Mississippi 7**

The Gators looked like it was the first game of a new season for most of the first half Saturday against S. Miss. Perhaps it was a combination of a hangover effect from the celebration of the 1996 National Championship team and the fact that the Golden Eagles came to play and jumped out to an early lead. Whatever the case, it took a while for both the offense and defense to find any sort of rhythm and take over the game.

On offense, an early mistake by true freshman Percy Harvin of cutting off his route too early led to an interception on the first series of the game. But after that – wow! Harvin has “it”. The kid has serious speed and acceleration, and saw seven touches and played very well, more than justifying the hype coming out of high school. Dallas Baker had a great night, and is definitely Chris Leak's go-to guy. His improvement even from late last year, is significant. It seems Leak spread the ball out to the receivers fairly well. The timing on the deep throws still needs a lot of work. It's good to see Coach Mullen call a handful of deep throws, but the players have to hit on a few to loosen up defenses. The running game was spotty. DeShawn Wynn started off very well, but now is a question mark after sitting out the entire second half with another in a long series of neck/shoulder injuries. Plus Markus Manson was dinged as well. Kestahn Moore carried the load in the second half, and he frankly looked rusty and a little slow after missing the majority of spring and fall practice with a back problem. The running game could be a trouble spot this year. It looks as if Coach Meyer and Drayton will try to get true freshman Mon Williams ready, after deciding in fall camp he would red shirt. Finally, the O-line played an okay game, but the absence of Ronnie Wilson at guard because of injury has caused Drew Miller to slide down to that slot, and Carlton Medder struggled both run- and pass-blocking. So did Phil Trautwein at the other tackle slot. Not a good sign. Miller had an excellent fall camp at right tackle until the re-shuffling, and this unit has to improve until all the original pieces are back in place. It was a good sign that the interior pass protection was good, with Leak not having to run for his life as he had to so often last year.

The defense got an early wake-up call after the interception of Leak. Southern Miss. went right to the air and scored in just a few plays. I think that stunned both the players and fans, and it took until the second quarter until the defense took over the game. I was surprised at the amount of blitzing from the corners so early in the season, but perhaps Coach Strong has simply decided to go for broke this year. I would have liked to see a more vanilla approach to give teams later in the schedule less to look at. The D-line played a solid game, but the absence of Steven Harris and Markus Thomas at tackle was obvious. Little push came up the middle on passing downs, and that may have forced the corner blitzes. The play of the tackles against the run was okay. Jarvis Moss was disruptive off the edge, coming close to a few sacks and drawing a couple of holding penalties. Brandon Siler was his usual self at linebacker, running sideline-to-sideline and making sure tackles. Earl Everett actually missed a few open field tackles, but made up for that with very solid pass coverage. It was interesting to see how many plays Brian Crum was removed and Kyle Jackson was inserted for a 4-2-5 alignment. I think we will see this a lot this season. Tony Joiner played a very nice game at strong safety, getting an interception and some pass breakups. Reggie Lewis and Ryan Smith were good in coverage, but there were a few times they blew some assignments on corner routes. Perhaps there were some communication problems with Reggie Nelson rotating over. But Nelson was a beast at free safety, getting a key end-zone interception to stop a drive in the third quarter, and flying all over to make sure tackles. If he stays healthy, he should make all-SEC this year.

The special teams kick coverage was very good. No big plays allowed, and sure tackling. Nelson looked like he could be a dangerous punt returner. The kickoff returns were surprisingly poor, though, and Coach Meyer said this unit would get lots of attention this week.

Overall, a solid performance for the first game, but with plenty of work to do to keep the players' attention this week.

Another bowl team from 2005 comes to the Swamp this week, UCF. They are favored to win their division in C-USA, and George O'Leary has instilled some toughness and confidence into their program. To be honest, Florida should enjoy a decided advantage in the trenches. There is a significant discrepancy in talent between the two teams. QB Steven Moffett has improved dramatically, and running back Kevin Smith is very good. Mike Walker is a solid wide receiver. However, the Gator D-line should wreak havoc, especially with the return of Thomas and Harris at defensive tackle. And Moffett still is prone to poor throws into coverage when under pressure. The Florida O-line should be able to establish an effective running attack because of its size and talent advantage. These first two games are solid preparation before the Gators travel up to Tennessee to face a resurgent Volunteer team that waxed California. Tim Tebow should get more reps, and some of the key starters should get the chance to play a little less to prepare for a key road test.
My prediction: Florida 38, UCF 14

**Visor Flings, Week 3:**
**UF 42, Central Florida 0**

The Gators certainly showed improvement from game one to game two, dominating UCF 42-0. Almost all phases played well, especially the blocking of the O-line and the improved pass-rush of the D-line. Of course, the return of defensive tackles Marcus Thomas and Steven Harris had a lot to do with that. The playmaking and depth of the skill position players, especially Percy Harvin and Dallas Baker, is exciting to watch right now.

UCF's defense had no answer for stopping either the run or pass. I thought it was interesting that they used only a three-man rush many times, which had no chance of really pressuring Leak or stopping any decent push by the O-line. The Gator defense dictated the tempo practically from the start. In fact, the first UCF drive of the game where they got out of the hole at their end to midfield before punting was the defense's worst series.

Another encouraging sign by the Gator offense was the distribution of the ball to so many backs and receivers. There are so many weapons for Leak to take advantage of right now that, if the O-line just gives him a little time, he should be able to move the ball against the Vols just enough to keep control of the game.

Now it's on to Tennessee, where the Volunteer fans are thinking they're all the way back and talking a big game. I will say that they should thank heaven that David Cutcliffe is back to coordinate that crappy offense from last season, and he has that group playing much better, especially in the passing game. Their wide receivers are big and physical, and will prove a challenge to the Gator cornerbacks. The Gator secondary just needs to prevent the big plays off of missed tackles that Tennessee has thrived on so far this year, and make Eric Ainge play mistake-free ball, which I don't believe he's capable of yet.

Tennessee's running game is actually only average this year, and if the Florida front four can hold its own without relying on too much help from the linebackers, the Gators should be in good shape. UT's O-line, while well-coached as always, is not as dominant as in years past, at least this early in the year. Florida's D-line is very strong and quick, and I have to believe it will make some big plays and cause a few turnovers.

It was good to see Air Force push Tennessee to the wire last week, making those guys sweat until the end and forcing the first-teamers to play the entire game. The Vol defensive front seven is nowhere near as strong, deep, or effective as last year, and the Gator O-line has to exploit this area. It's time for Coach Hevesy to show he can mold a unit that can perform effectively in a big road game.

I really feel Florida can win this game. The only thing preventing me from being even more confident is the fact that this coaching staff with these players has yet to prove they can win a big SEC road game. Everyone needs to push through that mental and emotional wall this week, or the wolves will start howling again.

Prognosti-Visor says: Florida 27, Tennessee 17

**Visor Flings, Week 4:**
**UF 21, Tennessee 20**

It was a true team victory at Knoxville against the Volunteers. The offense, defense and special teams, despite some occasional struggles or self-inflicted harm, each played a solid game. Even more important, however, was the maturity the team and coaching staff showed in the face of the adversity of a 10-point second-half deficit, pushing through a major emotional and psychological wall as far as winning on the road.

Chris Leak showed cool under fire in leading the offense on the two TD drives. Tim Tebow showed leadership and maturity in getting the clutch first downs he was asked to run for. Cornelius and Baker made the big receptions, especially sweet for Dallas after the embarrassment of 2004 in this game. The O-line is actually playing a little better than I had hoped, especially in establishing a solid rushing attack. DeShawn Wynn played his best game as a Gator, getting some nice gains and running for tough first downs in the fourth quarter. Even Dan Mullen, who I've criticized heavily so far, called a good game.

There are still some items to be improved on, and that should keep the players' attention. Leak needs to get rid of the ball to avoid unnecessary sacks, the O-line needs to continue to improve it's pass-blocking, and Wynn has to now show he can be a consistent performer each week.

The defense was hell on Tennessee's run game all night, outclassing the Vol O-line and forcing UT into a one-dimensional attack. The advantage in size and strength of the Vol receivers was exploited somewhat, but the Gator secondary followed the game plan of forcing long drives and sure tackling.

The D-line was getting a push against the run and pass, and Marcus Thomas showed why he is a difference-maker and an all-SEC talent (more on him later). Ray MacDonald is finally showing some of his pre-injury form again, both at tackle and end. Moss and Harvey are doing a good job of playing the run as well as the pass at defensive end.

The linebacker corps was very good all night. Earl Everett deservedly earned SEC Player of the Week honors for showing off his solid tackling and pass-coverage skills. Brandon Siler tackled well and made the play of the game, sacking Ainge on UT's last drive, which forced them into a difficult down-and-distance position.

Reggie Nelson showed why he is one of the top safeties in the country with his two big interceptions, while Lewis and Smith tackled well and didn't give up the big play at cornerback.

The special teams were frustrating even while showing some glimpses of something really big. Wilbur's punts were of the ugly variety, and Hetland missed his two field goals. Yes, they were long, but he shows the leg strength now to make those, and has to get on track. The really nice surprise was Brandon "Little Train" James, who had two dazzling punt returns, especially the 84-yarder called back on a very questionable block-in-the-back call. Coach Meyer loves to coach this unit, and I think we are about to get some more big plays out of this group this season.

Now it's on to Kentucky, with the cloud of disappointment hanging overhead at the indefinite suspension of Marcus Thomas due to a supposed second failed drug test. Whether it's a case of double-jeopardy or not, he will miss at least this game, and the team has to move on and focus on continuing to improve and taking up the slack. Kentucky is actually showing some life on offense this year, with it's best passing attack in a long time. Andre Woodson is a tough player at QB. UK could be hurt though with the questionable health status of its best running back (Little) and center. The Wildcat defense is still not SEC-caliber, though, and I expect the Gator offense to get its share of big plays and scoring drives. I hope the staff lets Percy Harvin rest his ankle injury this week, and even as much as possible next week against Alabama, if at all possible. There are plenty of reliable playmakers at wide receiver this year to get things done. Hopefully Wynn can continue to be effective and consistent, and the O-line can build on its early-season momentum.

Prediction: Florida 31, Kentucky 14

**Visor Flings, Week 5:**
**UF 26, Kentucky 7**

"The good, the bad, and the ugly" can summarize the uneven effort against the Mildcats on Saturday.

The Good:

The O-line is really coming together. The run-blocking was very good, and the tackles showed some hustle getting out in front of some wide receiver screens. A few pass-blocking missed assignments, but overall a solid effort.

Wynn and Moore ran well, finding the lanes created by the line and doing a fairly good job of running north-south. It's too bad neither has breakaway speed, because their were some big holes. We will have to accept that fact, and just hope they stay healthy and that the line continues to improve.

Chris Leak spread the ball around nicely and made some accurate throws. The yards after the catch (YAC) were excellent, especially for Dallas Baker. The downfield blocking by the receivers continues to yield results for all ball carriers. Tim Tebow really brought some energy into the game. He really has good feet for a big guy, and continues to do his job well.

Finally, the run defense continues to dictate the flow of the game. This group has been excellent.

The Bad:

Two fumbles, one each by Wynn and Moore. Unusual, but that's just the start of what was an unusual night. No true long runs given the opportunity.

Leak continues to hold the ball too long on occasion, missing chance at Baker and Caldwell.

Still too many false-start penalties by the O-line. No excuse, especially at home.

The play-calling by Dan Mullen left something to be desired. I'd like to see the QB that has led his team down the field finish the drive. I think the switching of QBs mid-drive is leading to some of the penalties and not finishing the drive off in the red zone. Also, it took way too long for Strong/Mattison to adjust the defense and call off the blitzes. The front four was dominant, and it wasn't until the third quarter that playing straight-up defense stopped the only thing working for UK – the screens and slants.

The Ugly:

Quite probably the worst display of tackling since Meyer and the new staff took over. Horrendous technique, and that's surprising. The defense took this game too lightly and lost focus early. The early scheme by Kentucky's offense was effective, but still too many mistakes.

And the kicking game on extra points and field goals has completely collapsed. That's shocking, especially with Coach Meyer spending so much time getting this unit personally ready. The blocking has been getting overrun right up the middle all season, and it hasn't been corrected.

It's now time for the toughest schedule in the country to come calling, starting with Alabama. It's obvious that the coaches will have the player's attention all week – both because of the sloppy effort against the Mildcats, but after last year's embarrassment against the Crimson Tide.

Once again, Bama's offense is safe and simple. Run the ball a lot (even if it's not always effective), and isolate their big receivers one-on-one. Unfortunately, I see them using the same strategy as Tennessee and Kentucky did, especially with a young QB on the road. Short, quick passes to bigger WRs, and attempting ball-control.

It will be interesting to see if Strong and Mattison blitz early and often again, or if they try and make John Parker Wilson read defenses. I think they lay back at first and try to get a read on Bama's intentions with the passing game. I'd definitely like to see the linebackers get better drops to help cut off the slant and square-in lanes.

I have to believe that the entire offensive staff, including Coach Meyer, are personally looking for some measure of redemption against Bama after the debacle last year. The Tide lost a lot of seniors off of last year's team, but are still very well-coached. It's time for this offense to raise it's level of play for the big-boy defenses it's going to see the next four games. I really don't expect to see a lot of mis-direction and trickery this week, because Bama is too smart for that. A lot of weird stuff shown against UK was, I believe, stuff just to make the Tide defense waste some practice time this week. Time to outwork and outplay another group head-to-head. The Gator defense should be able to control the flow of the game, but not too complacently. If they can rattle the young Bama offense early, everything else should fall into place.

As I see it: Florida 28, Alabama 13

**Visor Flings, Week 6:**
**UF 28, Alabama 13**

Another slow start, another strong finish for the 2006 version of the Florida Gators. It's a tribute to the improved toughness and resiliency of this team that they have been behind by 10 points to their two strongest opponents to date, yet have pushed through and overcome those obstacles.

Alabama's offense played better than anticipated, especially QB John Parker Posey, er, Wilson. Kenneth Darby ran hard, and the Brown and Hall got a lot of underneath yards at wide receiver. Yet for all that, their offense only managed six points. That tells you how strong this year's Gator defense is, even without the suspended Marcus Thomas.

The Florida offense continues to struggle early, and it may be time for Dan Mullen to loosen up the play-calling and quicken the pace in the first quarter to shake things up. The

95-yard drive near the end of the first half changed to entire complexion of the game, and the offense really dictated things after that. The combination of Leak and Tebow continues to be effective. It was another fine performance by the WRs, with Baker, Cornelius, and Caldwell all making big, clutch plays.

The Gator defense was able to once again cover the absence of Thomas along the line, getting three sacks and forcing some bad throws in the second half, the last of which was returned by Reggie Freaking Nelson to ice the game. The cornerbacks played hard, even though they were once again physically out-manned. The bend but don't break philosophy worked again, but it was nice to see the secondary playing bump-and-run in the fourth quarter, making Bama have to execute to make a big play.

Now comes the first of the two biggest tests on this year's schedule, back-to-back. LSU comes a-callin' to the Swamp, talking a big game after beating up another weak opponent, while getting stuffed by Auburn, the only decent team they've played.

The Tigers do have a legitimate group of skill players at QB and wide receiver. Bowe, Doucet, and Craig Davis are the closest WR corps to Florida's, and JaMarcus Russell is throwing deep effectively. Once again, Florida's defensive front seven has a chance to force some mistakes out of Russell, who still must show he can manage a close game. LSU's running game is nowhere near it past proficiency, and I think the Gators will make the Tigers one-dimensional on offense. The surprise return of Marcus Thomas from suspension will be a huge emotional lift, not to mention another quality player in the defensive tackle rotation.

The real challenge is on the Florida offense, which will be facing probably the best defense it will see in 2006, and that's saying something. LSU has a great secondary, and the Gator receivers have to prove they can beat them man-to-man. LSU has a solid front seven as well, but lost a lot of experience to graduation and aren't quite as good as last year. The Gator offensive line must establish some modicum of a running game, especially with the chance DeShawn Wynn doesn't play. Kestahn Moore is still a functional running back, and Brandon "Little Train" James and the forgotten one, Markus Manson, will have to pull their weight.

I really hope Percy Harvin can contribute at least a few plays, but I suspect he will mainly be a decoy. I just have the feeling that there are plays that have been saved for this game that could break things open. I believe that Coach Meyer has some special teams surprises as well. Even more than that, though, the Gators are getting NO respect nationally, and were even a home underdog until the announced return of Thomas! This is a slap in the face to the entire program, and I think they respond with a great performance against a very good LSU team in the biggest game of the season.

My prediction: Florida 20 LSU 17

**Visor Flings, Week 7:**
**UF 23, LSU 10**

A huge win for the good guys at the Swamp, which was rocking like it was 2001 again. That was a quality effort by all phases against a solid LSU team. It was obvious the players were invested in this game, and had a lot to prove to LSU and the nation (until the next game, when all of the doubters and haters come out again).

The Florida defense was outstanding in the clutch. Those were NFL-caliber receivers they were facing, as is Russell at QB. You can't expect them to hold LSU down completely, and they didn't. However, making the critical plays and forcing turnovers is what a great defense does, and this group is starting to look like that.

Reggie Freakin' Nelson will haunt the dreams of LSU's receivers for weeks, and Ryan Smith has been a godsend at cornerback. The return of Marcus Thomas was timely, and he played really well for missing 3 weeks of practice serving his suspension.

The Gator offense still moves in fits and jerks at times, but seems to be gaining some momentum now. The special packages for Tebow at QB are really giving opponents trouble. Leak was solid, but it's time for him to make some more aggressive passes downfield and let his quality WRs make some plays – they are more than capable.

It's a shame that the running game has stagnated somewhat, and the absence of Wynn really hurts. Mullen and Meyer will continue to shuffle other RBs and WRs at the tailback position to get by, and that's one of the hidden blessings of a spread option offense.

Now, on to the next "Game of the Year"...against the Tigers/War Eagles/Plainsmen/Whatevers of Auburn.

I really believe it's on the Florida offense to carry the day for this game. It's time to help out the defense by staying tied or actually having a first-quarter lead. It's obvious that Dan Mullen is adding a few new wrinkles and plays each week, capitalizing on the diverse talents of not just the QBs, but the other skill position players as well.

I think this game will be won by Chris Leak and his passing. Auburn's defense, while undersized, is the fastest the Gators will face all season. Slow-developing runs and stretch plays probably won't have much success against the Tigers. I could see more I-formation runs and play-action passes, to let the larger O-line play simple smash-mouth ball, while the receivers should out-talent Auburn's secondary. Yes, there may be something special thrown in when Tebow comes in, such as more passing, but I'd like to see more 'option' in the spread from him and the tailbacks, which I believe would have success against the Tiger defense.

Florida's defense will be tested by the very strong Auburn running game. Kenny Irons and the Tiger offensive line are very tough. The Gator linebacking corps will get it's biggest physical test to date. It will be interesting to see how well Earl Everett and Brian Crum respond to the physical pounding. The secondary should be able to control Courtney Taylor, Auburn's only real deep threat. It's how well Florida can recognize and control the play-action passes and patterns for the tight ends that will dictate how often they can get the

Tiger offense off the field. Control the Tiger running game and keep Cox from playing comfortably in the pocket, and this is a Gator win.

Once again Florida has to play a team fighting for its life to make it to Atlanta. I think there's enough left in the tank for this one, but the bye week will be much-needed after this battle.

Visorly Outlook: Florida 21, Auburn 17

**Visor Flings, Week 8:**
**Auburn 27, UF 17**

Implosion on the Plains.

A disastrous set of events, almost all self-inflicted, ruined the Gators' chance of a perfect regular season and re-opened the SEC East race. After playing an inspired first half of offense, and safe but surprisingly soft defense, the entire team – players and coaches, threw away all that was gained up until then and self-destructed.

It was especially painful to see seniors like Chris Leak and Eric Wilbur make freshman-like mistakes that cost Florida the win. Dropping a punt snap, fumbling in the red zone, and an egregious interception are completely unacceptable plays, and their teammates have to feel somewhat let down, despite the camaraderie this year's group has.

The entire coaching staff bears blame as well. The defense played extremely safe, soft pass coverage all night, allowing Auburn to control the momentum and the clock, while allowing the Gator offense to run only 45 plays – ridiculous. I was very disappointed in the play of Earl Everett and Brandon Siler against the run, repeatedly taking bad angles to the ball and often not even touching a running back, leaving the secondary to make the tackle downfield. Jarvis Moss had a critical penalty, completely brain-locking and roughing the QB well away from the play, while the defensive line had two more stupid offsides penalties. I can't believe the coaches wouldn't let the cornerbacks challenge Auburn's receivers off the line of scrimmage, instead sitting back and getting picked apart by a weak-armed QB.

The offensive staff made zero adjustments in the second half, never allowing Leak to roll away from the pocket to give him better vision to throw. Plus, a very talented group of WRs was basically wasted in the passing game. No aggressive downfield passing game all evening – shocking. Once again Dan Mullen seemed to outsmart himself, doing way too many cute things instead of playing a little more smash-mouth in the only trip to the red zone in the second half. Where is Tim Tebow running the “spread” part of the spread option in short-yardage situations?

This is a crushing loss, and Coach Meyer has to get the team to somehow mentally push forward from this. The off week is much-needed for this group to physically come back, but mentally they have two weeks to re-hash the game in their own minds while being reminded of it from everyone.

The goal of reaching the SEC championship game in Atlanta is still attainable, but there is zero margin of error now. A big season and BCS bowl are still possible as well. It will be very interesting to see the mental state of the team in two weeks in Jacksonville against Georgia. Florida is clearly a better team, but stupid mistakes and poor coaching adjustments can level any playing field.

**Visor Flings, Week 9:**
**Off Week**

The Gators have had to endure the off week to re-live their collapse at Auburn, and try to move on. At least the hated Puppies should be enough to get their full attention in Jacksonville.

Georgia is really struggling right now. Their offense has rotated three QBs this year, and true freshman Matthew Stafford looks like he'll start against Florida. Strong arm, a little mobility, but very little touch and suspect accuracy right now. I wouldn't be surprised at all to see Tereshinski sometime during the game – hopefully trying to lead a comeback after the Gators have taken it to Georgia.

Florida's offense must start to put together a full game of production. The majority of the second half against Auburn was a washout. It's time for Chris Leak to play like a senior leader and stop the stupid mistakes. Since there will apparently be no dominant running back this year, look for more carries by the receivers on sweeps, and maybe even Percy Harvin lining up at tailback more often. Sad, but true. Maybe Wynn will come off the bye much healthier and this won't be necessary, but I have little confidence in that happening right now.

The Gator wide receivers have a clear advantage over the Georgia secondary in terms of talent. These guys should get plenty of chances to make plays after the catch, and must do so. I expect there to be an expanded playbook for Tebow as well, with a few more pass plays put in for him.

It will be very interesting to see if the Florida defensive staff will play more aggressively, after letting Auburn control the clock decisively. Georgia has a weak receiving corps, and there is NO reason to have Reggie Freakin' Nelson lined up 30 yards downfield. It's time to cut these boys loose and hit people. The linebacker play against the run has been, frankly, disappointing. Brandon Siler needs to play better in filling the gaps. I hope Brandon Spikes starts to see more playing time as well, as Brian Crum has not impressed lately.

Coach Meyer had to be disgusted with the pathetic second half performance at Auburn, and I think he is going to do whatever it takes, either psychologically or personnel-wise, to shake things up and re-focus this team. And it needs to be done. The Gators have a lot to play for yet this year, and there is no room for error.

Prediction: Florida 28, Georgia 13

## Visor Flings, Week 10:
## UF 21, Georgia 14

It's always a good and a joyful thing to put the Puppies in their place, now 15 out of 17 times. But count me as one fan who is beginning to wonder if this team and staff really know how to put a team away and if they lack a killer instinct.

It was obvious early that Florida's defense was comfortable and in control, not allowing any sustained drives at all. Stafford looked uncomfortable, and was feeling the heat from the Gator pass rush. The linebackers played one of their best games against the run all year. I think they were somewhat embarrassed after the Auburn debacle, and came out with renewed energy. The secondary played tighter coverage as well, as they should have, against a less-talented Georgia receiving corps. The penetration provided by Thomas and RayMac really blew up any strategy Richt could come up with, even resulting in what proved to be the deciding score on the first play of the second half. The only disappointing thing about the Gator defensive effort was the inability to decently cover the tight end, and not playing disciplined football against the screen pass – especially since those are staples of the Georgia offense.

The offensive performance was very lackluster, and I'm afraid that at this point it won't get any better this late in the season. Leak played a little better than against Auburn, and was victimized by three or four dropped passes. But once again he threw a bad interception to let Georgia start its comeback, and is still throwing off his back foot when facing the blitz. After starting four years, I suppose we can't expect it to change now. It's frustrating to see how the staff has to cobble together a rushing attack, having to use Harvin and Caldwell so often, and not having a reliable running back to count on, unless Wynn gets back to full health.

The offensive game plan after getting the 14-0 lead lacked focus. Why Mullen continues to go into a shell is beyond me at this point. His play-calling was once again suspect, especially in the red zone. All Florida needed to do was pound away between the tackles to set up shorter attempts for Hetland to get insurance points, but too many horizontal calls netted negative yardage and allowed the Puppies to barely stay in the game. At the end, Florida showed it could get tough yards by playing smash-mouth and getting a few key first downs, but Mullen refused to employ that philosophy when it could have iced things early.

Now, it's on to Vanderbilt, and at this point I expect nothing but close games from this staff from here on out. There is no reason Florida can't concentrate on Bennett to slow down Vandy's passing game, and there is enough team speed to spy the QB and not allow him to extend drives on scrambles. The Gator offense has a huge advantage in speed, but will Mullen take advantage of it early, of will he be content to squeeze out a few scores and call it a day early – again?

Florida still controls it's SEC destiny, and still has a shot at sneaking into the BCS championship game if it wins out. I think Coach Meyer has just about had enough of the offensive struggles, and is going to kick some ass the next few weeks to keep the players' attention and try to stimulate some improvement.

Conservatively: Florida 27, Vanderbilt 14

**Visor Flings, Week 11:**
**UF 25, Vanderbilt 19**

Another Saturday, another sloppy win for the Gators. Once again, what could have been a comfortable win turned into nervous time late. It's apparent that after nine games, this Gator offense just doesn't seem capable of putting together a complete game, with just enough penalties and turnovers to allow anyone to stay close.

I was impressed with the D-line picking up the slack after the very disappointing news that Marcus Thomas was dismissed from the team. Derrick Harvey now leads the SEC in sacks, and Jarvis Moss is showing a versatile game, both dropping into coverage and playing the backside pursuit against the run very well. Earl Everett played good pass coverage again, while Brandon Siler made more plays against the run than he has in a while. Ryan Smith should start getting a lot of attention for some all-SEC votes. The guy is quick and smart, and also a special teams ace.

The Gator offense just can't seem to establish an identity, nor play consistently for four quarters. Chris Leak made some bad throws on two of his interceptions, plays a senior can't make. At least he had Dallas Baker and Bubba Caldwell running wild in the Vandy secondary to keep drives alive. The running game was underwhelming, again. DeShawn Wynn doesn't seem to be a good fit in the spread as far as reading a zone blocking scheme, but is still the only reliable back.

Now comes a huge game from many angles for the Gator coaches, players, and fans. Urban Meyer can put to rest a lot of the Spurrier worship that still permeates Florida fans, while the players can help wash away the stink of their performance at South Carolina last season, where they threw away a SEC East title. I think the fans give the old Head Ball Coach a rude welcome, and I hope the Gator team gives them even more reason to boo the Chickens off the field after getting pounded.

I expect the entire playbook from Spurrier. Rotating QBs, fade routes, trickeration. Fortunately, I think Florida's defense out-talents the Carolina O-line, and can play straight-up football and let the back seven control the passing game. If Florida could ever put together a complete offensive game, they would easily make USC one-dimensional and negate any possibility of the running game or Syvelle Newton being a threat. I think Blake Mitchell is good for at least two turnovers if he's pressured even moderately.

Florida's O-line has a few dings and little depth, and Siler is battling a knee injury. I really want a good ass-whipping, but at this point, it's just survive and advance.

Visor Vision: Florida 31, South Carolina 21

**Visor Flings, Week 12:**
**UF 17, South Carolina 16**

Was it any surprise that the Gators were in a death struggle with the ol' HBC? This team, whether it's the execution of the players, strange play-calling by the coordinators, turnovers, penalties, or suspensions, just refuses to put an opponent away of take advantage of good fortune. Instead, it's a weekly stomach-turning experience for everyone.

This was actually the best performance by the offense all season. Seven possessions, each of over 50 yards, but only 17 points. Chris Leak played perhaps his best game under Urban Meyer, toughing out the fourth quarter and calling his own number on some clutch runs. The threat of DeShawn Wynn gave the offense balance, and Percy Harvin was too much for the Gamecock defense to handle. The seniors on offense were solid as usual. Even the O-line played very well.

The Florida defense, however, really showed the wear of a brutal SEC schedule. Injuries to Siler and Everett and the suspension of Thomas softened the middle, and USC was able to establish a running game, which was the last thing Gator fans wanted. It opened up the pass in the fourth quarter, and the Gators had to rely on an incredible effort by RayMac and Jarvis Moss on special teams to save the day.

Of course, this was a HUGE statement game for Coach Meyer, beating down the legend of SOS in the Swamp. He showed real guts and faith by going for it on fourth down with six minutes left, and his motivation could be seen again in how this team made the plays it had to win. I'll never forgive Spurrier for coaching against the Gators each year in a position to ruin their conference hopes. He is a pariah until he retires...then he is welcome back home at Florida.

This was also a big-time recruiting weekend, with a host of four and five star recruits on hand to witness the victory. Expect a handful of future commitments to come from this group.

No apologies for welcoming 1-AA Western Carolina to the Swamp. Plus, this is a great opportunity to rest injured players and get quality playing time for Tebow, some young receivers, and inexperienced defenders. This will be nothing more than a glorified scrimmage. And the mantra for games like this remains the same – NO INJURIES!

Welcoming respite: Florida 45, W. Carolina 3

**Visor Flings, Week 13:**
**UF 62, Western Carolina 0**

The Gators destroyed the Catamounts 62-0 on Senior Day. It was a great way to send off the seniors, allowing them some early success, then getting their deserved ovations as they were pulled out early to let the young guys show a glimpse of the future.

It's always kind of strange to see how fast the four or five years have gone by for players like Chris Leak, Dallas Baker, Earl Everett, and company – guys who it seems have been around forever for various reasons.

The freshmen stole the show, however. Tim Tebow, Mon Williams, Brandon James, Jarred Fayson, and Riley Cooper stood out on offense, while Brandon Spikes, Dustin Doe, Brandon Antwine, and Markihe Anderson continued to show promise on defense. This is a great freshman class.

Now it's time for the final push, starting with a trip to Taliban City to try and drive another stake into the unconquered, I mean unranked, $emihole$. Despite this being a rivalry game, things are so bad up there that Florida would really have to self-destruct like they did in the second half at Auburn, for F$U to have a real chance at victory.

On offense, I hope to see the Gators play fast, attack, and use the middle of the field, not just play a horizontal game. Florida's O-line has the advantage, while the Gator WRs have a decided edge. If Dan Mullen isn't afraid to be aggressive early and often, I think the Gators will find enough success to keep F$U off-balance.

On defense, Florida doesn't need to worry much about a lousy $emihole running game. Yes, they will hit some jump balls to Greg Carr. The key is not to allow those plays to occur in the red zone. The area of most concern to me is the pass rush. Cohen and Harris need to step up their level of play – the loss of Marcus Thomas was really felt against South Carolina. The secondary needs to focus on stopping Chris Davis and Brandon Warren on slants and seam routes over the middle. The linebackers need to keep an eye on Slowrenzo Booker, who can actually do some damage out flat passes and wheel routes, both by design and on broken plays.

If the Gators strike early and continue to apply pressure, neither Weatherford or Lee worries me much at QB. I think Lee actually gives them a better chance because of his mobility, but Jeffy the SOB (Son of Bowden) is the great equalizer. Too bad he's not sticking around a few more years to further destroy what little is left of F$U's confidence.

The Gators still have a LOT to play for. It all starts with the coaching staff getting the team focused on a rivalry game this week, followed by the trip to Atlanta. Other than Dallas Baker being questionable with a sprained MCL (and I believe he will play), last week was a great break to give guys like Siler and Everett the week off, while playing other key players sparingly.

Time to go for four in a row over F$U (and yes, I will always count the 'Swindle at the Swamp' in 2003 as a win).

Crystal ball reads: Florida 27, F$U 17

**Visor Flings, Week 14:**
**UF 21, Florida State 14**

It's great to beat Florida State! Now it's four in a row (I'll always count the 2003 game as a win for the Gators). Another example of how mentally tough this year's group has become, never losing focus even after a dreadful third quarter caused by poor field position and questionable play-calling.

Chris Leak was finally allowed to expose an overmatched Nole secondary, as the Florida WRs were running free most of the day and making plays after the catch. The O-line played pretty well, despite the two holding calls. The real disappointment was the disappearance of the running game after Harvin and Wynn left with injuries. It's hard to believe the offensive staff has no confidence in anyone else to show a credible running threat.

Baker and Caldwell were terrific all game, making huge plays and scoring. Until Harvin was hurt, he certainly made his presence felt, and his direct-snap TD run was beautiful, as he left the Seminoles in his dust down the sideline. Even CI made a few clutch grabs as well to extend drives. This is definitely one of the top three groups in the country for 2006.

The defense was very impressive. I do not fault them for giving up only one big running play and one long jump ball completion. Those are to be expected. They did limit the number of big plays and made some huge interceptions to kill any momentum F$U tried to establish.

Once again, though, Dan Mullen's play-calling left something to be desired, as he continues to select plays that kill any offensive flow. It took Leak making two clutch plays to overcome another ill-fated wide receiver reverse call on the last TD drive, while the playbook for Tebow continues to be too predictable. The shotgun plays in their own end zone instead of lining up in the I-formation were very shaky.

Now it's on to the SEC Championship Game against Arkansas. It's been too long to be away from Atlanta for that game.

The Razorback running game will be far and away the best the Gators have faced in years. McFadden and Jones are NFL talents running behind a tough O-line. The only saving grace is that their passing game is almost non-existent. McFadden even lines up quite a bit at the QB position, which gives them flexibility to run some funky plays. This will be a huge assignment for Coach Strong and Mattison, and a real gut-check for the UF defenders, who will have to play their physical best on Saturday.

On offense, I hope Chris Leak gets the chance to open up the entire passing game and attack downfield against an overmatched Arkansas secondary. The Gator O-line and running backs had better be ready to pick up the blitz, as Defensive Coach Reggie Herring is not afraid to play man-to-man and bring the house. If Wynn doesn't play, the Gators will very likely have only a small threat of running the ball effectively, but so be it. Now's the time to lean on the senior leaders on offense and let them pull out the win.

On defense, I hope to see the Gators play "outside-in" and try to pinch the Hog running game to the middle of the field. They really like to hit the edges with direct snaps to McFadden, and use a lot of the jet-sweeps outside. Siler, Everett, Crum, Spikes, and Doe have to play a smart, physical game and tackle well. I expect Arkansas to run for over 100 yards easily; probably closer to 200. However, making just those few key plays to get them in long down-and-distance situations will make them very uncomfortable.

It really has to gall the players and coaches to hear all the dismissive talk about how the Gators are a "sham," and win ugly. It's incredible how the media has started to control perceptions and polls, and it's shameful. It's time for Florida to shut up a lot of people this Saturday.

Going with the Gut: Florida 28, Arkansas 24

## Visor Flings, Week 15:
## UF 38, Arkansas 28

It was a microcosm of the entire 2006 season for the Gators on display at the Georgia Dome against Arkansas. A quick start, followed by a ghastly 3rd quarter, followed by a tough fourth quarter performance to win the game. And another emotional wringer for the fans to go through.

Florida's coaches prepared a very nice game plan on offense and defense. On offense, Leak was given solid protection to throw, and Florida chose to abuse the Hog's 3-4-5 defensive backs. The great depth at WR really played out in that match-up. With Wynn basically out, Harvin and Moore were able to pick up the slack, with Percy making his claim as a freshman All-American with the game-winning home run early in the fourth quarter. The O-line played hard, and toughed out some painful injuries to Miller and Rissler. Not as much cute stuff called by Dan Mullen either. The shovel pass intercepted to give Arkansas the lead was poor execution by both Leak and Harvin. But the last TD to ice the game was a classic staple of the Spread Option – Tebow rolling left, then flipping the reverse pitch to Caldwell, who had the pass/run option. Great play.

The defense was tremendous against the running game. The Hogs' combination of McFadden and Jones is every bit as good as Auburn had in 2004 with Williams and Brown. Steven Harris has really blossomed in Thomas's old spot, while Cohen, Moss, RayMac, and Harvey played disciplined assignments, not allowing the breakaway scores that Arkansas has thrived on all season. And Brandon Siler was a beast in the middle, laying the wood to the running backs all night with sure, hard tackles. It was a little disappointing to see the Gators give up some big pass plays and penalties, but that happens against such a powerful running team, combined with the injury to Joiner. Munroe played well for a freshmen thrown into such a big game, but also got hit with two pass interference penalties.

Of course, the special teams were again just that, not allowing any big kickoff returns, executing a ballsy fake punt to break some of Arkansas' momentum, then completely turning the game around with the huge punt by Wilbur followed by the TD recovery by Pierre-Louis to re-take the lead. This group is coached hard by Meyer, and has been clutch virtually the entire year. It's interesting that the Gators' one loss came at Auburn, when Wilbur's fumbled punt exchange essentially lost the game. That's how big-time this unit has been.

Now all the whining from Michigan and the media is starting to die away, as Florida goes for the big prize in Glendale, AZ. I will be back soon to break down the BCS National Championship game against Ohio State.

Go Gators! SEC Champions for 2006!

**Visor Flings, Weeks 16-19:**
**BCS Preview**

After a year filled with down-to-the wire SEC thrillers, offensive struggles, and defensive excellence, it has all come together at season's end for Florida, with a final game in Glendale, AZ, against Ohio St. for the National Championship.

This game will be very hard to handicap, given the long break of 37 days for the Gators and 51 days for the Buckeyes since their last game, respectively. These layoffs, coupled with potential academic casualties, possible early-entry NFL chances, agents laying in wait, etc., make it extremely difficult for a team to get anywhere near it's regular season rhythm.

The Gators should be their healthiest since very early, with Tate Casey a game-time decision with a high-ankle sprain, and DeShawn Wynn still with a sore shoulder. Coach Meyer has been pleased with the preparations sine the SEC Championship Game, and final practices are wrapping up in Arizona today.

I'm of the opinion that the Florida offense has to carry the fight to the OSU defense, and will determine the Gators' success Monday night. They have to play fast and aggressively, and use the entire field to spread out the Buckeyes. The O-line will need to play it's best game of the year (at least since LSU) by attacking off the ball all night and not playing soft. The OSU front seven is the strength of their defense. They are a strong, disciplined group that really doesn't do anything fancy.

Florida has more weapons then any opponent OSU has faced all year, and should be able to exploit match-ups with their best receivers. The running game will again be a mixed bag of backs and receivers, with Percy Harvin the X-factor. Chris Leak will have to be ready to take his shots as well on some QB draws and zone reads – no timid play allowed. The OSU secondary can be exploited, as Michigan showed in the regular season finale on Nov.18. While James Laurinaitis is a great linebacker, the others have not been tested like they should be. The passing game will have to set up the run. Baker, Caldwell, and Cornelius should be able to get open. Leak will need to step into all his throws and be sharp. I believe Tebow will get to run some option plays out of the Spread look, and could hit a few big plays to get some momentum.

Florida's defense has been the constant for the success of the season, and will need to attain the same level of intensity and aggressiveness it displayed all year, especially against LSU and later Arkansas. Ohio St. has a balanced offense, led of course by Troy Smith throwing to Ted Ginn Jr. and Anthony Gonzalez. But OSU has struggled when it's running game, led by Antonio Pittman, has been slowed. The Gators must make the Buckeyes one-dimensional and place the pressure on the passing game. The close to two-month layoff has to hurt their timing. Yes, it could affect Florida's as well, but the two extra games played after OSU was done has to be an advantage. I think Ryan Smith and Reggie Lewis can do an adequate job, but how will Reggie Nelson be affected by the recent death of his mother? Hopefully he can find the focus to play his aggressive game while not trying to do too much. The entire unit has to tackle well and play a physical style. Earl Everett and Brandon Siler need to stuff the running game. I really feel the D-line can get some pressure against the pass, and can knock down some passes as well. RayMac will have to gut out his elbow injury, and Steven Harris hopefully will continue his surge at the nose position. Jarvis Moss and Derrick Harvey are the quickest pair of defensive ends OSU will have played, and I'm confident they will get pressure on Smith.

Ohio St. has two big advantages coming into this game mentally. Their players have plenty of BCS bowl experience (especially in Arizona), and Jim Tressel has won five championships previously (4 in D I-AA). They will not be overwhelmed by the hype leading up to the game, while Florida's players will have to show maturity and focus in the face of a media frenzy they haven't seen before. Coach Meyer and his staff really have their hands full trying to shelter the players as well as getting them game ready. Florida should have no trouble whatsoever feeling challenged, though, as they have been completely disrespected by the media all across the country the past month. They should play loose because of this, and I hope that if Florida can get an early lead, OSU will start to feel extra pressure.

In the final analysis, this Gator team has established it's identity as defense first, with special teams and the offense doing just enough to get them over the top. It's been a wild ride all year, with plenty of frustration thrown in, but this group has persevered all season. If the coaching staff and the senior leadership can keep the team in an aggressive, attacking frame of mind, I believe they can win the game in typical, late-game dramatic fashion.

Visor Envisions: Florida 21, Ohio St. 20

**Visor Flings, Week 20:**
**UF 41, Ohio State 14**

BEATDOWN! Florida completely dominated Ohio St. to win its second National Championship in Glendale, AZ. Only 82 yards allowed to Heisman-Trophy winner Troy Smith and the Suckeye offense. Derrick Harvey and Jarvis Moss will haunt their fans (and Smith) forever. The entire D-line destroyed O$U all evening except for a handful of Antonio Pittman runs. It was really almost too easy.

What a great moment when Earl Everett chased down Smith without his helmet and tackled him! At that moment I knew that this game was OVER, and that there was no way O$U would come back.

The Gator offense cut the Suckeye defense apart the entire first half. Chris Leak was very sharp throwing to CI, for whom O$U did not have an answer. And their defense was so concerned about the speed of UF's playmakers that they allowed Leak to kill them underneath all night, prolonging drives and wearing down the O$U defense. Harvin was too quick for the defense, and there were just enough running lanes opened to keep things honest.

So much for the great Jim Tressel – completely out-coached by Urban Meyer, and no adjustments really changed things. His panic call to go for it on fourth and one at his own 29 in the first half effectively ended the game. Amazingly short-sighted.

Man, the Ohio St. fans are the worst fan base I have ever seen. Rude, obnoxious, drunk, and just plain mean-spirited people who come from that hell-hole known as Ohio. That is saying something after putting up with F$U, scUM, Tennessee, and Puppy fans over the years, but the Suckeye fans were in a league of their own. Classless.

What a great ending for the 21 seniors who were the backbone of this tenacious Gator team all season, and held things together through a challenging season that could have been derailed with only a few mistakes. Reggie Freaking Nelson, RayMac, Steve Harris, Everett, Dallas Baker the Touchdown Maker, Steve Rissler, and of course Leak, all richly deserve this. As does Coach Meyer and his staff, who worked their asses off to toughen up these players and change the mindset from the Zook era.

That's it really. It was such a dominating win that there aren't that many points to make or plays to discuss.

National Champions in both football and basketball. It may never happen again, and very likely not in the rest of my lifetime. I am truly fortunate to have witnessed both. An amazing night in the desert for all of Gator Nation.

It's great to be a Florida Gator!

Very Truly Yours,
The Visor

# 2007
# Reloading the Young Guns

I suppose one could say that 2007 was the proverbial "rebuilding year" for the Gators, but in the broad view of things, rebuilding between championships this time around would only take one season, not ten.

Florida fielded a young team, and they played very well overall. Tim Tebow, in his first year as a starter, established himself as a force to be reckoned with, setting records for rushing and passing touchdowns and becoming the first sophomore to win the Heisman Trophy. Likewise, Percy Harvin strengthened his reputation as one of the best young players in the country.

Still, there were some bitter moments. The shameful, full-roster touchdown celebration by Georgia leaps to mind immediately. And while Tebow showed the LSU people what he is made of, after putting up with a week of personal attacks via his cell phone (someone had apparently gotten his number, so to speak), but nonetheless, a loss in Baton Rouge to the eventual national champions certainly put a dent in the season. And the bowl-game loss to Michigan wasn't exactly the capper we were looking for.

But we live and learn. Urban Meyer, our present and our future, looks like he plays for keeps, and if nothing else, we were assured that the old dark days were really done.

**Visor Flings, Week 1:**

## Preview and Predictions

It's all about youth and inexperience for this year's team, as a majority of starters and backups are true freshmen or sophomores. This is Urban Meyer's first go-around as a third-year head coach at one school, and he and the entire staff have a long road ahead of them this fall trying to put a cohesive unit on the field that doesn't self-destruct in big games with stupid mistakes.

OFFENSE

This group will need to show the way, as most of the experienced players returning from last year's National Championship squad are on this side of the ball. Tim Tebow has all the leadership skills imaginable, but now has to show he is the QB with the skills to really show what the true spread option offense can do. Fortunately for Florida the O-Line is talented and experienced, led by Drew Miller and Phil Trautwein. What a shame these guys are true seniors this fall, as Ron Zook wasted their freshmen years with just a few snaps of play. That being said, the starting five (including Medder, Watkins, and Tartt) are solid players, and should allow the offense to shine. There are a plethora of playmakers available, with Bubba Caldwell, Cornelious Ingram, and Percy Freakin' Harvin leading the way at wide receiver. Plenty of help will come from Riley Cooper, Louis Murphy, and Aaron Hernandez. Good luck to defensive coordinators trying stop these guys. Running back is still by committee, with Kestahn Moore getting the first crack as the starter. He's the best pass-blocker of the group, meaning he will be in for most crucial plays. Jared Fayson may actually be #2 right now, and is a real talent running the ball, even though he is more of a natural receiver at this point. Freshman Chris Rainey has a lot of hype and moves, but is a small guy with zero experience. Tebow's running ability will actually help this group look better, as defenses will have to honor his ability on option runs.

Dan Mullen has hopefully greatly reduced the number of brain cramps in play-calling he had last year, as poor decisions led to the end of quite a few good drives. He has all the personnel in place to run what he wants now, and that alone should make him more comfortable. Given how young and inexperienced the defense is, the offense has to show consistency and score enough to take the pressure off, especially early in the season. Look for long, clock-eating drives to help out the defense.

DEFENSE

Wow. Only two starters back – Tony Joiner and Derrick Harvey – and question marks and inexperience everywhere else. Harvey is an all-SEC talent at defensive end, but will the other linemen play well enough for him to show off that ability? Undersized Jermaine Cunningham gets the first chance at the opposite DE slot, with the staff hoping his great speed off the edge offsets his lack of bulk against the run. A lot of the Gators' #1-ranked recruiting class will be shown off here, though, as Carlos Dunlap, Justin Trattou, Jaye Howard, and Duke Lemmens will all have the opportunity to see the field early (and perhaps often if deserved). Great talent, but raw. The tackle position is led by Brandon Antwine, Lawrence Marsh and Clint McMillan, with no history (yet) of achievement or big-game success to be found. True freshman Torrey Davis will be counted on a lot to provide quality snaps from early on. He is a beast and has impressed in fall practice, but SEC play is where you earn your keep. Terron Sanders has shown flashes in fall practice but is another guy who was red-shirted and hasn't seen a live snap yet. John Brown is a rock as well, but missed Summer B and fall practice getting his grades in order so he could qualify and enroll this fall. Another great talent, but he may have to red-shirt after the late start.

The linebacker corps is led by sophomores Brandon Spikes and Dustin Doe, the only two starters who saw any time on the field last year. A.J. Jones gets first crack at the Will position, but true freshman Lorenzo Edwards is my pick as a stud athlete who will be a starter before mid-season. Ryan Stamper, John Jones, and Brandon Hicks are all good, quick athletes, but have no experience. Another true freshman, Jerimy Finch, has impressed the staff this fall at LB after being a top 100 player at safety in high school, and it appears he will not be red-shirted and will get a good look.

Scary situation. But not as scary as...the inexperienced secondary. Markihe Anderson gets the start at one cornerback slot. He saw limited action last year, mainly on special teams. True freshman Joe Haden gets first shot at the opposite CB position. Thank goodness he was an early enrollee, as he was able to get training during spring practice at CB after playing QB and WR in high school. He has the best physical skills of the group, but will have to play through the mistakes he will certainly make early this fall and keep his confidence up. Former running back Markus Manson and special teams key player Wondy Pierre-Louis are the backups, with no starting experience. Jacques Rickerson was a much-touted recruit in 2006, but is just another in a long list of guys with zero game experience. Yikes.

The safety position is an embarrassment of riches, led by Joiner at strong safety. Kyle Jackson gets a shot at reviving his career as a senior, but I will not be surprised at all if he loses his free safety job to a combination of sophomore Dorian Munroe and true freshman Major Wright. Munroe has perhaps practiced better than KJ this fall, while Wright has impressed with his hitting ability and hustle. Red-shirt freshmen Jamar Hornsby and Bryan Thomas are in the mix as well. Both are great athletes and very fast.

## SPECIAL TEAMS

Coach Meyer will have even more fun with this group this year, starting with the new kickoff rule that kicks must be moved back from the 35 to the 30. Look for the Gators to be able to use a variety of their playmakers, old and young, on kickoff returns. Also, look for more front-line defenders on the KO coverage unit, as field position will be at an even larger premium. Jared Fayson, Kestahn Moore, Brandon James, and true freshman Chris Rainey will terrorize opponents this fall on returns, and I can't wait to see them unleashed.

Joey Ijjas won the placekicking job in fall practice, and gets first crack at being a reliable field goal kicker. Jonathan Phillips may get some work as well, but I'm not counting on any reliable production until it's proven. This is an unacceptable situation for Florida to be in. True freshman Chas Henry, a top recruit, will be the punter. He was inconsistent in fall practice, but has a big-time leg. There will be growing pains here as well.

## PREDICTIONS

This year's edition is actually a faster team than Meyer's previous two, but is startlingly young and inexperienced on the two-deep depth chart. Tim Tebow's leadership skills will be invaluable to the offense, as that group will need to carry the load through September while the young defense tries to gel and find it's identity. Fortunately, Tennessee and Auburn are at the Swamp in September, with a trip to Mississippi before Auburn comes a callin'. LSU will be the biggest test the week after Auburn, then a twist in the schedule with the normal off week before Georgia moving up to after the LSU game. Then comes an interesting visit to Kentucky, who are talking a big game in the preseason. This could be a trap game for such a young team before playing the Puppies in Jacksonville. Vanderbilt visits for Homecoming, followed by another emotional trip to South Carolina against the Ol' Ball Coach. This may be the one season the Gamecocks can make some real noise, with the Big 3 in the East -- Florida, Georgia, and Tennessee, all in transition. Then of course F$U visits the Swamp to close out the regular season.

Despite all the talent on hand, there is just too much youth and inexperience at key positions on the defense to expect a huge season. Right now I'm leaning toward a loss at home to Auburn, followed by a road loss at L$U. That means the Kentucky and Georgia games will make or break a decent, good, or very good season. Coach Meyer and the entire staff will have their hands full coaching up this year's team through another tough SEC schedule. I'm going to be pessimistic and predict a loss at Carolina as well, although I think they are a little overrated right now. I do think that the team will re-group to beat F$U for a fifth straight year (I'll always count the 2003 game as a win).

Florida is fortunate to have an incredible coaching staff on hand. This group works as tireless recruiters, and has proven with inexperienced and lightly-regarded players the past two years that they can elevate their play to championship levels. It's hard to predict three losses, but if there is one staff that can teach and motivate this young group to exceed my expectations, it's this one.

This team will stumble a few times this fall, but I'm not worried about the short or long-term. Urban Meyer is stockpiling the talent for a consistent powerhouse starting in 2008. This season will be a transition year, even in a slightly weaker, but more balanced, SEC. My educated guess is the Gators will go 9-3 for the season and 5-3 in the SEC.

As for the season opener against Western Kentucky, this is the first year in Division 1-A football for the Hilltoppers, and it will look that way in the Swamp. I expect some sloppiness from the Gators, but I also expect to see a ton of young guys get some experience. Florida's talent and speed will overwhelm WKU, and I expect the Gators to comfortably pull away starting in the second quarter. The only real disturbing news heading into this game is the injury status of Markihe Anderson (sprained MCL) at cornerback and Phil Trautwein (fracture in foot) at offensive tackle. It appears neither will play Saturday. Anderson will hopefully be back for the Tennessee game, while the news on Trautwein is more disturbing...potentially out 6-10 weeks. Just more opportunities for guys with little or no game experience to get their feet wet. Yeesh.

Most importantly...no more injuries.

**Visor Flings, Week 2:**
**UF 45, WKU 10**

It was a solid debut for an extremely young and inexperienced Gator team, as they dominated WKU 49-3. It was amazing (and a little sobering) to see all of the freshmen and sophomores on the field with the first units, and then to see an even younger team in the second half. Talent and speed abounds, but this team has a long way to go in order to compete successfully in the SEC.

The offense was fun to watch, especially since it now takes on such a different look with Tim Tebow running the show. Much more of the true spread option was on display. It was good to see so many long passes, which will give future opponents something to consider before loading up the box to stop Tebow and the running game. The offensive line played well, especially given the fact they had less then two weeks with the new lineup in place after Phil Trautwein's injury. Maurkice Pouncy looks like a future star at guard, even as a true freshman. Drew Miller seems to be comfortable snapping the ball now. The pass protection was good as well, even given an outmatched opponent. Very few mix-ups were evident in the blocking. Kestahn Moore looked just like I expected him to – functional, but no real breakaway threat. But as long as he has corrected his fumbling problems, that's okay. There will be a lot more option looks with Tebow as the season progresses – I'm sure Dan Mullen has a lot of the playbook still on hold until the SEC season starts. The receivers looked very good. Riley Cooper has all the physical talent you could want, and may wind up seeing a lot more snaps than anticipated. He's a great blocker, which is a must to play in this offense. Bubba Caldwell will be a terror on deep routes, which will loosen up the intermediate spaces. And it's hard to believe that Percy Freakin' Harvin (PFH) had only three touches and that CI had only one catch. Too few touches for these two, but I think that will change starting this week.

The defense, statistically, looked very good. Allowed only two third-down conversions, 48 rushing yards allowed, 12 TFL. But the coverage in the secondary was way too soft. I don't see Wondy Pierre-Louis remaining a starter as soon as Markihe Anderson returns from injury. Joe Haden looked like a true freshman, but he's still going to be a good one. Coach Heater has a ton of work to do before Tennessee comes to the Swamp. Derrick Harvey was unblockable at one end, and a lot of the true freshmen defensive ends saw action as well. But there was minimal push up the middle from the tackles, and I'm afraid that will be a trouble spot most of the season. I look for Torrey Davis to start seeing a lot more playing time, and soon. Brandon Spikes and Dustin Doe were all over the field at LB, but must tackle better. I think it's more of a mental issue to overcome, as they need to realize these aren't high school guys they are tackling now, and must do a better job of wrapping up. Kyle Jackson still scares me at free safety, and I think Dorian Monroe will take over that position soon. The talent at safety is just sick. True freshman Major Wright looks like a brutal hitter, and once he learns the coverages, look out.

Special teams coverage was excellent, and Joey Ijjas looked comfortable kicking extra points. I'd like to see him get a few chances at FGs before the Tennessee game, but if that means the Gators are scoring TDs, then I'll get over that! Jarred Fayson got some valuable experience returning punts, but Brandon James should be back this week as the main kick and punt returner. The kickoff coverage was very good, but once again there are a lot of young guys on that unit, and the new kickoff rule of kicking from the 30 means more returns this year, and more opportunities for mistakes. Coach Meyer will be working this group very hard all season, looking for the right personnel combinations and correcting mistakes.

This week the level of competition ramps up considerably, as a solid Troy team with no fear of ranked teams comes to Gainesville. Troy has played a lot of good teams closely the past five years, and will probably expose some of Florida's inexperience this week. I do expect the defense to show improvement overall, but I really hope to see a better pass rush from guys other than Harvey. I also expect to see a little more work on the running game, and perhaps more work on the short and intermediate passes. Omar Haugabrook is just another of hundreds of Florida kids that wind up all over the country at various sizes of schools, and does a very good job with Troy's version of the Spread. They will throw the ball a lot Saturday, and the Gator secondary will be tested (and will probably look bad occasionally). Troy had a difficult time with Arkansas' running game, and while Florida does not have the same powerful Razorback running attack, that bodes well for the offense being able to stay balanced. This will be an excellent test before Tennessee and its passing game comes to Gainesville, and I see a close game through halftime.

Prediction - Florida 38, Troy 17

**Visor Flings, Week 3:**
**UF 59, Troy 31**

It was definitely a tale of two halves against Troy. Total domination followed by an ugly, disinterested effort. The offensive production in the first half was very impressive to watch, as all facets of the spread option were in view. Moore and Tebow had their way running the ball, CI was unleashed on crossing routes, and Harvin and Caldwell wreaked havoc on direct snaps. The O-line played very well, opening holes and providing a wall of pass protection for Tebow.

The third quarter was brutal to watch, though. It's obvious a bunch of young kids were already thinking ahead to the Tennessee game, and played perhaps the worst quarter of football seen at the Swamp since before Spurrier came to UF in 1990. That clearly shows that this year's team has zero room for error, and must play at or near peak efficiency and intensity against any SEC opponent in order to win. The pass coverage is scary bad right now. Poor drops by the LBs, and the safeties are really struggling with their zone defense assignments. Troy had guys wide open all day in 15-18 yard square-ins and crossing routes.

The D-line had its moments, and did a solid job of stopping the run. But there is still little push up the middle from the DTs, and that has to change, starting now.

The pre-season is over. Time to see what this very young and inexperienced Gator team can do in a big-game environment. Tennessee has an offensive coordinator in Cutcliffe and QB in Ainge that will try and control the clock with a no-huddle, short-passing game. Unfortunately, I see them having some success, putting a lot of pressure on the Gator offense to score early and often. The Vol O-line is no where near its past performance but is still serviceable, and combined with an inexperienced Gator D-line means that it could be a frustrating afternoon trying to get Tennessee's offense off the field. It will be interesting to see how much Torrey Davis plays at DT, and how effective Trattou and Dunlap are in the DE rotation. Each and every freshman has to come up big to help out the few experienced guys. Derrick Harvey has to play like an all-SEC performer. Spikes and Doe are playing well at LB, but the backups are very shaky right now, especially in pass coverage. Anderson should get more playing time at one cornerback spot, but Haden, WPL, and Rickerson will see a lot of action against plenty of three and four wide-out sets. Tony Joiner has to get the other safeties in proper position, and all of them have to tackle better.

The Gator offense looks better than I had hoped with the loss of Trautwein. The O-line has been great so far, but must stay healthy and consistent. The Tennessee defense has had plenty of trouble when opponents spread the field and in pass coverage, so if the O-line gives Tebow decent protection, I have to believe Florida scores a lot of points. Moore is still the #1 running back right now, but this game is where Tebow will be unshackled, and allowed to run as often as necessary on option plays and allowed to scramble whenever the pocket breaks down. The loss of Caldwell really hurts, as he looked better than ever with the ball in his hands last week. It looks like Riley Cooper will get first crack at the outside WR slot in his absence, and he certainly is a good blocker and has proven he can get open deep. This may be the game that Percy Harvin blows up after a quiet start. He has been struggling with the tendonitis issue in his Achilles and knee, but it's time to nut up and explode. If the Vols play a lot of zone, then CI will have to make plays over the middle.

Prediction: Florida 35, Tennessee 31

**Visor Flings, Week 4:**
**UF 59, Tennessee 20**

What a beatdown of the Vols! That was better than just about anyone could have expected, and now raises expectations to ridiculous levels. Florida simply ran around and over the Tennessee defense with a display that had to be frightening to future Gator opponents. All elements of the spread option were on display – the option, the WRs involved in the running game, CI creating mismatches over the middle, and the deep ball. Tim Tebow is quickly dispelling the hopes and wishes of critics in the media and in the camps of opponents in terms of his throwing ability. Percy Harvin was finally unleashed in full effect. And everyone can now see what a QB with Tebow's running ability can do to a defense who has to account for him on every snap, whether it be run or pass. Who knew you could use a play-action fake with no one but the QB in the backfield!

The offense was explosive, ripping off chunks of yards and full of big plays. Lost in all the hype about the skill-position players is the great job done by the O-line. Even the early loss of Maurkice Pouncey didn't cause a drop-off, as Mo Hurt replaced him seamlessly. Kestahn Moore is the 'glue-guy' who does a little of everything to help out – run the ball, pass block, catch balls out of the backfield, and even serve as lead blocker on kickoff returns. Cooper and Murphy kept the Vol secondary loosened up with the deep receptions, and CI is a freak…what a stud. Mullen and Meyer have all the components in place to attack any defense with success.

The defensive philosophy of keeping everything in front and making Tennessee work for every yard paid off with some turnovers and frustration. I was a little concerned that the defense couldn't come up with some third and fourth-down stops, but the overall result was very good. Losing Markihe Anderson so early was disappointing, as he showed in less than one quarter of work why he is considered the best CB by the staff. Big interception by him to stop an early Vol drive. Joe Haden tackled very well and showed good speed and toughness. The tackling of Jacques Rickerson and Kyle Jackson was poor, though, and it looks like KJ may have lost his starting slot to Major Wright, who came in and made plays immediately. Brandon Spikes and Dustin Doe continue to defend the run well, and Doe had the play that completely turned the momentum back Florida's way on his fumble return for a touchdown. The other disappointment was seeing Jerimy Finch's season end after making a great interception. The kid seems to have the knack, and will be a future star.

Special teams were exactly that, as this group looked like the best unit in the country. Brandon James just has 'it' when it comes to returning kicks. Great weapon. The kickoff coverage struggled a little bit, but improved as the game went on (they had enough practice!). The loss of Finch will be felt, though, as he was already emerging as a leader. Moore's lead blocking on kickoff returns is excellent, and James made sure to credit all of his blockers for a great performance.

The next game at Mississippi will be a challenge for such a young team in terms of both being on the road, and the very early start time (11:30 local). Coach Meyer is already looking very hard at keeping some sort of routine for the players, which is especially important with all of the underclassmen on the roster. Ole Miss has struggled to date and is coming off of a 14-point loss at Vanderbilt. Their starting QB (Seth Adams) will probably start but play hurt. He has had some success in the passing game, as the Rebels are averaging over 200 yards a game. They also have a very good and tough RB in BenJarvus Green-Ellis. The wild card could be if Brent Schaeffer plays at QB. He's a great runner, and I could see Florida's inexperienced DEs allowing him to break containment and make big plays running or throwing. Ole Miss is re-building their defense, and that unit can be exploited. I'm sure the game will be a sellout and the local crowd will be loud and hostile early, but this is where

the offense can take charge of the game early and set the tone for a win. I don't see having to use all the various plays needed against Tennessee in order to have success – the basics should get the job done. I suspect the young defense will lose some focus and allow some big plays, but not enough to lose the game.
Florida can't afford any more injuries with Auburn and L$U coming up next. Hopefully Caldwell and Pouncey will be back by then (not sure on Anderson), and Cooper should be close to 100%.

Prediction: Florida 35, Mississippi 17

**Visor Flings, Week 5:**
**UF 30, Ole Miss 24**

As expected, a sluggish win at Ole Miss, highlighted by breakdowns by the young defense and a myriad of silly penalties. Any road game in the SEC can get dicey, especially when you combine inexperience with a less than focused attitude and effort. It's a testament to this staff and the few leaders on this team that the Gators still pulled out the win.

Tim Tebow was a man against boys, and Percy Harvin was, well, Percy Harvin, a player the Rebels could not stop when needed. Tebow put the offense on his shoulders in the fourth quarter and ground out two long drives to ice the game, but that was way too much punishment to take and expect to survive the SEC schedule. The final offensive numbers were quite impressive, with another 500+ yard performance split almost evenly between run and pass. But you could see how the absence of both Caldwell and Cooper affected the play-calling, as well as Ole Miss dropping eight in coverage and daring the Gators to methodically drive the length of the field. Fortunately the O-line was once again solid and got the job done, but the false-start penalties have to stop. This unit has too many veterans to allow that to continue (I hope). Dan Mullen really reined in spreading the ball around when things got tight, meaning CI, Fayson, and Moore did not get enough touches.

The defensive secondary finally showed its youth and cracked a few times, allowing two long pass plays to get Ole Miss back in the game. Part of that was caused by the continued poor play of Kyle Jackson at safety, who may have lost his job to true freshman Major Wright. I can't fault Joe Haden for getting burned deep, given the fact that he didn't start playing CB until spring practice. The tackling was a little shaky in the secondary as well, as Joiner missed quite a few, including the Ole Miss fake punt near the end of the game that fortunately Cunningham cleaned up. Still no effective push by the DTs in the pass rush, but they continue to stuff the running game fairly well. Spikes and Doe were their usual selves against the run, but Doe has to improve his pass coverage in space.

It didn't help that the long kickoff return by James to open the game went to waste, as a poor three downs by the offense led to a missed FG. It was revealed during the game that Ijjas was kicking with a groin pull, and here's hoping he can get healthy soon, because

Phillips just flat out stinks. His missed extra point was almost the difference in the game. Still some shaky decision by James on fielding punts in traffic, and the kickoff return coverage was only average – the loss of Finch from that unit was felt.

Now it's payback time against Auburn, after that music-filled, replay review marred game last season. No doubt the few Florida players remaining from last year have all the motivation to focus on this game, and Coach Meyer himself said the Gators owe them one.

I hope that Strong and Mattison allow for some more press coverage, as Auburn lacks playmakers in the WR corps. The Tigers will try to establish the running game, because there's no way Brandon Cox will lead them to a win throwing the ball. They have a stable a good running backs as usual, but because of injuries they may start up to three freshmen on the O-line. Auburn's defense is its usual fast self, but I expect the Gators to play a little smash-mouth football early, both to soften them up for later and to help neutralize Quentin Groves, the Tiger's best DL. He's a great pass-rusher, but the ability of Tebow to run will help slow him down a little.

Florida is still banged up somewhat, with Caldwell out and Cooper questionable on offense, and Anderson out on defense. Plus, it will be a game-time decision as to who starts at FS – Jackson or Wright. I think the Gators tough out a win, but are still not at full strength.

Prediction: Florida 28, Auburn 17

**Visor Flings, Week 6:**
**Auburn 20, UF 17**

> A baffling, ugly effort led to a bitter loss to Auburn. I've reminded myself before every game that this team is incredibly young and inexperienced, and that they could lay an egg at any time. But because of how well the staff has coached and the high level of talent, it still was very disappointing to see the Gators lose that way at home.

I do believe that a significant amount of fault lies with the coaches. The defensive play the entire first half was entirely too soft and safe, while the play-calling by Mullen on offense was questionable at best. The penalties are the biggest beef I have with the players right now, especially the false starts by the O-linemen who do have experience.

The first half was, simply, a nightmare. Once again a mediocre Auburn QB is made to look like a star, because Strong apparently didn't recognize that Auburn has zero playmakers. Once the heat and pressure were turned up, the Tigers struggled to only six points in the second half, but by then the damage was done.

It's a testament to the talent and hustle of this team that they still had possession in a tie game with a chance to win in the fourth quarter. That's when Mullen failed the team by not letting Tebow run the off-tackle play behind the pulling guard, which was killing the Tigers the second half. Then an option call on 2nd and 16? Terrible. All of those mistakes, and it still took Auburn playing its best game of the season just to barely win. That's why this loss – at home, no less – is so galling.

Now it's on the road to L$U. The Tigers are hungry after last year's Gator win, and their defense is as good as it gets in college. The Florida staff has its hands full with getting this team re-focused and re-energized. Last year's team was mature enough to respond to adversity. But no one knows how such a young team will respond. Add in the Tony Joiner drama which takes some of Coach Meyer's attention away from game-planning, and the tea leaves are not yielding a good forecast.

The Gator defense has enough speed to challenge L$U's offense, especially if Early Doucet does not play at WR. But L$U's O-line has developed into a fine power-running unit, and this is the worst match-up for Florida's D-line right now. The Gators have played pretty well against the run so far, but Auburn was able to exploit some problems up the middle, and I have to think L$U will try early to do the same. Matt Flynn doesn't seem to be 100% running the ball, which could limit the play-calling when he's in, but Ryan Perriloux will be an x-factor running or throwing. The Tigers have a stable of solid RBs big (K. Williams) and small (T. Holliday). Their WR corps has talent, but without Doucet is young and thin in depth.

The O-line will get its biggest challenge of the year from Glen Dorsey and a powerful Bengal Tiger front seven. This unit has to stop the stupid penalties and play a strong, smart game. No doubt that L$U will make a lot of plays on defense, some of them big. But this is as much a mental challenge for the offense as a physical one as they have to fight through the crowd noise and the best defense they will see all year.

I do think that the Gators will play a solid game, but there is still too much youth and inexperience on the defense to pull off an upset in Baton Rouge.

Prediction: Florida 17, L$U 31

**Visor Flings, Week 7:**
**LSU 28, UF 24**

That was a great effort against L$U on the road. A bunch of young kids were not intimidated by a very loud and hostile environment, and actually outplayed the Tigers for three quarters before turnovers did the Gators in. The staff did a great job of getting the team ready, and had a winning game plan in place.

The O-line played by far its best game of 2007. They controlled the line of scrimmage all night, and ran directly at the supposedly all-world L$U front seven. Jim Tartt and Maurkice Pouncey neutralized Glen Dorsey and co. against both the run and pass. The Tigers had to blitz to get any pressure on Tebow, and he usually made them pay by getting away and scrambling to make plays. Kestahn Moore played the game of his life – it's too bad his fumble at the end of the third quarter, though not leading directly to a L$U score, started the ball rolling to a fourth quarter loss. It's painfully obvious that the injuries to Caldwell and

Cooper have hampered Florida's ability to stretch the field vertically, allowing opponents to bracket Harvin the entire game and limiting big-play opportunities. Caldwell was not in game shape yet. Tebow was a man on the field. You could see how he relishes a big-game atmosphere and challenge, and brought it to the Tiger defense all night. I loved it when he taunted the L$U student section by dialing the imaginary cell phone to mock them. They had somehow gotten his number and left threatening and crass messages for him and about his family all week – pathetic.

The defense played valiantly, but the D-line wore down in the fourth quarter and just could not seem to make one key play on third or fourth down to win the game. Joe Haden and Major Wright continue to impress, especially as true freshmen. Spikes and Doe did okay against the run, but were gassed late in the game. Cunningham is still undersized, but incredibly was in on 17 tackles. The other freshmen DEs blew some contain assignments that allowed Flynn to kill Florida with key scrambles on third down. The defensive staff is doing a remarkable job with this unit, but they lack the physical maturity and game experience to win a game on their own yet.

The week off came at a great time to allow the team to re-focus and re-energize. And they will need to be ready for another tough match-up – this time at Kentucky, who is coming off a surprising win over L$U. It looked like the Tigers had little left in the tank after playing Florida, and the Wildcats outplayed them most of the second half and in overtime.

Kentucky will be led by QB Andre Woodson and a solid group of WRs, but its offense is not just a passing game anymore, balanced by a solid running game. If Rafael Little returns to go along with backup Derrick Locke, the Gator defense will really be challenged. TE Jacob Tamme is very good and a tough match-up as well.

Florida must continue to pound the run, especially with its WR corps still missing key players and not completely healthy. I think that the O-line, if it can bring the same focus and intensity it had at Baton Rouge, can control the line and allow Tebow the time to hurt the Wildcats running and throwing.

The running game of Florida and its run defense will decide this game, despite all the talk of the Gator pass defense and it's struggles. If Kentucky is forced into being one-dimensional on offense, that should be enough of an advantage to let the Gators get out with a win. Yes, the Gators have won 20 in a row in this series, but this is the best Wildcat team in a long time, and they are very experienced.

One other factor will be how the team responds to the tragic death of Michael Guilford in a motorcycle accident. 'Sunshine' was a valuable member of the scout team and a popular teammate. Plus, Joe Haden's girlfriend, who was riding with Guilford, was also killed. Joe will be hard put to focus completely on the game. Just a terrible thing to have happen.

Prediction: Florida 35, Kentucky 31

**Visor Flings, Week 8:**
**UF 45, Kentucky 37**

The game against Kentucky wound up being just like one of those shootouts from the '80s featuring BYU. I don't like the fact that the Gator defense was shredded so easily by the Wildcats, but perhaps Woodson and co. are just that good this year. It certainly puts a lot of pressure on the offense to continually score, knowing that one mistake and not scoring could lose the game, but they came through like champs.

The offense scored every time it had the ball except for three times, and those were three-and-outs. In other words they sustained drives all afternoon. Great play-calling by Mullen and execution by the players. Once again Tebow had 20 carries, but I already stated weeks ago that it's crunch time in the SEC East now, and to get used to it. He did sustain a shoulder bruise that was really hurting him at the end, but he should be close to 100% this week. Moore did another serviceable job running the ball, but it's painfully obvious that a top-flight RB with some breakaway speed would have been able to rip off a handful of 10-20 yard gains. It was nice to see Bubba Caldwell contribute, and he looks around 90% now. You could see how his presence as another playmaker opened things up for Harvin and Murphy. The O-line did a great job, but I'm not sure how good Kentucky's D-line really is. Hopefully Medder's heel injury improves before the Georgia game, but Marcus Gilbert did a serviceable job as his replacement. Tebow is clearly the most valuable player for his team in the country right now, and should be the front-runner for the Heisman.

Where to start on the defense? The D-line actually had a great sack day, with six. But when Torrey Davis came in at tackle in the rotation, UK gashed the Gators right up the middle on running plays. He sorely needs more experience, as it's obvious right now that his main task is to get into the backfield as fast as possible. Spikes had another solid tackling day, but both he and Doe did not do their best job of reading the running lanes. The staff has to coach the players better on disguising blitzes, at least until right before the snap. They continually showed their hand early, and were exposed by those simple screens to the WRs that went for big yardage. I was hoping that Markihe Anderson would be red-shirted this year. I guess I'm glad I was wrong, as Pierre-Louis went out for a while with a shoulder injury, and Anderson was sorely needed. The tackling was poor, and has to improve. The broken thumb suffered by Major Wright could be a big blow to the secondary – he's questionable for the Georgia game.

Now it's on to Jacksonville, as the Gators have the SEC East lead and will guarantee a return trip to Atlanta with wins in their next 3 games.

The Puppies are a hard team to get a handle on as far as what kind of performance to expect. They are also 5-2, but have an ugly loss at home to S. Carolina, an even uglier loss at Tennessee, and escaped two weeks ago at Vanderbilt – a game they should have lost. Matt Stafford seems to be an improved player this year judging by his reduced number of turnovers, but is still only a 56% passer right now. Their running game is down to basically Knowshon Moreno, who is very good but has not carried the load for an entire game. Once again Georgia has a middling set of WRs, who seem to still have a lot of drops. One thing Mark Richt does do that is effective is devise a solid screen-passing game and also use the TEs, both areas that the Gator pass defense has struggled against. Once again, stop the run, make the Puppies one-dimensional, and the chances for a win are much better.

Prediction: Florida 35, Georgia 24

**Visor Flings, Week 9:**
**Georgia 42, UF 30**

What can I say? The defense sucked, and the Gators didn't respond like a championship-caliber team. Injuries certainly gutted the D-line and hampered Tebow's running effectiveness. But it was incredibly disappointing the see this young team not respond to the indignity of that classless celebration by the Puppies after they scored.

So many missed opportunities on offense, and the continued inability to get the opponent off the field on third down were crushing blows. Tebow struggled in the first half against the blitz, missing hot reads and simply holding the ball too long. Kestahn Moore's fumble set the tone for the entire afternoon, killing a promising opening drive. The defense was abysmal, allowing Georgia over 200 rushing yards, and allowing over 200 yards on just four big plays. Even experienced players like Tony Joiner lost their poise occasionally and simply played poorly. Ingram continued his recent trend of dropping passes. The WRs missed some key blocks. The O-line missed blitz pickups in the first half. There were a few highlights, though. Percy Harvin is simply one of the handful of players in the country that no one really has an answer for. He terrorized the Puppies each time he had the ball. The secondary improved in the second half, until the staff had them play soft coverage on critical third down plays. Tebow did a better job reading the blitz. Jared Fayson made some big plays.

What's lost in the aftermath of all the failures is that even with all the poor play, the Gators were right there against a decent SEC team, showing just what potential this young team has. Too bad the growing pains I feared have come to fruition. I think a lot of people were blinded by the beat-down of Tennessee and overrated this year's team after that.

There's no doubt that stupid Mark Richt just upped the ante for future games, and there is no way Meyer will forget what happened.

It will be a mish-mash on defense against Vanderbilt. Mike Pouncey will actually get snaps at DT, after one week of practice at a new position. What does that tell you about the state of the Gator D-line? This is one beat-up and downtrodden unit, and they somehow have to make themselves respectable for the stretch run. Vandy's running game has struggled most of the season, which helps, plus both of their QBs will play hurt. Receiver Earl Bennett is once again their only real weapon, and employing bracket coverage on him should slow down their entire offense.

I believe Brandon James and Jared Fayson will handle most of the RB load, as Kestahn Moore may be in the doghouse (pun intended) until 2008. Tebow will be playing hurt the rest of the regular season, and I think Mullen will tailor the game plan to account for this. I look for Percy Harvin to continue to show why he's one of the most unstoppable forces in college football. The Florida passing game should have a big day against Vandy, despite the fact they are a decent defensive unit, as South Carolina can attest.

It's gut-check time for this very young team. Hopefully the coaching staff can re-focus them on trying to win out and finishing strong. It all starts with the D-line's performance.

Prediction: Florida 35, Vanderbilt 20

**Visor Flings, Week 10:**
**UF 49, Vandy 22**

That was a much-needed win for the Gators against Vanderbilt, given the shaky emotional and physical state of the team after the Georgia debacle. All units played hard and very well, even given the fact that Vandy was simply out-talented.

The offense continues its dominant ways. The only real opponent to this unit has been itself this year with occasional penalties, fumbles, and poor execution. Tebow was very sharp throwing the ball, and seems to be improving at seeing the field and reading defenses. He did run enough to keep the Commodore defense honest, but took advantage of serious mismatches of the Florida WRs vs. the opponent. Percy Freakin' Harvin showed again why he is such a special talent, tearing up Vandy from the tailback position by exploding thorough small holes and making tacklers look silly on his way to the end zone. He's also proven to be a tough guy as a receiver over the middle as well. Bubba Caldwell is back to close to 100%, and his big day shows how much he was missed against Auburn, L$U, and Georgia. The O-line had a solid day, despite two bad snaps that were drive-killers. Even Fayson and James got more touches, making playing the Gator offense a nightmare.

The real story was the improved play of the defense. Yes, Vanderbilt is a step down from Georgia and two steps down from Kentucky's offense, but the players seem more under control, as additional film study helped. Michael Pouncey was a revelation at DT. For just one week of practice on defense, he was disruptive and got into the backfield. Honestly, I think it's best for Florida that he remain on defense the rest of 2007, and perhaps his entire career. The secondary did a fine job of slowing down Earl Bennett, who had torched the Gators the past two years. Once he was contained, the rest of Vandy's offense was slowed as well.

Brandon James is unreal as a kick returner. He's just one of those guys that have the knack for returns, and is as important a weapon as Harvin and Tebow, especially when he can flip the field and set up the Gator offense. I would like to see the pooch kickoffs abandoned – the coverage team consistently allowed Vandy to start outside the 40-yard line, which is unacceptable. Let Ijjas kick it deep and cover.

Now it's on to my least-favorite game of each season since the 'Ol Ball Coach became a pariah at South Carolina. And once again the Gators come to Columbia desperate for a win to perhaps win the SEC East, just like 2005. The Gamecocks are out of the East race with three straight conference losses, but that could allow them to play fast and loose against Florida. While I believe that the Gator coaching staff is completely over the SOS angle, there's no doubt that this game means a little something extra, especially for Meyer.

The Gamecock defense is really hurting right now, not just physically. They were crushed by Arkansas' rushing attack and the top NFL talent Darren McFadden. Their pride was taken away, along with some potentially crucial injuries in their secondary. Munnerlin and Moody may play, but will be less than 100%, which could possibly make their staff resort to a safer defense, hoping the Gator offense stops itself on longer drives. Tyrone Nix does get his guys to play hard each week, but they are up against it if the Gator offense is on its game. The formula is pretty much established by now – spread the ball around to utilize the entire field, but emphasize Harvin more in the running game at tailback. I was worried seeing CI limp around last week, wondering why he was even on the field against Vanderbilt. If he's even near 100%, he's a match-up nightmare for Carolina. The game film from the Vandy game will give the Gamecocks plenty to worry about, which could allow Mullen to throw in a few wrinkles to set up a few big plays.

But the real key for a Florida win is simply this – stop the running game of Corey Boyd and Mike Davis. They have not done it the past two seasons, and it's almost cost them twice. Even with Jared Cook becoming a dangerous option in the passing game to go along with Kenny McKinley, the running game is what makes the Carolina offense go. The Gator defense is still too young and inexperienced to try and deal with an offensive attack that Spurrier can put together if the running game is working. That's when the corner routes and seam patterns open up downfield, and then it's over. Looks like Blake Mitchell will get start. If the Florida defense can just get pressure on him, he is not a good scrambler, and will make mistakes. Unfortunately, that's a big if.

Prediction: Florida 38, S. Carolina 35

**Visor Flings, Week 11:**
**UF 51, So. Carolina 31**

The Tebow-for-Heisman campaign picked up a lot of supporters, as the Gators played dial-a-score against the Lamecocks. The offense could only be stopped by one thing – itself – all night, despite Percy Harvin not even making the trip due to illness. It seems as if Urban Meyer is now completely out from under the Steve Spurrier shadow, as he should be, given he's the head coach of Florida, and Spurrier is nothing more than a pariah.

The news that Harvin didn't even make the trip was shocking, even though the rumors were circulating as early as Friday. But the entire offense came together and didn't miss a beat. Tebow was a man amongst boys, running and passing at will. If not for a case of the drops by Louis Murphy, he would have had two more TD throws on deep balls. He again spearheaded the running game with 26 carries, but Brandon James, Kestahn Moore, and Jarred Fayson each contributed a handful of good carries to spread the wealth. Bubba Caldwell continues his late-season surge, showing once again how good he is when healthy, and how much he was missed when he was out. The WRs were open short and deep all night. Even Aaron Hernandez showed a glimpse of what he will be doing in the future with a 55-yard catch-and-run. The O-line didn't miss a beat when Maurkice Pouncy went down on the third play of the game. Maurice Hurt filled in admirably once again, while Drew Miller and the others continued the best O-line play in the SEC.

The defense had its moments as well, but still lacks consistency and confidence at times. They did do the key thing in order to win the game – stop the running of Boyd and Davis, who had hurt Florida the previous two years. And it was nice to see Blake Mitchell play like he usually does and not like an NFL QB – decent play, but inconsistent. The D-line got some decent pressure against the pass, but it is what it is with this group the rest of the season. Spikes tackled well at LB, but Jones and Doe still disappear occasionally. This group has to be improved next year as well. The secondary came up with two big plays – Joiner's interception and Wright giving Davis an out-of-body experience on a crushing hit that led to a fumble. He will be fun to watch as he continues to hurt opponents the next three years.

Overall, just a dominating offensive performance, with just enough defense thrown in to get a big win. That has been the formula for 2007. Now, it's time to come back home to the Swamp, beat up on FAU, and get ready for F$U. I will get a lot of satisfaction if the Gators can put a hurting on Howard Schnellenberger after his antics from when he was the Hurricane coach in the early '80s. FAU has played a few teams tough, including S. Florida at home, but are outclassed in this game. They will be up for it because it's the Gators and an in-state battle, but I think some shock and awe awaits them. It looks like Harvin will miss this game as well, and I'm starting to worry that nothing has been specifically diagnosed. Pouncey can hopefully sit out, but some more shuffling along the O-line may take place as Hurt is dinged up as well. It looks like Cam Newton may get some significant snaps at QB, which is much-needed.

Prediction: Florida 45, FAU 10

**Visor Flings, Week 12:**
**UF 59, FAU 20**

Florida simply out-talented the FAU Owls on their way to a blowout win. Despite a very sloppy effort, including a ton of silly penalties and an obvious lack of focus at times, the

Gators were just too good to be seriously challenged. The defense, unfortunately, seemed to take a step back, and now injuries have popped up again in the secondary at CB. Even Tebow was a little high and wild, but that just shows how high the bar is set for him after a spectacular season.

There isn't really much to say about the offense, except that they performed almost as expected. FAU had no answer for the passing game, but did surprise the Gator O-line with more blitzing than expected. It was great to see Bubba Caldwell attain the career receptions record, breaking the mark of the Cuban Comet, Carlos Alvarez. A well-deserved record for Bubba, who has had to battle injuries most of his career but kept working hard. The run blocking was a little lazy as well, but the game plan was a vanilla one, which was all that was needed.

It's rivalry week!

It's too bad the Gator defense is such a question mark right now, or else Florida would probably win by four touchdowns without too much difficulty. F$U is that bad on offense, despite all of the rhetoric coming out of Taliban City about 'the greatest coaching staff ever assembled'. The fact is that their QB play is mediocre, and almost always inconsistent. Their O-line is still average at best. Their running game has been so-so, and the jump ball is still their best way of attacking downfield. I look for a lot of passes to Antoine Smith and Preston Parker (their best playmaker) out of the backfield. It looks like Parker will line up at tailback some as well – their imitation of Harvin. They will take advantage of Florida's weakness at CB, between guys trying to play hurt (Haden, Anderson) and the inexperienced ones. The Gator linebackers have to come up big in this game both in stopping the run and in coverage. I would not be surprised to see more 4-2-5 looks to try and offset the physical play of Carr and Fagg with a decent coverage safety like Munroe.

On offense, it appears that Percy Harvin will return, although it's difficult to know how well he will play. The rest of the unit has adjusted well to his absence by elevating their play, but he's a special talent that causes the defense to worry about him on each snap. Tebow will need to be patient early and not get too hyped up throwing the ball. He has been high and wide recently, and turnovers are the great equalizer. If and when F$U blitzes (and they will), the option play to the edges and quick passes to the hot reads have to be executed well, success in these plays will slow down the pass rush and allow the Gators to run the ball occasionally. I expect it to be difficult to run the ball early, but as long as the score is manageable Mullen has to stick with it somewhat.

Tebow needs to show patience on offense. Take the check-downs if they're available and move the chains. He'll get his opportunities for the deep ball later. A few option plays and quick-hitters should slow down any blitzing. I think a few roll-outs are on tap for this game as well to help out.

I'm concerned about what Meyer said about 'too much' in practice for the offense during the week. I think that they should have a relatively simple game plan on offense and let the guys play fast. They are talented enough to beat F$U without resorting to a too-complicated game plan. I'm sure they will have a few 'special' plays ready, but don't over think it, Coach Mullen.

The defense will have to play with a lot of emotion, because, quite frankly, it's an average unit at best this year. The pass defense will get burned a few times – get ready for it. But three-and-outs are critical Saturday. It's a shame that the crappy F$U offense will actually pose a threat to
this defense.

The Gators are such a young team that you wonder if they will be too hyped. I can see them getting stupid penalties and getting pulled in to retaliation-type penalties. I hope they play 'beyond their years' and play smart.

By the way, I hope Geno 'Taze' Hayes gets a nice crack-back block from Hernandez or CI, and that the O-line punishes him all day.

Prediction: Florida 35, F$U 24

**Visor Flings, Week 13:**
**UF 45, F$U 12**

BEATDOWN!

It was more than fun to watch the Gators crush the Seminoles at the Swamp. So much talk from punks like Geno Tayes, er, Hayes about how Tim Tebow was 'going down'. Yeah – down the field. Down in the history books. Typical clowns from the clown school. They were manhandled on both lines, and it was apparent by late in the first quarter that Florida was the dominant team and program in the state.

The Gator defense has shown improvement the past month since the debacle against Georgia. The move of Mike Pouncey to DT really solidified the middle. Cunningham and Harvey were unblockable, as the Turnstiles (formerly known as the F$U O-line) were spun again. Spikes has really improved in pass coverage. I would say that this was Joiner's best game of the season. He anticipated run and pass plays very well and was in position to make big plays all night. Jacques Rickerson stepped in for Haden at CB and played very well. He could be one of those guys that doesn't always practice well but turns it on on the field. The only playmaker that F$U has is Preston Parker, who is the only reason they moved the ball in the first half. Good luck with Jimbo Fisher as OC and Head-Coach-in-Waiting, 'Nole fans.

The Gator offense toyed with the Seminoles. The O-line whipped F$U's D-line all game long. Percy Harvin was electric at RB. If he can just stay healthy for an entire season – look out. Tayes had all of one tackle; what a joke he is. And F$U's LBs and DBs wanted no part of Tebow in the open field. Murphy has really developed into a reliable weapon at WR. CI was healthy again, and he was available anytime Tebow needed a play – a complete mismatch for F$U. They just punished the Seminoles the entire game – a wonderful thing. And Tebow showed again why he's the best QB in the country. His deep throws are money, and when he decides to run he's a load.

This game was once again the springboard to a big recruiting class. It's obvious to even the most jaded F$U fan or recruit watching this game that Florida's talent level is far beyond F$U's. And the coaching at Florida is superior. Players are developed and perform at a high level, while the Seminoles don't have a clue on offense and have been exposed on defense. Despite smaller numbers than in 2006 and 2007, the Gators should reel in another Top 5 class in 2008.

And now it's another off-season of discontent in Taliban City, as Blobby desperately hangs on to stay ahead of Paterno in the win category, while Head Clown-in-Waiting Jimbo Fisher gets ready to take over…maybe. What a farce. And all this uncertainty just widens the gap between the Gators and Seminoles. More beat-downs to come!

Florida will next play Michigan in the Capitol One Bowl in January. Michigan has had their share of problems this year, with the unsavory distinction of being on the short end of one of the biggest upsets in college football history when they lost to the Appalachian State Mountaineers in their season opener. All in all, I don't expect them to be able to compete with this Gators team.

Prediction: Florida 35, Michigan 17.

**Visor Flings, Week 17:**
**Michigan 41, UF 35**

What a huge letdown after a strong finish to the regular season. The defense collapsed completely in its worst performance of the year, allowing Michigan to do whatever they wished. Their imitation of a sieve put the Gator offense into the tough position of knowing it had to score almost every time it had the ball, which is too much pressure, even for a team with the Heisman Trophy winner and Percy Harvin on its roster.

Granted, I knew that Michigan would be extremely motivated after they had been roasted by their own fans and nationally for their poor performance both early and late in the year. Unfortunately, the combination of that, their head coach in his last game, and all of their offensive weapons finally healthy all at once, was too much for a painfully young Gator defense to overcome. The Wolverines have four guys that will be drafted in rounds one through three into the NFL, and it showed. Jake Long led a dominant OL performance, as he overpowered anyone Florida had to offer.

A lot of the defensive players popped off before this game about how they would control Michigan, and they were embarrassed. What a weak effort – those guys need to shut up and learn to play a lot better. They have not endeared themselves to the coaching staff, and it's going to be a long off-season with brutal conditioning drills and a wide-open depth chart in spring practice.

Some criticism will be leveled at Tebow for his below-average numbers, but he still accounted for four TDs. He did not look nearly as sharp as he did the second half of the season, and I wonder if all of the Heisman obligations really did affect his preparation. Percy

Harvin was the best offensive talent on either sideline, and terrorized Michigan's defense all day. As I alluded to earlier, though, when you know you have to score every time, you start to press, and even the best offense will make mistakes. Untimely penalties and drops in the red zone left at least 10 points off the scoreboard, and that was the difference. Aaron Hernandez made some big plays, and he could be a serious factor next year along with Cornelius Ingram at TE.

Coach Meyer, Coach Strong, and the rest of the defensive staff have a mountain of work to do to improve the defense for 2008. The raw talent is there, but those players have to get faster, stronger, and very simply, play a lot better. The Gators will have one of the top offenses in the country next year, but championships are won with defense, especially in the SEC. I wouldn't be surprised to see some new faces, maybe even some of the early enrollees, see the field some next season.

Well, as bad as the end of 2007 was, there is a lot of hope for 2008. I do believe in Coach Meyer's ability to get the most out of his players and coaches, and I have to think this game will be fuel to bounce back in a big way. It's time to reclaim the SEC. There are some serious challengers in the way, including Georgia and LSU. We'll see how Tebow bounces back and how he leads the Gators next year.

Go Gators!

Very truly yours,
The Visor

# 2008
# True to his Word

Strange how some images just stay with you. For me, there were a number of moments during the 2008 season that re-defined Florida football in the present era. For instance, I won't soon forget Tebow's speech to the media after the loss early on to Ole Miss. A lot of players in his place at the time might have *said* those things – that we would never see any player work harder to help his team win from that point on, and so on – but how many of them could have actually gone out and done it, as Tim did? And then to see him the following week before the Arkansas game, out there in his coat and tie, leading the cheering. It brought back images of legends: Knute Rockne, Nagurski, Byron White…Steve Spurrier.

I admire the way he willingly changed his role for this team this year. He clearly never had any interest in his own stats or his own chances at a second Heisman; he was the spiritual leader, an emblem of human willpower and what it can do, and once everyone – the coaches as well as all the great players surrounding Tebow – once they knew exactly what had to be done, they did it with tenacity and iron resolve. I think that any unbiased and intelligent college football fan who watched UF's last three games this season, against F$U, Alabama, and Oklahoma, would admit that he saw a masterpiece in the making. He would have to say, "Yep, that's how it's done. That's how you win it all."

Some people had talked about an undefeated season for the Gators, but I think the loss to Ole Miss was really the key. Without that stunning moment of devastation and crushed pride, we would have had nothing to try and make up for, nothing to overcome. All great stories are like that.

Besides, Urban Meyer and Tebow and the rest of the boys may still get their shot at an unmarred record. Tim has already promised to return for his senior year, and in keeping with his deep Christian beliefs, he has a very clear idea of himself as a person of destiny. Although he and his teammates have already added a couple of great chapters, the story is not finished.

But for now, let's talk about what happened in 2008. It's worth reliving.

**Visor Flings, Week 1:**
**Preview and Predictions**

It's that time of year again! Heeeeeeere come the Gators!

After a disappointing and discouraging end to 2007 in the Capital One Bowl loss to Meat-chicken, Florida is re-energized and improved heading into 2008.

Any discussion about the Gators' chances for any kind of championship run in 2008 starts with the defense. Last year the Florida defense was its worst in over 30 years. Injuries, inexperience, and a lack of quality depth were too much for even a dynamic offense to overcome, leading to a four-loss season that could have been so much more.

The defensive line will get the most scrutiny, especially the tackle position. It appears that Lawrence Marsh, Terron Sanders, and JUCO transfer Omar Epps will be the rotation to start the season, as John Brown battles through a broken wrist. Torrey Davis may not even play this year due to off-the-field issues that have him buried in Coach Meyer's doghouse. Freshman Omar Hunter has the ability to contribute, but a back injury has slowed him in fall practice and put him behind the others. It all starts with this group, and Coach McCarney has to develop a functional unit that can withstand a SEC schedule.

The defensive end position looks like potentially one of the best groups in the SEC, and could be even better than that with some quick development by talented guys with little experience. Jermaine Cunningham is undersized, but utilizes great quickness and technique to make plays. Carlos Dunlap could be a monster this fall if he learns to go 100% each play. He possesses all of the physical tools to dominate. Justin Trattou really played well as a true freshman, and shows great pursuit and coverage ability. True freshman Matt Patchan will get some snaps this fall, moving over from playing offensive tackle in high school. He's got a great motor and knack for making plays, even as a young guy. Jaye Howard will play inside and out as needed.

The linebacking corps has some promise this fall, finally developing some depth to support a starting unit that simply wore down in games last year. Brandon Spikes is the leader of the entire defense in the middle, and plays both the run and pass equally well. Dustin Doe will be counted on to show improvement this fall, while Brandon Hicks and Lorenzo Edwards battle for the other starting spot. Ryan Stamper played very well last year backing up all 3 positions, and is a valuable player. AJ Jones played most of last year with a broken hand, slowing his development. He should be a solid contributor this fall. John Jones has a chance to be a situational pass-rusher, to utilize his quickness off the edge.

The secondary will be improved. New Coach Vance Bedford has really pushed this group to play more physically, and they have responded. Joe Haden and Wondy Pierre-Louis will start at cornerbacks, but are being pushed by Markihe Anderson. True freshmen Janoris Jenkins and Jeremy Brown will play this fall, and their early enrollment in January gave them the benefit of Spring to both get acclimated to college, but also an extra 20 practices to move ahead of the others. At safety, injuries have taken their toll in the off-season, as both Dorian Munroe and John Curtis suffered torn ACLs and are out for the season. Major Wright will lead a very young and inexperienced unit, playing both safety positions as the situation warrants. Ahmad Black gets first crack at the other position, and has good football instincts. However, look for true freshman Will Hill to get a lot of playing time this fall. He has the talent, and will have to get on-the-job training. Justin Williams has moved over from WR, and has already surprised the staff will how quickly he's picked up things. He could be a pleasant surprise and contribute a lot.

The Gator offense was dynamic in 2007, averaging 40+ points a game, and was efficient in third down conversions and in the red zone. This unit will hopefully not have to carry as large a load in 2008, but definitely can if called upon.

The offensive line looks to be the best one in Coach Meyer's tenure at UF. Coach Addazio has molded what could be a dominant group that could be one of the best in the country. The interior, consisting of the Pouncey twins at center and right guard, and Jim Tartt at left guard, will punish opponents all season. Phil Trautwein could actually be the most important player on offense in 2008, returning from a foot injury that sidelined him all of 2007 to start at LT. If he can stay healthy, he is one of the best tackles in the SEC. Jason Watkins returns at RT to protect Tim Tebow's blind side. There is finally quality depth developed now, with Marcus Gilbert, Carl Johnson, and Maurice Hurt cross-trained at multiple positions.

The running back group has been over-analyzed all off-season, as many are wondering if a quality rotation will finally emerge to take some of the load off of Tebow. New RB coach Kenny Carter seems to have connected with a diverse group led by senior Kestahn Moore and USC transfer Emmanuel Moody. Moore and Chris Rainey appear to have the ability to make big plays at tailback, and Moore will see action at both tailback and fullback, to take advantage of his solid pass-blocking and receiving skills. Mon Williams has recovered physically from his ACL surgery in 2007, but is lagging behind the others right now while he struggles to go 100% and not worry about the knee. I really think this group will be solid in 2008.

The receiver lineup at Florida this fall could be the best group ever. It is headlined by Percy Harvin, one of the top playmakers in college football. His radical Achilles heel surgery has slowed him in fall practice, but he should be 100% by the start of the SEC schedule. Louis Murphy really developed into a threat in 2007. The combination of Riley Cooper and JUCO #1 WR Carl Moore will do well over the middle. And we haven't even mentioned Deonte Thompson, who red-shirted in 2007 as one of the fastest players in the country out of high school. The loss to an ACL of Cornelius Ingram is devastating personally for him, but fortunately for the team, Aaron Hernandez is going to prove to be a beast at tight end this fall, and Tate Casey is a capable fill-in at the other spot. This unit, barring injury, will be one of the best in the country this fall.

Then there's the QB position, manned by returning Heisman Trophy winner Tim Tebow. What a luxury for the team to have one of the most respected leaders in college football at the helm. He spent most of his off-season working on becoming a better decision-maker both running the option and reading pass coverages. I seriously doubt his rushing statistics will approach what he accomplished in 2007, but that is actually best for the overall offense. Expect to see both Cam Newton and John Brantley to see action backing up Tebow this fall. Coach Meyer thinks that Newton is a real red-zone threat as a runner, while Brantley is a smooth passer who has improved both physically and in his running ability. Hard to find a better depth chart in college football then what's in Gainesville.

The special teams will once again be dynamic in 2008. They are headlined by junior Brandon James, who terrifies opponents returning both kickoffs and punts. He is one of top return guys in the country. And there are a ton of great talents that back him up, including Murphy, Haden, and Rainey. Wow. Chas Henry could develop into one of the top punters in the SEC this fall, and is solid. The real competition is being waged at place kicker between senior Jonathan Phillips and true freshman Caleb Sturgis, who already possesses one of the strongest legs in college football. It appears that Phillips will get first chance at field goals this fall, but Sturgis will handle kickoffs. Coach Meyer personally handles this unit, and it shows. Great production every year.

As usual, any SEC schedule is physically and mentally challenging. But compared to 2006 and 2007, the schedule this fall is as manageable as it can be for Florida. Hawaii and Miami open the season at the Swamp. Expect the Gators to physically wear down the Warriors, while there is a ton of payback due for scUM. Expect Coach Meyer to have the team motivated to dispose of the 'Canes. There is an open week before the trip to Tennessee, which will be interesting because Phat Phil has decided to open up the offense with a Spread look. Florida is the better team, but the game being at Knoxville could keep it close. Ole Miss follows back in Gainesville, led by a former commitment at QB, Jevan Snead, and a new head coach in Houston Nutt. Another road trip follows at Arkansas, who also has a new head coach in Bobby Petrino. Then a major test back at the Swamp against defending National Champion L$U. Another open week follows to rest up for the push to the end, starting at home against Kentucky. Then the grudge match against the Puppies in Jacksonville. Another road trip to Vanderbilt follows, then two more home games against South Carolina and Steve Spurrier, and then the Citadel. Finally, the regular season ends in Taliban City against F$U.

The open weeks fall at good times, and many of the teams during the first half of the season are breaking in new QBs, which bodes well for Florida. No way Hawaii or Miami challenge the Gators in the Swamp. After last year's beat-down of the Vols, hopefully the team is not overlooking them on the road. Ole Miss will not win at the Swamp. The trip to Arkansas could be a 12:30 snoozer-type game, but the Gators have historically struggled in facing West Division opponents on the road. The loss of Darren McFadden and Felix Jones is probably too much for them to overcome. The game against L$U may once again prove to be the SEC game of the year. There is still too much talent on both the O-line and D-line for the Tigers, and they will challenge anyone, anywhere. The Gators will need that open week to refresh themselves. Kentucky will not be the challenge they were last season, and then the showdown in Jax. I personally don't believe the Puppies will be undefeated by the time they arrive, but the record won't matter to a VERY motivated team and coaching staff. That classless celebration last season will be repaid. I expect a win at Vandy, and then the pariah returns to Gainesville for another beat-down. Finally, the Gators go to Taliban City to continue the Semiholes' misery.

Pre-season injuries have taken a toll, and the defense, while improved, may still slip up a few times. It's really hard to say where, but I just don't expect the defense to be championship-caliber in 2008. Maybe they don't have to be if the offense once again is dominant, and maybe they are good enough for a trip to Atlanta and a possible SEC title, but I just can't see a run to Miami for the BCS championship this year.

My forecast: Regular Season 11-1 and an SEC championship.

The Gators will open 2008 against the Warriors of Hawaii. It will be a tough environment for UH – not just the Swamp fans, but the oppressive heat and humidity of a 12:30 kickoff in August. Brutal. I expect Hawaii to score some points, but Florida is going to physically wear them down with numbers and talent in the heat, and should score a comfortable win.

Prediction: Florida 45, Hawaii 17

**Visor Flings, Week 2:**
**UF 56, Hawaii 10**

That was a solid win for an opener against Hawaii. Of course, the usual rough patches as far as execution and penalties are expected, but it was encouraging to see all three units contribute.

The defense played a lot of a 3-3-5 alignment to offset the Spread attack of the Warriors, and all of the stunts and blitzing from different angles was enough to disrupt the timing of their passing offense. Florida had way too much speed for UH to counter – welcome to the SEC. Lawrence Marsh proved the coaches comments about his fall practice with a good game at nose tackle, while Cunningham, Dunlap, Trattou, and co. made life miserable for UH off the edges. Ryan Stamper and Dustin Doe filled in nicely for the injured Brandon Spikes. The best development, though, was the aggressiveness of the secondary, both in coverage and tackling in the open field. Haden, Wright, and Wondy all played very well, while Janoris Jenkins, as a true freshman, showed why the staff is so high on him. Being an early enrollee was key to his development.

The offense was efficient, and was content to pound away with the run most of the day. It gave the fans a glimpse of the future playmaking ability of Rainey and Demps. Tebow was actually not very sharp throwing the ball, and the O-line was only average at picking up the blitz, but it was just the first live game, and I'm sure the line will be ready for the next game.

The special teams were already in mid-season form. Brandon James is a dynamic returner, and if he stays healthy has to be an All-American candidate. Chas Henry is a great athlete at punter, evidenced not only by his fake audible for a first down, but punting the ball both short and deep. The only area that looked below average was the kickoffs, which caught everyone by surprise. After a great fall camp, Caleb Sturgis looked ordinary, with no real deep kicks. This has to improve.

Now, it's time to beat down the Hurricanes, as scUM comes to Gainesville for a long-awaited visit. Their players and fans are delusional right now, thinking that a bunch a young guys, a weak offense, and two QBs with no college experience are going to do damage in the Swamp. Plus, head coach Randy Shamnon is due a punch in the face, as he spreads his lies on the recruiting trail, and shows no real coaching prowess in a big-game atmosphere. Jacory Harris and Robert Marve will both take snaps, and will wish they hadn't when this one is through. Their O-line is a weak spot, and will be exposed Saturday. They have to rely heavily on Javarris James and Greg Cooper in the backfield to have big games, but they will have only limited success.

The scUM defense will look to pressure and blitz a lot, but they will get burned by Florida's myriad playmakers all over the field. Expect some quick throws the to flats and the edges to slow any blitzing. The Gator O-line will pound and wear down the 'Canes front seven as the game progresses.

The 'Canes have no clue what's going to hit them when they enter the Swamp, which will be electric at night. The fans will make it impossible to hear any signals, and intimidate them. Plus, it appears that Harvin, Spikes, and Tartt will see some action, which will be an emotional lift to the Gators.

This is a big recruiting weekend as well, as a ton of 2009 and 2010 prospects will be attending to see Florida dominate another in-state opponent. Coach Meyer knows when to bring certain kids to the Swamp to see a real team take care of business.

Prediction: Florida 38, Miami 14

**Visor Flings, Week 3:**
**UF 26, Miami 3**

Well, it wasn't quite the beat-down I had hoped for, but it was still a good win over scUM. Actually, the game never was as close as the score, as Miami's offense had no chance to seriously threaten the end zone all night. It was the curious lack of offensive adjustments by Dan Mullen until late in the third quarter that kept the score close. Once those adjustments were made, the floodgates opened, and it was just a question as to how much Florida would win by.

Florida's defense dominated all evening, allowing the 'Canes inside the 30 only once (after a 4th down conversion), and across midfield only one other time. Granted, the pathetic offense put together by Patrick Nix, with a QB making his first collegiate start, was a bad combination heading into the Swamp, but there are some playmakers on the 'Cane offense, and they were entirely shut down. They knew a pounding running game was the only way to shorten the game and keep things close, even though it was painful to watch. The Gator defense this year exhibits much more team play and hustle to the ball, and a D-line that, while still average at DT, is still an improvement over 2007, with a little depth being developed.

The Gator offense was strangely ineffective most of the game until the aforementioned adjustments were made in blitz pickups and in quick passes to the open spots on the edges and in the zones. The O-line, quite frankly, stunk most of the evening, but I have to place more blame on the coaches than the execution. Once an extra blocker was set up to counter the constant blitzes, Tebow and the passing offense really took off and exposed the scUM secondary. Louis Murphy turned a nightmare game into a decent one with a solid fourth quarter. Aaron Hernandez is beginning to show how dangerous a weapon he can be, and just enough of a jolt from Percy Harvin and his explosiveness was enough to rally the offense in the second half.

The Florida special teams were dominant once again, and may be the best in the country. Brandon James continues to terrorize opponents on kick returns, and the punt block team is dynamite. Caleb Sturgis did a much better job on his kickoffs, and Chas Henry was efficient again, pinning the 'Canes inside the 20 many times, and once at the 1-yard line.

Randy Shamnon is bitching about the late field goal, and saying it will help scUM in recruiting. That guy is such garbage. The same person who tells recruits his friend Walter Odom, who played TE at Florida, was shot and killed in Gainesville to show that Gainesville is as dangerous a place to live as Miami, when the truth is Odom died of cancer in a South Florida hospital. He's a punk and a liar, and I can only hope some kids are smart enough to see through him over time. Classless person, fans, and program.

Suck on this one until 2013, scUM fans.

The biggest game of the year comes this Saturday for the Gators. Yes, that's right – a win sets the table for a run at Atlanta and a BCS game, while an ugly loss derails early a season of big expectations.

There is some concern about Florida's offense, and it's justified. The O-line has plainly struggled. Trautwein has not knocked off the rust of missing last season due to injury, Tartt may see his first action this week, and the blitz pickups have been very poor. The running game against Miami was poor, and the tailbacks remain a mystery somewhat. Moore is mainly a pass blocker now, Demps and Rainey are not between-the-tackles guys, and Moody has been both dinged up and in the doghouse. What else could be holding him back?

Percy Harvin is still the best running back at Florida, and the staff may have to just accept it and let him run wild. He's practiced well the past two weeks, and seems as healthy as he's ever been. He can certainly make plays even without stellar run-blocking, and can still serve as an outlet in the passing game if Tebow needs to check down.

It would go against Coach Meyer's plan to win, but it may be time to unleash Tebow and the passing game, and just bomb away at the Vol secondary, which still remembers how it was torched last year. It would certainly break tendency, but may be what the offense needs early to get going. Tebow is always a solid last resort if the pocket breaks down, as he can still make some big plays with his legs if necessary. Cooper, Murphy, and Thompson can all get deep, and Hernandez is starting to show flashes of being a playmaker at TE.

This will be the first real test for the Gator secondary. There is definite improvement over last year, and Coach Bedford has instilled more aggressiveness and confidence into this unit. But they are still very young, even with all of the on-the-job training they had in 2007.

Wright and Black have played the majority of snaps, but I expect Will Hill to start seeing more action. At cornerback, Haden has been a stud so far, and Pierre-Louis, Anderson, and even Jenkins look markedly improved. The linebackers have played well so far, but have some injury concerns. Doe is not 100% with a groin injury, Stamper still has a cast on his broken thumb, and Spikes has only played one game after sitting out the Hawaii game with a toe injury. This group has to play it's best, because it will be challenged by Tennessee's running game and short-passing scheme.

Honestly, I give the Vols a serious chance only because this game is at Rocky Top. I feel they have a fragile psyche after their debacle against UCLA, and they still slept though some of their game against UAB. They will be jacked for this one, as they know their season could go downhill in a hurry, with Auburn and Georgia following this game.

Florida has some doubts about its running game right now, and its defense will get its first legitimate test Saturday. Time to play with confidence and ratchet up the intensity – this is a huge game for the Gators.

Prediction: Florida 28, Tennessee 24

**Visor Flings, Week 5**
**UF 30, Tennessee 6**

It was a surprisingly easy win on Rocky Top Saturday, as the Gators toyed with the Vols in a 30-6 beating. It's not looking good for The Great Pumpkin right now, and Krispy Kreme stores throughout the southeast will mourn the day he is let go.

Brandon James again set the tone early, as Tennessee's coaches were dumb enough to kick to him again and again. The opening kickoff return set up the Gators in Vol territory, and the offense immediately punched it in with another classic jump-pass from Tebow to Hernandez. You know opponents are waiting for it, but each time it comes from a new formation, and works.

Then, true freshman Janoris Jenkins causes a fumble on Tennessee's first possession, and that leads to a FG. Another stop, another punt to James, and...game over! What an awesome return, with BJ juking six guys, then blowing right up the seam into the end zone.

After the first quarter, it was another Coach Meyer plan-to-win blueprint. Control the clock, stay efficient on offense and dominate field position. I am impressed with the consistent play of the defense so far, but was shocked at how bad Compton looked at QB – he has definitely regressed since David Cutcliffe left for Duke. The Gator secondary looks very good for now and the future, with Jenkins, Haden, Wright, Black, and co. showing huge improvement over last year. Credit goes to Vance Bedford.

Of course, the overhead shots of Neyland Stadium after Tebow and Harvin closed out the game late in the third quarter were satisfying – another empty SEC stadium after the Gators roll the home team.

Now, an interesting match-up comes up at the Swamp this week, as Houston Nutt brings the Ole Miss Rebels to town. They look like a much more balanced and solid team than the past few years, and have very good line play on both sides. Former Gator commit Jevan Snead has played decently at QB, but still lacks experience yet. You never know what you'll get from one of Nutt's teams from week to week, and he has sprung some stunning road upsets in the past. The Rebel defensive line is very good, but the back seven is poor, and has been repeatedly exposed so far. The Gator offense should be able to exploit match-up problems all over the field and control the action.

This is still a young team, so I don't expect a completely solid effort week-to-week just yet, and a letdown could come, especially with another snoozer 12:30 kickoff time. It may take a little while for the team to get up to speed, but I expect the Gators to pull away in the second half. There is a lot of hand-wringing about the performance of the offense so far, but between the early leads and the new clock rules, there's no way they will approach last year's output, but the good thing is that they probably won't have to, either.

Prediction: Florida 35, Mississippi 17

**Visor Flings, Week 6:**
**Ole Miss 31, UF 30**

Fools Gold?

Fool me once (2007 Tennessee), shame on you.
Fool me twice (Tennessee 2008), shame on me?

Once again, the Gators blow out UT, and then lay a huge egg in the Swamp. Florida is not acting like a top-shelf team...yet. False hope...again, even with a defense that is better. Man, does that suck.

Yes, the defense IS better. And, yes, they gave up two big plays. But, they did OK, even with the offense in meltdown mode in the third quarter.

Tebow is right – he has to work harder...but he's got to get better. Yes, better. His deep throwing really killed the Gators today.

I suppose Tartt is the MVP of this team, because it appears we have no running game with him out. The injury to Moody was critical as well.

Will Coach Meyer adapt? It's time for him to either let Mullen turn things loose, or else turn Mullen loose. This is crazy that so many talented kids get so few touches. NO IDENTITY yet for this year's offense. Hey, at least last year it was no secret that it was the Tebow and Harvin show...and that worked okay.

Plan to Win (or is it Lose?)...Yeesh. Please, start blowing away these inferior teams from the outset of the game, and stay after them. I'm frustrated, as are all Gator fans. But seriously, it's time to open up things a little and unleash these talented playmakers.

Folks, it's time to cut this entire team loose. I'm glad they have a game next Saturday, so they can try to move on. And actually, I'm glad it's on the road, so the team can close ranks and re-focus on playing better and getting the job done right.

The staff has a lot of work to do, both in improving it's coaching and game-planning, but also in building the players' confidence back up. It looks like Tartt may only be available every two or three games the rest of the year. Gilbert is injured as well, so Carl Johnson gets the start at left guard. It's also time to get James Wilson and Ronnie Wilson ready to play. Dustin Doe is out for 3-4 weeks with hernia surgery, so Brandon Hicks becomes the starter at SLB. Here's hoping Lo Edwards starts seeing more action as well. It also looks like Hunter will get more snaps at DT.

Tebow and his receivers have to communicate and play better. There are too many big plays being left out on the field, plays that can put away an opponent much earlier, and not let them stick around into the fourth quarter. The injury to Moody may mean some significant change in the play-calling, since no one else seems to have success running inside except for Harvin on occasion. It's time to run more option plays, and incorporate more swing passes and screen in order to get more playmakers in space. The offense is stale, which is unbelievable to me given the talent. Dan Mullen has done a poor job in 2008 with this group.

The season can still be a very good one...but it's going to have to start with the head coach and the staff, and then on down to the players, to make it happen. This is still a young team, and honestly, I expected 2009 to be the next run for a title. But don't give up on this bunch yet.

Prediction: Florida 35 Arkansas 17

**Visor Flings, Week 7:**
**UF 38, Arkansas 7**

> Despite a 38-7 win, that performance was like putting lipstick on a pig (or in this case, a hog). The Gator offense once again struggled for most of three quarters, and even the defense started to show some cracks, especially against the run. The hangover from the debacle against Ole Miss took a long time to recover from, as mistakes in execution and penalties plagued Florida most of the afternoon.

The offense still is searching for its identity. The ball was spread around a little more both running and passing, but the long ball is almost non-existent, as Tebow continues to struggle with his accuracy. Murphy had a decent day, and it was good to see Thompson start getting some throws his way – that guy is too dangerous to be an afterthought. Harvin was pretty quiet, partially because of a sprained ankle. But Rainey and Demps more than picked up the slack with a combined three long TD runs. Tebow continues to be the only dependable short-yardage back, but at least the home run threat of the others keeps opposing defenses a little honest. The play-calling by Dan Mullen is still questionable, as he does not seem to want to throw any screens, and only uses the swing pass to a back on rare occasion – a perfect opportunity to get one of the myriad playmakers in space. The O-line played a little better, actually, as Carl Johnson did an adequate job at LG. I also saw guys like Ronnie and James Wilson getting more reps, and it's about damn time. Those guys need some experience with the tough part of the schedule coming up.

Of more concern was the defense, which was pushed around most of the day against the run. he D-line is still not SEC-caliber at DT, as they were gashed for repeated big plays all day. The adjustment to the crossing routes also took way too long to happen. What was Coach Strong (not) seeing? It looks like Torrey Davis going to be back in the rotation now, and he's needed desperately. He's still green with little experience, but gets the best penetration off the ball, even though he still takes himself out of some plays. I did see him hustle down the line to make some tackles, which is an improvement. March and Sanders were MIA, though – very disappointing. At LB, there were a lot of missed tackles by the outside guys – another position of disappointment. Hicks is getting better, but is plagued by inexperience. The absence until garbage time of Lorenzo Edwards is a huge letdown – great athlete, and smart, but apparently in Coach Meyer's doghouse right now. The secondary was solid again, giving up no long throws and making Arkansas keep everything short. Haden and Jenkins are fine pair of young corners, and just keep getting better. Major Wright still has to improve his pass coverage, but did not get out of position this week. Black may be the best tackler other than Spikes on the defense.

Now, the SEC season is on the line at the Swamp this Saturday night against LSU. It's a shame it's come to this, but that's what a terrible home loss to a bad team will do to your fortunes. LSU has to have a lot of confidence, as they have already gone on the road and won a tough game, at Auburn. Their QB situation may be more settled right now with Jarrett Lee as the starter, but he's still a red-shirt freshman, and I just want the Gators to make that guy have to make plays in the passing game. The problem with that is that the Tigers have a powerful running game led by Charles Scott, and he's backed up by quality guys like Keiland Williams. I have to believe they will try and pound the Gator D-line, and, frankly, I see them having some success doing it. That would mean crowding the box and putting the CBs on an island. Well, even though the guys are still young, I think that's the best strategy, and they can probably hold up. LSU's receivers, led by Brandon LaFell, are good, but still inconsistent, and will drop the ball.

The Gators need to play with the lead, as they have not exhibited the ability to consistently come from behind, especially in the 4th quarter. Partly because of poor execution, but more so because of mediocre coaching and play-calling. The offensive staff has let down these players so far, and have to come up with a better game plan and prepare the team better. It's time to ditch the five-wide formation, and give Tebow some more protection. LSU's secondary is no where near what they were the past three or four years, and they actually made Auburn's pathetic passing game look decent a few weeks ago. Mullen has to be able to at least get as much out of this group of talented playmakers. Hopefully Harvin is healthy, as he will be the main tailback with Moody still out. And even if the run gets stuffed a few times, Rainey and Demps only need a little seam to go the distance in one big play.

A few points to consider:

1) Break tendencies on offense early. Throw more on first down. More swing passes to Rainey/Demps/James, and maybe a few WR screens to Harvin.
2) The Gators may show a 5-2-4 on defense, or even a 3-4? That could shake up Lee's reads early, and cause some blocking scheme problems for LSU.
3) Man-to-man defense by Florida. I really think Bedford has these guys at a level to do this, because I'm just not overly impressed with the Tigers' WR corps. LaFell has actually improved, but they still drop a lot of balls.
4) Attack LSU's secondary deep. Those guys have allowed a lot of receivers to get open deep. Hey – even Auburn had a good passing half! Tebow has struggled on his deep throws, but there will be chances to score this week.

The Swamp will have to come alive Saturday night, as this team is still searching for it's confidence, and needs the crowd the entire game. Any faint hope of an appearance in the BCS championship is on the line, and any chance of a trip to Atlanta and the SEC championship would be severely damaged with a loss.

Prediction: Florida 27, L$U 24

**Visor Flings, Week 8:**
**UF 51, LSU 21**

It was definitely a statement at the Swamp Saturday night, as the Gators announced that they are still in the mix for SEC and national recognition. That was the most complete performance across the board since perhaps 2006. The crowd was electric, and there was another big-time recruiting "who's who" in attendance.

There was no doubt from the opening drive that the Gators were ready to play. The long TD pass to Harvin was just the thing to get the fans even more into it. Then the defense forces two straight 3-and-outs, and the offense drives again and again. That eventually proved too much for LSU to overcome, and paved the way to a beat-down.

The success of the running game and overall play of the O-line was the most important development of the entire game. The little guys only need a little crease to make a huge play, and until Moody returns, Tebow will have to be the short-yardage back again. The Gators controlled the LSU D-line better than anyone else in the SEC for the second year in a row. Tebow has time to actually read the defense and set his feet. The option plays are key to keeping the defense honest, and Demps is a dangerous man when he gets loose. Excellent ball distribution, as many players had touches.

The D-line obviously took it as a personal challenge to slow down the Tiger running game – mission accomplished. Charles Scott never could get going. I'm actually surprised that Andrew Hatch didn't get more playing time, as he moved them pretty well mixing in the option plays and getting some running game going. Brandon Spikes made his case for All-SEC and All-American teams this year. He is a beast, and has excellent coverage skills as well. Props to Janoris Jenkins as well. It's amazing that the kid is right out of high school, and is starting, breaking up pass plays, playing in single coverage, and reading screens and making tough tackles.

The bye week comes at a good time, despite the idea that you would want to keep the momentum after such a big win. This team is beat up right now. Tebow, Harvin, Murphy, Cooper, Moore, Rainey, Moody, some OL, some LBs, and Sturgis really need to heal up for the second half of the season. In my opinion, Tebow has been playing hurt since the start of the year – he is continually stretching his lower back and hips the entire game, and not running with either the speed or power he did last year. Hopefully Meyer will figure out what the heck is going on with the kickoffs and coverage, which have, quite frankly, been the worst in his four years at Florida. There are still areas that need improvement and tightening up, so the staff should be able to keep the attention of the team.

Game balls to: Coach Addazio (OL)
Coach McCarney (DL)
Spikes
Jenkins
Demps
The O-line
The D-line

After a week off to heal up and get focused on a run to Atlanta, the Gators host Kentucky. Another 12:30 kickoff – brought to you by the Official Network of the Florida Gators – Raycom. Yeesh. These 12:30 games are snoozers for everyone, and almost always give the underdog a better chance.

I hope Florida doesn't have to play Harvin, Rainey, Stamper, and a handful of others too much – they will need to be at full strength on Nov. 1 in Jacksonville. Kentucky is nowhere near as strong on offense this year. They are more of a ball-control offense with Hartline at QB, throwing safe possession passes. They still have a decent running game led by Derrick Locke. I'm sure they want to lull the crowd to sleep with one of those ugly early afternoon games. It's up to Florida to come out with some fire early and jump on the Wildcats from the start. It would be a refreshing change to see it happen for a day game.

Actually, Kentucky is really beat up for this game. Receiver Dicky Lyons Jr. is out for the year, Locke is doubtful, and three or four defensive starters probably won't play. For a change, the opponent has bigger injury problems than Florida.

Unfortunately, I expect a pretty vanilla scheme on both sides, as the staff wants to play it safe in preparation for Georgia. Actually, I'd like to see a wide-open first half, get a big lead, and then grind it out in the 2nd half.

Prediction: Florida 38, Kentucky 14

**Visor Flings, Week 10:**
**UF 63, Kentucky 5**

> Pretty much a perfect recipe for what you want for Homecoming, and a week before the showdown for the SEC East and a trip to Atlanta. It was a great sight to see the team focused early on whipping an injured opponent, making big plays on special teams and offense, and taking them out of the game in the first quarter. A lot of backups got significant time, and the starters got to rest and stay healthy.

Once again, Florida showed why it arguably has the best, most complete special teams in the country. Blocks, returns, kicks, and improved kickoff coverage – the total package. And continued evidence of how that makes winning so much easier. There are some future studs making huge plays – William Green, Will Hill, Jeffrey Demps. It's amazing how Coach Meyer has so many players buying in to playing special teams, and they are certainly excited to do it.

It was an efficient, businesslike approach by the offense. Solid O-line play, nothing too fancy – just overpowering a defense that isn't as talented. Carl Johnson seems to have settled in nicely at guard, and the whole unit seems to have cut down on the penalties. Demps and Rainey continue to terrorize defenses, and now the added feature of short passes leading to big plays is just one more way to slow down the rush and freeze the linebackers. Tebow has found a groove now, and seems ready to make a big run the rest of the season. Harvin looked healthy as well, which will be huge in Jacksonville.

The defense was once again solid, as the Mildcats had no real weapons to threaten seriously. Solid tackling, good ball pursuit, and a pretty vanilla scheme were all that was needed. Kentucky was missing two starters on the O-line, and they were dominated.

Now, the game of the year is here. I just hope the players don't get too hyped up after that debacle last year when the Puppies rushed the field in that idiotic TD celebration. There's too much on the line to get so emotional that you don't perform your assignments. The Gators have to play their best game of the season in all phases.

On offense, Florida should have some success. They had plenty of big plays and yards last year, and Georgia's front seven is not as good or as healthy. The option threat with Demps, Rainey, and Harvin should keep them honest, as LSU piled up a ton of yardage last week. The development of the short throws to dangerous guys like Demps, Rainey, and James should help Tebow keep the chains moving and spread out the defense. I don't think Georgia will allow the deep ball, as most of Florida's opponents haven't, either. As long as the O-Line stays healthy and continues to pick up blitzes and cut down on the penalties,

Florida should put up 30+ points. I do expect the Puppies to blitz often like last year, to try and disrupt the timing of the offense. Look for it especially on the plays where the Gator O-line has the wider splits, which they started to employ in the Arkansas game. This year, though, I believe Tebow has improved his reads enough to be able to check to slants and swing passes to counter the pressure.

The Gator defense has its biggest challenge of the season. It's unfortunate the D-line, while improved, is not playing so well that it can fully take advantage of an inexperienced, thin Puppy O-line. Of course, slowing down the running game led by Knowshon Moreno is key. Winning first down is crucial to help dictate the action. Stafford has a strong enough arm that he will complete some throws even into good coverage, but he wants the deep ball, and after giving up too many long plays last year, I think Coach Strong will try and make him stay patient and throw underneath. That's why it's so important to control the running game and down-and distance. Can Stafford stay patient? Time for the secondary to prove they are vastly improved from last season. Haden and Jenkins will get their sternest test of the season, and Wright and Black must stay in proper position at safety. Too many big pass plays killed them in this game last year.

No motivational speeches needed this week. Just do your job, play hard four to six seconds at a time, and line up and do it again. If the Gators can limit mistakes and stay efficient on offense, I think they win the game.

Prediction: Florida 38, Georgia 31

**Visor Flings, Week 11:**
**UF 49, Georgia 10**

Forget "paying it forward." The Gators paid back the Puppies Saturday in a way that was a dream scenario for all players, coaches, and fans. After a year of their yapping and all the motivation bullcrap about the TD celebration, Florida reminded everyone that they own this series.

No fancy plays, no stupid celebrations, no joke. The focus of the team was apparent from the start – just a few penalties, no turnovers, and solid fundamentals throughout.

As expected, it was obvious that the Gator offense could move the ball both running and throwing from the start. The difference in this game was the Gator defense growing up from last season. There was no way that they were going to shut down Georgia's offense, as they have too many playmakers. But the defense always rose to the occasion when they were challenged in the red zone, making the right reads, getting in the proper position, and coming up with clutch stops and turnovers.

It was also encouraging to see the linebackers finally adjust to the deep square-ins and slants in the third quarter, as that was the only play that was hurting them up until then. Dustin Doe had his best game as a Gator, getting one interception and causing another. Brandon Spikes set the tone early with a monster hit on Knowshon Moreno in the second play of the game, and showed effectiveness as an edge rusher – a new wrinkle in the game plan. The pass rush was decent all game, and the D-line would have had a few more sacks if the officials would ever call holding.

The Florida offense did not have much success running inside, but that constant threat kept the defense honest, and set up the option runs and play-action passes. I was surprised Harvin did not get more touches, as he was certainly efficient when he did. But his presence is enough to open up other things. The O-line did a nice job picking up the blitz, and Tebow, unlike last year, had time to pick his receivers out. Another deadly-efficient game from him, accounting for five more TDs.

I would be remiss in not pointing out how overrated Coach Helen Hunt of the Puppies is, as she once again made stupid decisions like allowing the Puppies to throw on second-and-two and third-and-two at the Gator 12-yard line in the first quarter, and then trying that idiotic onside kickoff in the second quarter, leading to a short TD drive and a 14-3 lead for Florida. When will the media start picking up more on this? I hope she enjoyed those last two timeouts at the end of the game, as Coach Meyer once again reminded her of her place in this series, and that Florida calls the shots.

Now the table is set for Florida to get to Atlanta, starting with a visit to Nashville to take on Vanderbilt. The Commodores got off to a hot start and look to become bowl-eligible, but lately have lost momentum, and the Gators need to help them continue that trend.

Vandy has alternated QBs quite often this year, and have never achieved consistency there. They have relied on an opportunistic defense and turnovers this year, so Florida just needs to continue it's recent style of play, stay efficient on offense, protect the football, and let it's talent and playmaking ability overwhelm the Commodores.

The Gators seem to have come out of the Georgia game healthy, and should be ready to continue their roll. The loss to Ole Miss is a constant reminder of what a loss of focus can do, and the coaches will use that as motivation the rest of the way. While I don't expect a huge win this week, I would be very disappointed in a sluggish effort.

Prediction: Florida 38, Vanderbilt 14

**Visor Flings, Week 12:**
**UF 42, Vanderbilt 14**

So much for a "trap game". The Gators went to Vanderbilt and crushed them from the opening kickoff, dropping 42 straight on the 'Dores to start the game. Great focus displayed by the players. Remember, this is still a young team, but fortunate to have stellar leaders like Tebow, Harvin, Watkins, and Spikes.

There isn't much analysis necessary from the game – just total domination in all phases. Tebow has looked better running the ball the past two weeks than he has all year.

The O-line is really jelling. The defense is still opportunistic, and wasn't really challenged by Vandy.

Now, the Pariah returns to the Swamp, trying once again to screw his former team out of a shot at a national championship. I'm sure their team will draw upon their performance from two years ago in getting ready for the game, but this Gator team has a much stronger and balanced offense now. I don't care one bit about his history at Florida – I'm hoping for another beat-down. The Gators always come first.

South Carolina's running game is not where it was the last two seasons, leaving its young, inexperienced QBs to learn under fire. They are still turnover-prone, leading the SEC in giveaways. They do have a solid WR in Kenny McKinley, and a quality TE in Jared Cook. Plus the old HBC can still scheme up some good plays. But the Gator defense now has enough individuals at LB and in the secondary to man up and cover these guys, forcing the QB to look for other targets. It's key to take away any comfort zone from the Gamecocks – they will turn the ball over under pressure.

I think Carolina keeps it close until the second half, but I have faith that this year's Gator team has the playmakers on both sides of the ball to pull away in the second half.

Prediction: Florida 34, South Carolina 17

**Visor Flings, Week 13:**
**UF 56, South Carolina 6**

> Wow. Florida made the Lamecocks look like nothing more than chickens with their heads cut off, handing the Pariah his worst defeat – ever. Too bad SOS – you made a mistake going there, and now the Gators are making you realize it.

Complete, utter domination in all phases. The defense set the tone by stuffing USC early, and starting the scoring barrage by forcing two consecutive turnovers, which in turn forced the ol' Head Ball Coach's hand to try a throwback on the kickoff return, which in turn pretty much doomed them. Carolina's defense was tough in the interior early, but their heart was cut out after it was 21-0, and then the Gator offense found its rhythm and blew them out in the second half.

Percy Harvin was sick, making it look so easy (as usual) to take it to the house in just one play – twice. The O-line is playing its best ball in Meyer's tenure, making great blocks on the inside counter play, while also running option plays and pass-protecting. This offense is the most versatile one in college football, and strikes fear into anyone now. Tebow just had to manage another solid effort, and is not carrying the load anymore. He's still fresh this late in the season, and his running looks that way. It's difficult for all of the playmakers to have to share the touches, but these guys have been unselfish all year, and the results speak for themselves.

The Gator defense completely shut down anything Carolina wanted to do. These guys are in position, making plays, forcing turnovers, and scoring themselves. This is quite a turnaround just one year removed from a disastrous performance in 2007, and the entire defensive coaching staff – Strong, McCarney, Bedford, and Heater – have to be considered one of the best staffs in the country. Spikes' int. return for the first score really shook up USC, followed immediately by Black's sixth pick. That kind of performance destroyed the confidence of Smelley and Garcia.

And don't forget the special teams, probably the best in the country as well. James Smith made a huge play on the kickoff throwback, James was dangerous again on punt returns, and the kickoff coverage team seems to have finally got its act together the past month.

The mantra for Senior Day is this:
No injuries.
No injuries.
No injuries.

Time to game plan early for F$U and Alabama. Oh, yeah, and no injuries!

Prediction: Florida 56, Citadel 10

**Visor Flings, Week 14:**
**UF 70, Citadel 19**

Well, the plan for Saturday almost went off without a hitch. Great day for the Gators, the seniors were honored and some scored touchdowns, and the bench was emptied. But, Lawrence Marsh and Matt Patchan getting knee injuries was a bad deal. Patchan is probably out until the bowl game, while Marsh's status is up in the air for this week at least.

The offense came right out and went for big plays early to put this one out of reach quickly. It was obvious they wanted to work some on the long passing game, as it has been pretty much shelved due to playing SEC opponents as well as the importance of winning out. Also, Rainey and Moody got in some more work, which will be advantageous when they are called upon the next 2 games. The Bulldogs were completely overmatched on defense.

Actually, the Citadel offense has some good plays, and ran some stuff we should see this week from F$U. That will give the coaches more things to keep the player's attention this week. Overall, the Gator defense was clearly physically superior, but they did play with aggressiveness most of the game, which shows that the young guys are starting to get it as far as practice habits and coming to play each week.

Now it's time to go for six in a row at Ron Zook Field this week. After winning last week, the Semiholes are already talking again about how they are “back,” and pointing out their improved offensive statistics. Well, that's mainly the result of playing in the Almost Competitive Conference. It will be a whole new experience when the Gators line up against them Saturday, and deep down they know it, and are fearful.

Offensive keys:

1) If F$U tries their usual bully tactics on defense by rushing straight up the field and blitzing (as they can get away with this against the lousy ACC offenses), the option and swing passes will KILL them. Just the threat of the option should make the F$U LBs play more assignment football, which is an advantage for Florida.

2) Attack the safeties! They have been below average there since 2005, and Florida should really have a big advantage there. I see Murphy on the weak side making a big catch or two, and Percy in the slot deep down the middle.

3) Tebow must be on his game reading the LBs. If they sit back, then the Gator O-Line should be able to push the F$U D-Line back and get solid gains. I'm not too sure if the crossing routes will work well against their LBs – they are quick.

4) I think we could see more of Aaron Hernandez and Riley Cooper in the possession passing game this week. Also, I hope the WRs are on their game reading the blitz, and give Tebow a safe hot read to throw to. I do not expect much bump-and-run coverage from their CBs – they have been torched too often the past few years.

5) I'm also encouraged by the development of some screen passes the past month. Once again, this will slow down the F$U pass rush, and if Demps or Rainey get in open space…forget it

6) Now is no time for hurt feelings. I would not be surprised at all to see Harvin get a lot of snaps at tailback – he's the best player on the team. Tebow will be prepared to carry the ball as well. As much as it's been beneficial to spread the ball around this year, if any of the young guys struggle, you have to ride your horses.

Defensive keys:

1) The Gator D-line should at least hold their ground on most plays, and should get good penetration a decent amount of the time on their own, without blitzing from the LBs. The DEs could really have a big day against F$U's tackles – they are weak. I still suspect we see Marsh get at least 8-10 snaps.

2) Ponder has struggled reading coverages. Win first down, and F$U is in serious trouble in passing situations.

3) This will be a big game for the Gator CBs. F$U will throw a lot of short passes and slip screens, so the CBs have to play physical.

4) The development of Will Hill the past month is very important. He has the speed to play in coverage against some of F$U's big WRs, but also has the size to help play some run support – especially as Ponder will try and run off of the read option, and can scramble.

Special Teams:

1) Brandon James has been playing with a hurt ankle for about a month now. I believe he's close to being back to 100%, which means big trouble for F$U. Opponents have been kicking away from him recently, but the trade-off is good field position, which is a main part of the Plan to Win.
2) Phillips and Henry have been consistent all season. Sturgis has to come up big on kickoffs. The kickoff coverage team had been improving, but seemed to slack off last week – the tackling has to be sound, as well as lane assignments.
3) Coach Meyer has developed one of the top groups in the country, and views these next 2 games as the perfect opportunity to prove again how important special teams are.

The Gator coaching staff has done a great job so far this year developing this team. There are still a lot of young guys on this team that weren't around in 2006, and have not experienced this game, or an SEC Championship Game. The staff has to find the right balance of encouragement while keeping the players on edge and focused on the game at hand, not looking ahead, and not wound too tight. The Gators are fortunate to have some tremendous leaders on the field in Tebow, Harvin, Murphy, and Spikes, and CI has been on the sideline for every game providing encouragement. It's time to reach out and take what is attainable now, and not wait for it to happen.

Prediction: Florida 31, F$U 21

**Visor Flings, Week 15:**
**UF 45, F$U 15**

The Gators put forth a professional effort in Taliban City, hammering F$U despite the terrible weather and field conditions. The gap in talent and coaching between the team continues to widen, and it's too bad Florida didn't put up 60 points. Just a total manhandling from the start, with no change to the offensive play calling despite the elements. The F$U coaching staff (aka "the greatest staff ever assembled") was totally outclassed, and between their ineptness and the shadow of NCAA sanctions hanging over their program, they will continue to wallow in mediocrity.
Tebow did a great job of managing the game in that weather. His passing was accurate, his option reads were spot on, and the ball security was excellent. He truly is the best leader in college football, and has the Gator offense on a tremendous roll going into Atlanta. The O-line was solid, as they blew open holes all game long to lead to 300+ rushing yards again, and now Florida leads the SEC in rushing. The WRs did their usual good job of downfield blocking, and held on to the ball very nicely in the wet conditions. The loss of Harvin was not felt, which is a testament to the preparation and talent of the players and staff. Coach Mullen did a nice job of going for the home run after turnovers, and called enough long passes to keep the F$U defense honest.

The defense did a great job despite being put into difficult situations with terrible kickoff coverage and the one offensive turnover. They shut down F$U's running game, and there was no way the Seminole QBs had the ability to pass effectively against the Gator secondary. Janoris Jenkins did a fine job against the bigger F$U WRs, breaking up multiple passes, and the overall tackling was sure. The D-line did a nice job of controlling the action, despite the constant holding and poor field conditions. Carlos Dunlap is thriving in the scheme of moving him all across the line of scrimmage, both in a stance and as a stand-up rusher. Spikes continues to make big plays, with another interception to start the third quarter that led to the TD which iced the game. Coach Strong continues to develop effective game plans, and the entire defensive staff has to be commended on an excellent job developing this young group into one of the top defenses in the country this year.

Now it's on to the Game of the Year against Alabama. This will be the biggest SEC championship ever in terms of what's at stake for the teams. There will be an incredible amount of buildup and media hype for the showcase conference championship game in college football.

Alabama comes in undefeated, led by a tough-as-nails running game and efficient QB play from John Parker Wilson. Julio Jones is one of the top freshman WRs in the nation, and is their leading receiver. Bama also utilizes the tight end effectively off of play-action, which has served them well all season as no one has completely shut down their running game. Glen Coffee and Mark Ingram have been tough RBs all season, even as freshmen. The rotation has kept them fresh. Andre Smith at left tackle and Caldwell at center are all-SEC players. Their defense is solid and stays pretty basic. Safety Rashard Johnson and LB Rolando McClain are the leaders. Coach Saban and Coach Steele are two of the better defensive coaches in college football, and their coaching ability is apparent in the performance of this unit. Few mistakes, few penalties, get turnovers.

The Florida offense does so many things well right now that I honestly feel that there is no special game-planning necessary, except for perhaps juggling the personnel if Harvin can't go or is ineffective this week. There are so many options in the running game, as well as the threat of the deep ball and the TE in the passing game. Mt. Cody may prove to tough to run on in the A gap, but that just means the option plays to the edges will be utilized, and I think the spreading out of the defense and the running required of the D-line will wear him down. There is no doubt that the Gators have the best and deepest collection of skill players in the country, and I just cant see Bama shutting them down. I expect a lot of 2-deep coverage by the Tide, and them trying to make Florida stay patient and work the ball down the field without big plays. It's the best strategy I can think of against Florida, but the execution has been so good that no one has managed it. Tebow and the O-line have improved their recognition of the blitz, and swing passes or screens to Demps and Rainey should slow that down as well, if Bama decides to come after the QB.

The biggest discussion all week is how the Florida D-line and defense can slow down Alabama's running game. I have a lot of respect for the Tide O-line, and fully expect them to have some occasional success. I do expect the Gators to play Major Wright or Will Hill closer to the line if necessary, which leaves man coverage in the secondary. At this point in the season, however, I'm confident in the coverage ability of Jenkins, Haden, and Black. The Gator cornerbacks are physical and skilled enough to stand up to the pressure, and are all sure tacklers as well if needed. Either because of stopping the run or scoring early, Florida will try and make John Parker Posey beat them with the passing game. He's been comfortable with a lead or in short-yardage situations, but even now still struggles when the run is not a threat. The WRs and TEs are solid, but lack a real deep threat. The pass protection of Bama's O-line is not their strong suit, and opponents have been effective in rushing the passer.

The special teams battle will be interesting. Both teams have a great punt returner. The Tide's Javier Arenas is one of the country's best, as is Brandon James for Florida. The Gators have a great punter in Chas Henry, but Bama's punt game can be had. Christenson gets the ball off slowly, and expect to see some rugby-style punts to offset the punt-block team of Florida. The one area the Gators have struggled in most of the year is on kickoff coverage. Injuries have affected this unit, but the inconsistent kicking of Sturgis has hurt as well. I would hope that the indoor conditions and turf field should help him get his kicks deeper to assist the coverage guys. Jonathan Phillips has been money all season, although never being put into a critical pressure field goal situation. His being a fifth-year senior has to help, though.

The Tide have had few close games, with the overtime win at LSU their closest call. They have pretty much imposed their will on their opponents most of the year, as a rugged running game tends to do that. They also have quite a few seniors, and that leadership cannot be overstated, as evidenced by Florida's run to the National Championship 2006. Their confidence is high right now, and their play has been consistently strong all year.

Much has been made of the contrast in styles, especially on offense, between the two teams. I find that funny, and also wrong. The Gators have a great running game as well led by a big, physical O-line, and their opponents will attest to that. The media has played the "finesse, soft" angle all week, and that will provide more motivation. The Florida defense is among the best in yards and points allowed, as well as turnover margin. The Gator coaching staff has really developed a "team" this season, and their performance has been consistent week to week.

Florida has fared better overall with common opponents, and I'm going with the team on a bigger roll right now. The stakes could not be higher, and will make this game a classic.

Prediction: Florida 31, Alabama 21

**Visor Flings, Week 16:**
**UF 31, Alabama 20**

Instant Classic

The Florida Gators are SEC Champions for the second time in three years and the 11th time overall (yes, I count 1984, 1985, and 1990), after a great 31-20 win over Alabama in the Florida Dome on Saturday.

Tim Tebow fulfilled his promise to the Gator Nation, as the Gators crushed everyone in their path after losing to Ole Miss. It was gut-check time for Florida in both the second and fourth quarters, and both times they responded with clutch drives and big plays on defense to retake the lead. Tebow, of course, led the way in the absence of Percy Harvin, as the offense took on a little more of the look of the 2007 team, with Tim carrying the ball a lot in the first half to keep drives alive. However, the difference in this year's team came through in dramatic fashion, as Demps, Murphy, Hernandez, and Cooper all contributed huge plays, while the offensive line showed that they were the equal of Bama's. Even with the occasional dominance of the Tide running game, Florida ran the ball right at them when behind in both halves, and went on consecutive scoring drives when absolutely necessary, with many of the plays being runs.

Tebow may not win the Heisman Trophy a second straight year, but no one in the Gator Nation would trade him for any other player. His development as a passer was on display this game, as he threaded some beautiful throws into tight coverage near the goal line, as well as showing nice touch on long throws to Cooper and Murphy. It was definitely the signature game for him and the entire Gator offense this season, despite the blowout wins over LSU, Georgia, and Florida State. When a championship is on the line and you are trailing, there is no room to hide, and it's put up or shut up time. Their performance, with Harvin being out, is only enhanced, with all the other guys filling for his various roles and making big contributions.

The Florida defense struggled some against Bama's running game, but honestly that was no real surprise. Credit has to be given to the Tide O-line, as they dominated in the running game all season with two All-Americans in Smith and Caldwell. Coffee was a beast as well at tailback, especially as a freshman. This was on top of the Gators dealing with losses due to injuries that affected the depth and quality of the DT rotation at the worst time. However, enough big plays and stops were made to prevent Bama from completely taking over the game. The real heroes were the cornerbacks, Haden and Jenkins, who were asked to play man coverage all game long in order for Florida to put eight in the box as often as possible. Julio Jones, who is a monster, made them pay with some big-time catches and plays, but that was the tradeoff, and overall it paid off. When the Tide was forced to pass, the advantage clearly switched to Florida's side, as Cunningham, Dunlap, Trattou, and Spikes were able to apply good pressure on John Parker Wilson.

With the switches in momentum from quarter to quarter, and with Florida coming through in such a big way when trailing in the fourth quarter (surprisingly, a first with Tebow as QB), this SECCG has to rank as one of the top few games in it's 17-year history. The added significance of having the two top-ranked teams playing essentially an elimination game in order to advance to the BCSCG probably places this game at the top. This game will always be one of the most important and memorable in Florida's football history – simply an incredibly clutch performance.

I'll be back with a preview of the BCS game in Miami in a few weeks. There is much to discuss, unfortunately not all strategy, as there are coaching staff changes in the works. But right now, I'm going to enjoy this SEC Championship immensely.

Go Gators!

**Visor Flings, Week 17:**
**Oklahoma Preview**

It's time to settle the debate this Thursday night in Miami, as the Gators go for their second National Championship in three years. There has been much talk about the weak defenses in the Big 12, and so far this bowl season, that has been the case. However, Oklahoma has demonstrated the most balanced and effective offense, and could give Florida all it can handle. Also, Bob Stoops has to want some redemption for four straight BCS bowl losses – some blowouts, and one huge upset to Boise St. two years ago.

UF Defense vs. OU Offense:

Florida must do two things exceptionally well to win: line up correctly against the no-huddle offense, and tackle in space. I do think that the Gators will play a decent amount of man-to-man coverage, as they have the athleticism and depth to match up with the Sooner WRs. OU will have some success when its passing game gets in rhythm, but the Gators must stay focused and not panic. Assignment football is key. The D-line will be on its own mostly to stay in the proper rush lanes to pressure Sam Bradford; I don't believe we will see a lot of blitzes unless the Gators fall behind and have to force the action. OU's running game is still effective somewhat even with Demarco Murray out with an injury, but Florida's DL have played well all season against the run.

I hope to see the LBs and safeties punish the OU receivers at every opportunity, to wear them down physically and mentally. TE Daryl Gresham is a favorite target for Bradford, and I expect to see AJ Jones, Brandon Spikes, and either Major Wright or Ahmad Black to play close coverage on him to disrupt timing. OU has had too easy a time with quick-hitting passes all season, and some effective tight coverage early could rattle their offense and prevent long drives. I also think we will see some 3-4-4 and 3-3-5 looks, in order to clog up the short passing zones, and to keep the DL rotation fresh, as the no-huddle does not allow as many opportunities to substitute.

UF Offense vs. OU Defense:

It's put up or shut up time for Oklahoma, as their defense has been abused often this year. They are definitely weak at LB, especially in the middle, where they will play two or three different guys after Ryan Reynolds went out for the season against Texas with a knee injury. Unless their D-line outplays the Gator OL (which I doubt), they are going to have a lot of trouble stopping the option running game and short passes. It's too bad they have had a month to prepare, because they would have been in serious trouble earlier. I would not be surprised at all to see OU roll the dice early by playing close to the line, pressuring the running lanes and blitzing, to force the Gators and Tebow to prove they can pass effectively. The blitz pickups and pass protection by Aaron Hernandez and the RBs needs to be solid. Stoops and Venable have to be feeling the heat after their defensive meltdowns the past two years, which is surprising given their respective coaching abilities.

As usual, the success (or lack thereof) of the Gator running game will probably dictate the outcome. The threat of the speed of Demps and Harvin, even running inside, has to occupy a lot of the Sooners' attention. Moody should finally be 100% as well, and has proven to be the hammer in the second half as the opponent's defense starts to tire. The Florida OL is tough, physical, experienced, and should find some success – they have played against some of the best competition in the nation that past two years. The spread option also gives Tebow enough discretion to take things to the edge himself or pitching, putting constant extra pressure on Oklahoma's front seven to consistently execute – which they haven't proven all year. In single-coverage match-ups, the Florida WRs have a marked advantage as well, as the Sooner secondary has been abused consistently this season. Tebow should, as usual, spread the wealth to Murphy, Cooper, Hernandez, and Thompson.

The one potential x-factor is Dan Mullen splitting his time between preparation for this game and starting his own regime at Mississippi State. Coach Meyer, newly-promoted OC Steve Addazio, and Billy Gonzales have all contributed to the game planning as well, so hopefully that offsets any potential problems. If Florida can solve any wrinkles shown by OU early, then I expect 30+ points, and I really don't see anything unusual required in either the game plan or play-calling, other than breaking some tendencies for particular down and/or distance scenarios. One area I could see utilized more than usual is throwing to the RBs, either on swing passes or screens.

UF vs. OU special teams:

This is a big advantage for Florida. The return ability of Brandon James is well known, while Chas Henry and Jonathan Phillips have been rock solid all season. The loss of Murray hurts OU, as he was their #1 KO returner and a big-time threat. The Sooner kickoff coverage has ranked near the bottom all year and has struggled mightily – they have to be very concerned right now. Expect some directional kicks to contain any possible big returns by Florida, but that should still yield very good field position. Coach Meyer will undoubtedly have some trick plays ready just in case, and the punt-block unit is one of the best in college football.

Oklahoma is talking a good game right now, but I really think they are emotionally fragile. If Florida can jump out to a 10 point or more lead early, the Sooners will start to press. Also, if the game is a close one throughout and into the late third quarter/early fourth quarter, once again OU will be in uncharted territory and feel the pressure. The Gators should enjoy a decided advantage with the crowd – I expect a 2:1 or 3:1 ratio in favor of

Florida. The return of Percy Harvin certainly could help, but I suspect he's still not close to 100%, and may not get his usual number of snaps. His presence, though, should occupy enough OU defenders to open up the field for others. Murphy and Rainey are dinged up as well...it's going be a chess match for Mullen and Addazio to mix-and-match these guys for spot duty. I suspect that Florida will be run-heavy early in this game, partly by design, partly due to injuries.

Both teams have plenty of motivation for different reasons, so it should be a spirited fight. I will lean towards Tebow and Meyer in this game, based on their performance in the clutch and in pressure situations, and their previous championship success.

Visor Vision Says... Florida 35, Oklahoma 31

**Visor Flings, Week 18:**
**UF 24, Oklahoma 14**

Champions again! Florida reached elite status in the college football world with its tough, thrilling 24-14 win over Oklahoma. This was one championship game in recent years that lived up to the hype, as the Sooners and Gators went at it for the entire game, until Florida was able to finally impose its will in the fourth quarter – similar to what it had done to Alabama to win the SEC Championship.

Even in a team victory such as this, one unit has to be recognized as most responsible, and it was the Gator defense led by Coach Charlie Strong. Once again, the rest of the country had to be reminded that defense in the SEC rules college football. Despite all of the glitzy stats piled up by Sam Bradford and the OU offense in 2008, they had seen nothing like the speed and quality of Florida. The Sooners were held to 200+ yards and 40 points below their average heading into this game. But even more important than those simple numbers was the clutch performance in the second quarter, denying Oklahoma any points on two goal line stands. This completely changed the complexion of the second half, and certainly rattled their psyche. This was something that they just had not experienced all season, and they would never overcome it.

The Gator secondary was asked to play tough man coverage, and they delivered all night. The OU receivers never established any consistency despite some first down plays. They were physically punished the entire game, especially by Major Wright, whose monster hit on the second play from scrimmage let the Sooners know they were going to get hit all game long. The play of the secondary allowed Coach Strong to mix looks and coverages, and blitz Bradford more than he'd seen all season. Carlos Dunlap announced himself to the college football world, as he showed his great quickness and pass-rushing ability from both the down and stand-up positions. There were plenty of big plays spread throughout the entire defense, the two biggest being Torrey Davis' stuffing Brown on 4th-and-goal in the second quarter, and then Ahmad Black's interception after Florida had taken a 17-14 lead in the 4th quarter, stealing the ball away from Iglesias and setting up the game-winning drive.

Oklahoma made a great adjustment in the second quarter, going to the running game and hurting the Gators. Brown was rolling, but then Florida rose up on the goal line stands. In the second half, though, OU seemed to go away from the run, and that was a mistake. They had a huge, senior-laden OL, and should have stayed with it. But that's on the Sooner coaching staff, and is another example of which was the better team. Once the Gators got the option running game going, they controlled the clock the entire second half, and forced OU's hand. The Sooners started throwing almost exclusively, and that played into Florida's hands, as they had the personnel to handle OU better than anyone else, and took control of the game.

It was great to see how the Gators handled Tebow's two interceptions in the first half, continuing to play solid defense and getting the running game going, all the while not panicking and sticking to the game plan. Oklahoma has to be given credit for committing to stopping the inside running game all night. They kept 8 men in the box until late in the 3rd quarter, when Florida finally got the option game going with Tebow by hitting the edges, and unleashing Harvin for two of his signature big plays. This was a game of patience, and the leadership of Tebow was critical in keeping the confidence of the entire offense up during a rough first half.

Oklahoma joins a long line of teams that talked trash about Tebow, saying he's one-dimensional and disrespecting his overall game. That same long line is now full of losers, as he once again tore their heart out in the clutch. But it wasn't all Tebow's doing, as many others contributed significant plays to put the game away in the second half. Harvin played with guts and toughness as always, as he was hurting the entire game. Even at well less than 100%, his ability was enough to make some huge runs, both in critical situations. Aaron Hernandez was huge on the shovel passes off of the option, and killed OU with many third down conversions on TD drives. Riley Cooper made some big receptions to extend drives, and then David Nelson came up with his 2 catches in the fourth quarter, the last of which iced the game on a different twist of the jump-pass from Tebow. Just awesome clutch plays by all of these guys. Of course, once Tebow got rolling running the ball, it got him pumped up, and then he got the crowd into it, and the swell overwhelmed Oklahoma.

The final touchdown drive by Florida will go down into the annals of Gator football as one of the two or three most clutch ever. Knowing a three-point lead was tenuous, the Gators drove the ball right down the throat of Oklahoma, executing key plays, eating up the clock, and crushing the dreams of the Sooners and their fans.

Coach Meyer now has two BCS crystal balls, something no other coach has (that includes you, Pete Carroll). And Florida has passed a handful of schools in the count of National Championships (including leaving F$U in the rearview mirror). The program has reached new heights in just the past four seasons, and is at the point right now where they can reload in talent each season and always be title contenders – the true mark of an elite program. It is truly, "great to be a Florida Gator!"

Postscript: Now that Tebow and Spikes are returning for their senior year, it's hard not to already look ahead to what could be a run for the Roses in 2009. The entire two-deep returns on defense, while the loss of Harvin to the NFL can be offset by spreading the ball around to the returning playmakers. If the team can stay healthy first, and motivated, they will be favored to repeat as SEC Champions and go for a second straight National Championship. It's going to be another exciting year in the Swamp.

Very Truly Yours
The Visor

## The Visor's All-Time Gator Greats

The Visor was ruminating about all-time Gator greats, and quite a few players came to mind. Here's a conversation starter. I'm only counting college performance and contribution to the program, though. That's what really counts most to us, right?

OFFENSE

**Quarterbacks:** Danny Wuerffel; Steve Spurrier; Shane Matthews/Rex Grossman (tie); Chris Leak; Tim Tebow. Danny for the titles; SOS for the national recognition; Shane for the first official title; Rex for pure production; Leak for being the ultimate winner; and Tim Tebow, who as of this writing has already won the Heisman, been part of one BCS championship and led the Gators to another, while achieving legendary status, for sheer willpower and strength of character. Other notables: John Reaves; Wayne Peace
**Running backs:** Emmitt Smith; Neal Anderson/Errict Rhett (tie); Fred Taylor/Larry Smith (tie). Emmitt is in a class by himself; Neal and Errict were highly productive; Fred showed why he should have played more before his senior season; Larry contributed to the first Orange Bowl win (can't forget all the old-timers). Others: Willie Wilder; Terry Jackson; Doug Dubose
**Fullbacks:** John L. Williams; James Jones. John L. was a great talent and did it all; James was a fine athlete and clutch in big games
**Wide Receivers:** Tough calls here – Wes Chandler; Carlos Alvarez; Ike Hilliard; Jabar Gaffney; Percy Harvin. Wes was dangerous every time he touched the ball and returned kicks; Carlos was always a deep threat; Ike was smooth, found the end zone, and made a solid contribution as a true freshman; Jabar's production was at such a high level it can't be overlooked, and he ran great routes; Percy Harvin's legend is still being written. Others: Ricky Nattiel; Cris Collingsworth; Jaquez Green; Jack Jackson; Willie Jackson (This is a tough group to pick from, and there are many others I've left off).
**Tight Ends**: Kirk Kirkpatrick; Chris Faulkner; Mike Mularkey; Erron Kinney; Ben Troupe. Kirk dominated his only year in the Spurrier system; Chris was very productive, despite injuries, in Mike Shanahan's system; Mike was on the same team as Faulkner (what a pair) and has done quite nicely as Offensive Coordinator of the Steelers; Erron was a great blocker, and made big plays the occasional times he touched the ball; Troupe was one of the best Gator players from the Zook years.
**Offensive Linemen:** Another tough group. Lomas Brown; Jason Odom; Jeff Mitchell; Donnie Young; Jeff Zimmerman. Lomas dominated opponents; Odom was a two-time Jacobs award winner, started as a true freshman and played at a high level even then; Jeff was our finest center; Donnie was tough, played hurt, and was an inspirational leader; Jeff Z. started from his freshman year. Others: David Williams; Mike Pearson; Mo Collins; Kenyatta Walker, Phil Trautwein

**Special Teams:** Ray Criswell (P); Bobby Raymond (FG - with tee); Jeff Chandler/Judd Davis (without tee); Ricky Nattiel/Lito Sheppard/Reidel Anthony (tie); Ivory Curry. Ray was the most consistent and clutch punter (and a good athlete); Bobby the most accurate on FGs (a big reason for the SEC title in 1984); Jeff/Judd were accurate and clutch in big games; Ricky/Lito/Reidel all were dangerous and found the end zone; Ivory was a dangerous punt returner (also a fine cornerback). Others: Shane Edge; Brian Clark; Carlos Yepremian.

DEFENSE

**Defensive Linemen:** Very tough list. Jack Youngblood; Tim Newton; David Galloway; Ellis Johnson; Kevin Carter. All these guys were All-SEC, All-American, etc. Others: Trace Armstrong; Brad Culpepper; Reggie McGrew; Robin Fisher; Tony McCoy.
**Linebackers:** Wilber Marshall; Ralph Ortega; Alonzo Johnson; Jevon Kearse. Less of an overall talent pool in numbers then other positions, but an outstanding group. Others: Scot Brantley; Jerry Odom; Godfrey Myles; Clifford Charlton; Mike Peterson; Johnny Rutledge; David Little; Travis Carroll.
**Defensive Backs:** Historically the weakest group. Jarvis Williams; Fred Weary; Tony George; Lito Sheppard; Louis Oliver; Reggie Nelson. Others: Bruce Vaughn; Anthone Lott; Will White; Larry Kennedy; Tony Lilly; Ivory Curry

I know I've left off a bunch of names, but that always happens when you try to make a list like this.

www.ingramcontent.com/pod-product-compliance
Lightning Source LLC
LaVergne TN
LVHW061220100826
845148LV00004B/811

* 9 7 8 0 9 7 5 5 1 0 4 3 8 *